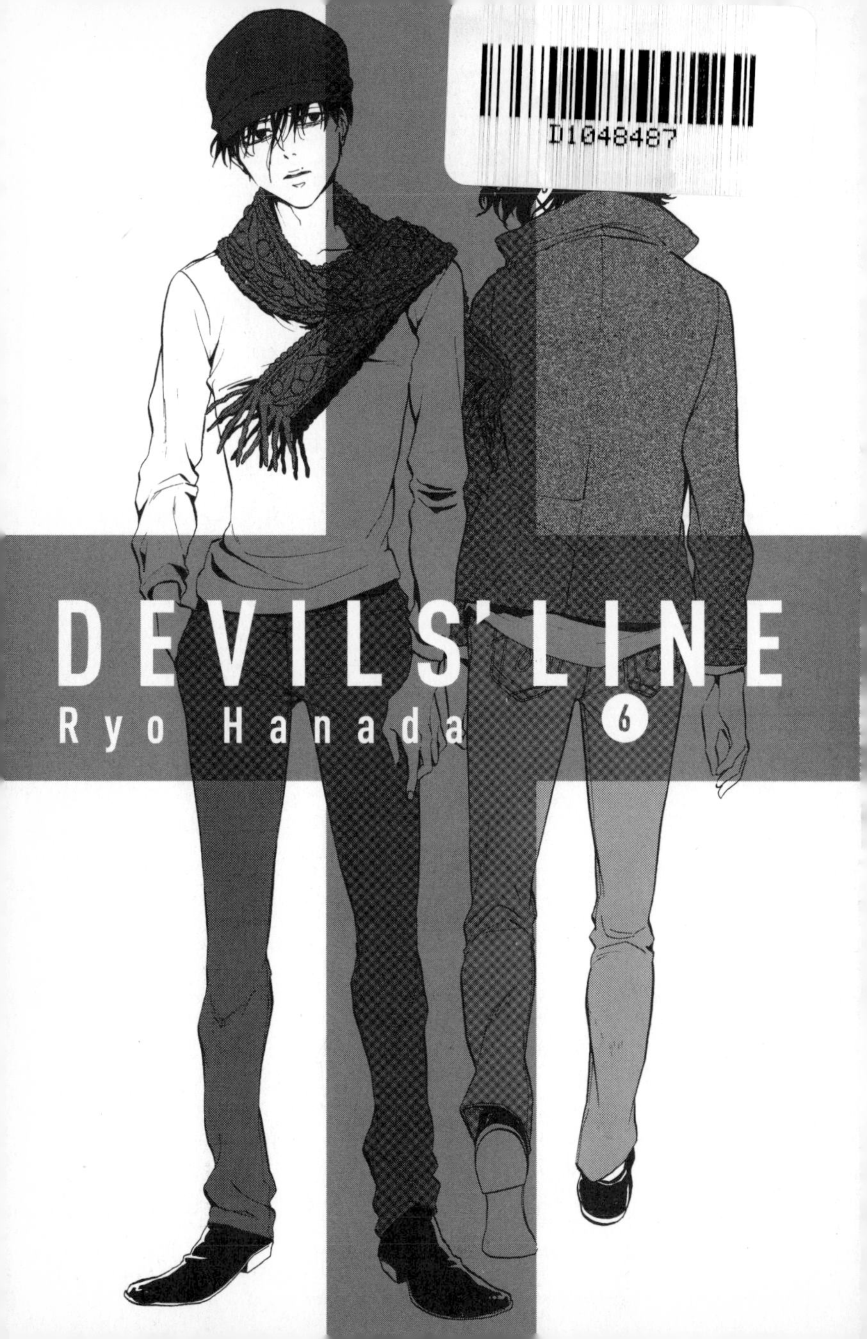
DEVILS' LINE
Ryo Hanada
6

MPD PUBLIC SAFETY DIVISION 5

C SQUAD

NAOYA USHIO
(Zero Five)

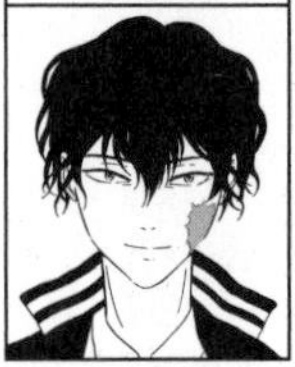

A member of the CCC along with Kikuhara and Makimura. He attacked Tsukasa in a hotel.

B SQUAD

TAKESHI MAKIMURA
(Zero Six)

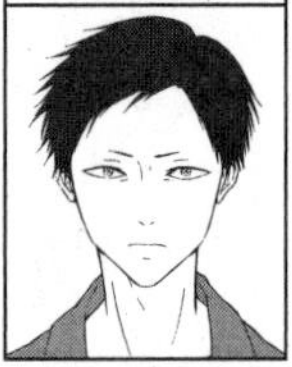

Secretly a member of the CCC. He previously instructed Zero Seven in sniping.

A SQUAD

KIRIO KIKUHARA
(Zero Two)

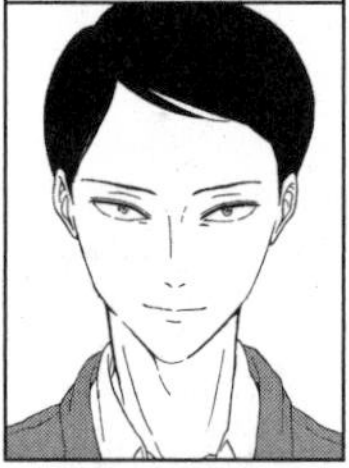

The leader of A Squad, he's also secretly the commander of the CCC, an organization dedicated to the extermination of devils.

YUUKI ANZAI

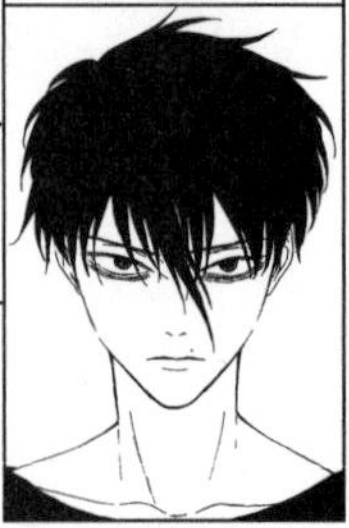

Half-devil, half-human police officer. He was pessimistic regarding the coexistence of devils and humans, but his thinking has been changing since he met Tsukasa.

MEGUMI ISHIMARU

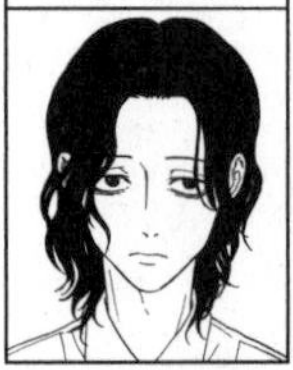

New F Squad leader. Since he came to F Squad at the recommendation of Kikuhara (Zero Two), he is suspected of being a spy.

TAKASHI SAWAZAKI

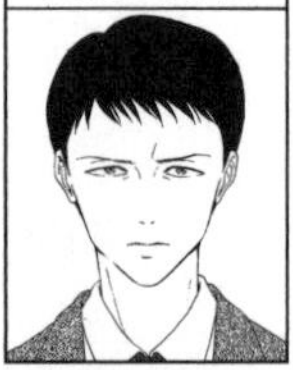

Former F Squad leader, his inability to control his devil subordinates was regarded as problematic, and he was demoted from his position as leader.

YOUSUKE ASAMI

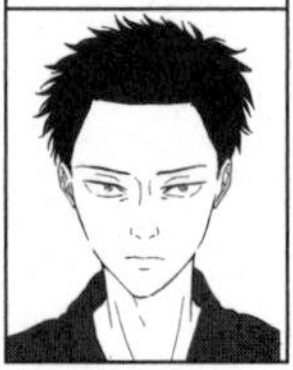

A member of Investigation Division 1, he was assigned temporarily to Public Safety Division 5, where he is part of the ongoing investigation.

JULIANA LLOYD

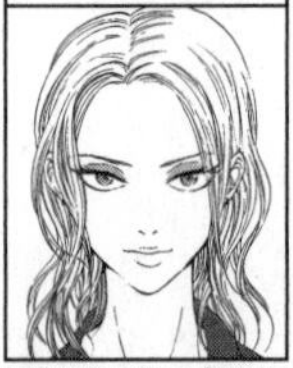

Devil police officer. Born and raised in Japan. She skillfully uses make-up to hide the bags under her eyes.

RYUUSEI YANAGI

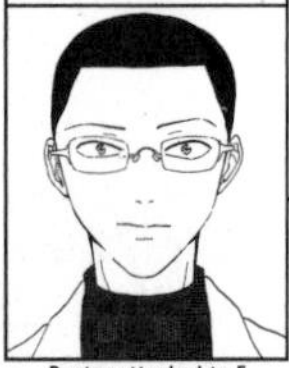

Doctor attached to F Squad specializing in the hematology of the redeye race, he was apparently a punk in his youth.

AKIO KANO

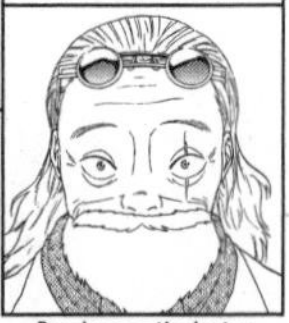

Psychosomatic doctor specializing in devil care, he is also a member of R2PC, a committee that works to protect devil rights.

*A more detailed *Devils' Line* Character and Relationship Diagram created by the author can be viewed online. (Japanese only.)
http://hanada.coln.biz/diagram/realpart/topmenu.html

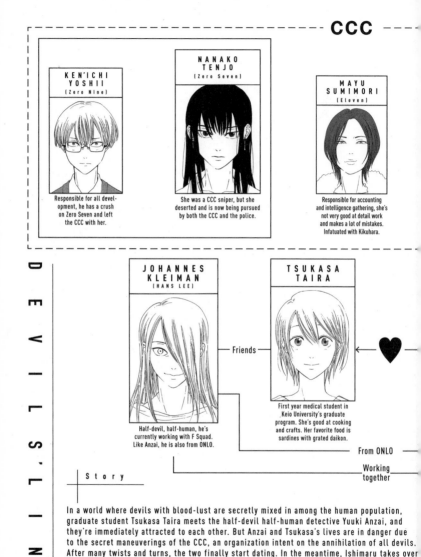

CCC

KEN'ICHI YOSHII
(Zero Nine)

Responsible for all develop-
ment, he has a crush
on Zero Seven and left
the CCC with her.

NANAKO TENJO
(Zero Seven)

She was a CCC sniper, but she
deserted and is now being pursued
by both the CCC and the police.

MAYU SUMIMORI
(Eleven)

Responsible for accounting
and intelligence gathering, she's
not very good at detail work
and makes a lot of mistakes.
Infatuated with Kikuhara.

DEVIL'S LINE

JOHANNES KLEIMAN
(HANS LEE)

Half-devil, half-human, he's
currently working with F Squad.
Like Anzai, he is also from ONLO.

Friends

TSUKASA TAIRA

First year medical student in
Keio University's graduate
program. She's good at cooking
and crafts. Her favorite food is
sardines with grated daikon.

From ONLO

Working
together

Story

In a world where devils with blood-lust are secretly mixed in among the human population,
graduate student Tsukasa Taira meets the half-devil half-human detective Yuuki Anzai, and
they're immediately attracted to each other. But Anzai and Tsukasa's lives are in danger due
to the secret maneuverings of the CCC, an organization intent on the annihilation of all devils.
After many twists and turns, the two finally start dating. In the meantime, Ishimaru takes over
the squad that Anzai belongs to, Public Safety Division 5's F Squad, which was previously led by
Sawazaki. Ishimaru opens a thorough investigation into the CCC. The battle between the CCC
and F Squad, plagued by half-truths and falsehoods, has begun.

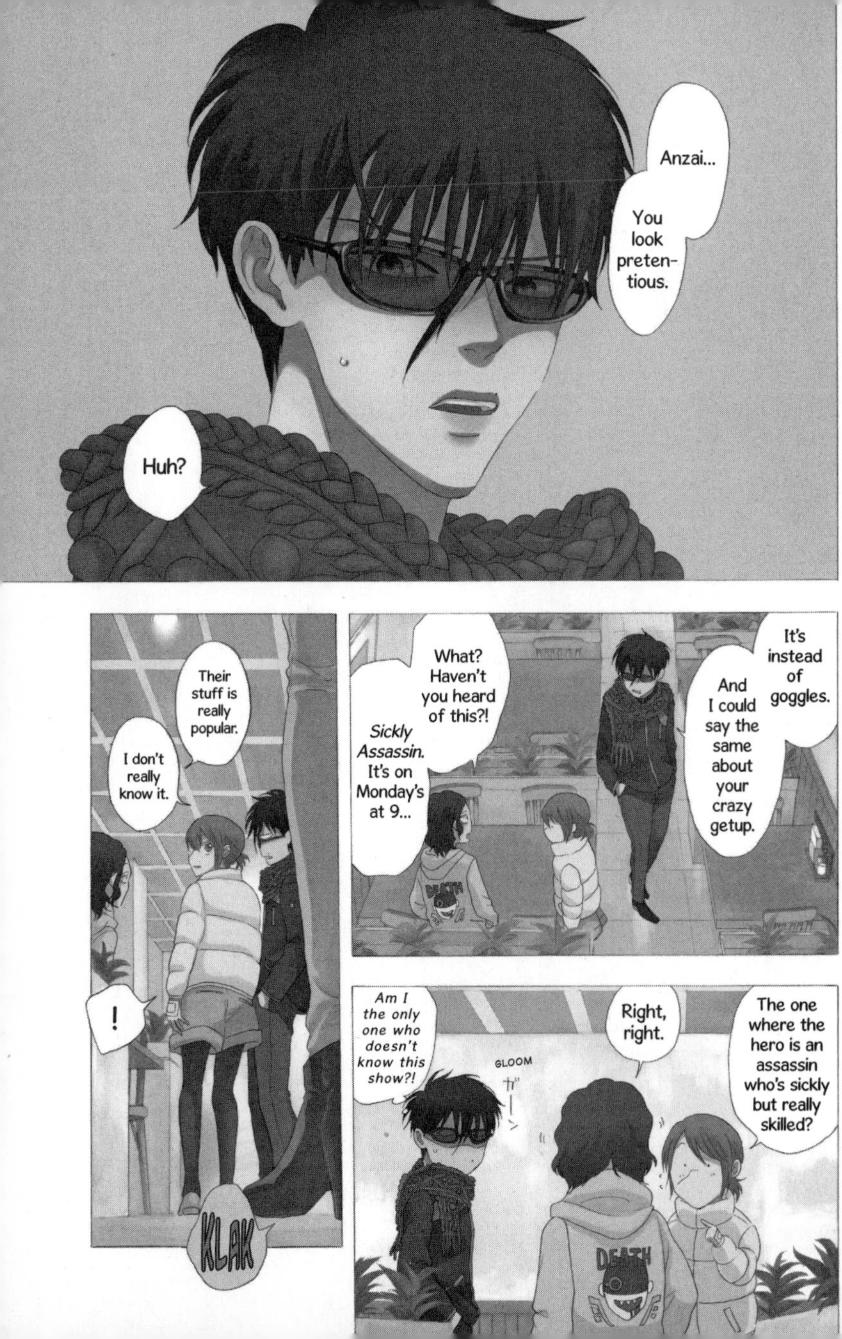
Anzai...
You look preten-tious.
Huh?
It's instead of goggles.
And I could say the same about your crazy getup.
What? Haven't you heard of this?!
Sickly Assassin. It's on Monday's at 9...
The one where the hero is an assassin who's sickly but really skilled?
Right, right.
GLOOM
Am I the only one who doesn't know this show?!
Their stuff is really popular.
I don't really know it.
!
KLAK

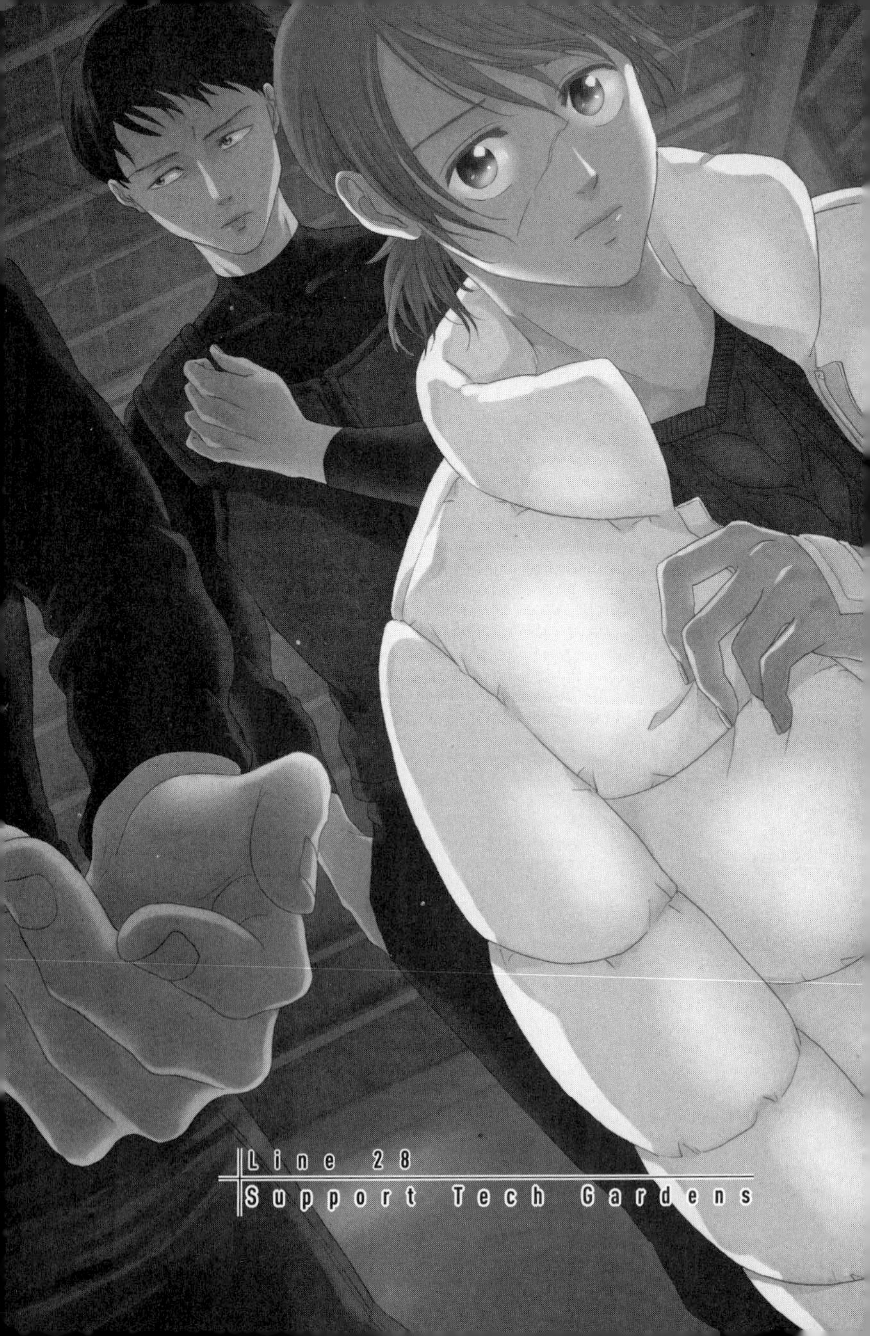
Line 28
Support Tech Gardens

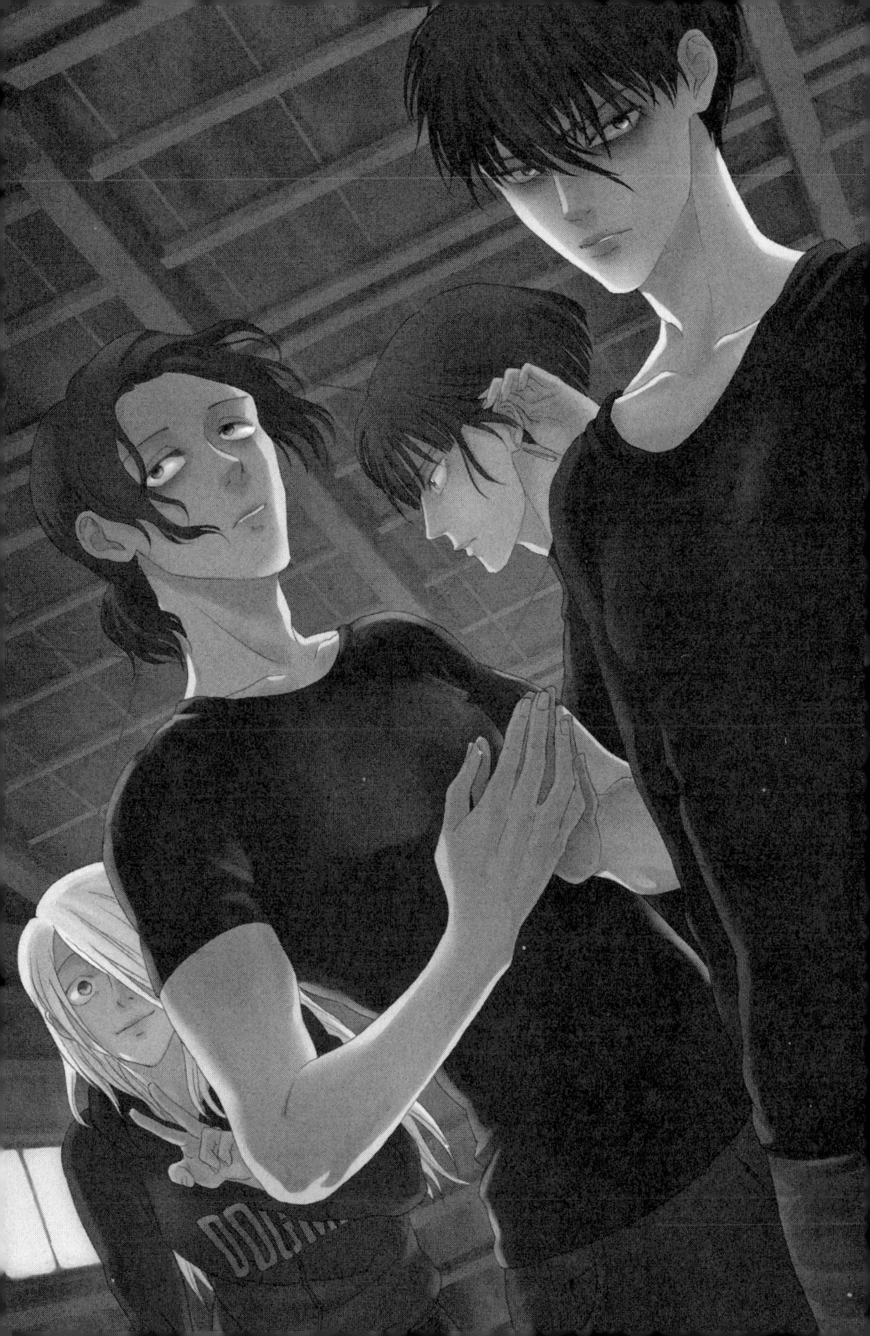

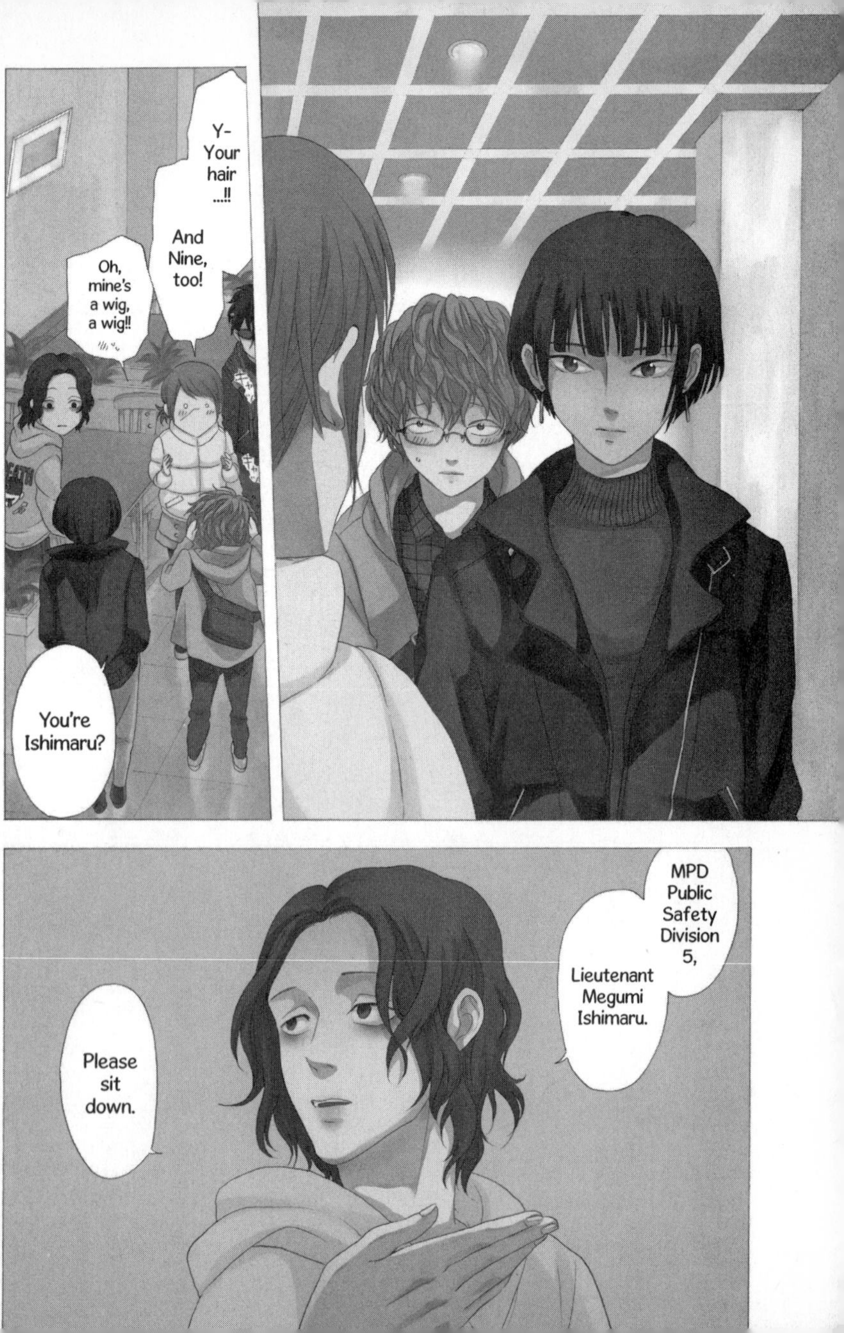
Y- Your hair ...!!
And Nine, too!
Oh, mine's a wig, a wig!!
You're Ishimaru?
MPD Public Safety Division 5,
Lieutenant Megumi Ishimaru.
Please sit down.

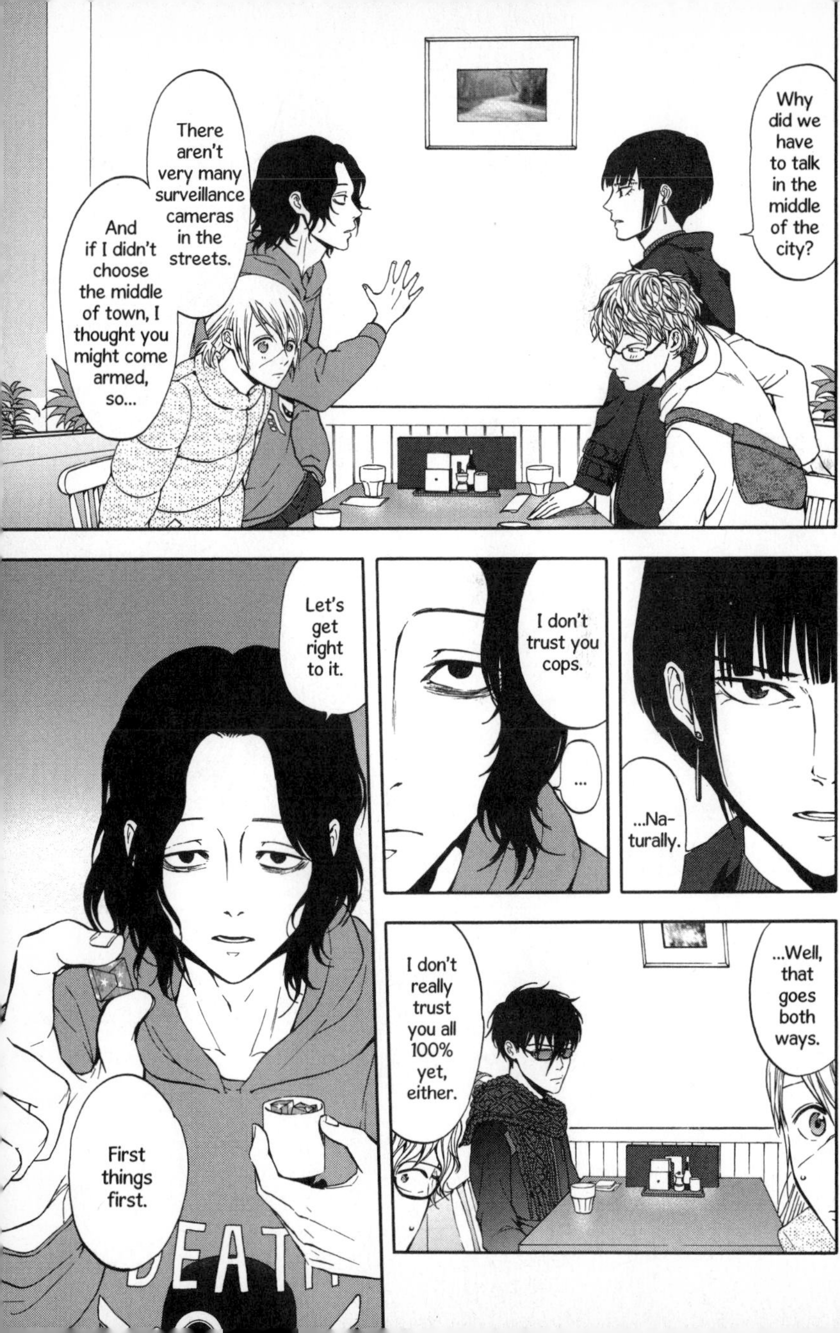
Why did we have to talk in the middle of the city?
There aren't very many surveillance cameras in the streets.
And if I didn't choose the middle of town, I thought you might come armed, so...
...Na-turally.
I don't trust you cops.
...
...Well, that goes both ways.
I don't really trust you all 100% yet, either.
Let's get right to it.
First things first.

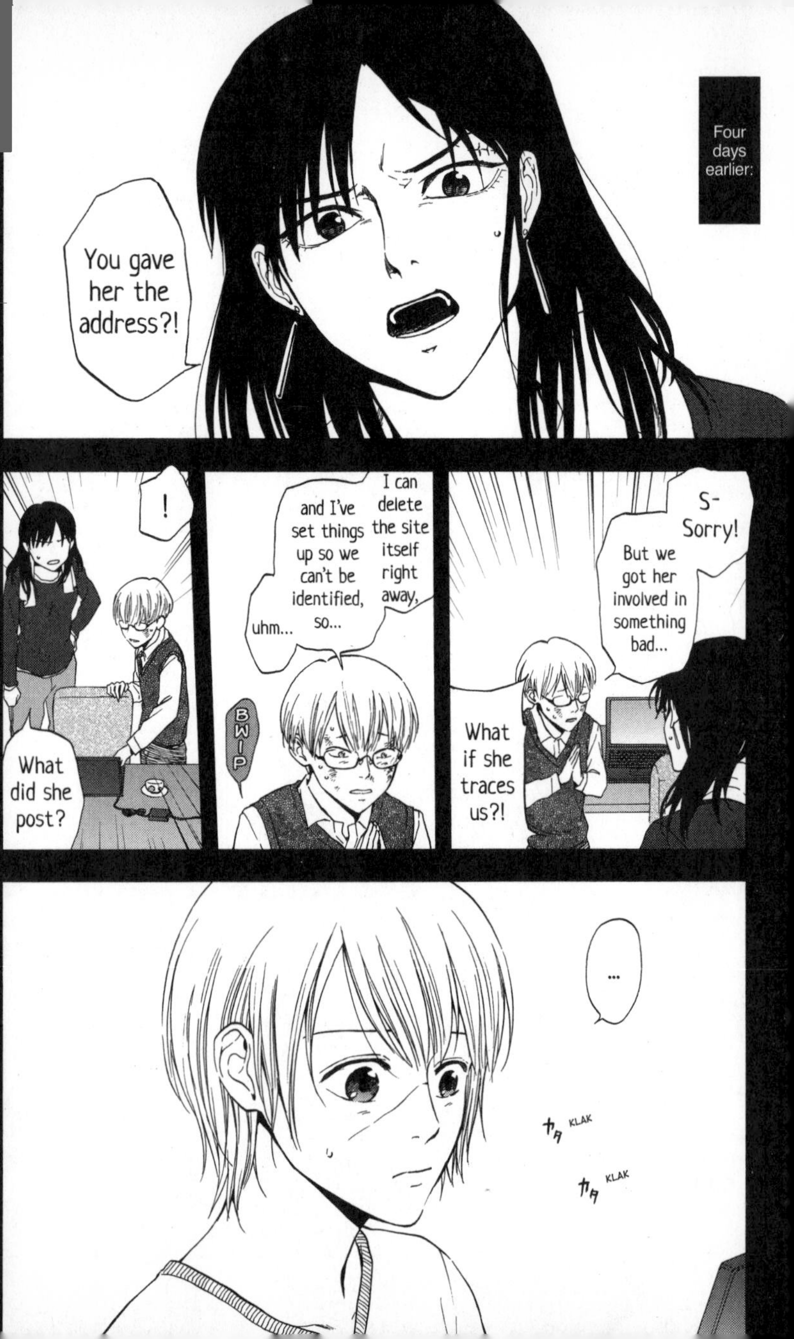
Four days earlier:
You gave her the address?!
S- Sorry!
But we got her involved in something bad...
What if she traces us?!
I can delete the site itself right away,
and I've set things up so we can't be identified,
uhm... so...
BWIP
!
What did she post?
...
カタ KLAK
カタ KLAK

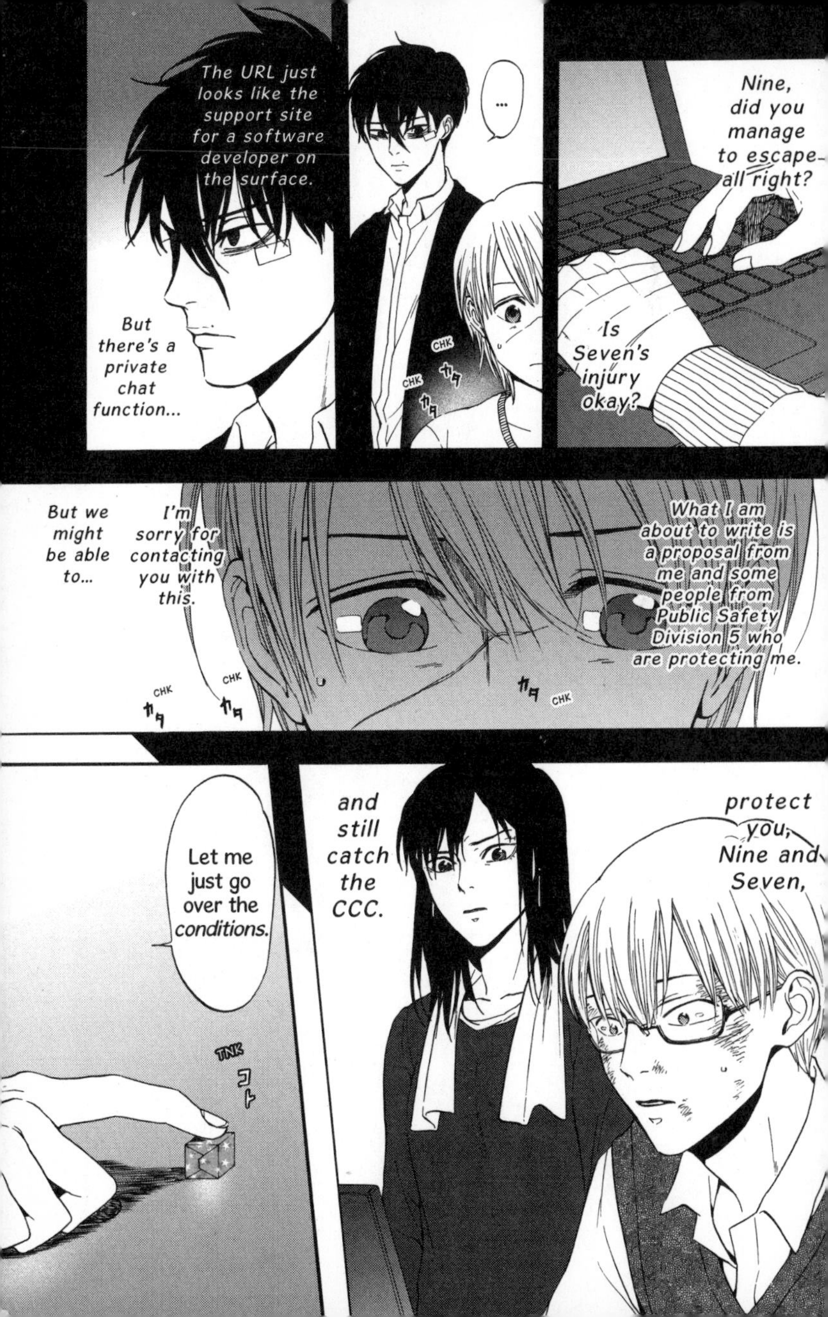
Nine, did you manage to escape all right?
Is Seven's injury okay?
...
CHK CHK
The URL just looks like the support site for a software developer on the surface.
But there's a private chat function...
What I am about to write is a proposal from me and some people from Public Safety Division 5 who are protecting me.
CHK
I'm sorry for contacting you with this.
But we might be able to...
CHK CHK
protect you, Nine and Seven,
and still catch the CCC.
Let me just go over the conditions.
TNK

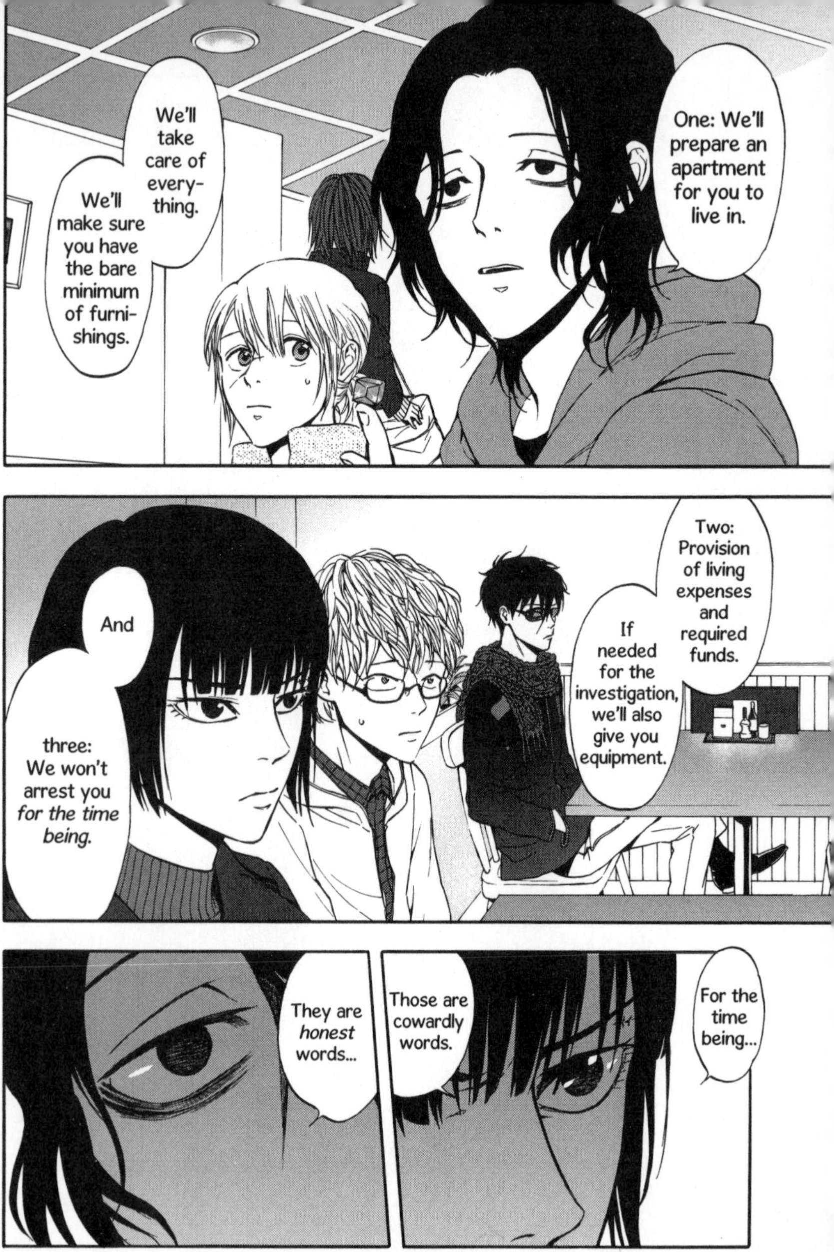
One: We'll prepare an apartment for you to live in.
We'll take care of every-thing.
We'll make sure you have the bare minimum of furni-shings.
Two: Provision of living expenses and required funds.
If needed for the investigation, we'll also give you equipment.
And
three: We won't arrest you *for the time being.*
For the time being...
Those are cowardly words.
They are *honest* words...

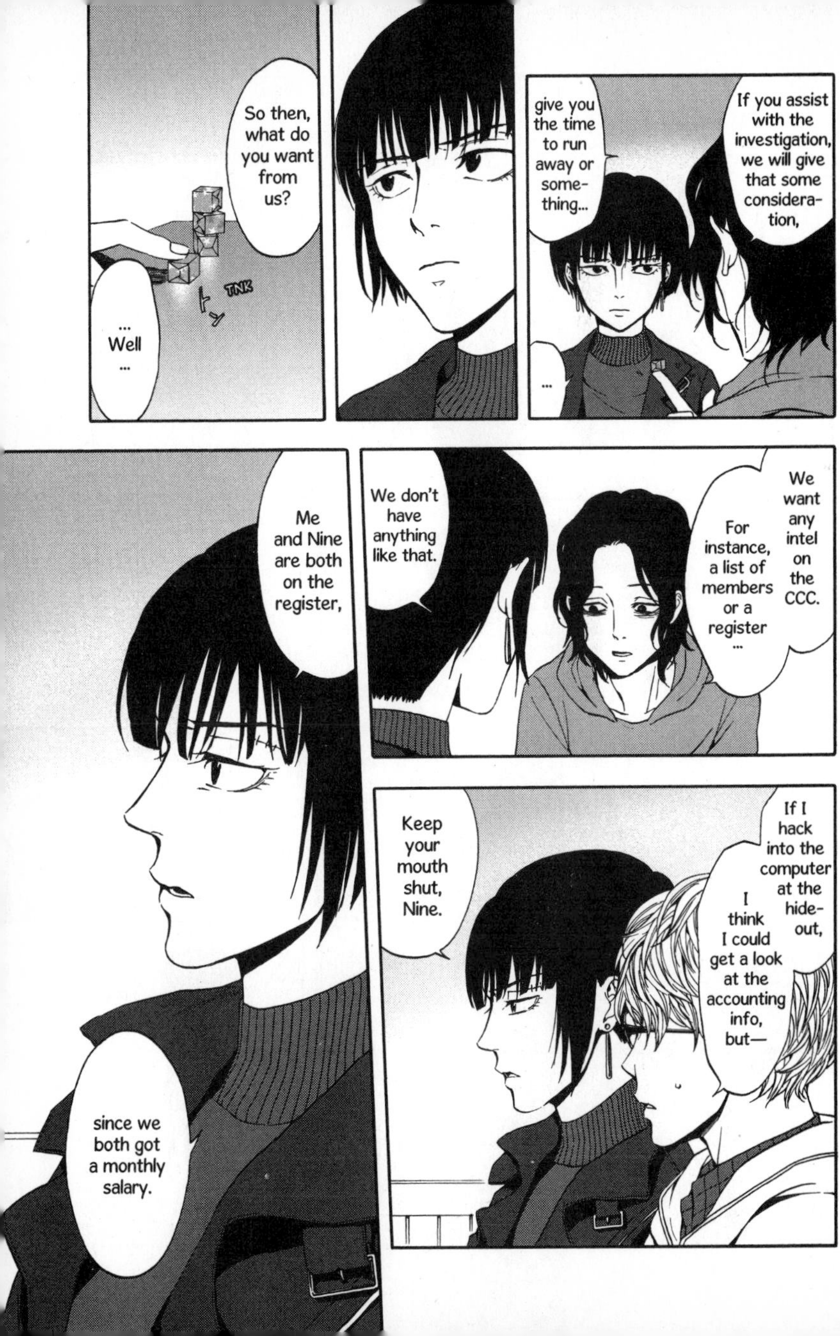
If you assist with the investigation, we will give that some considera-tion,
give you the time to run away or some-thing...
...
So then, what do you want from us?
TNK
...Well...
We want any intel on the CCC.
For instance, a list of members or a register...
We don't have anything like that.
If I hack into the computer at the hide-out, I think I could get a look at the accounting info, but—
Keep your mouth shut, Nine.
Me and Nine are both on the register,
since we both got a monthly salary.

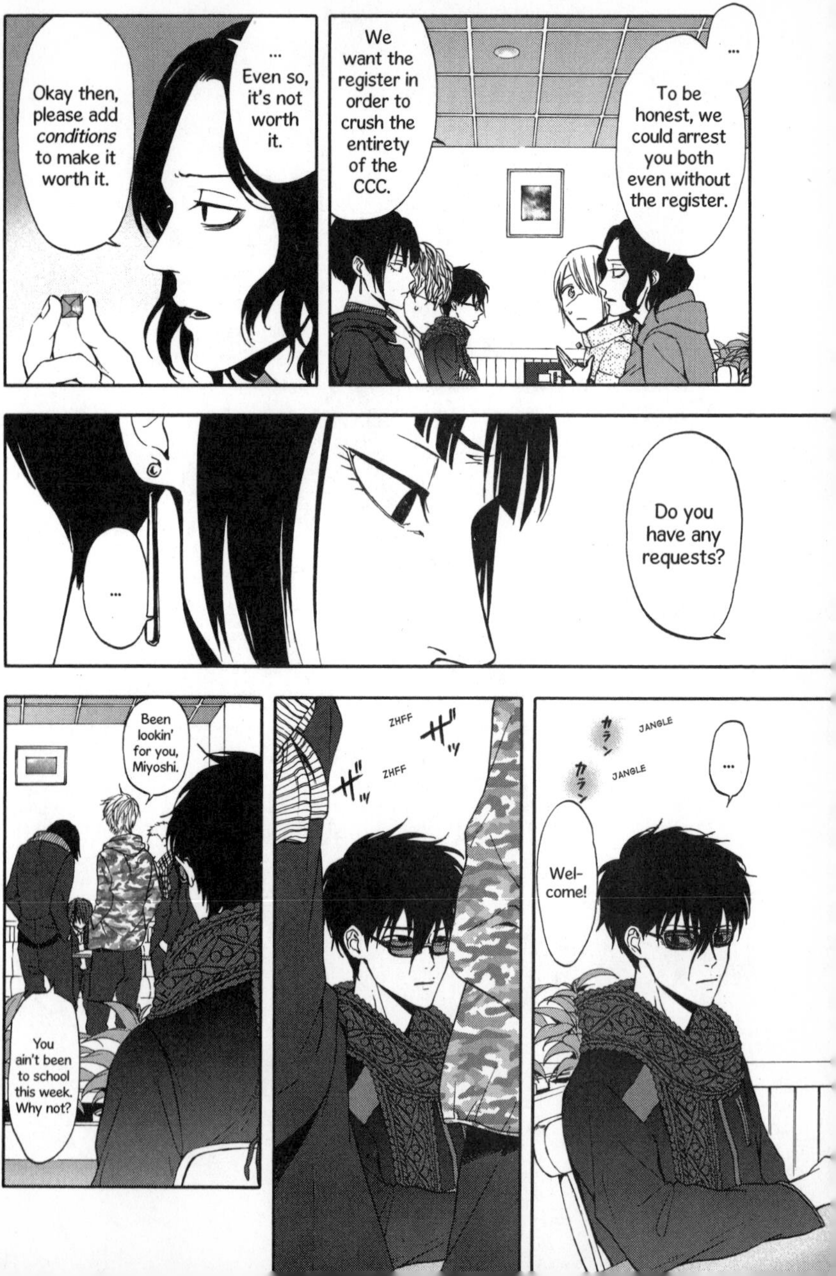
...
To be honest, we could arrest you both even without the register.
We want the register in order to crush the entirety of the CCC.
... Even so, it's not worth it.
Okay then, please add *conditions* to make it worth it.
Do you have any requests?
...
カラン JANGLE
カラン JANGLE
...
Wel-come!
ザッ ZHFF
ザッ ZHFF
Been lookin' for you, Miyoshi.
You ain't been to school this week. Why not?

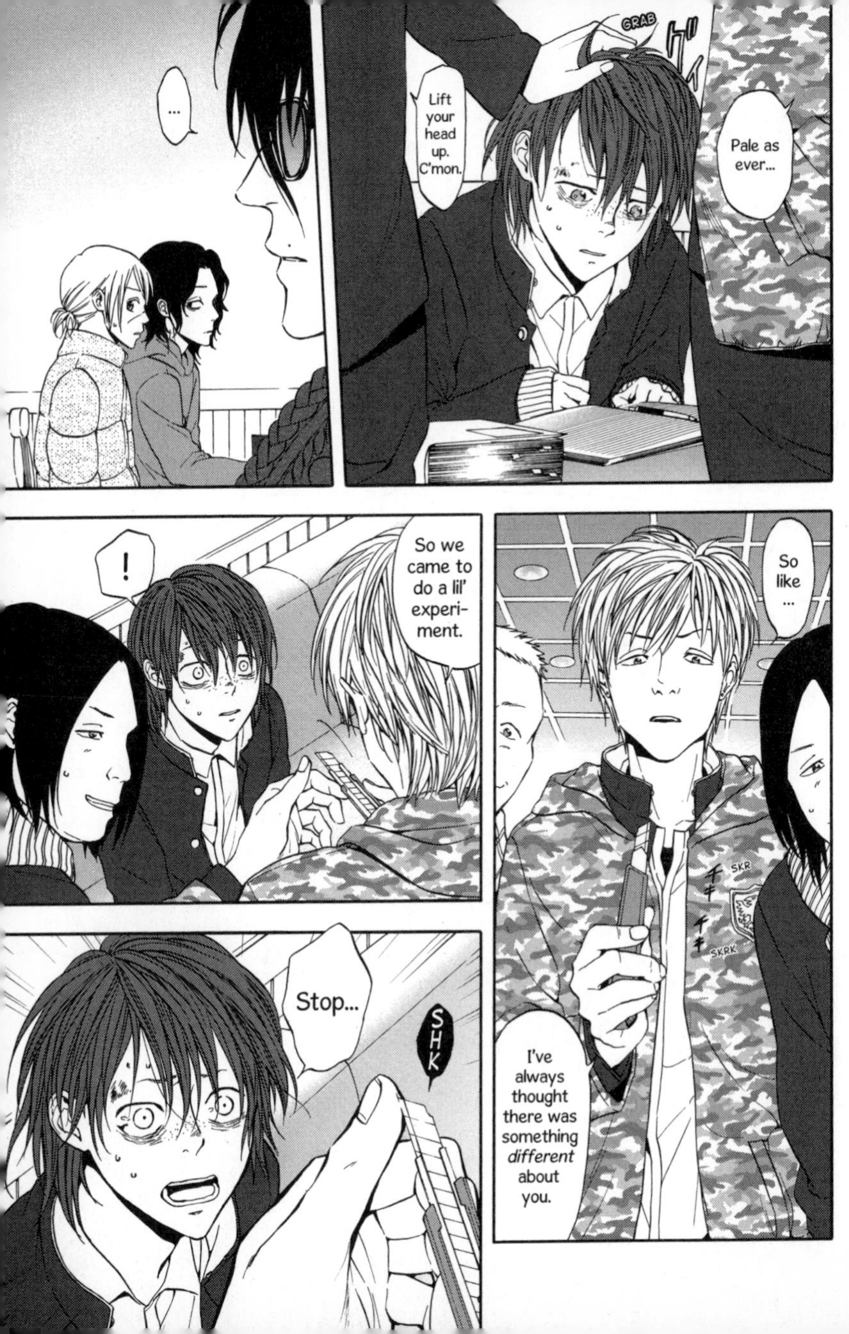
Pale as ever...
GRAB
グイ
Lift your head up. C'mon.
...
So like ...
SKR
チキ
チキ
SKRK
I've always thought there was something *different* about you.
So we came to do a lil' experiment.
!
Stop...
SHK

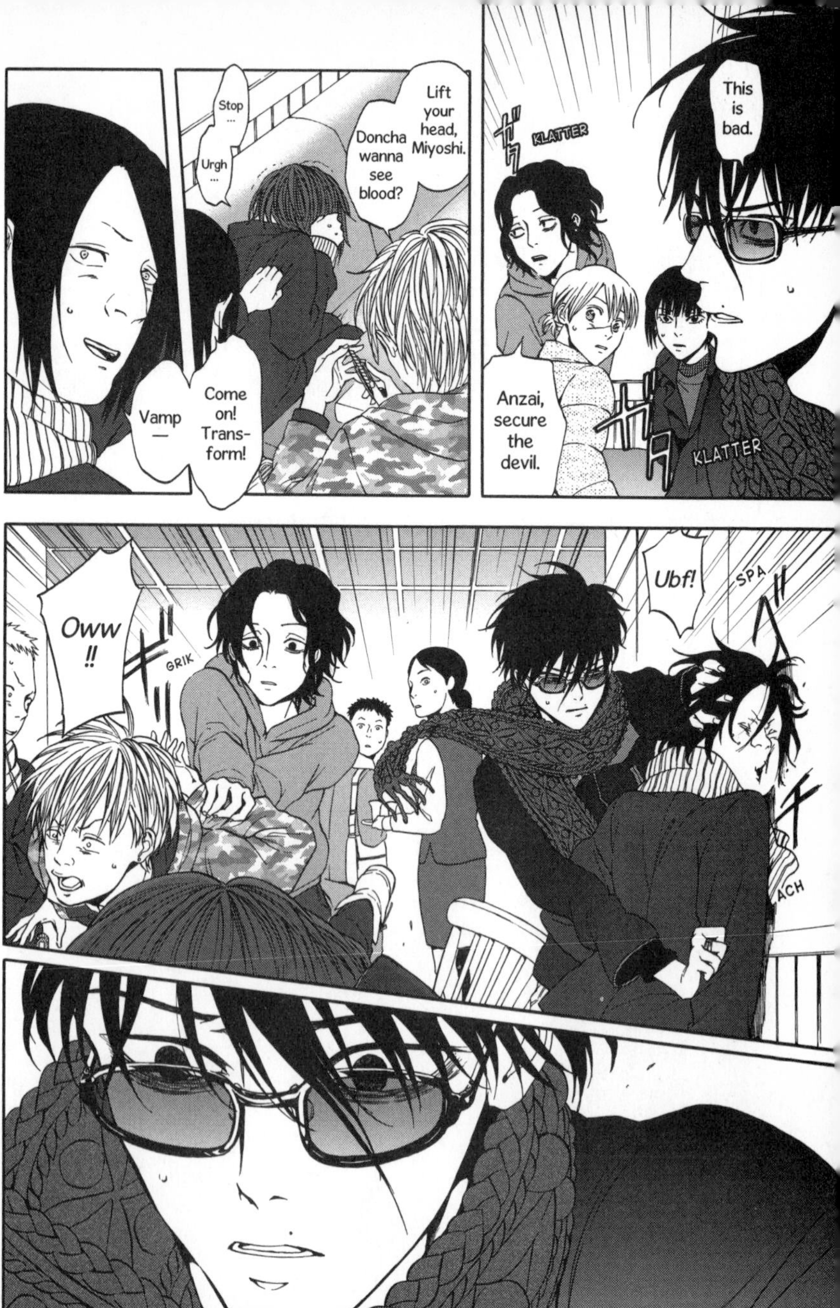
This is bad.
KLATTER
KLATTER
Anzai, secure the devil.
Lift your head, Miyoshi.
Doncha wanna see blood?
Stop ...
Urgh ...
Come on! Transform!
Vamp —
Ubf!
SPA
ACH
GRIK
Oww !!

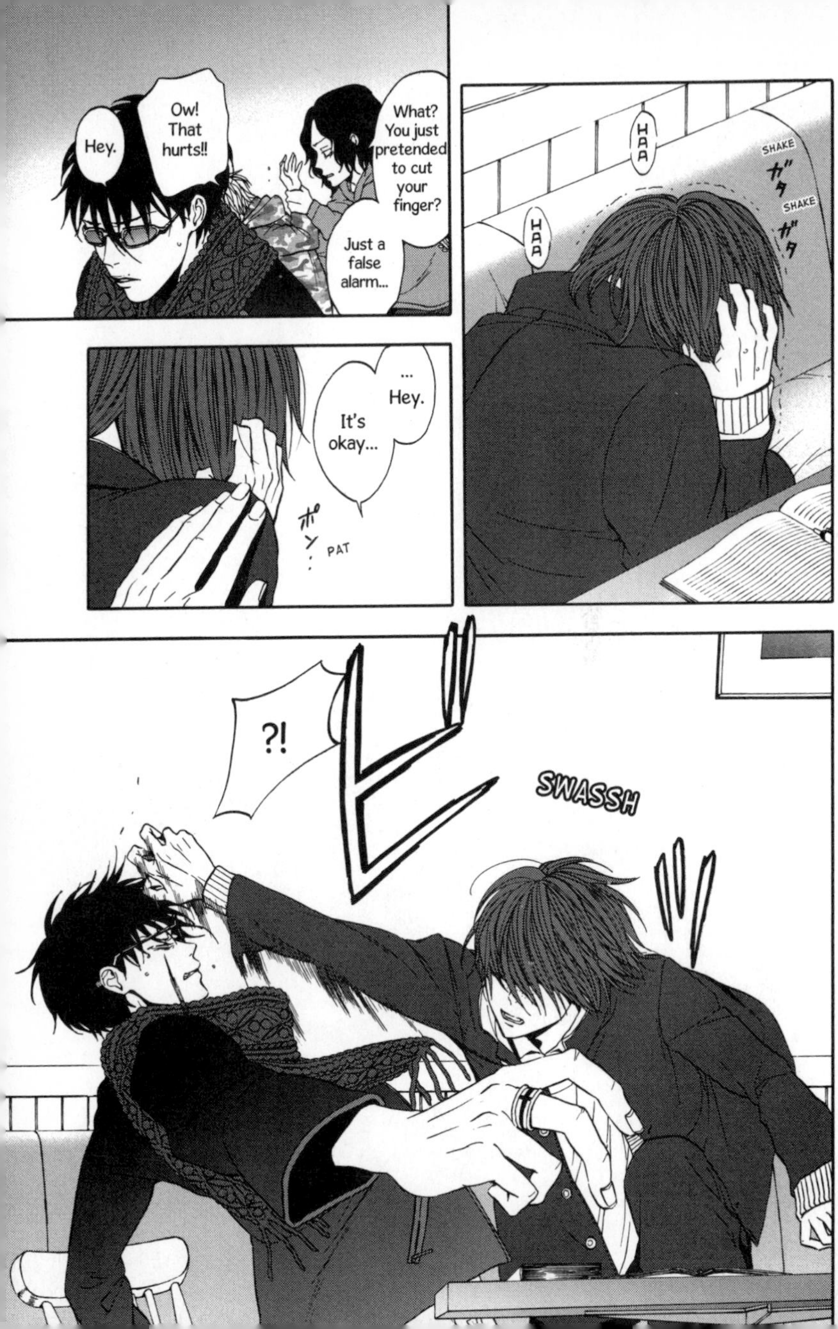
HAA
HAA
SHAKE
ガタ
SHAKE
ガタ
What? You just pretended to cut your finger?
Just a false alarm...
Ow! That hurts!!
Hey.
... Hey.
It's okay...
ポン
PAT
?!
SWASSH

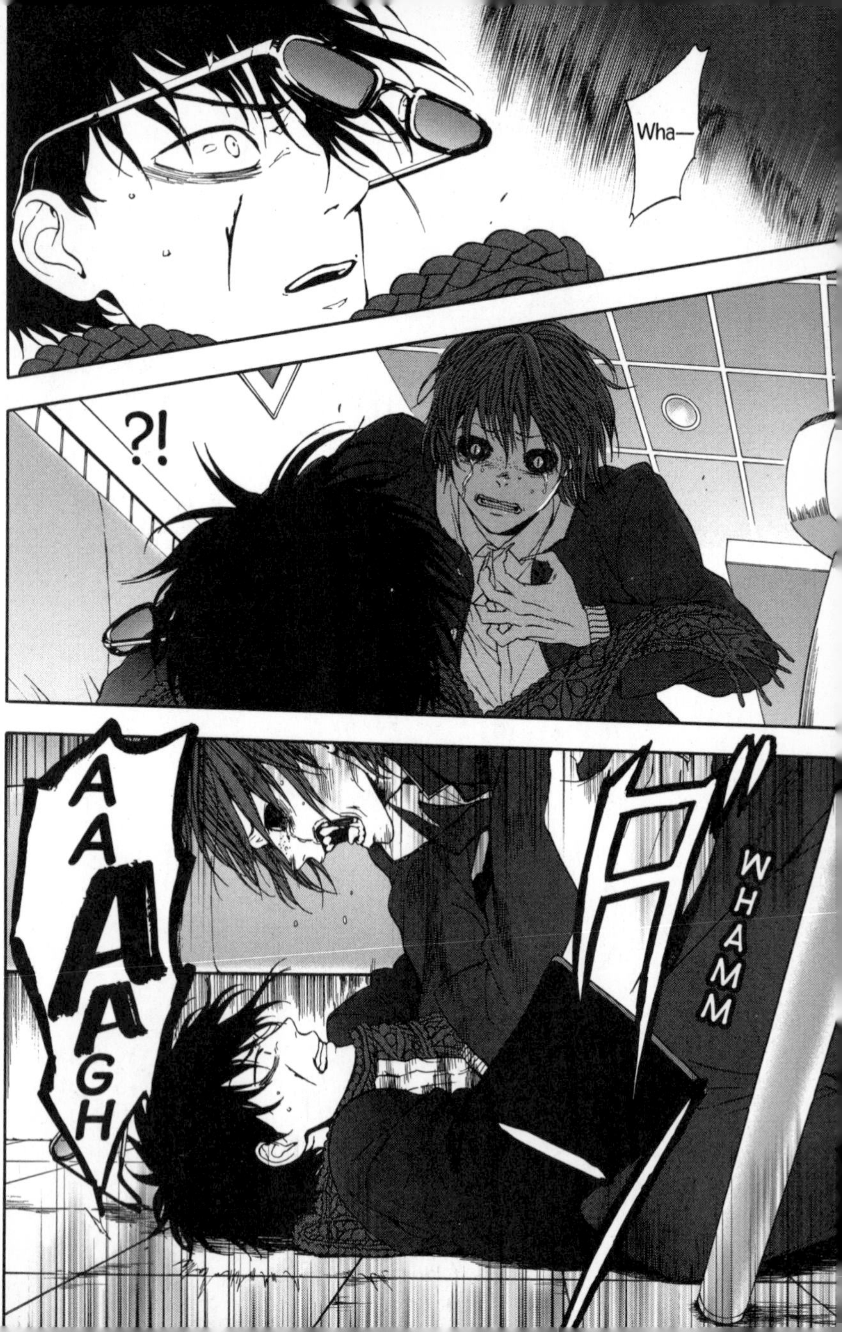
Wha—
?!
WHAMM
AAAAGH

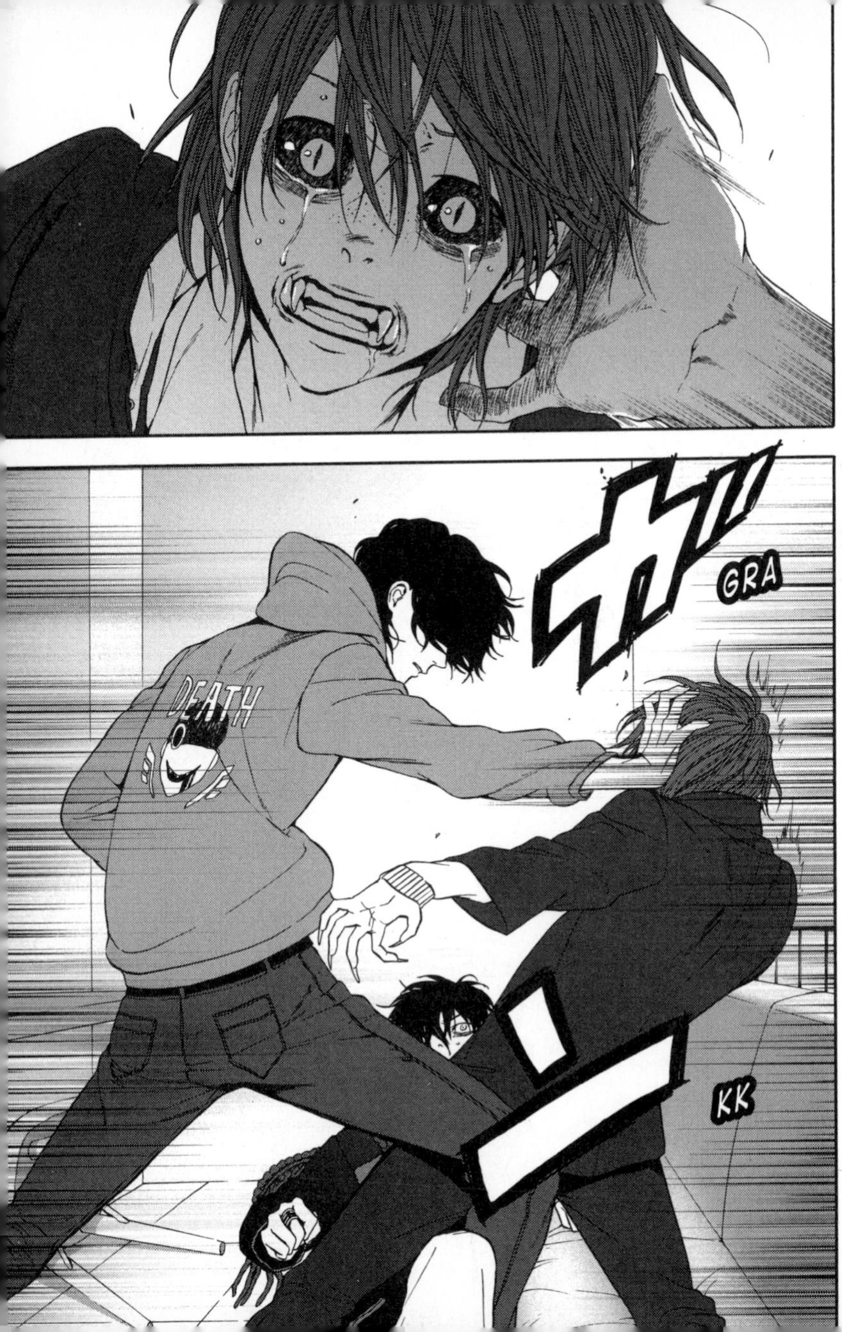
GRA
KK

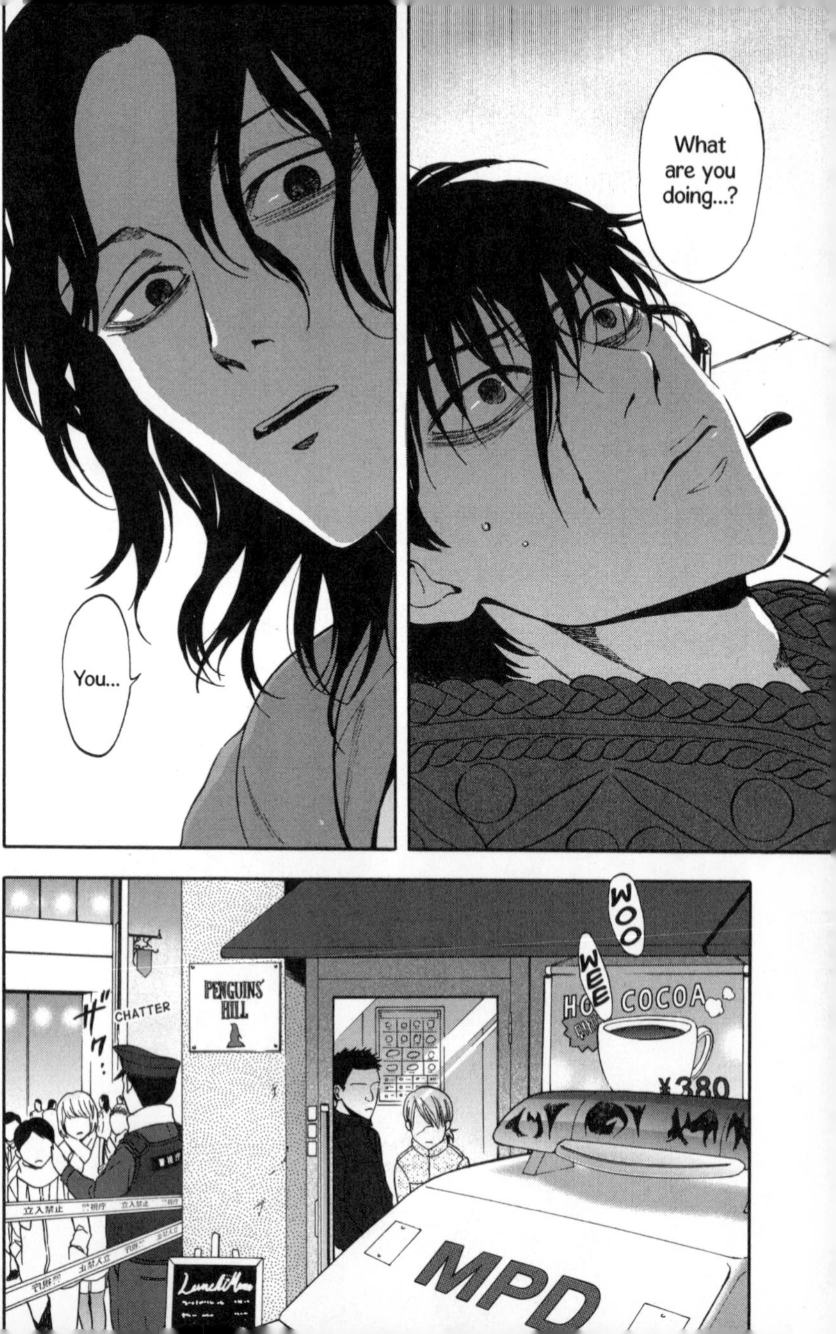
What are you doing...?
You...
WOO
WEE
COCOA
¥380
PENGUINS' HILL
CHATTER
MPD

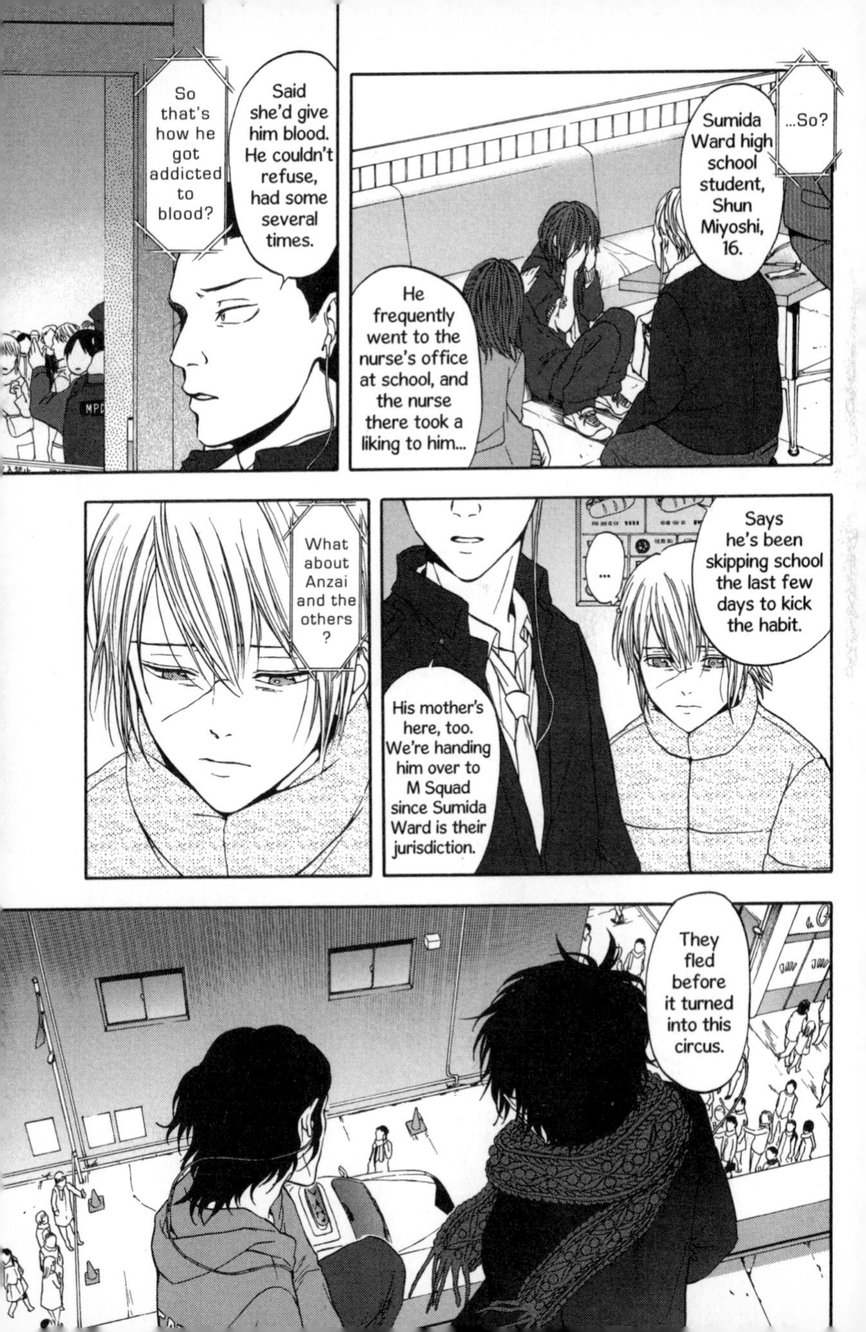
...So?
Sumida Ward high school student, Shun Miyoshi, 16.
He frequently went to the nurse's office at school, and the nurse there took a liking to him...
Said she'd give him blood. He couldn't refuse, had some several times.
So that's how he got addicted to blood?
MPD
Says he's been skipping school the last few days to kick the habit.
...
His mother's here, too. We're handing him over to M Squad since Sumida Ward is their jurisdiction.
What about Anzai and the others?
They fled before it turned into this circus.

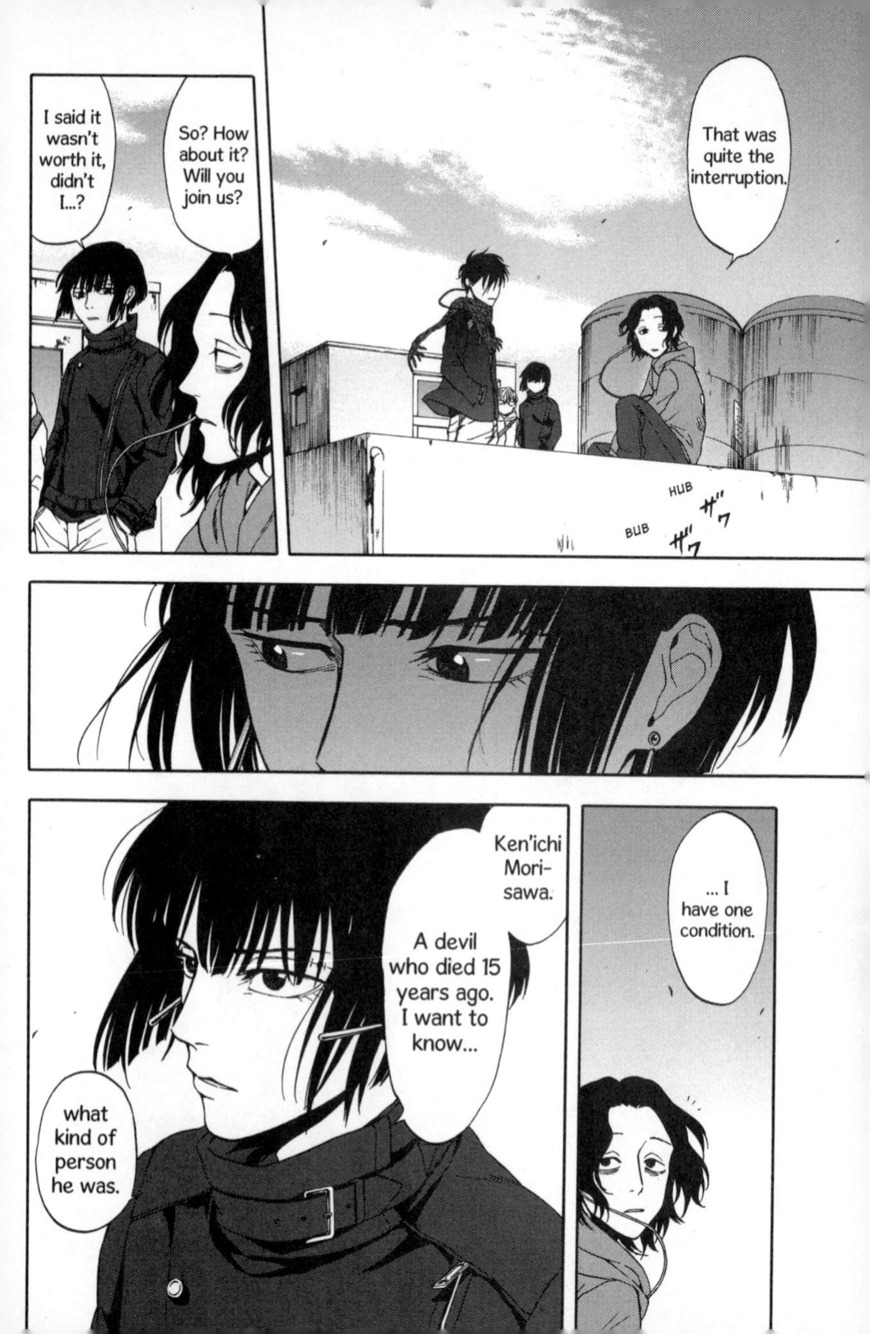

That was quite the interruption.
HUB
ザワ
BUB
ザワ
So? How about it? Will you join us?
I said it wasn't worth it, didn't I...?
... I have one condition.
Ken'ichi Mori-sawa.
A devil who died 15 years ago. I want to know...
what kind of person he was.

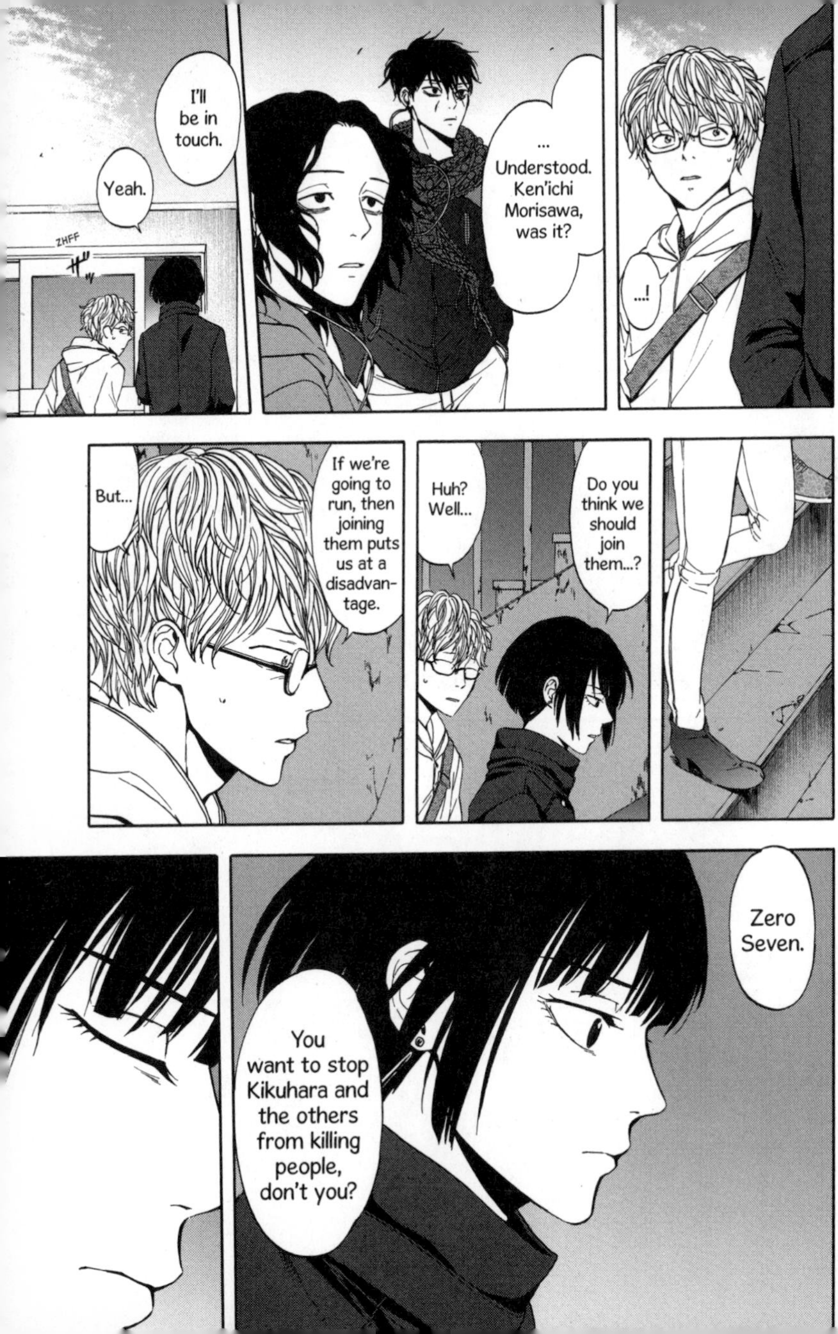
...!
...
Understood. Ken'ichi Morisawa, was it?
I'll be in touch.
Yeah.
ZHFF
Do you think we should join them...?
Huh? Well...
If we're going to run, then joining them puts us at a disadvantage.
But...
Zero Seven.
You want to stop Kikuhara and the others from killing people, don't you?

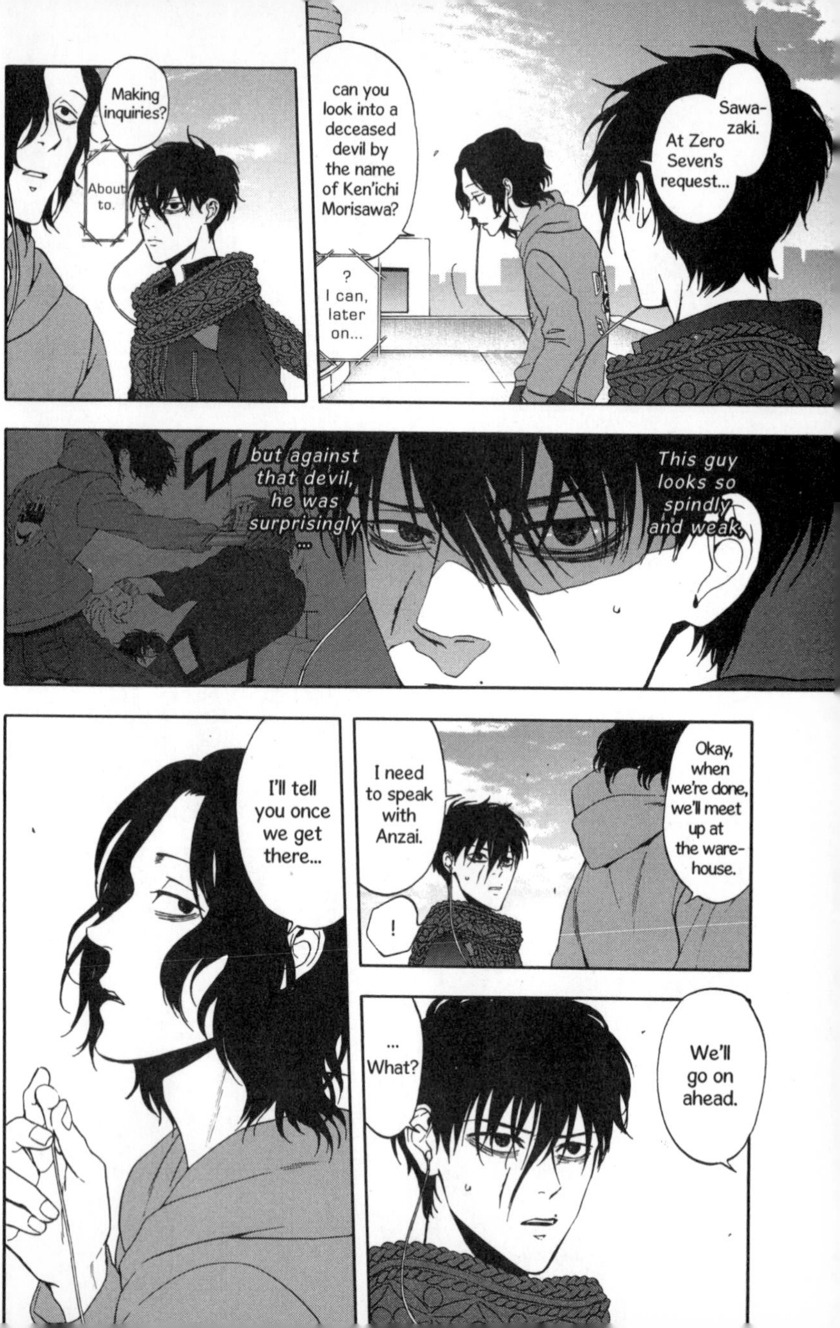
Sawa-zaki. At Zero Seven's request...
can you look into a deceased devil by the name of Ken'ichi Morisawa?
? I can, later on...
Making inquiries?
About to.
This guy looks so spindly and weak,
but against that devil, he was surprisingly ...
Okay, when we're done, we'll meet up at the ware-house.
I need to speak with Anzai.
!
We'll go on ahead.
... What?
I'll tell you once we get there...

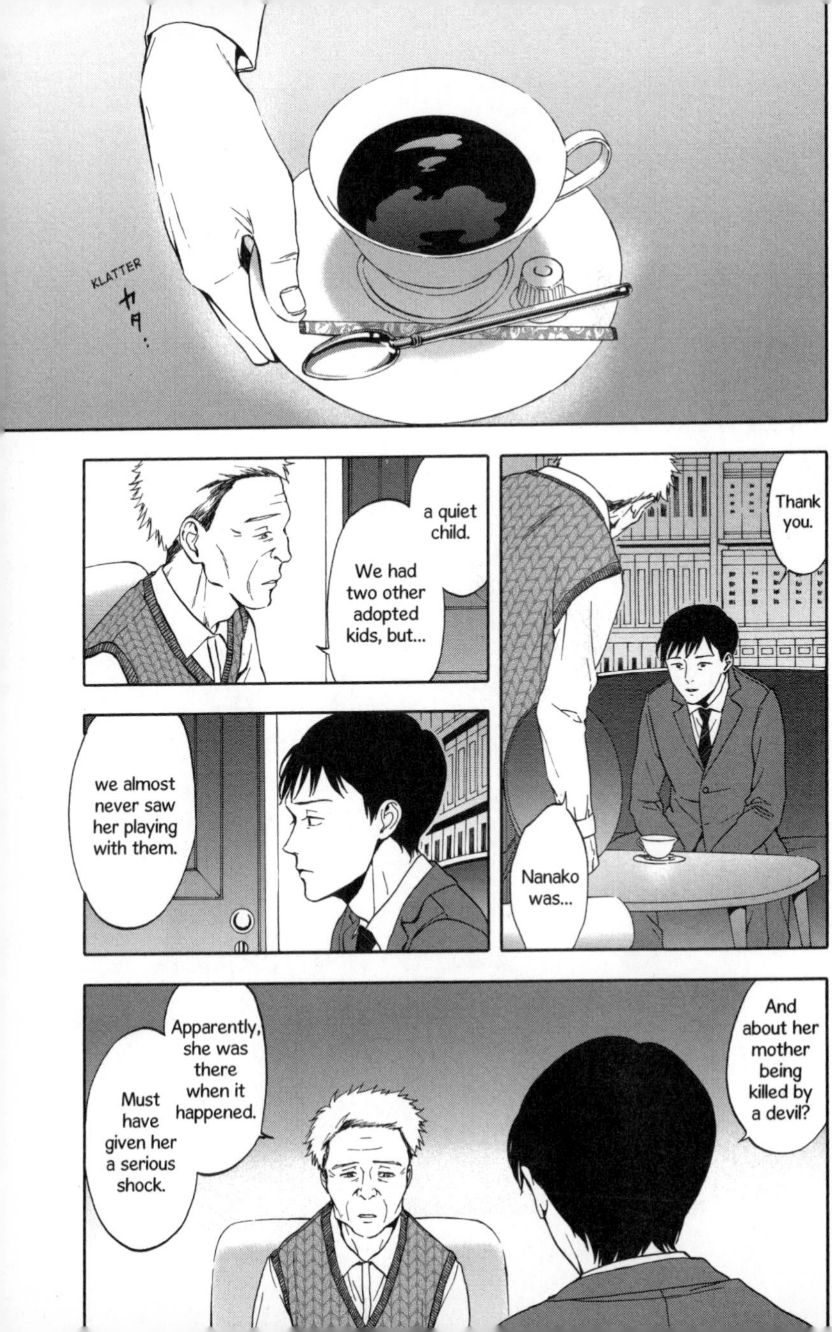
KLATTER
カタ..
Thank you.
Nanako was...
a quiet child.
We had two other adopted kids, but...
we almost never saw her playing with them.
And about her mother being killed by a devil?
Apparently, she was there when it happened.
Must have given her a serious shock.

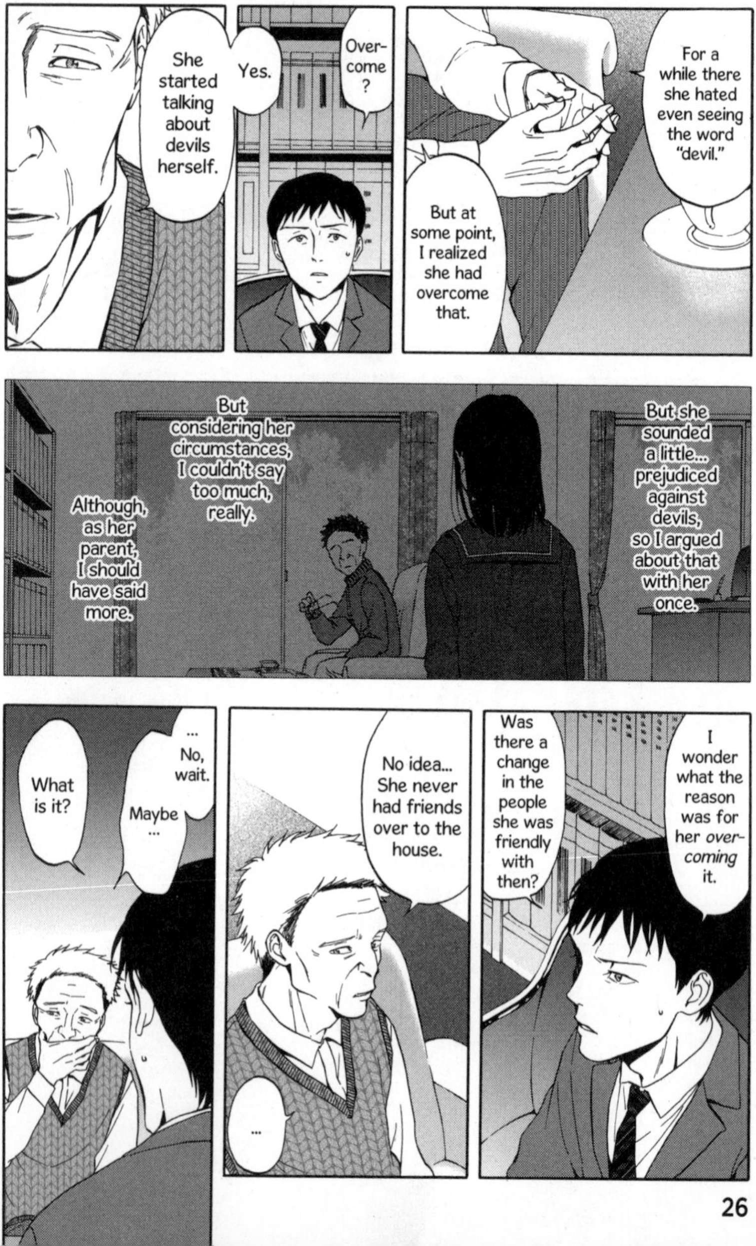

For a while there she hated even seeing the word "devil."
But at some point, I realized she had overcome that.
Over-come?
Yes.
She started talking about devils herself.
But she sounded a little... prejudiced against devils, so I argued about that with her once.
But considering her circumstances, I couldn't say too much, really.
Although, as her parent, I should have said more.
I wonder what the reason was for her *over-coming* it.
Was there a change in the people she was friendly with then?
No idea... She never had friends over to the house.
...
... No, wait.
Maybe ...
What is it?

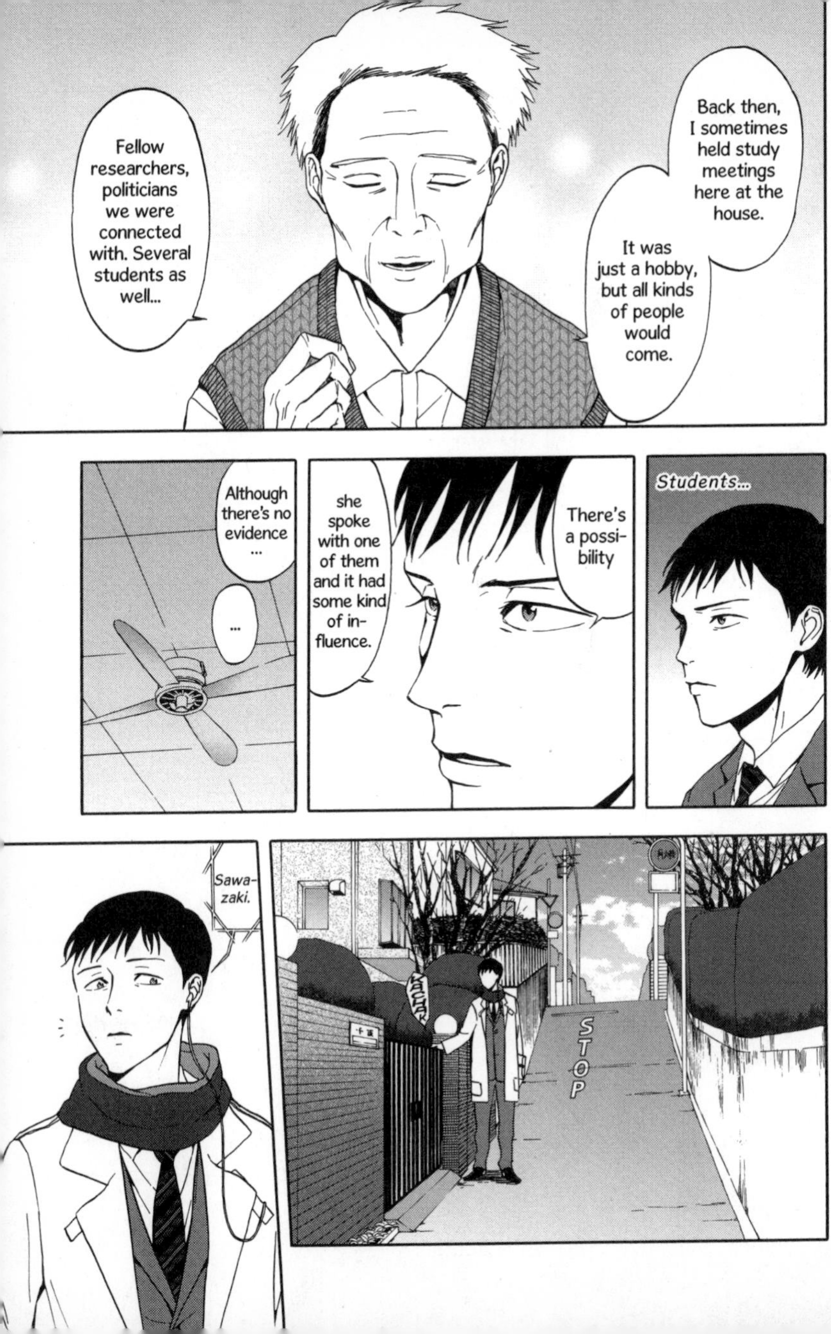
Back then, I sometimes held study meetings here at the house.
It was just a hobby, but all kinds of people would come.
Fellow researchers, politicians we were connected with. Several students as well...
Students...
There's a possi-bility
she spoke with one of them and it had some kind of in-fluence.
Although there's no evidence ...
...
STOP
Sawa-zaki.

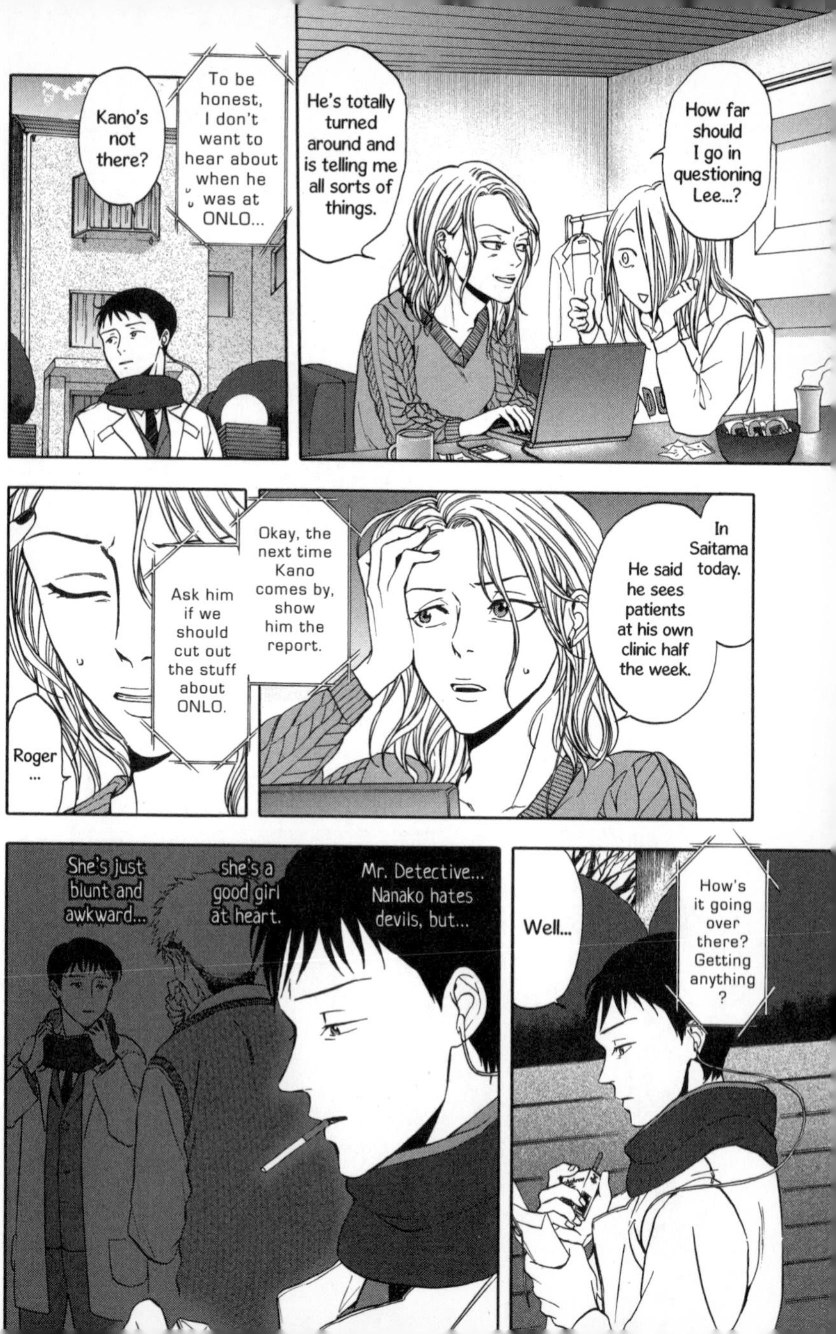
How far should I go in questioning Lee...?
He's totally turned around and is telling me all sorts of things.
To be honest, I don't want to hear about when he was at ONLO...
Kano's not there?
In Saitama today.
He said he sees patients at his own clinic half the week.
Okay, the next time Kano comes by, show him the report.
Ask him if we should cut out the stuff about ONLO.
Roger ...
How's it going over there? Getting anything ?
Well...
Mr. Detective... Nanako hates devils, but...
she's a good girl at heart.
She's just blunt and awkward...

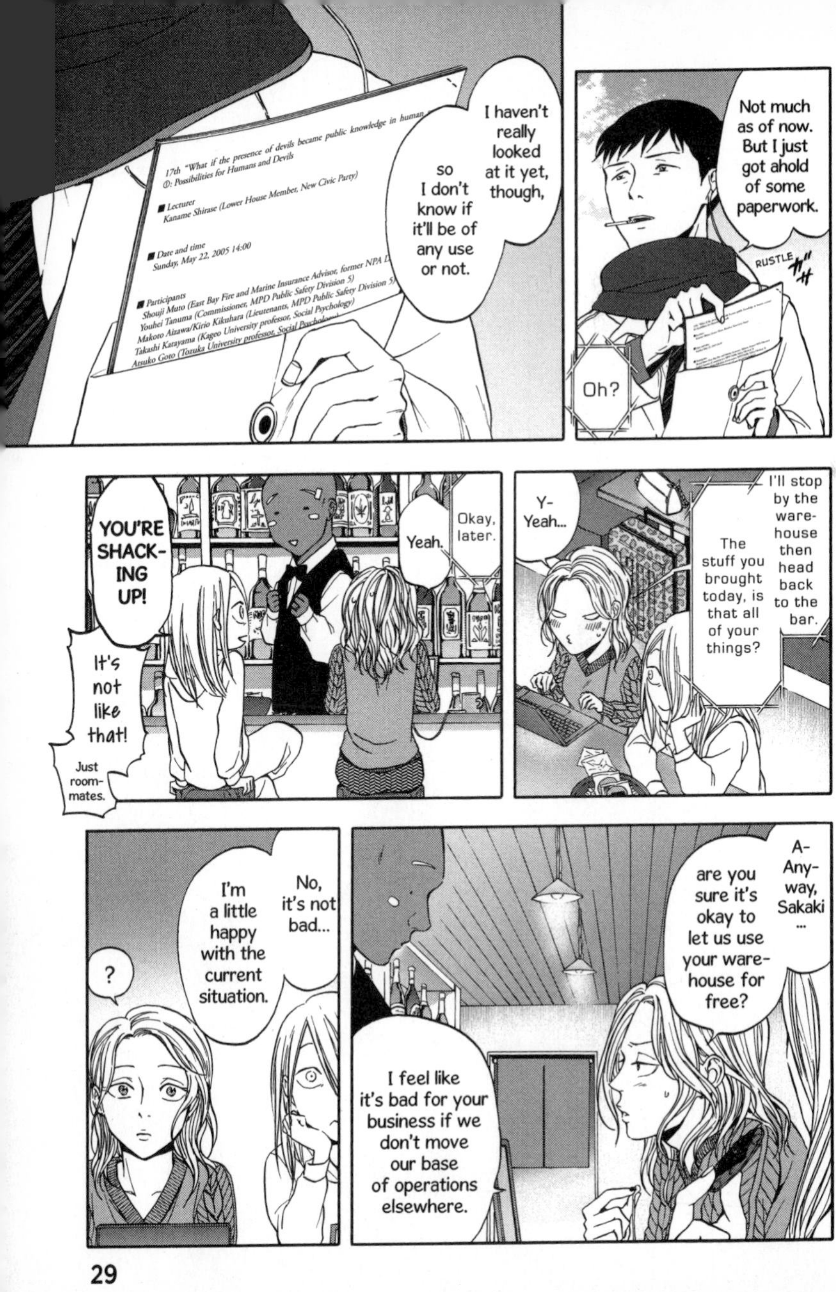
Not much as of now. But I just got ahold of some paperwork.
RUSTLE
Oh?
I haven't really looked at it yet, though,
so I don't know if it'll be of any use or not.
17th "What if the presence of devils became public knowledge in human
①: Possibilities for Humans and Devils
■ Lecturer
Kaname Shirase (Lower House Member, New Civic Party)
■ Date and time
Sunday, May 22, 2005 14:00
■ Participants
Shouji Muto (East Bay Fire and Marine Insurance Advisor, former NPA
Youhei Tanuma (Commissioner, MPD Public Safety Division 5)
Makoto Aizawa/Kirio Kikuhara (Lieutenants, MPD Public Safety Division 5)
Takashi Katayama (Kageo University professor, Social Psychology)
Atsuko Goto (Tozuka University professor,
I'll stop by the warehouse then head back to the bar.
The stuff you brought today, is that all of your things?
Y- Yeah...
Okay, later.
Yeah.
YOU'RE SHACKING UP!
It's not like that!
Just roommates.
A- Anyway, Sakaki...
are you sure it's okay to let us use your warehouse for free?
I feel like it's bad for your business if we don't move our base of operations elsewhere.
No, it's not bad...
I'm a little happy with the current situation.
?

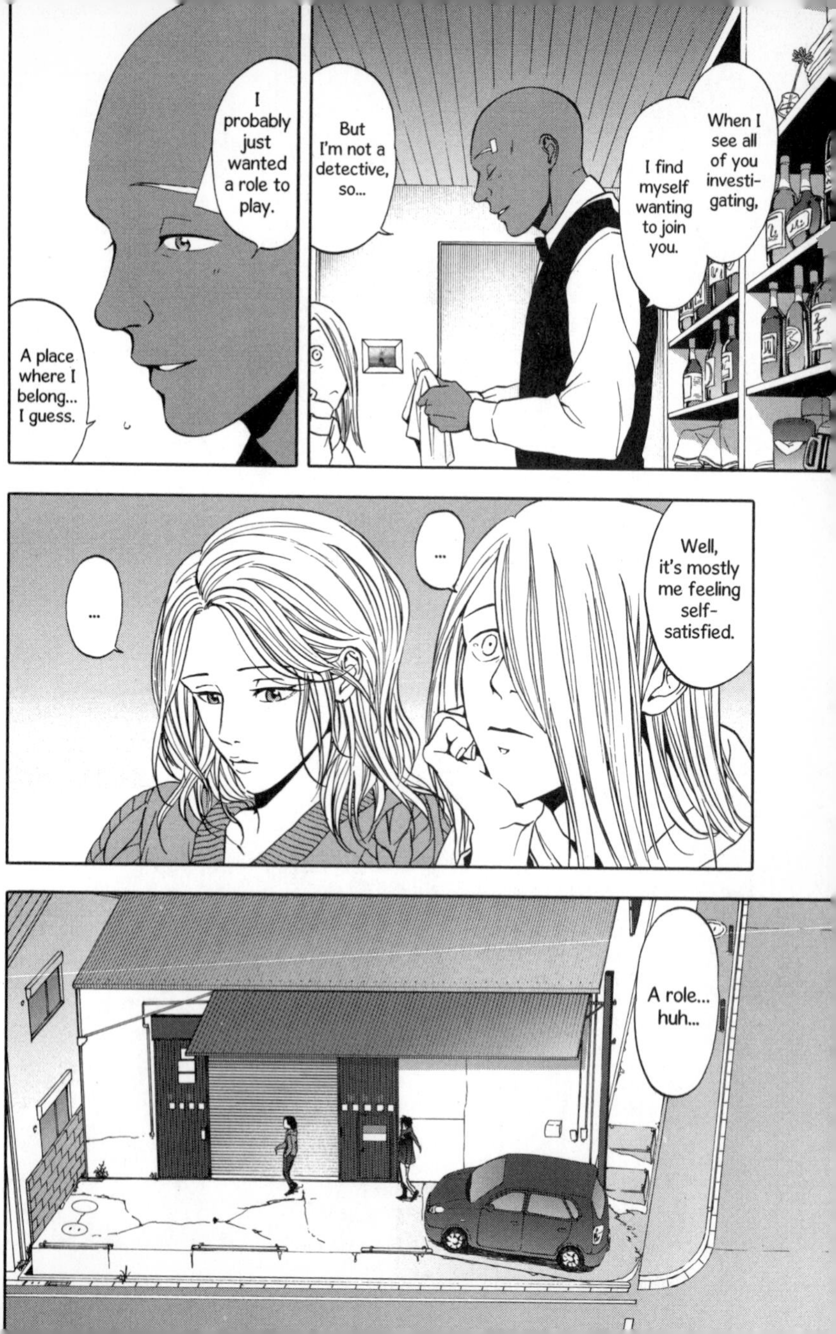
When I see all of you investigating,
I find myself wanting to join you.
But I'm not a detective, so...
I probably just wanted a role to play.
A place where I belong... I guess.
Well, it's mostly me feeling self-satisfied.
...
...
A role... huh...

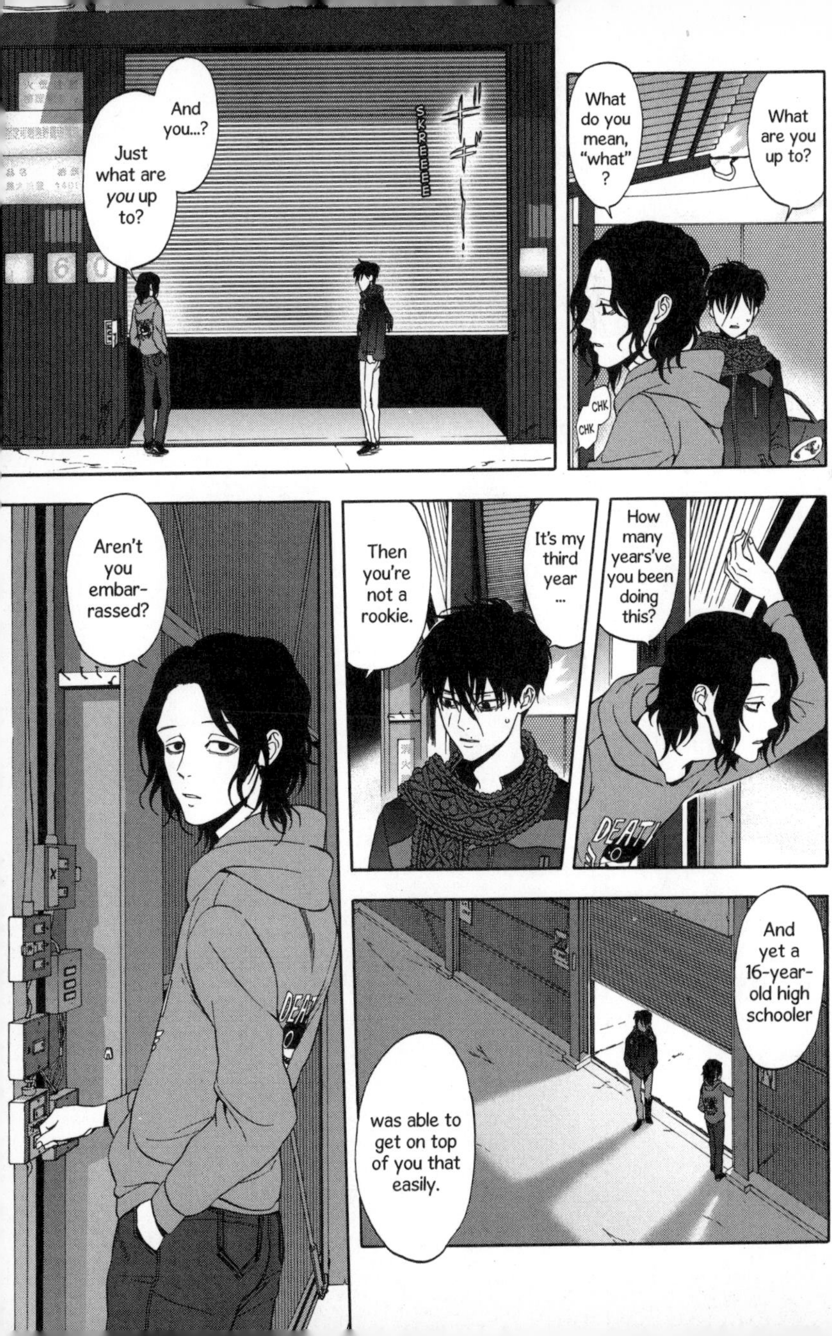
What are you up to?
What do you mean, "what"?
CHK
CHK
SKREEEE
And you...?
Just what are you up to?
How many years've you been doing this?
It's my third year ...
Then you're not a rookie.
And yet a 16-year-old high schooler
was able to get on top of you that easily.
Aren't you embarrassed?

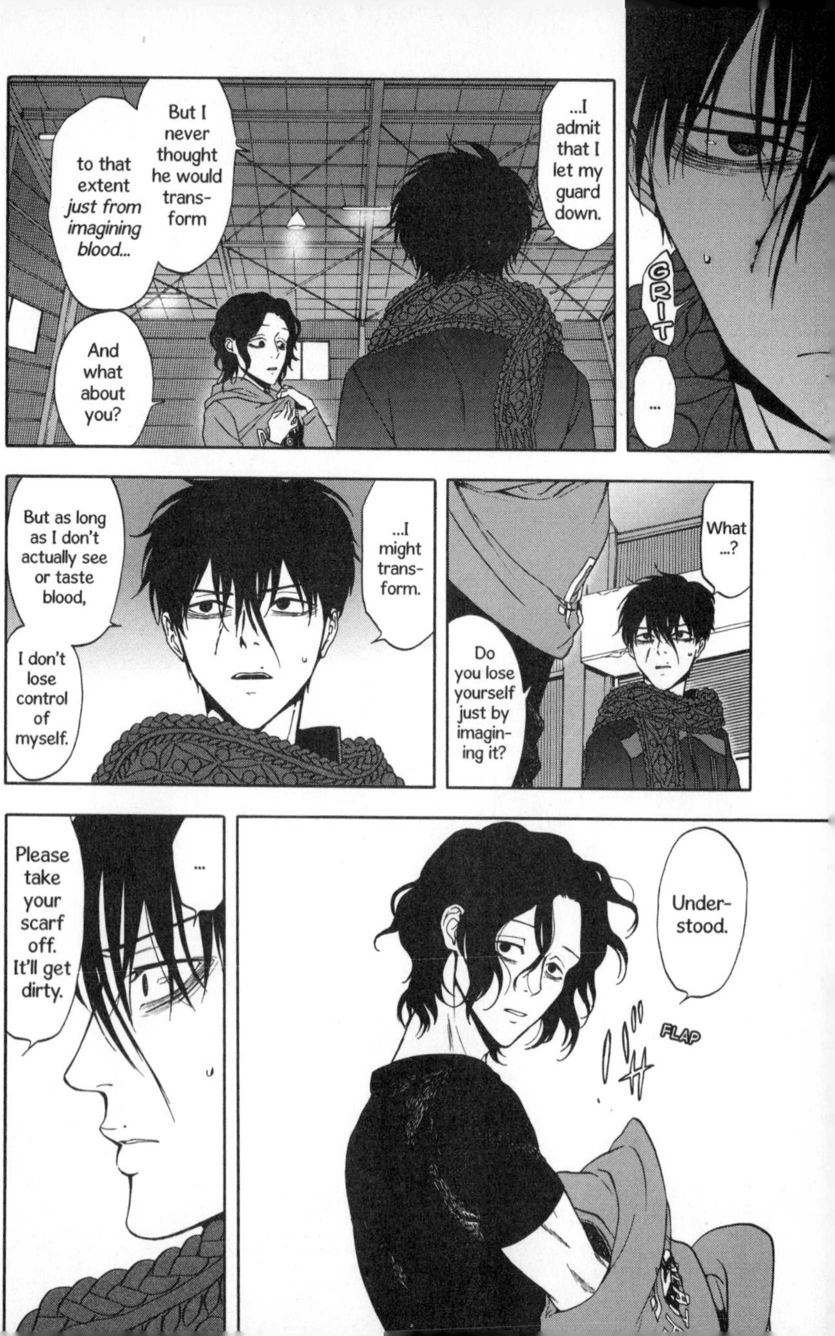

GRIT
...
...I admit that I let my guard down.
But I never thought he would transform
to that extent *just from imagining blood...*
And what about you?
What...?
Do you lose yourself just by imagining it?
...I might transform.
But as long as I don't actually see or taste blood,
I don't lose control of myself.
Understood.
FLAP
...
Please take your scarf off. It'll get dirty.

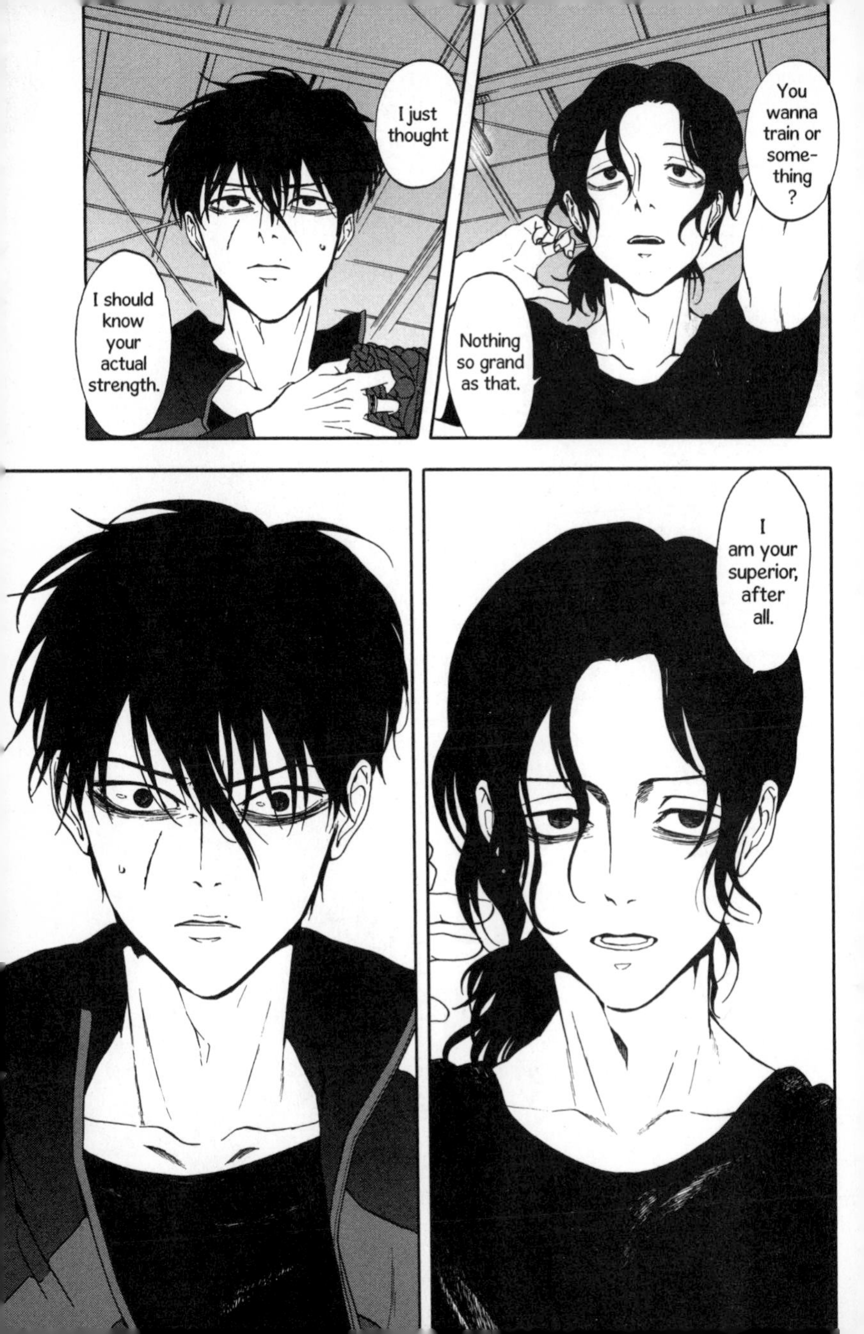
You wanna train or some-thing?
Nothing so grand as that.
I just thought
I should know your actual strength.
I am your superior, after all.

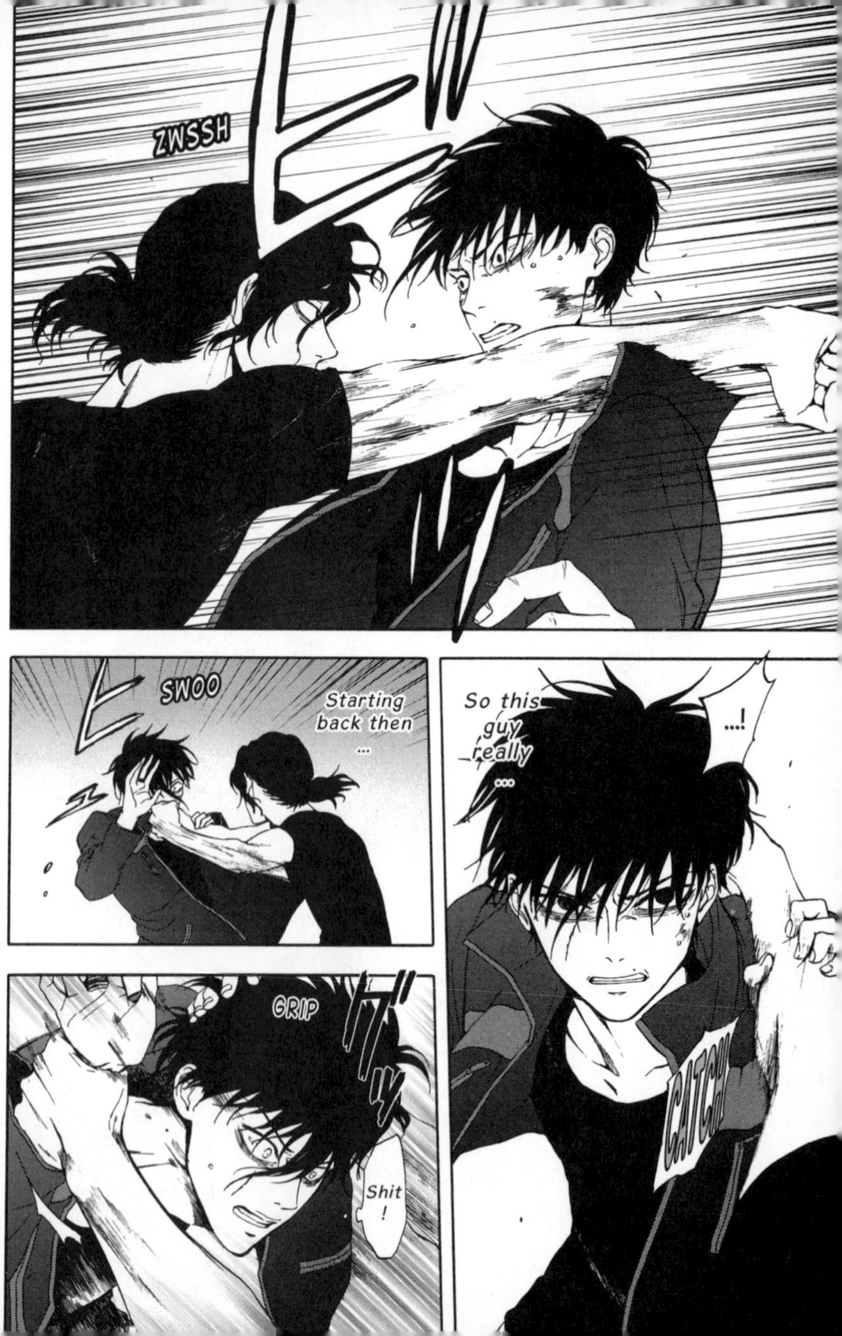
ZWSSH
So this guy really ...
...!
CATCH
SWOO
Starting back then ...
GRIP
Shit!

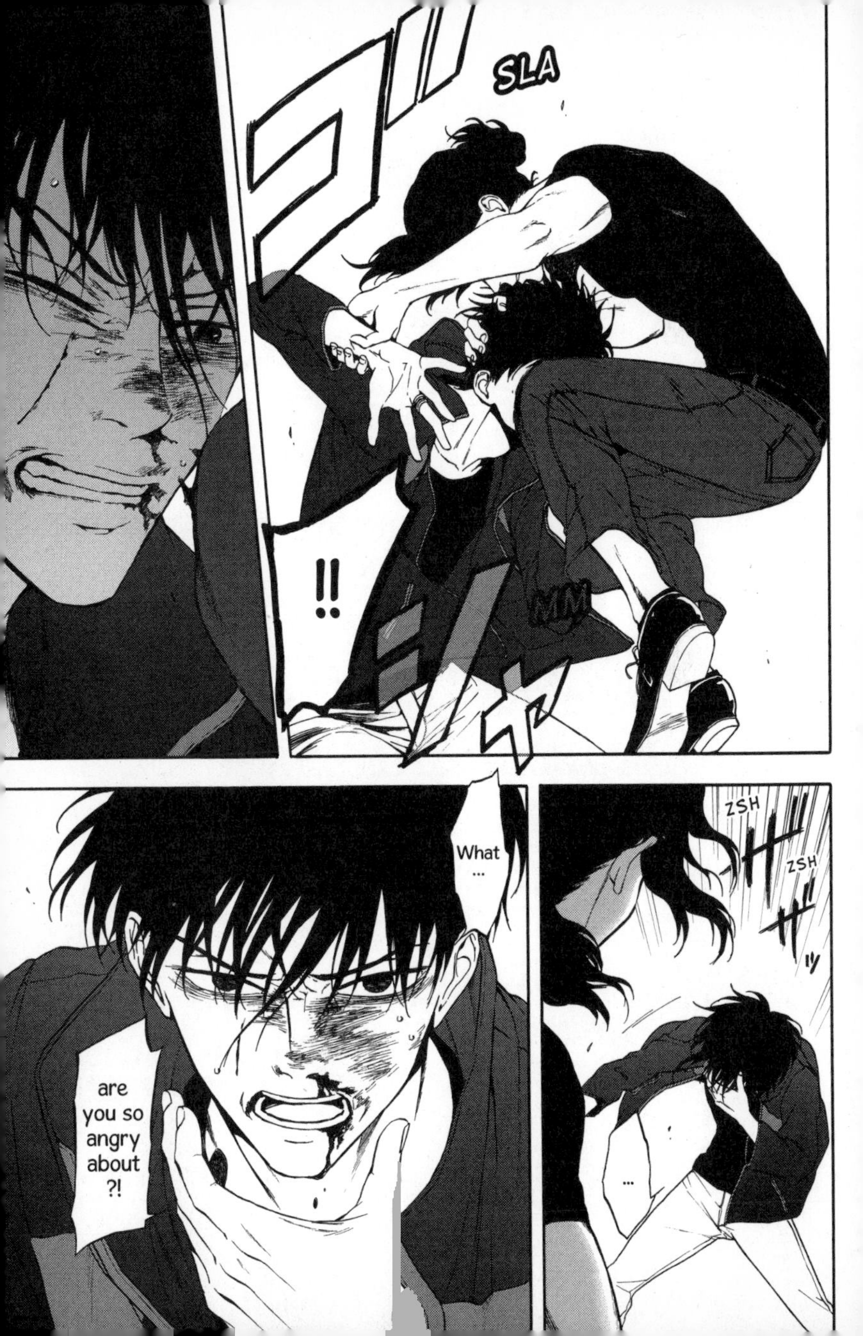
SLA
!!
MM
ZSH
ZSH
...
What ...
are you so angry about ?!

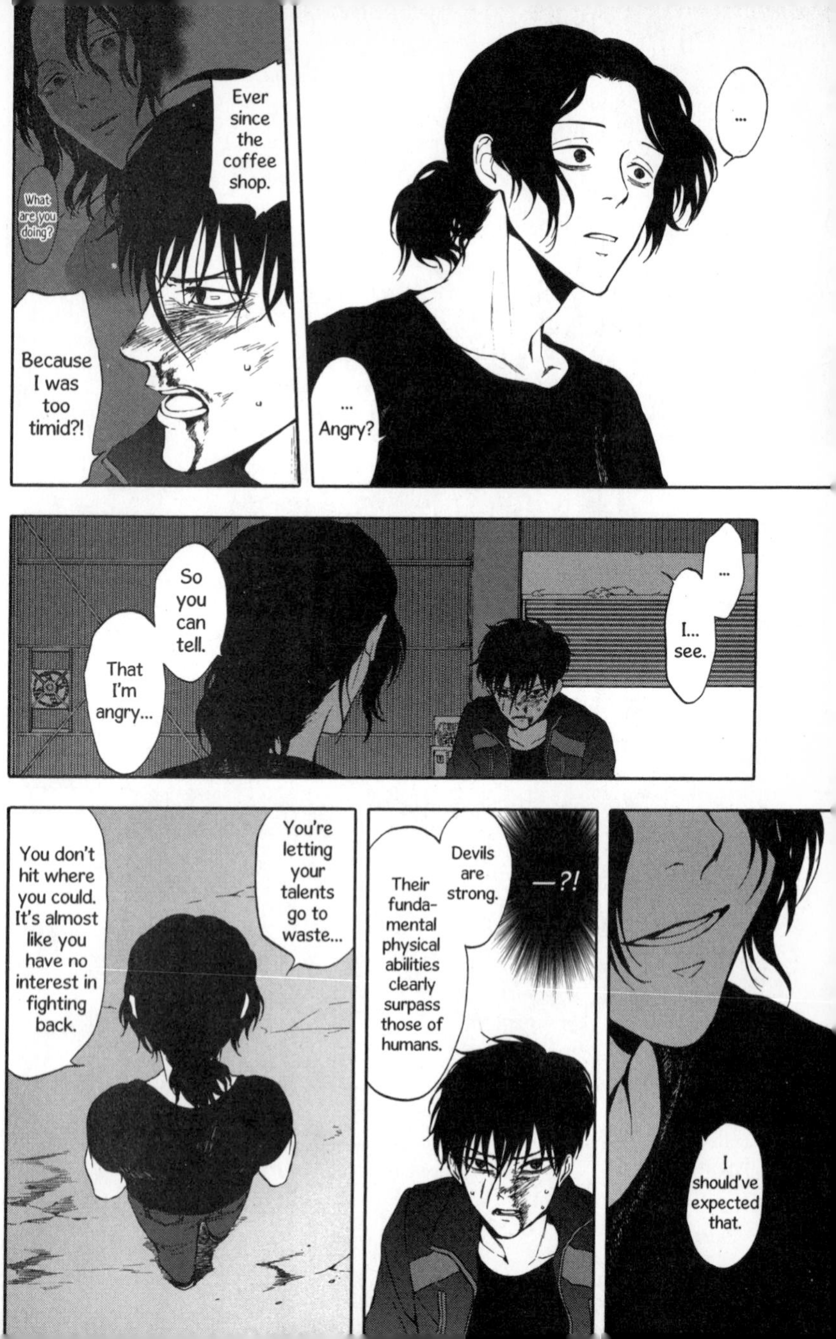
...
...
Angry?
Ever since the coffee shop.
What are you doing?
Because I was too timid?!
...
I... see.
So you can tell.
That I'm angry...
I should've expected that.
—?!
Devils are strong.
Their fundamental physical abilities clearly surpass those of humans.
You're letting your talents go to waste...
You don't hit where you could. It's almost like you have no interest in fighting back.

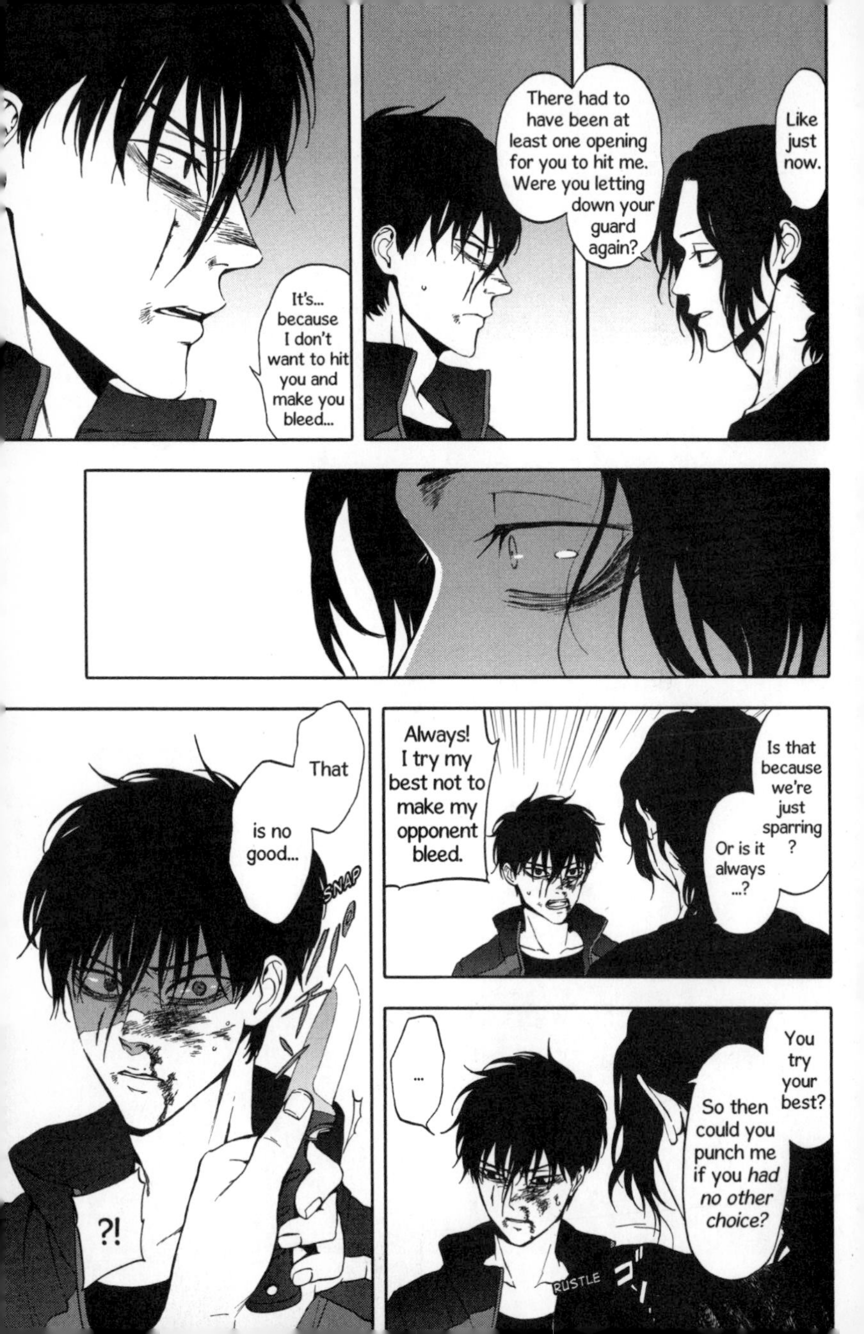

There had to have been at least one opening for you to hit me. Were you letting down your guard again?
Like just now.
It's... because I don't want to hit you and make you bleed...
Is that because we're just sparring?
Or is it always ...?
Always! I try my best not to make my opponent bleed.
You try your best?
So then could you punch me if you *had no other choice?*
...
RUSTLE
That is no good...
SNAP
?!

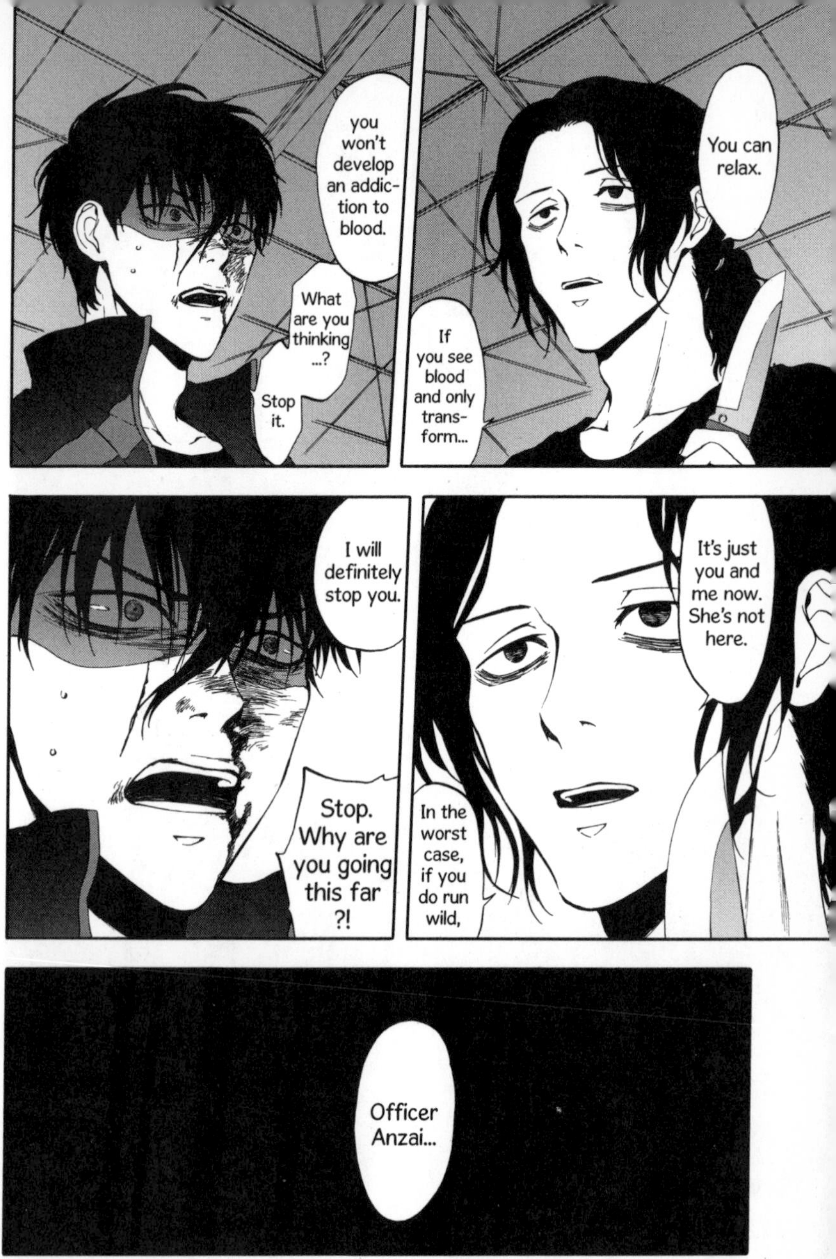
You can relax.
If you see blood and only transform...
you won't develop an addiction to blood.
What are you thinking ...?
Stop it.
It's just you and me now. She's not here.
In the worst case, if you do run wild,
I will definitely stop you.
Stop. Why are you going this far ?!
Officer Anzai...

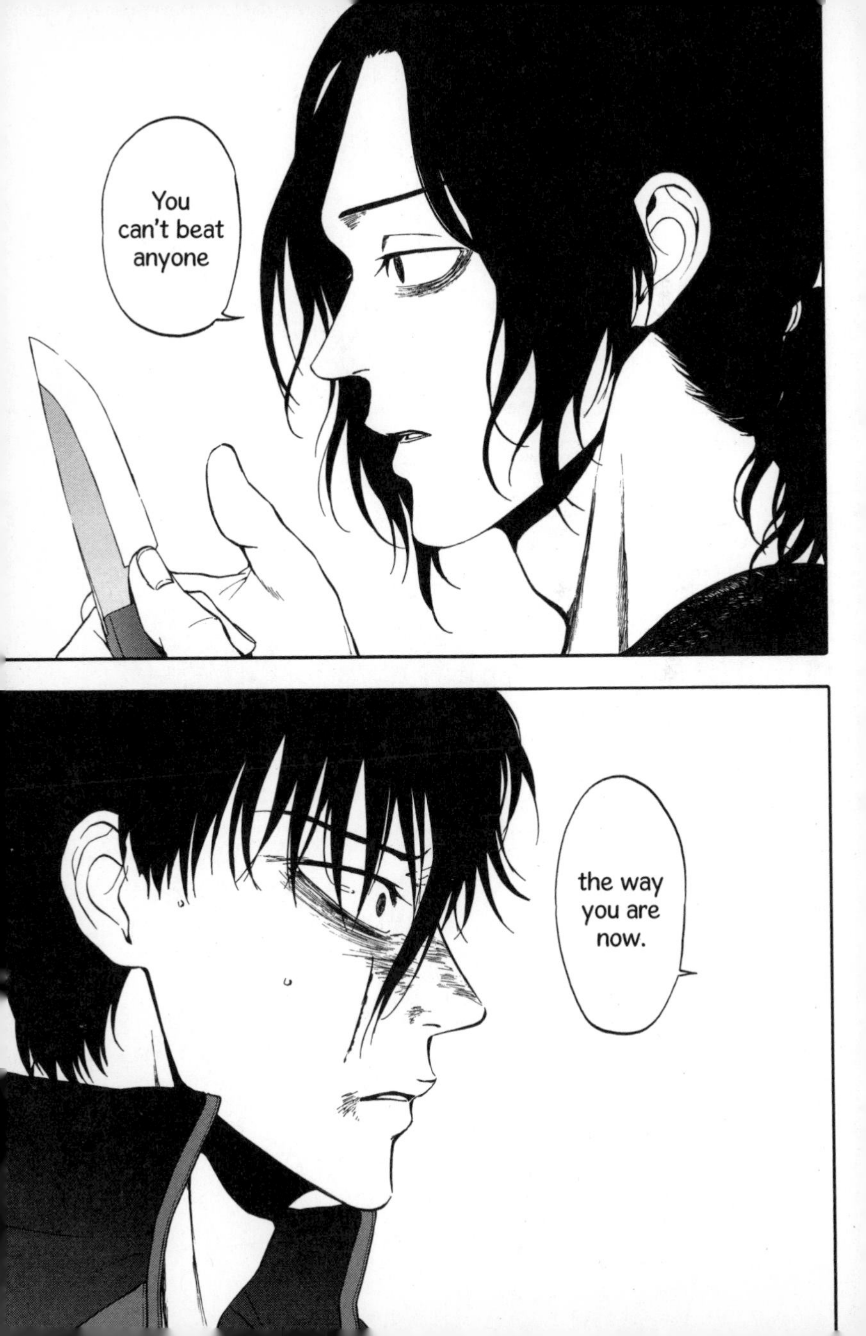
You can't beat anyone
the way you are now.

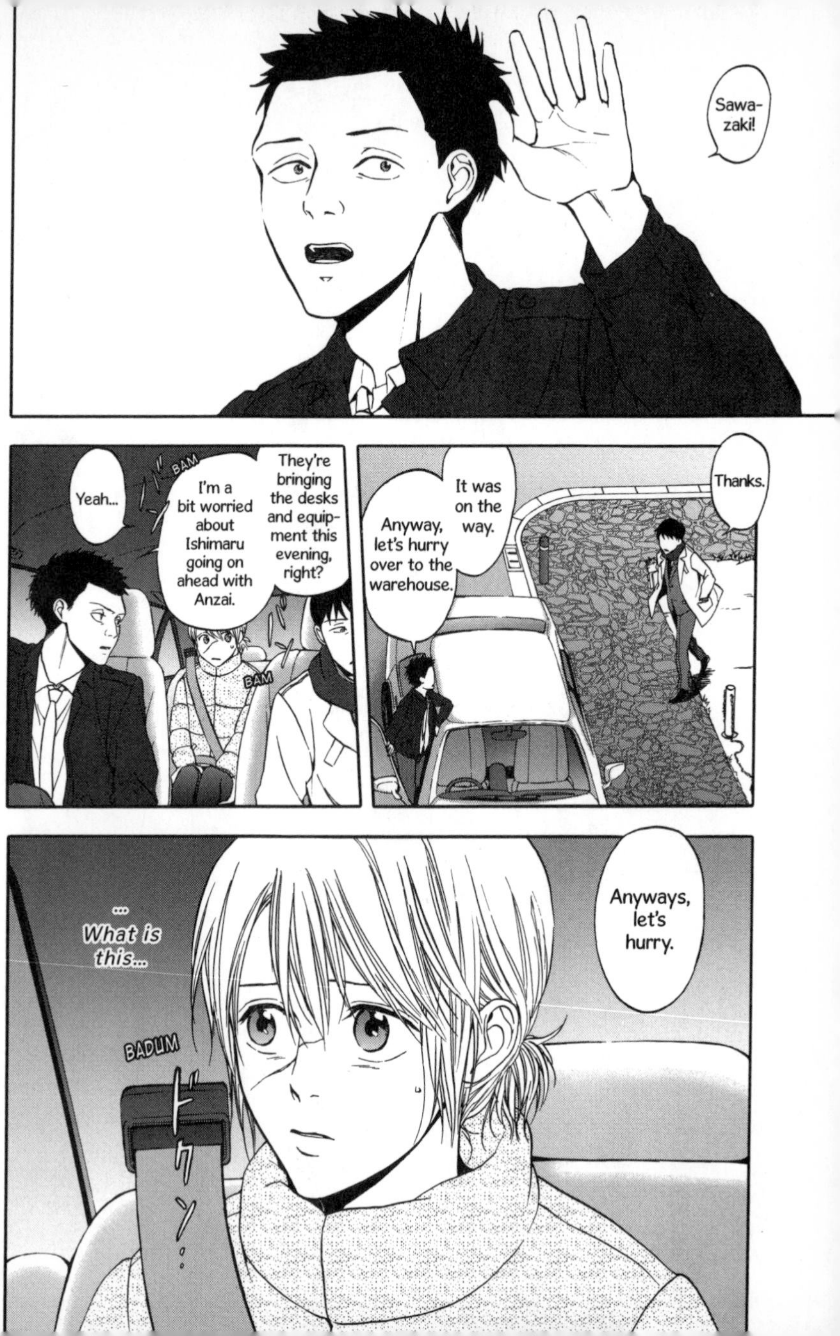

Sawa-
zaki!
Thanks.
It was on the way.
Anyway, let's hurry over to the warehouse.
They're bringing the desks and equip-ment this evening, right?
BAM
I'm a bit worried about Ishimaru going on ahead with Anzai.
Yeah...
BAM
Anyways, let's hurry.
... What is this...
BADUM
ドクン

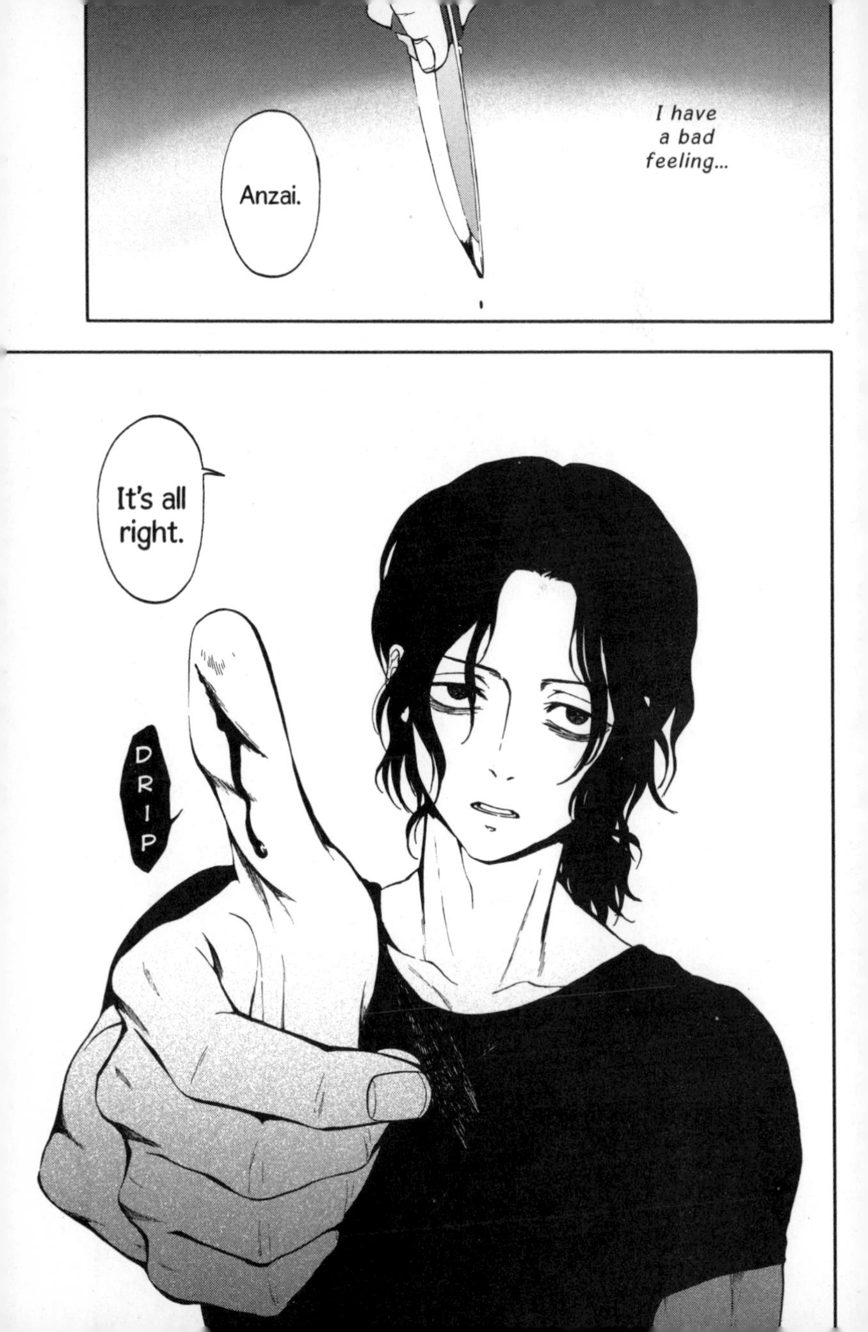
I have a bad feeling...
Anzai.
It's all right.
DRIP

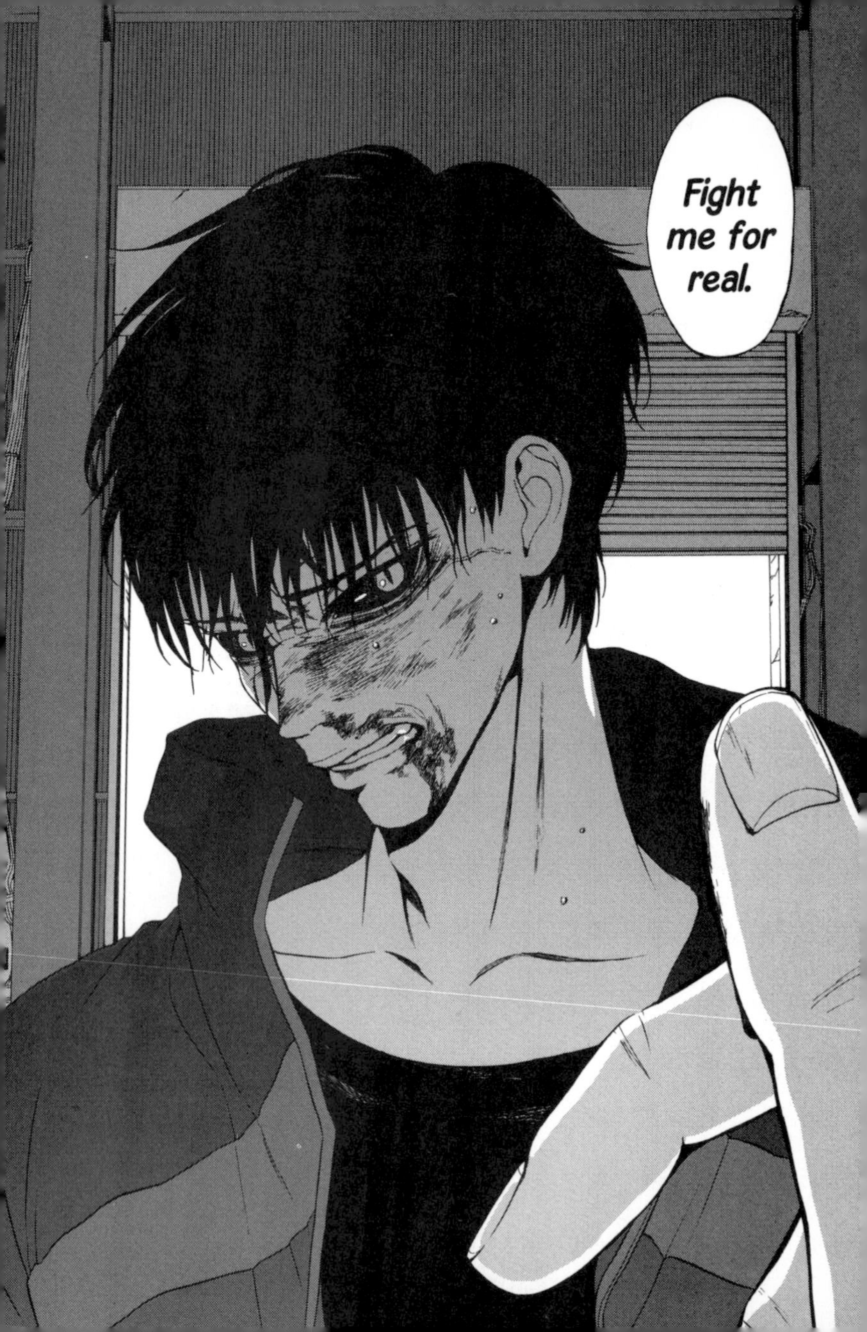
Fight me for real.

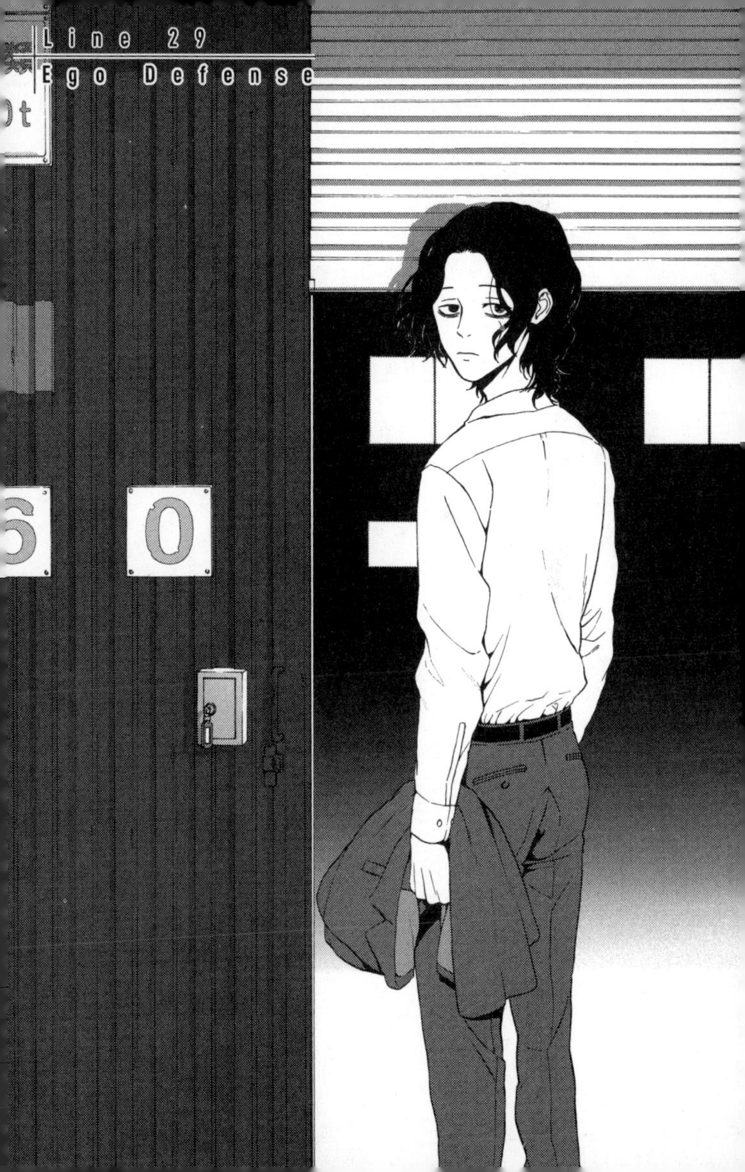
Line 29
Ego Defense

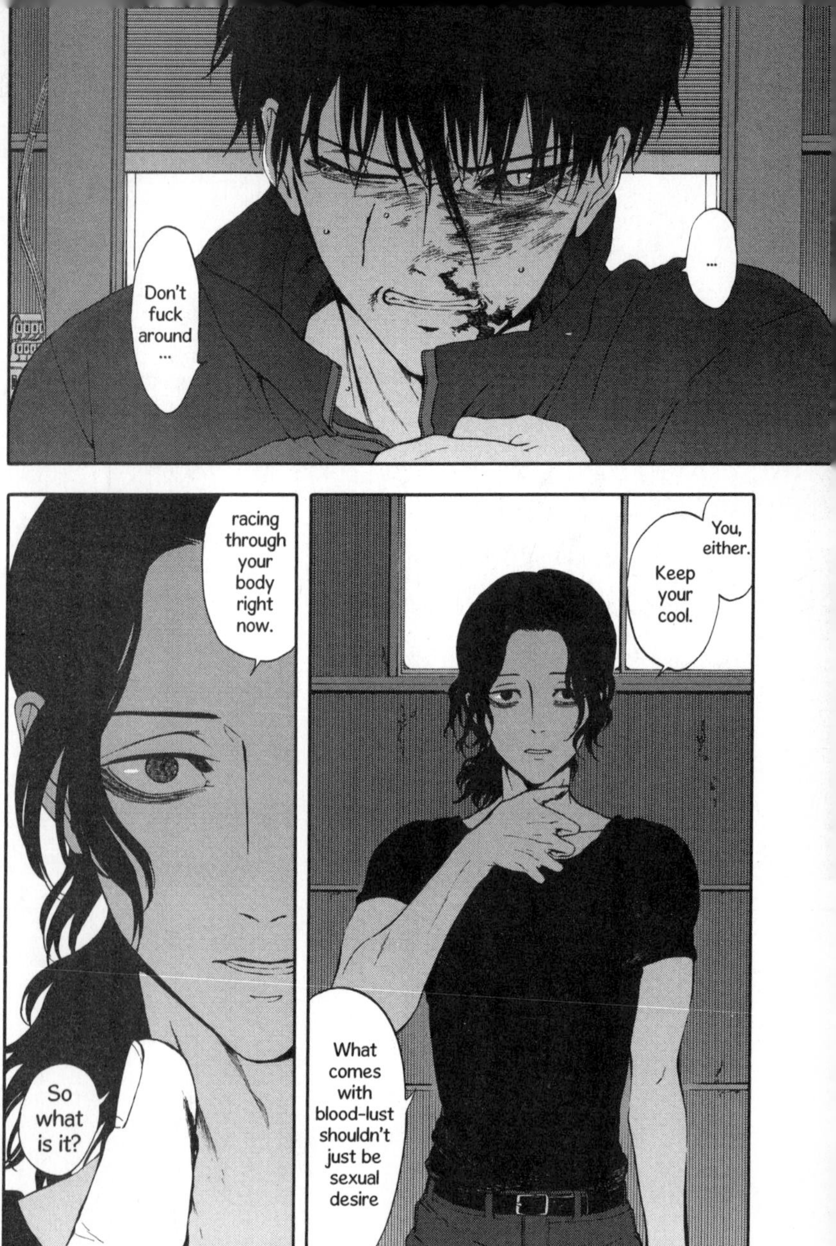
...
Don't fuck around ...
You, either.
Keep your cool.
What comes with blood-lust shouldn't just be sexual desire
racing through your body right now.
So what is it?

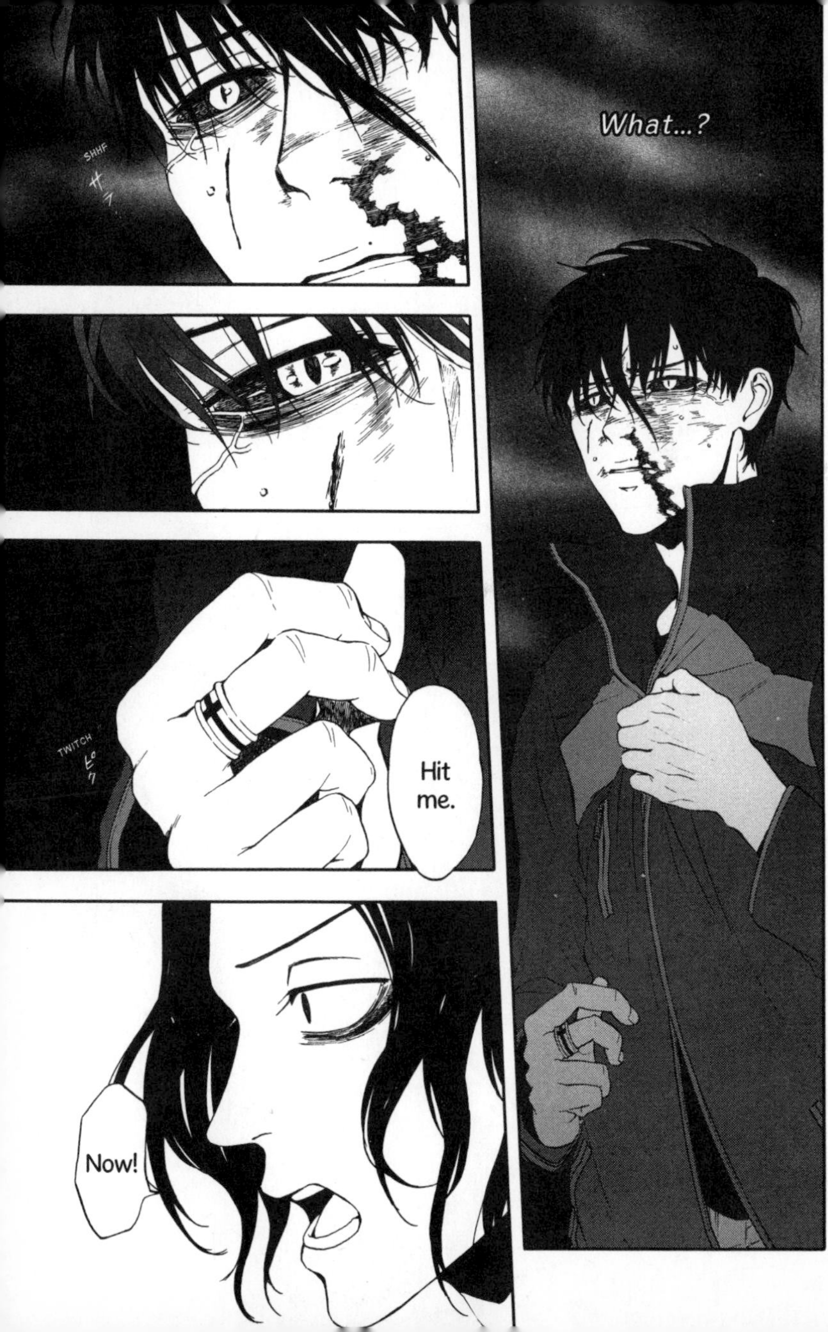
What...?
SHHF
Hit me.
TWITCH
Now!

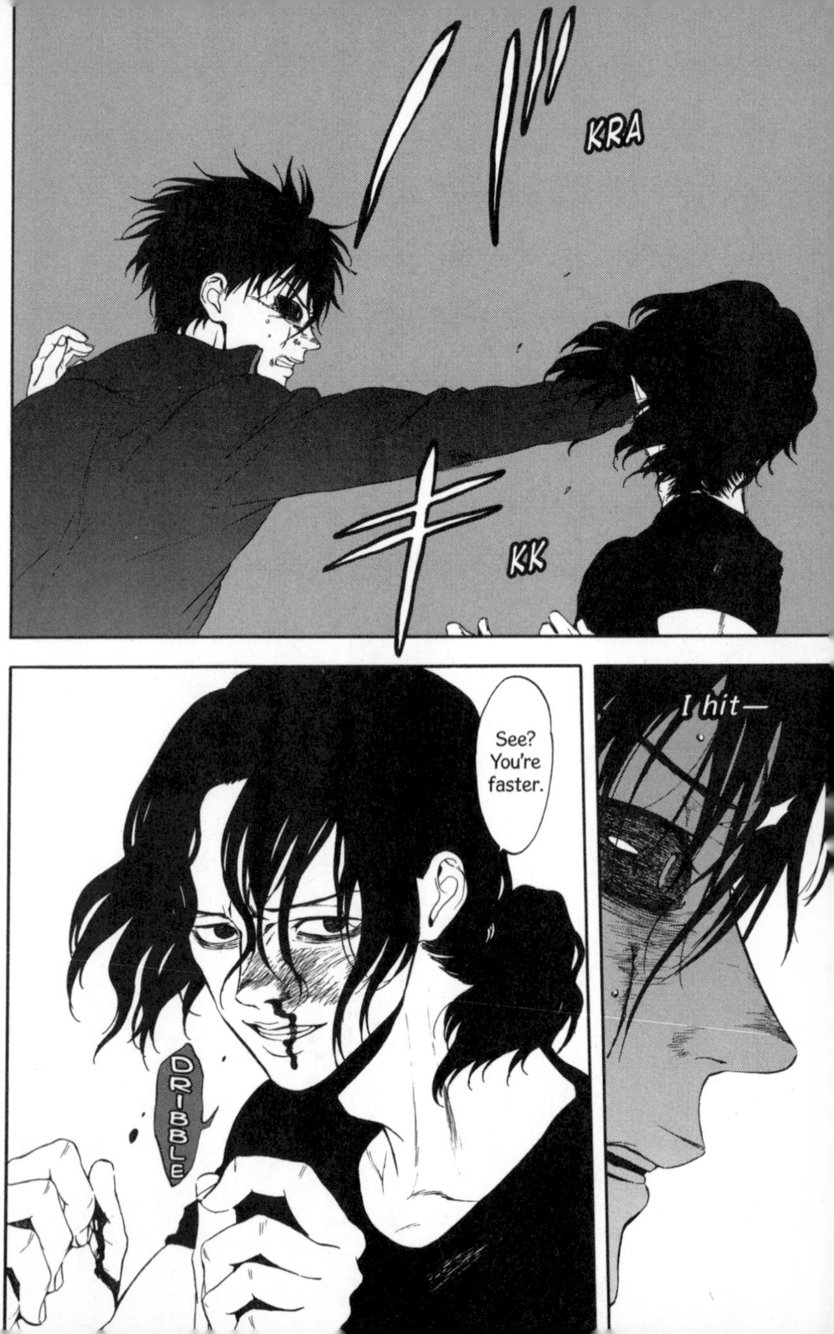
KRA
KK
I hit—
See? You're faster.
DRIBBLE

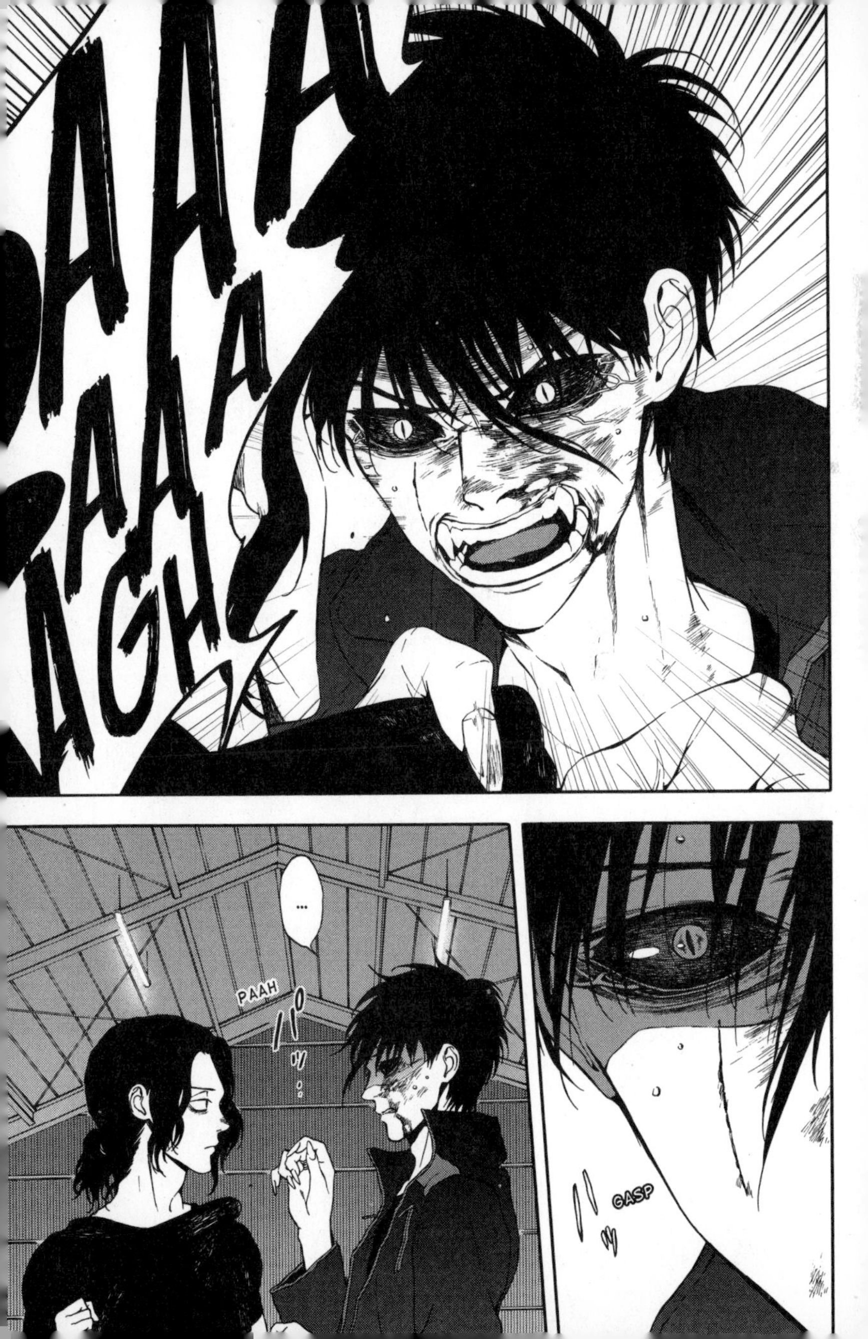
GASP
...
PAAH

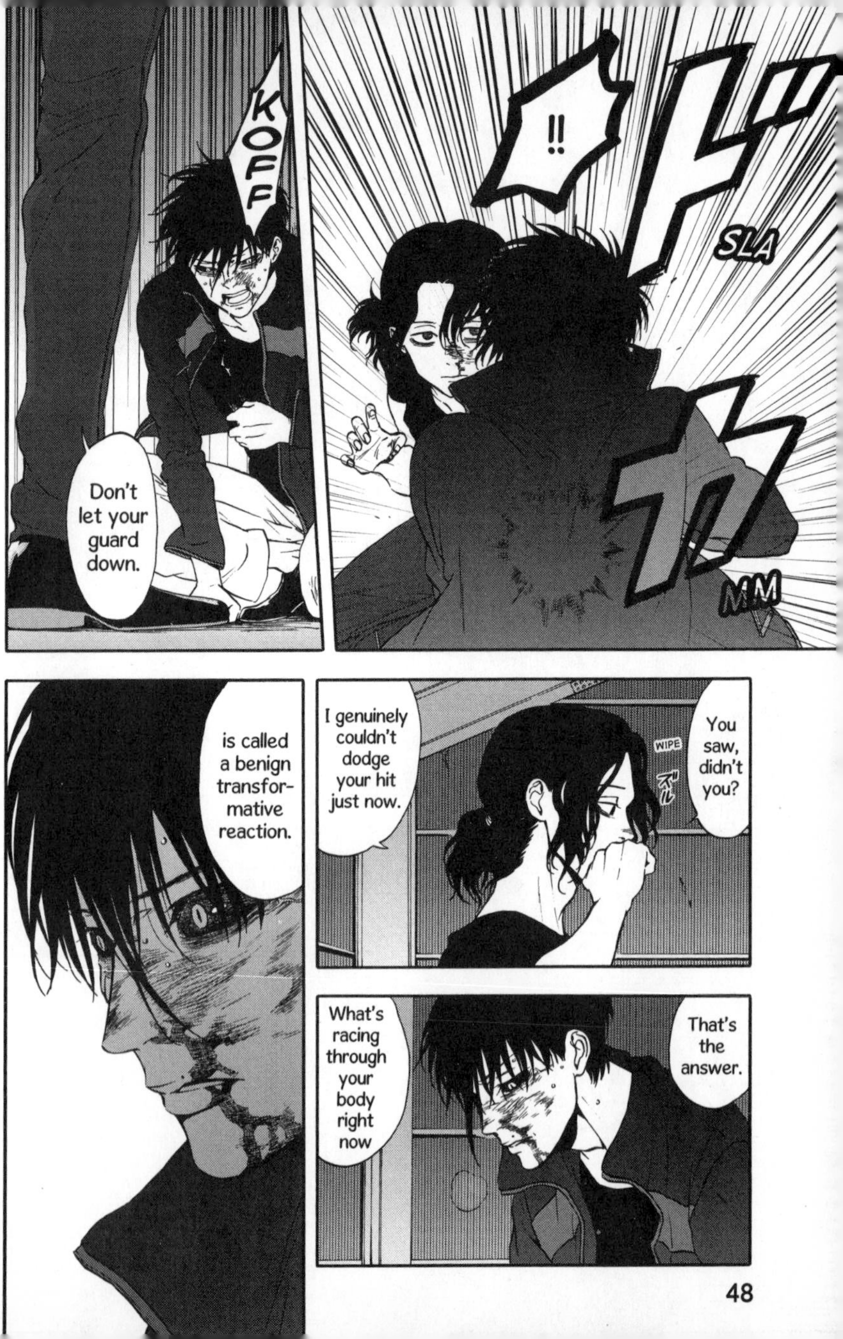
!!
SLA
MM
KOFF
Don't let your guard down.
You saw, didn't you?
WIPE
ズル
I genuinely couldn't dodge your hit just now.
That's the answer.
What's racing through your body right now
is called a benign transfor-mative reaction.

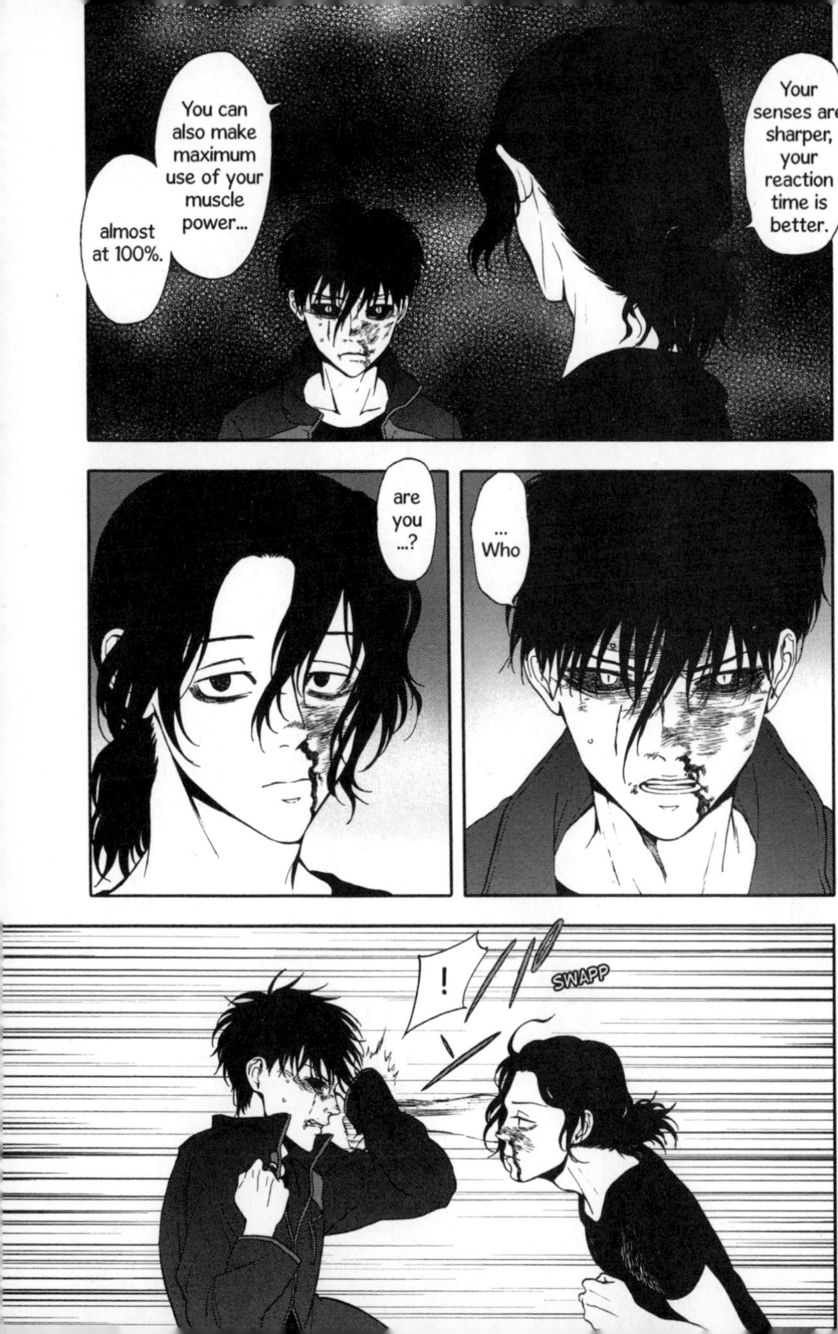
Your senses are sharper, your reaction time is better.
You can also make maximum use of your muscle power...
almost at 100%.
... Who
are you ...?
!
SWAPP

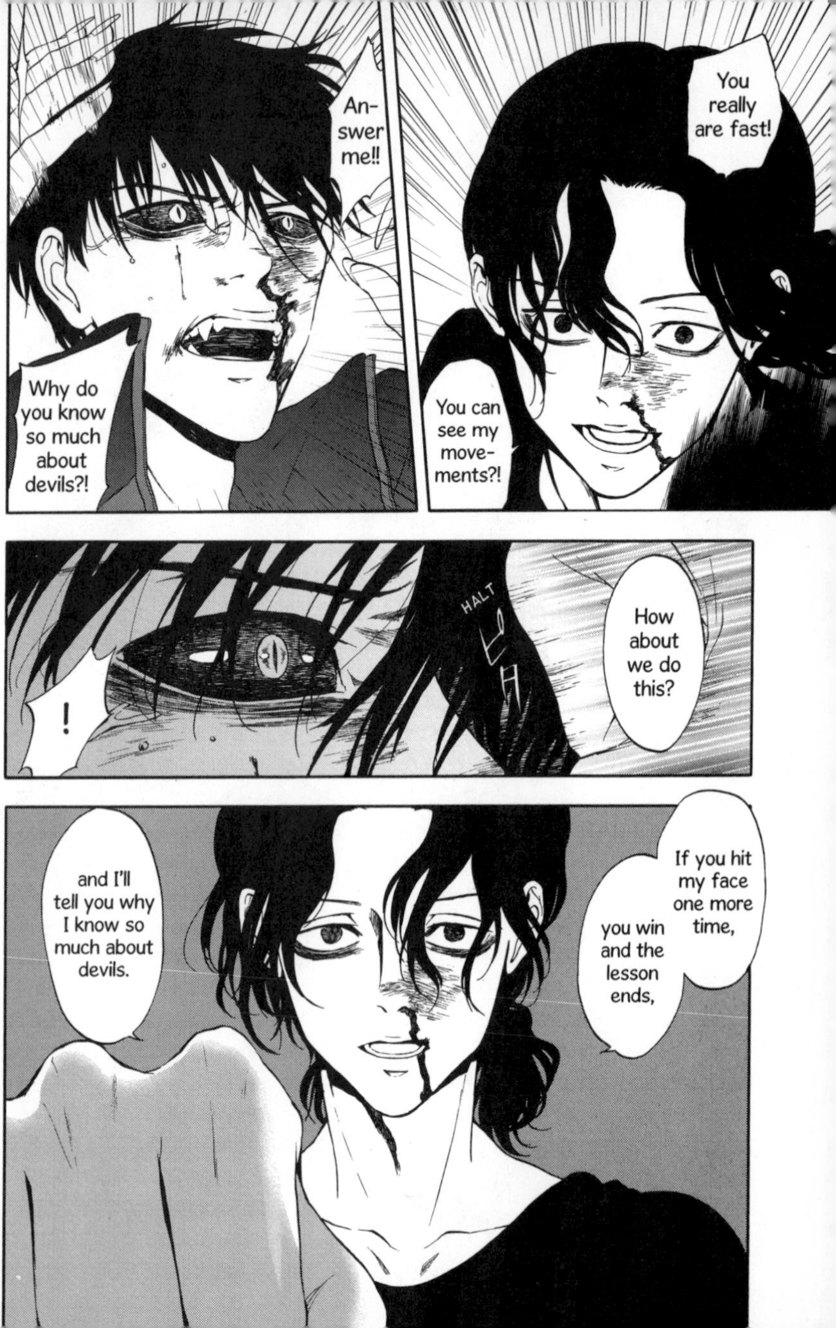

You really are fast!
You can see my movements?!
An-swer me!!
Why do you know so much about devils?!
How about we do this?
HALT
!
If you hit my face one more time,
you win and the lesson ends,
and I'll tell you why I know so much about devils.

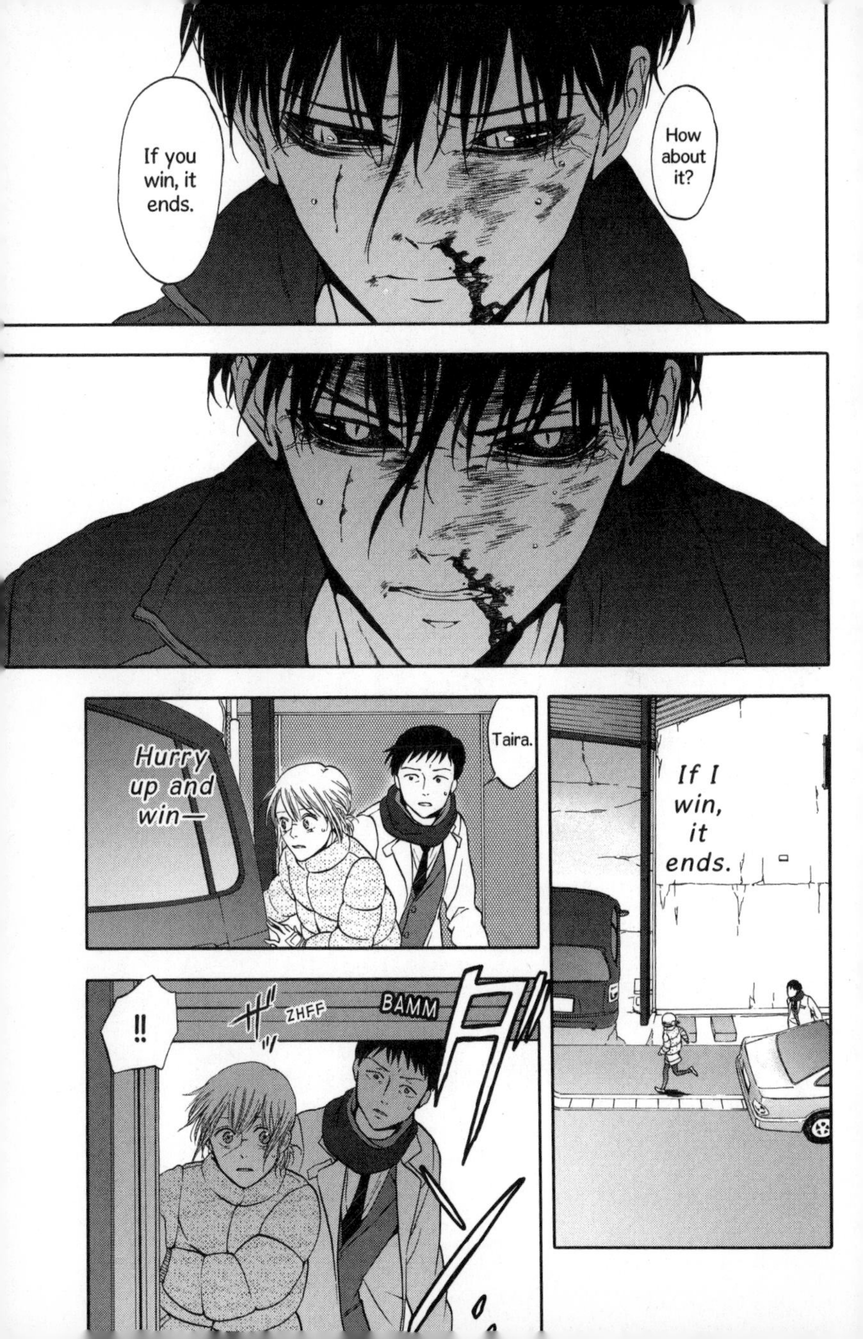
How about it?
If you win, it ends.
If I win, it ends.
Taira.
Hurry up and win—
BAMM
ZHFF
!!

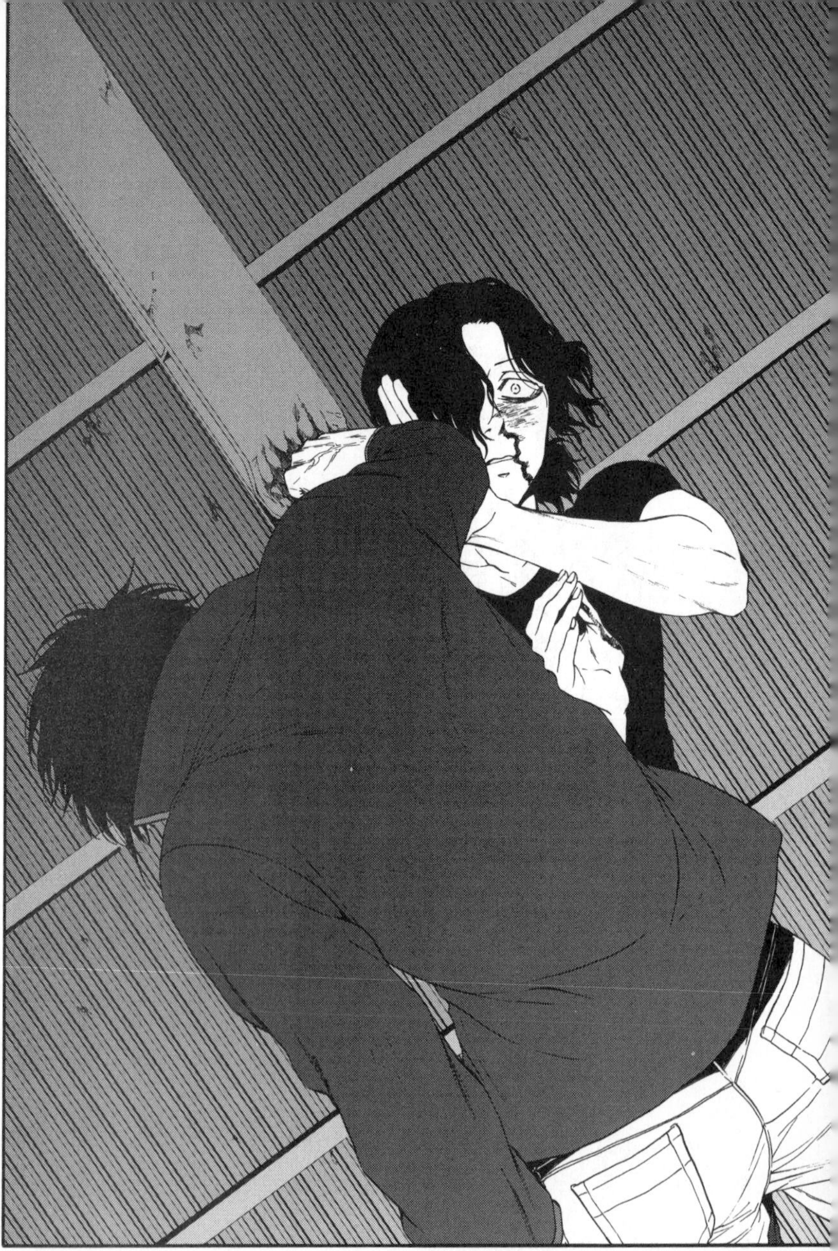

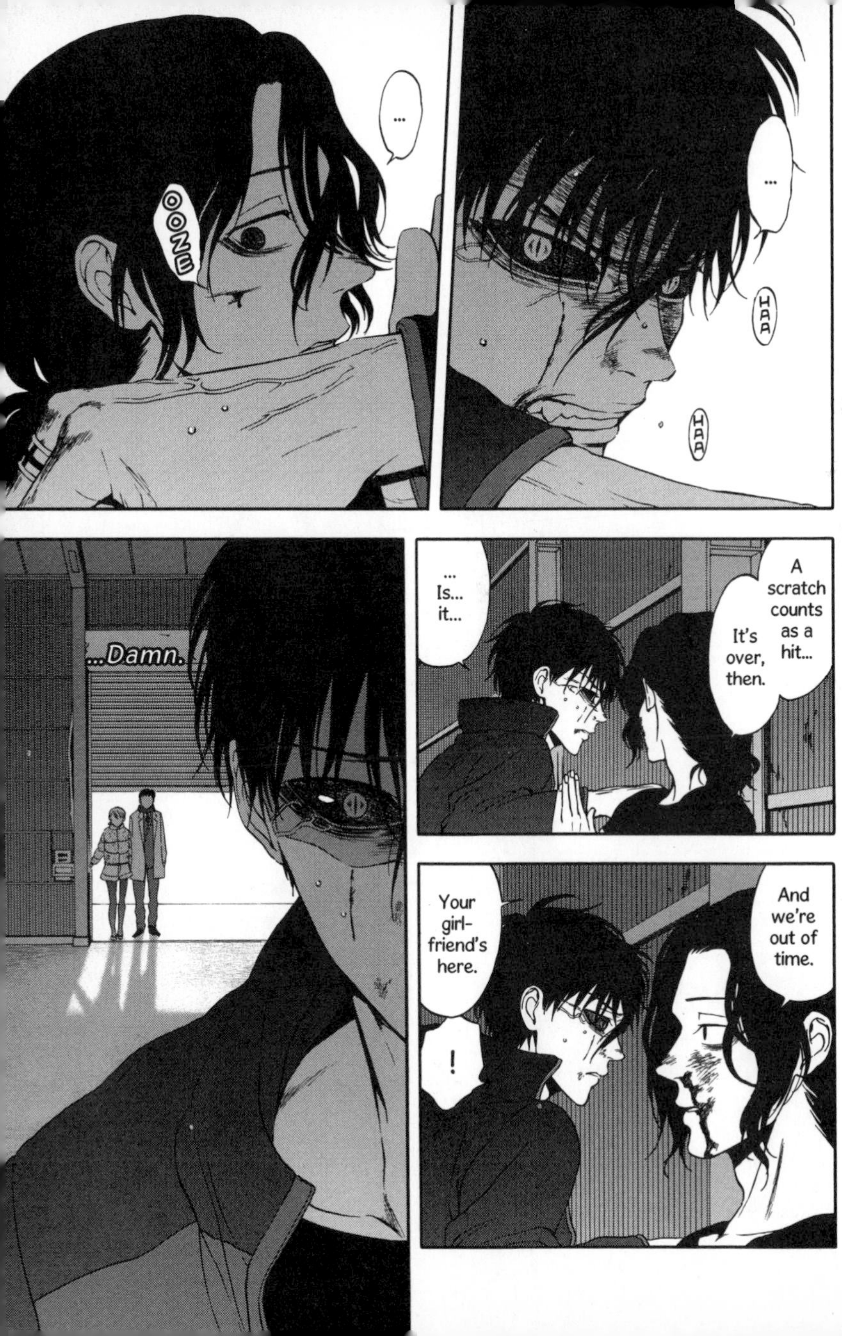
...
HAA
HAA
...
OOZE
A scratch counts as a hit...
It's over, then.
... Is... it...
And we're out of time.
Your girlfriend's here.
!
...Damn.

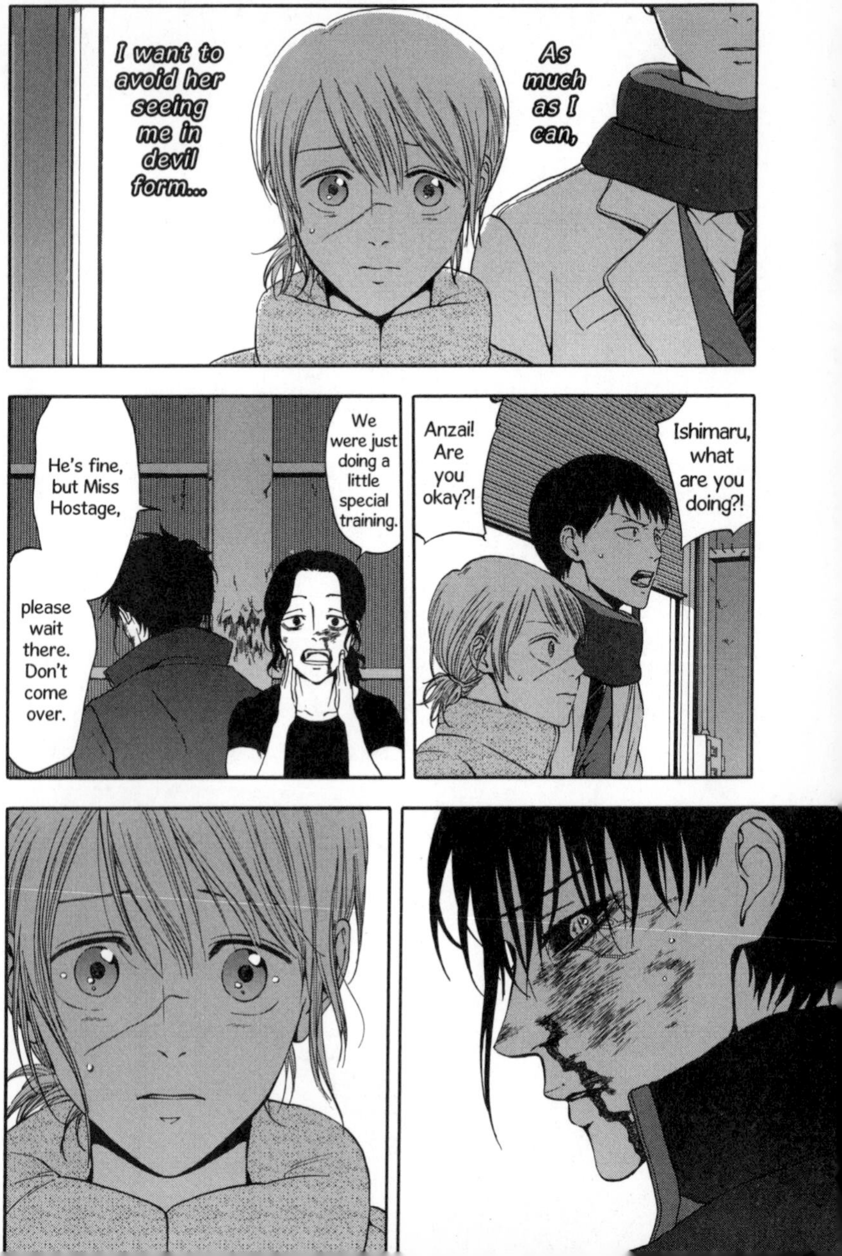
As much as I can,
I want to avoid her seeing me in devil form...
Ishimaru, what are you doing?!
Anzai! Are you okay?!
We were just doing a little special training.
He's fine, but Miss Hostage,
please wait there. Don't come over.

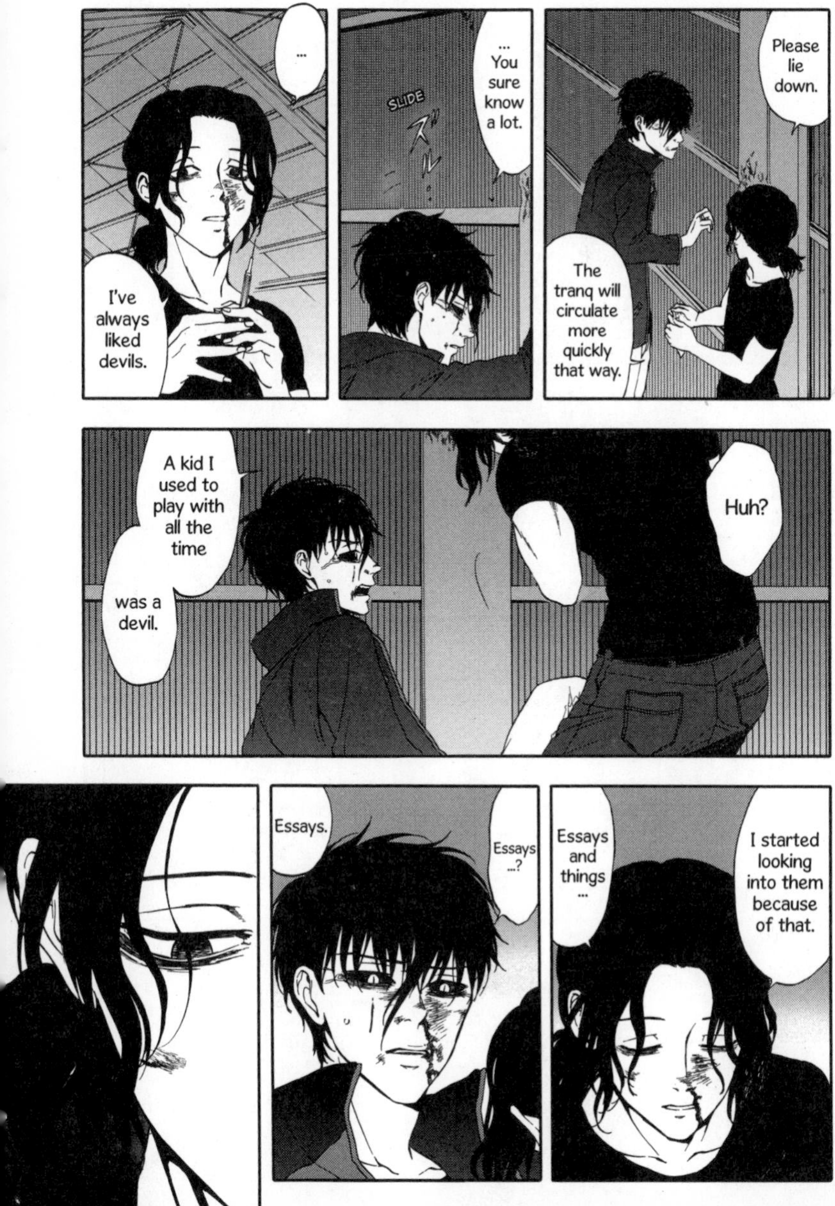
Please lie down.
The tranq will circulate more quickly that way.
... You sure know a lot.
SLIDE
ズル…
...
I've always liked devils.
Huh?
A kid I used to play with all the time
was a devil.
I started looking into them because of that.
Essays and things ...
Essays ...?
Essays.

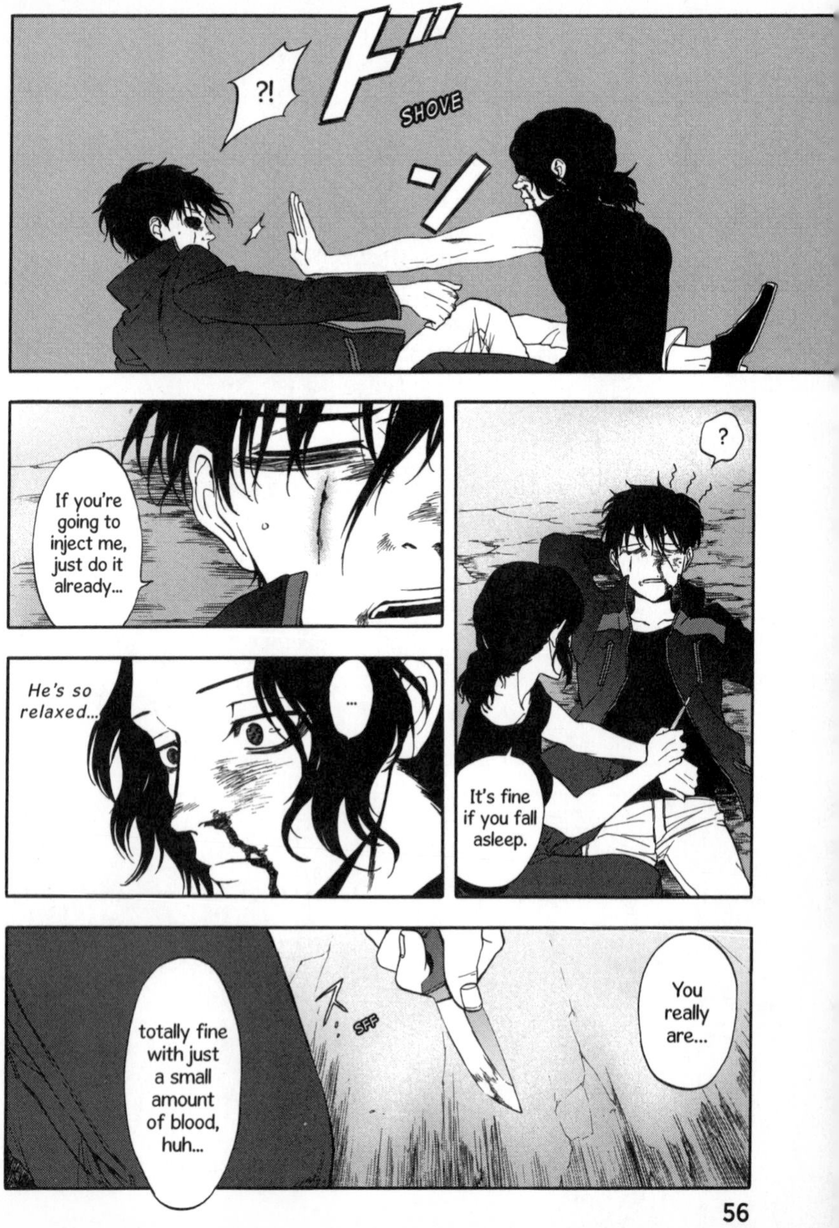

?!
ド
SHOVE
?
It's fine if you fall asleep.
If you're going to inject me, just do it already...
He's so relaxed...
...
You really are...
ス
SFF
totally fine with just a small amount of blood, huh...

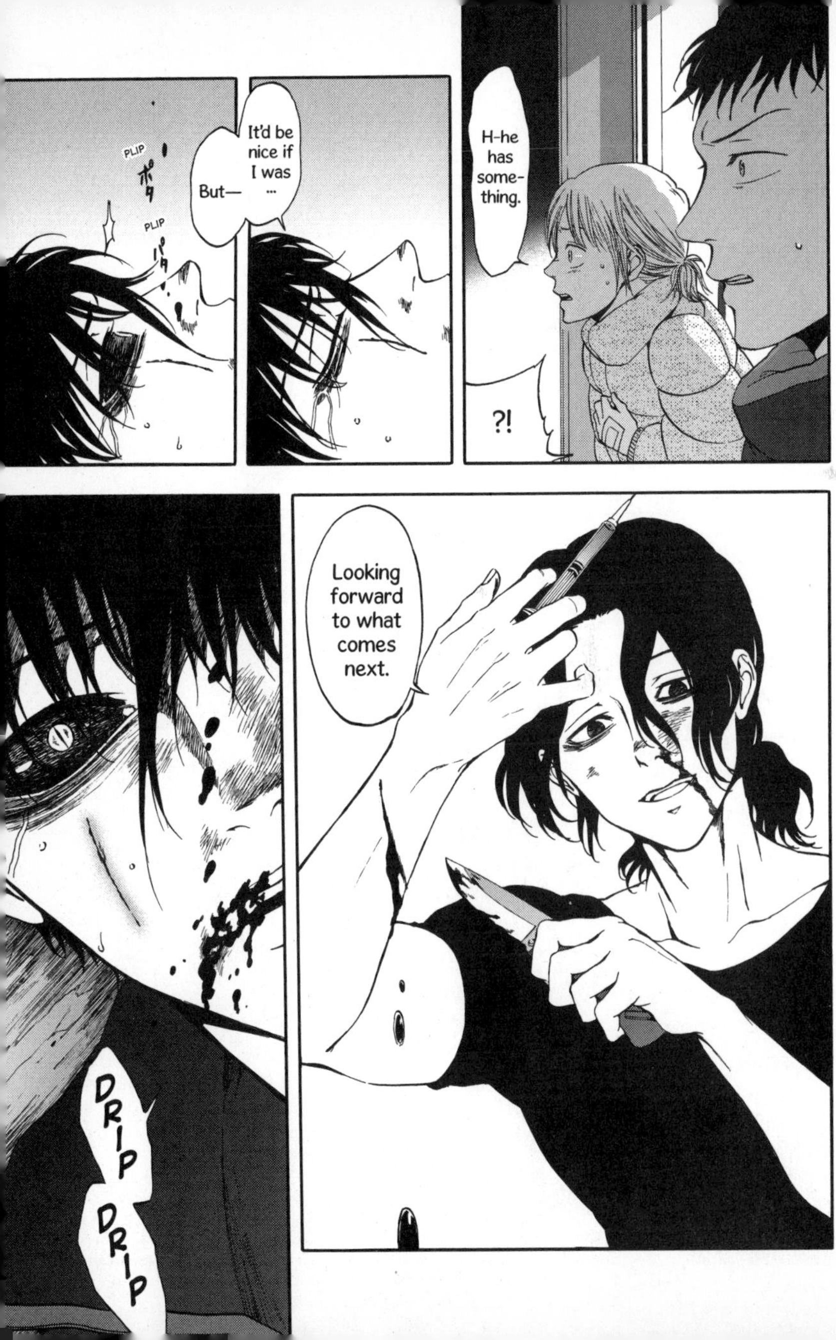
H-he has some-thing.
?!
It'd be nice if I was ...
But—
PLIP
ポタ
PLIP
パタ
Looking forward to what comes next.
DRIP DRIP

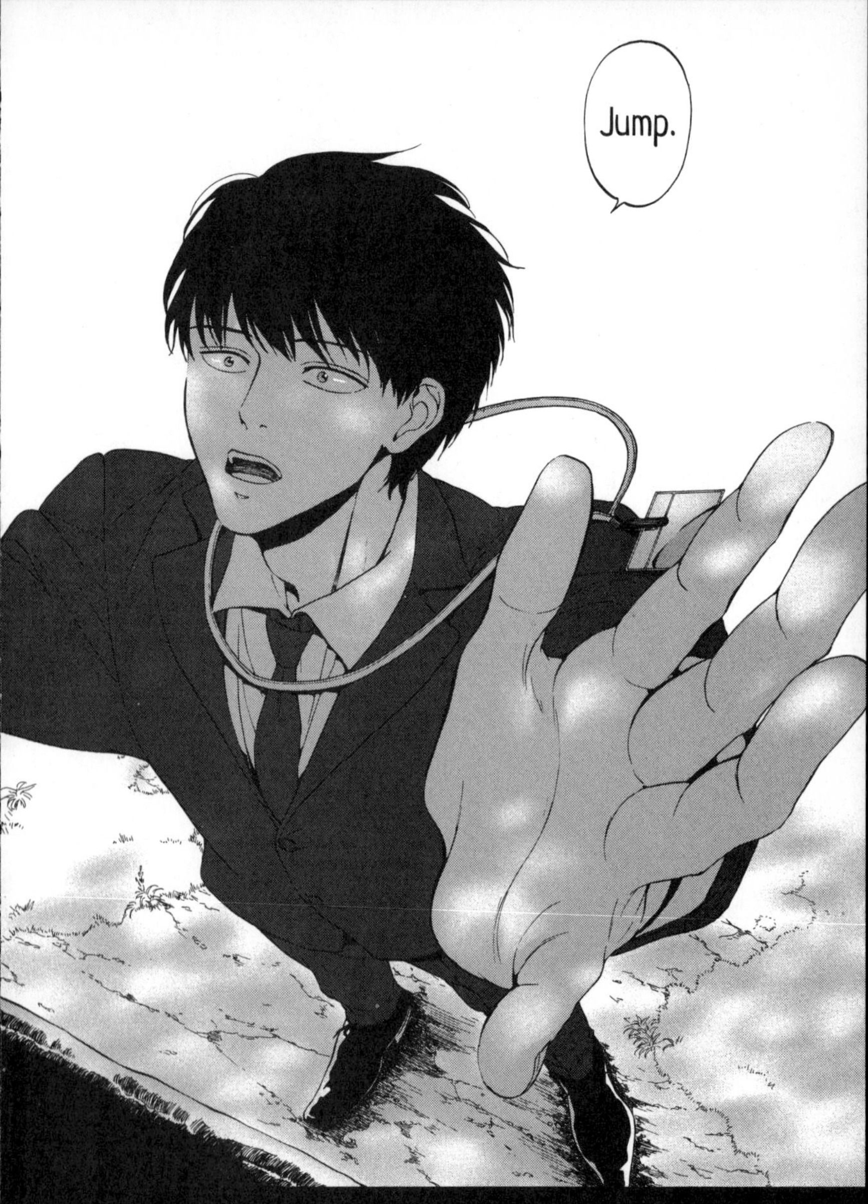
Jump.

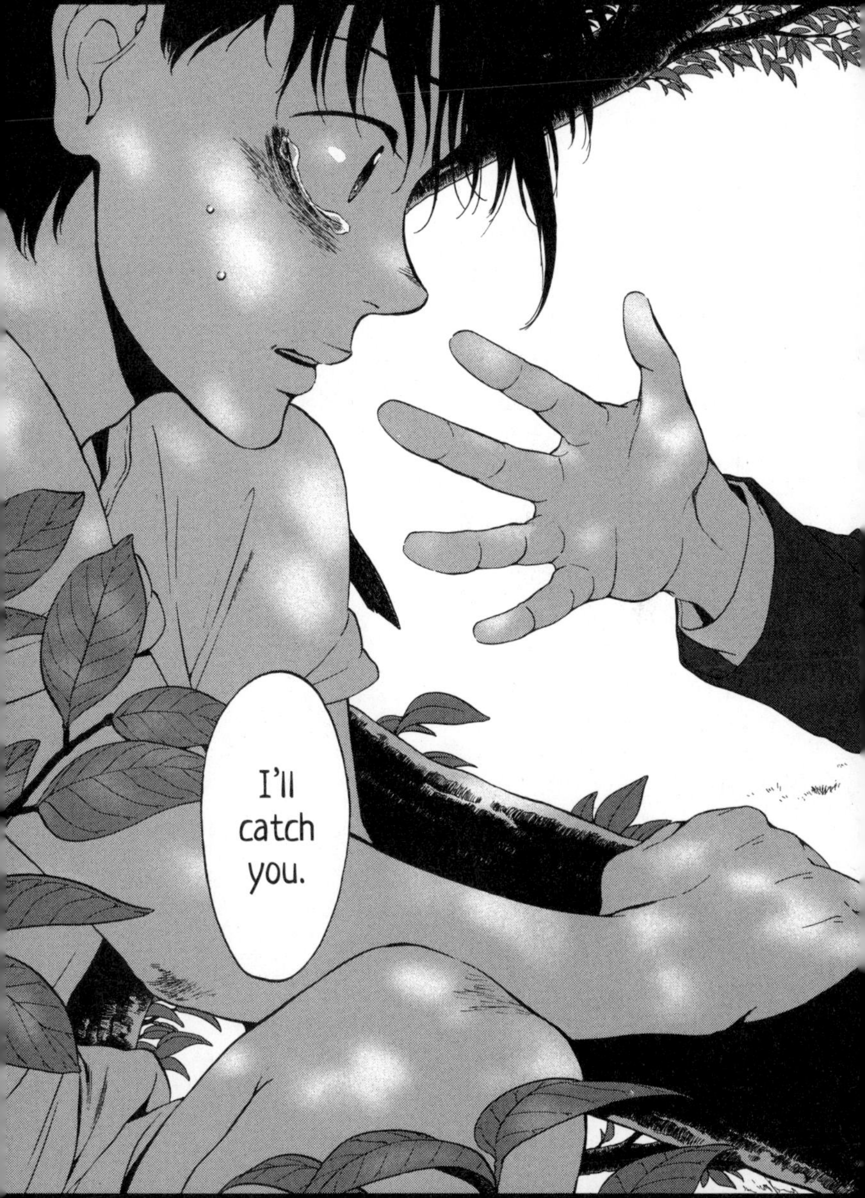
I'll catch you.

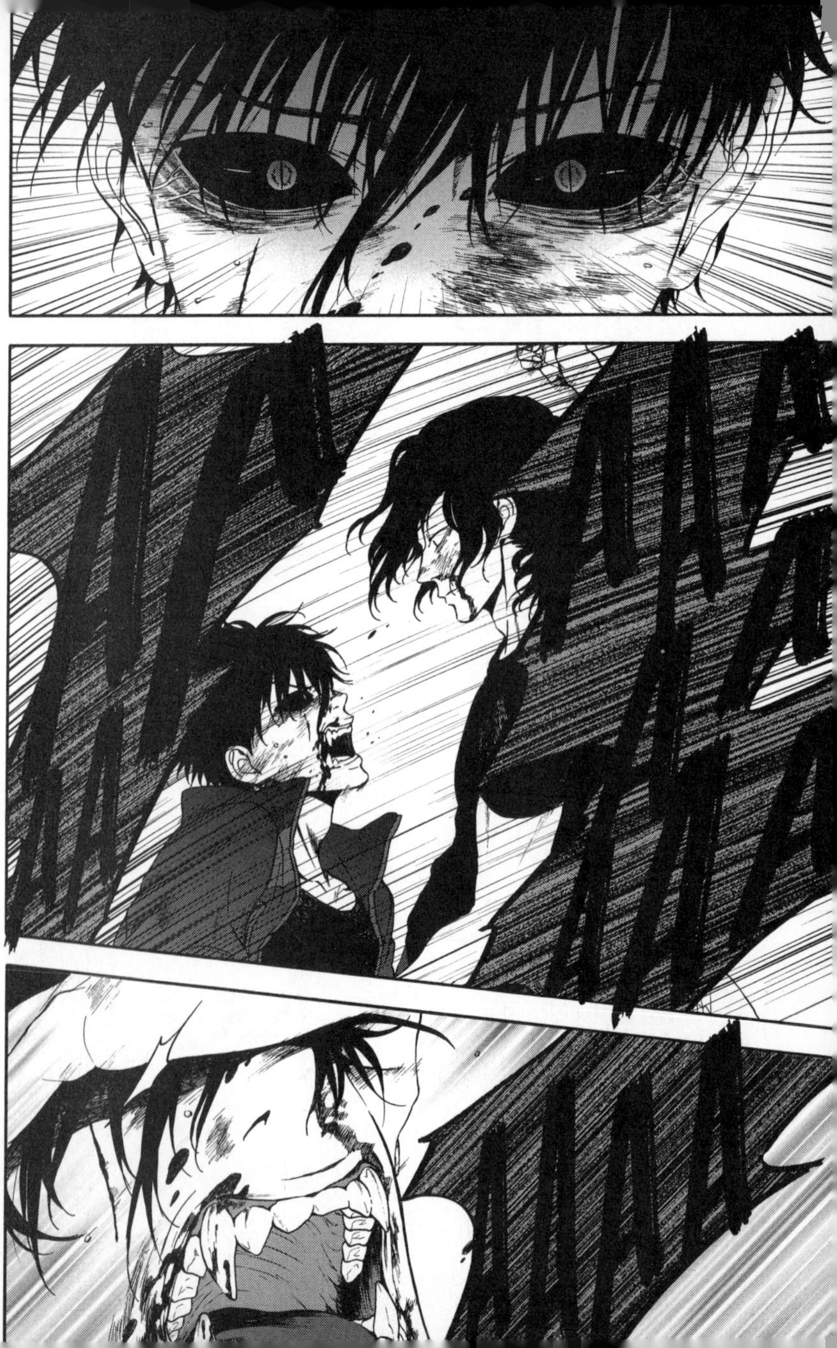

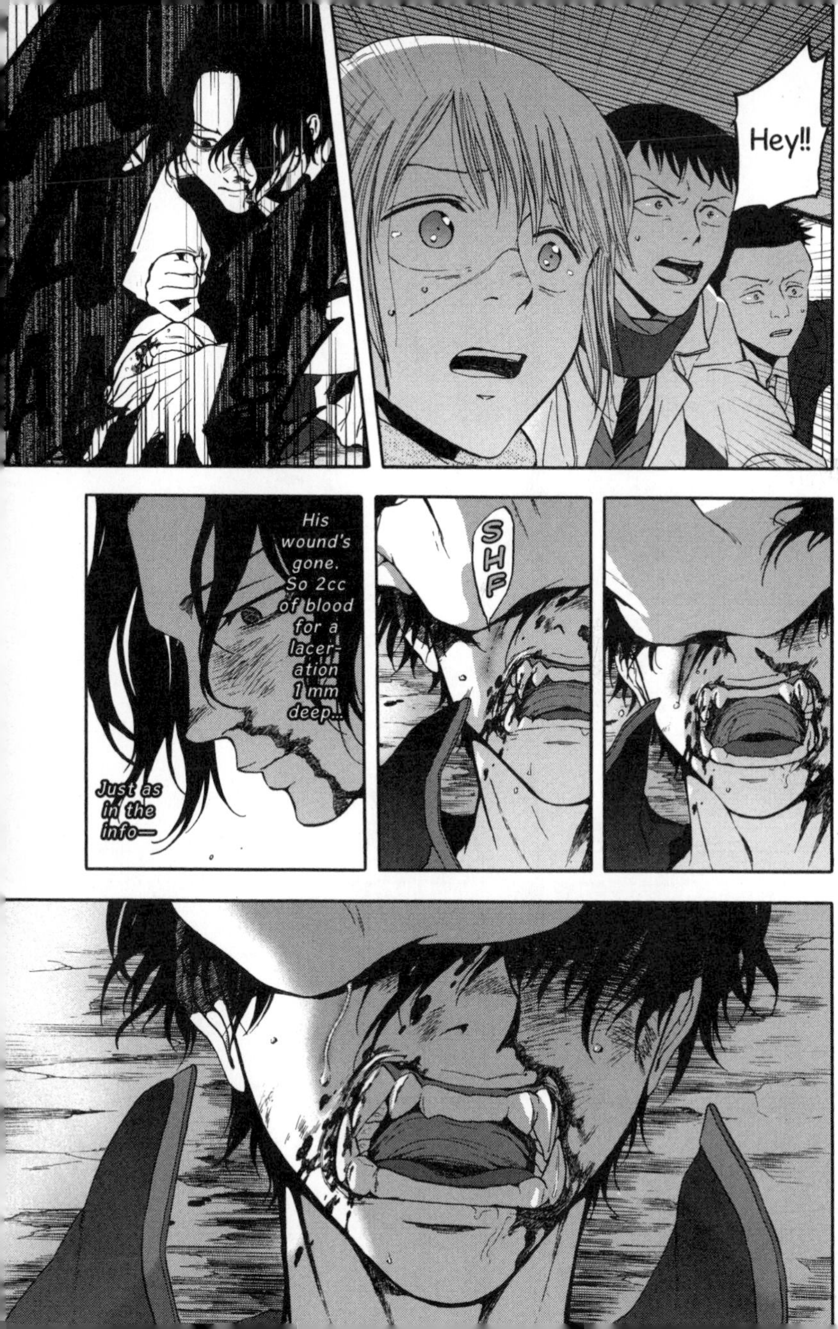
Hey!!
SHF
His wound's gone. So 2cc of blood for a laceration 1 mm deep...
Just as in the info—

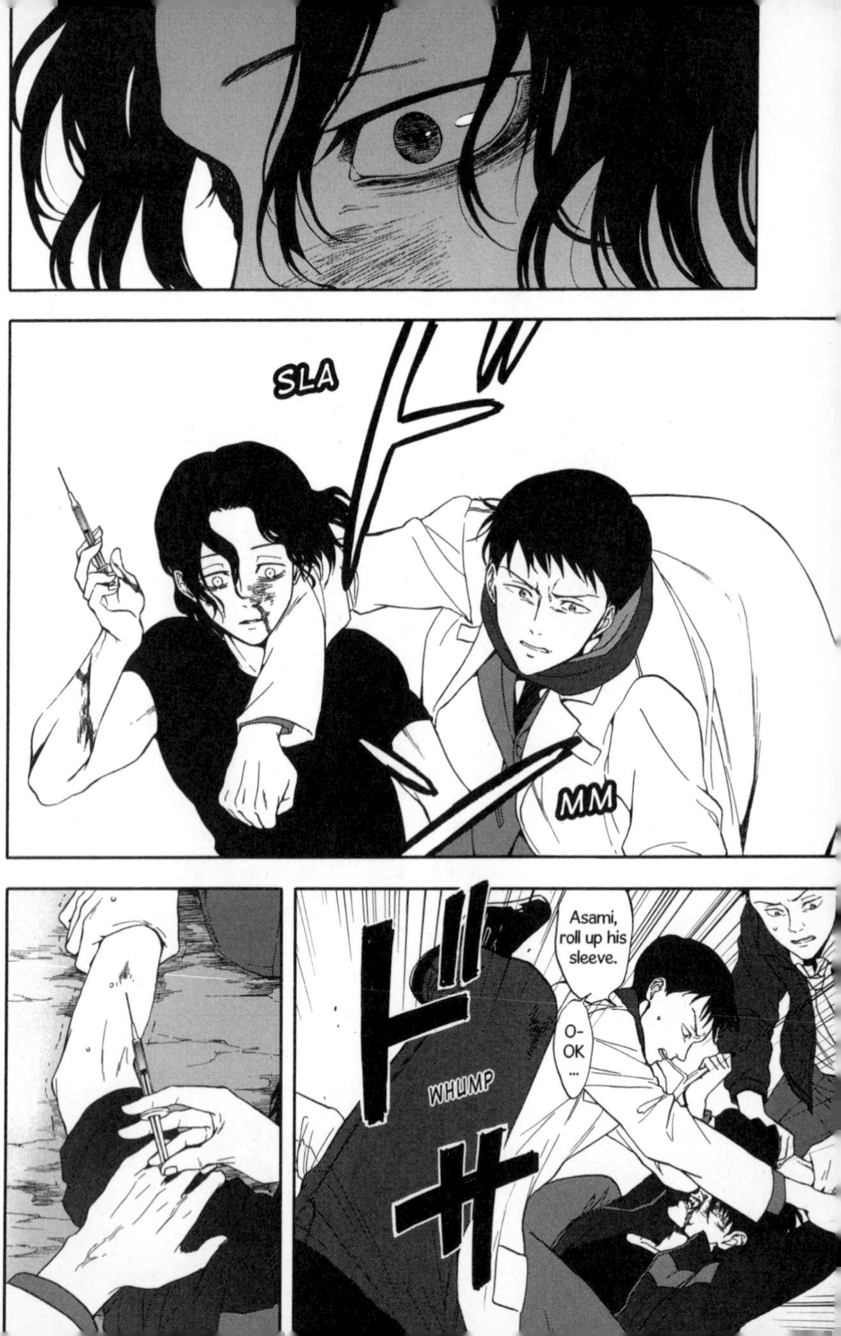
SLA
MM
Asami, roll up his sleeve.
O-OK ...
WHUMP

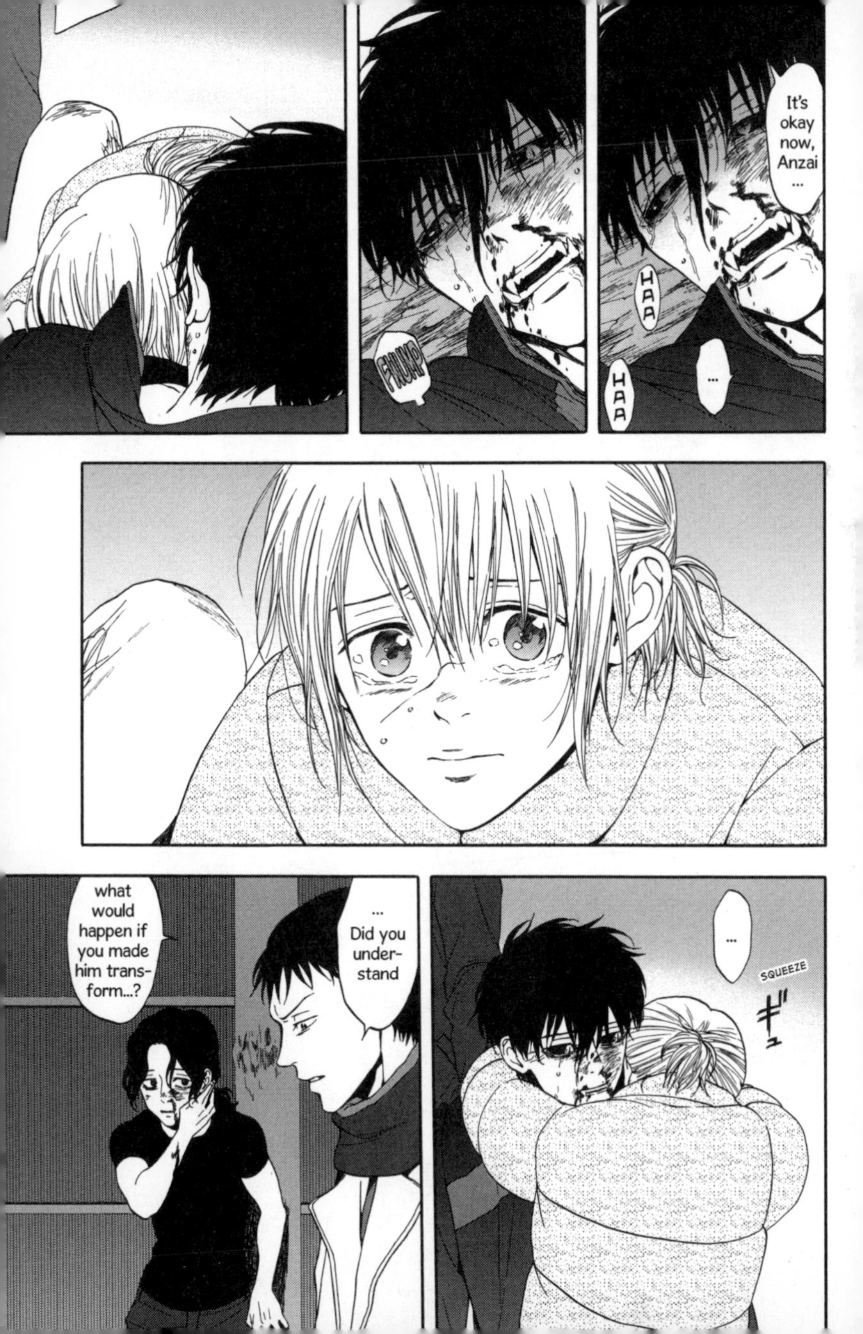
It's okay now, Anzai ...
HAA
HAA
...
FNUMP
...
SQUEEZE
ギュ
... Did you understand
what would happen if you made him transform...?

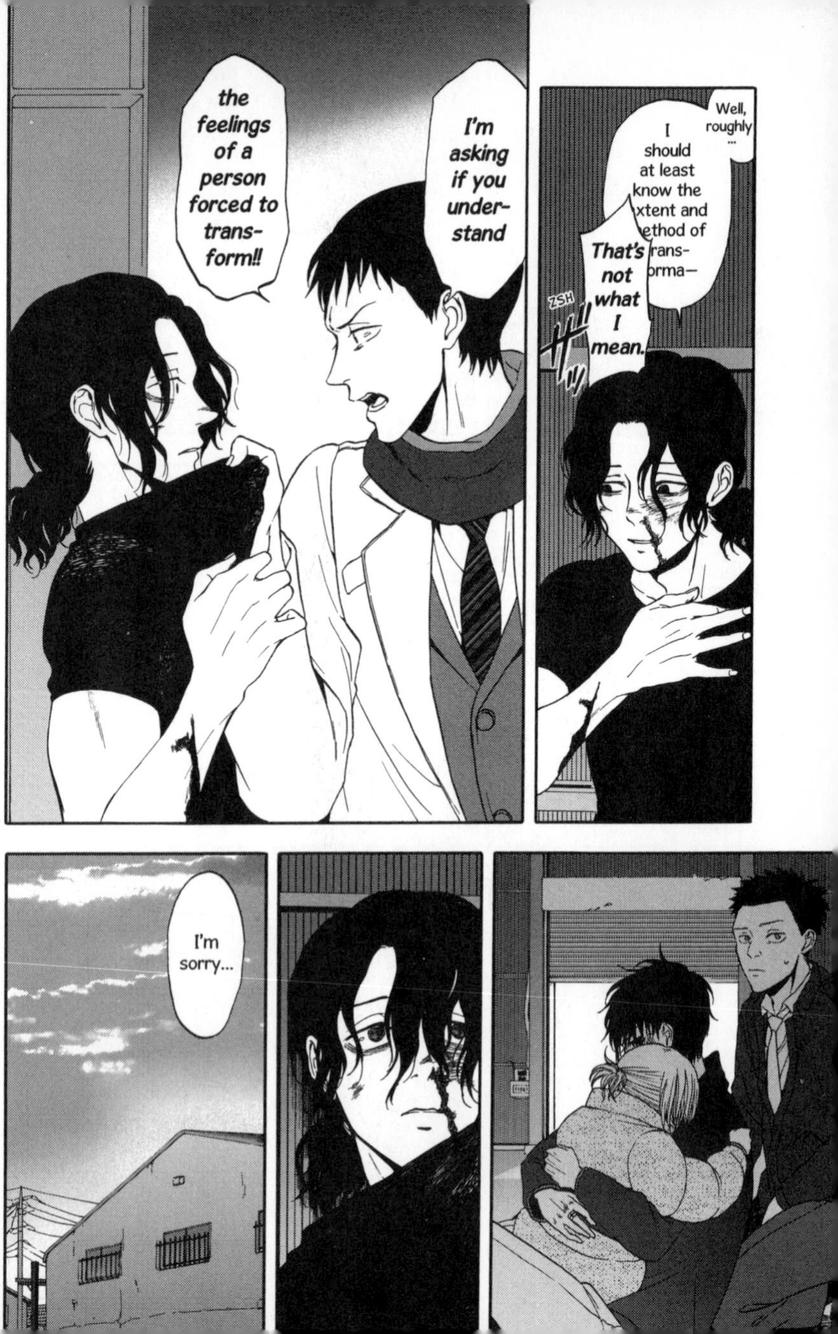
Well, roughly...
I should at least know the xtent and ethod of rans- orma—
ZSH
That's not what I mean.
I'm asking if you under- stand
the feelings of a person forced to trans- form!!
I'm sorry...

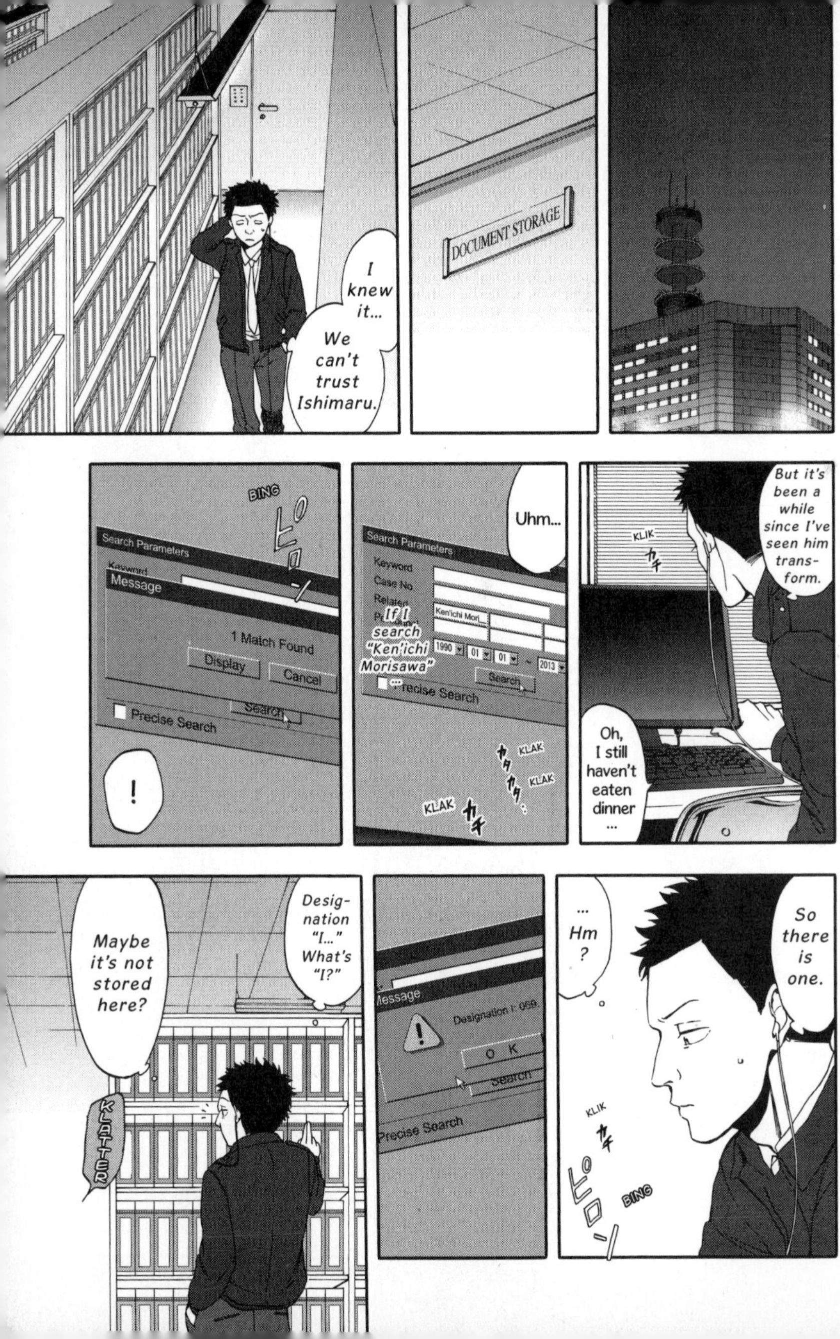
DOCUMENT STORAGE
I knew it...
We can't trust Ishimaru.
But it's been a while since I've seen him transform.
KLIK
カチ
Oh, I still haven't eaten dinner ...
Uhm...
Search Parameters
Keyword
Case No
Ken'ichi Mori
1990 01 01 ~ 2013
Search
If I search "Ken'ichi Morisawa"
...
Precise Search
KLAK
カタ
KLAK
カタ...
KLAK
カチ
BING
ピロー
Search Parameters
Message
1 Match Found
Display
Cancel
Search
Precise Search
!
So there is one.
... Hm?
KLIK
カチ
ピロー
BING
Message
Designation I: 069,
O K
Search
Precise Search
Designation "I..." What's "I?"
Maybe it's not stored here?
KLATTER

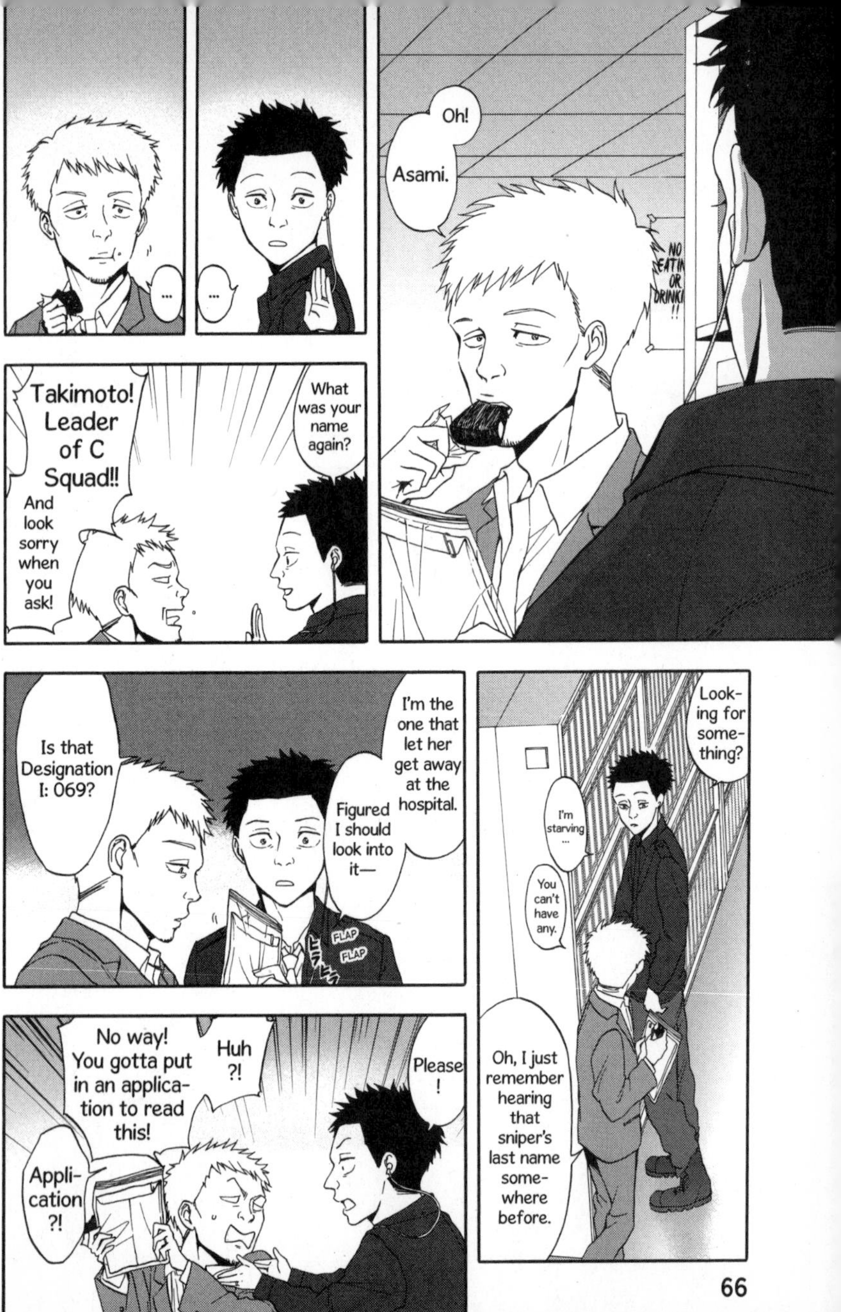

Oh!
Asami.
NO EATIN OR DRINKI !!
...
...
What was your name again?
Takimoto! Leader of C Squad!!
And look sorry when you ask!
Looking-ing for some-thing?
I'm starving...
You can't have any.
Oh, I just remember hearing that sniper's last name some-where before.
I'm the one that let her get away at the hospital.
Figured I should look into it—
Is that Designation I: 069?
FLAP
FLAP
Please!
Huh?!
No way! You gotta put in an applica-tion to read this!
Appli-cation?!

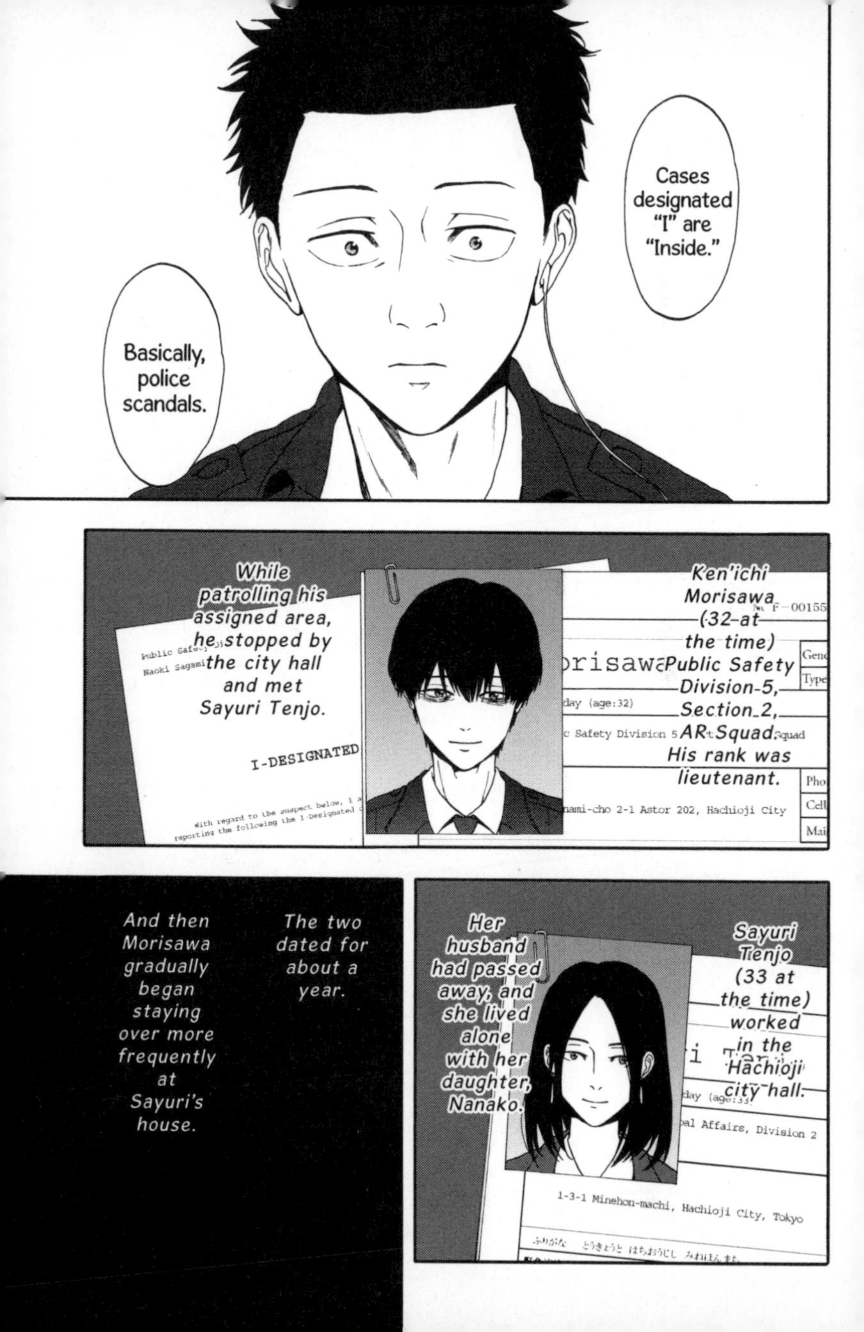
Cases designated "I" are "Inside."
Basically, police scandals.
Ken'ichi Morisawa (32 at the time) Public Safety Division-5, Section 2, AR Squad. His rank was lieutenant.
While patrolling his assigned area, he stopped by the city hall and met Sayuri Tenjo.
I-DESIGNATED
nami-cho 2-1 Astor 202, Hachioji City
Sayuri Tenjo (33 at the time) worked in the Hachioji city hall.
Her husband had passed away, and she lived alone with her daughter, Nanako.
1-3-1 Minehon-machi, Hachioji City, Tokyo
The two dated for about a year.
And then Morisawa gradually began staying over more frequently at Sayuri's house.

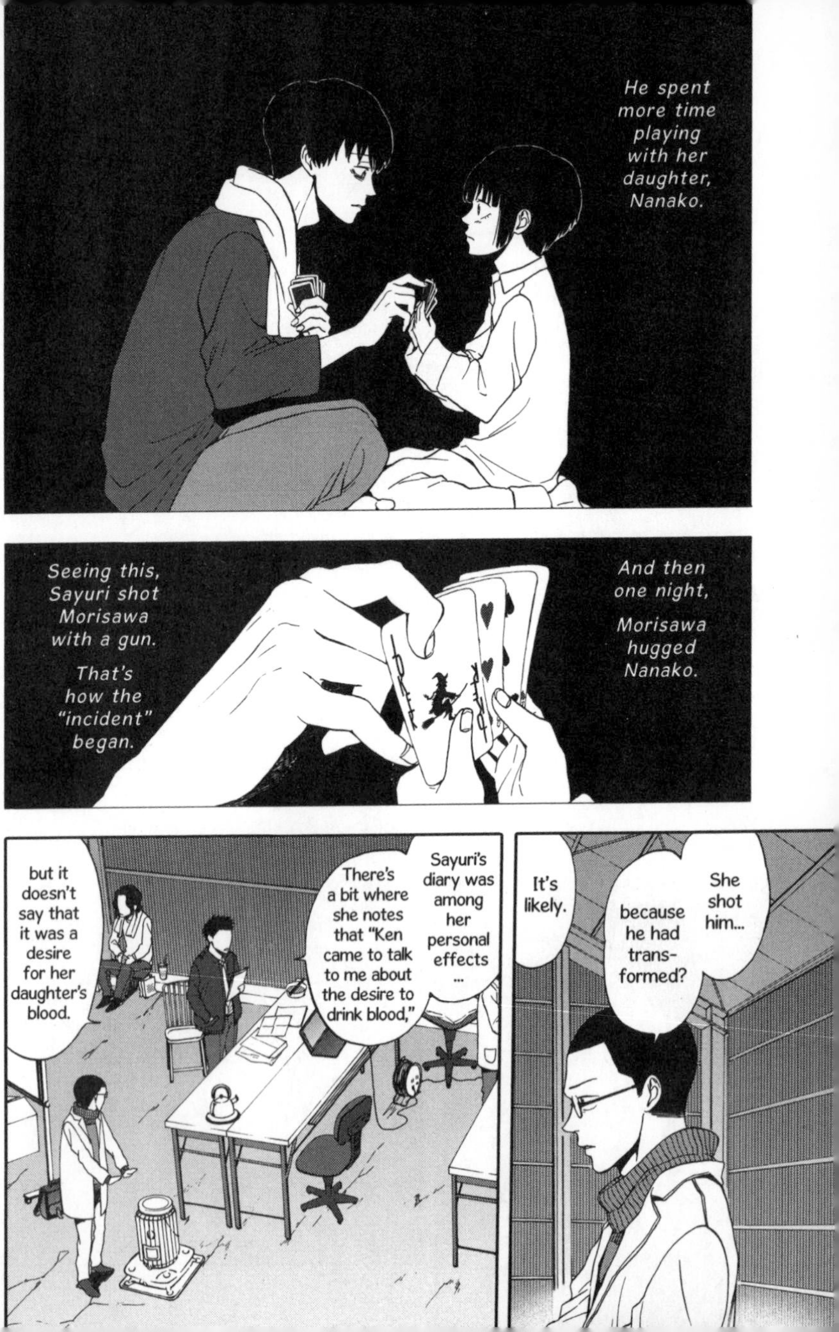
He spent more time playing with her daughter, Nanako.
And then one night, Morisawa hugged Nanako.
Seeing this, Sayuri shot Morisawa with a gun.
That's how the "incident" began.
She shot him...
because he had transformed?
It's likely.
Sayuri's diary was among her personal effects...
There's a bit where she notes that "Ken came to talk to me about the desire to drink blood,"
but it doesn't say that it was a desire for her daughter's blood.

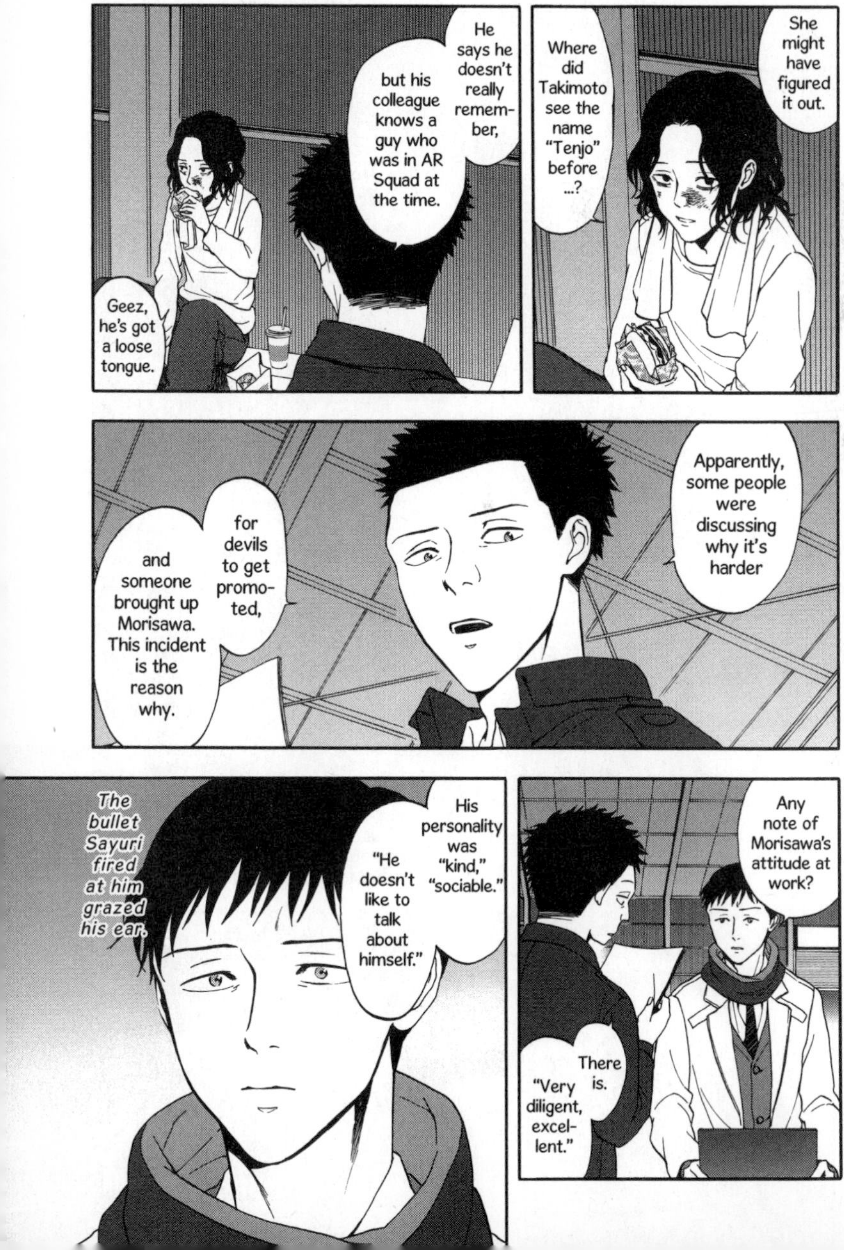
She might have figured it out.
Where did Takimoto see the name "Tenjo" before ...?
He says he doesn't really remember,
but his colleague knows a guy who was in AR Squad at the time.
Geez, he's got a loose tongue.
Apparently, some people were discussing why it's harder
for devils to get promoted,
and someone brought up Morisawa. This incident is the reason why.
Any note of Morisawa's attitude at work?
There is.
"Very diligent, excellent."
His personality was "kind," "sociable."
"He doesn't like to talk about himself."
The bullet Sayuri fired at him grazed his ear.

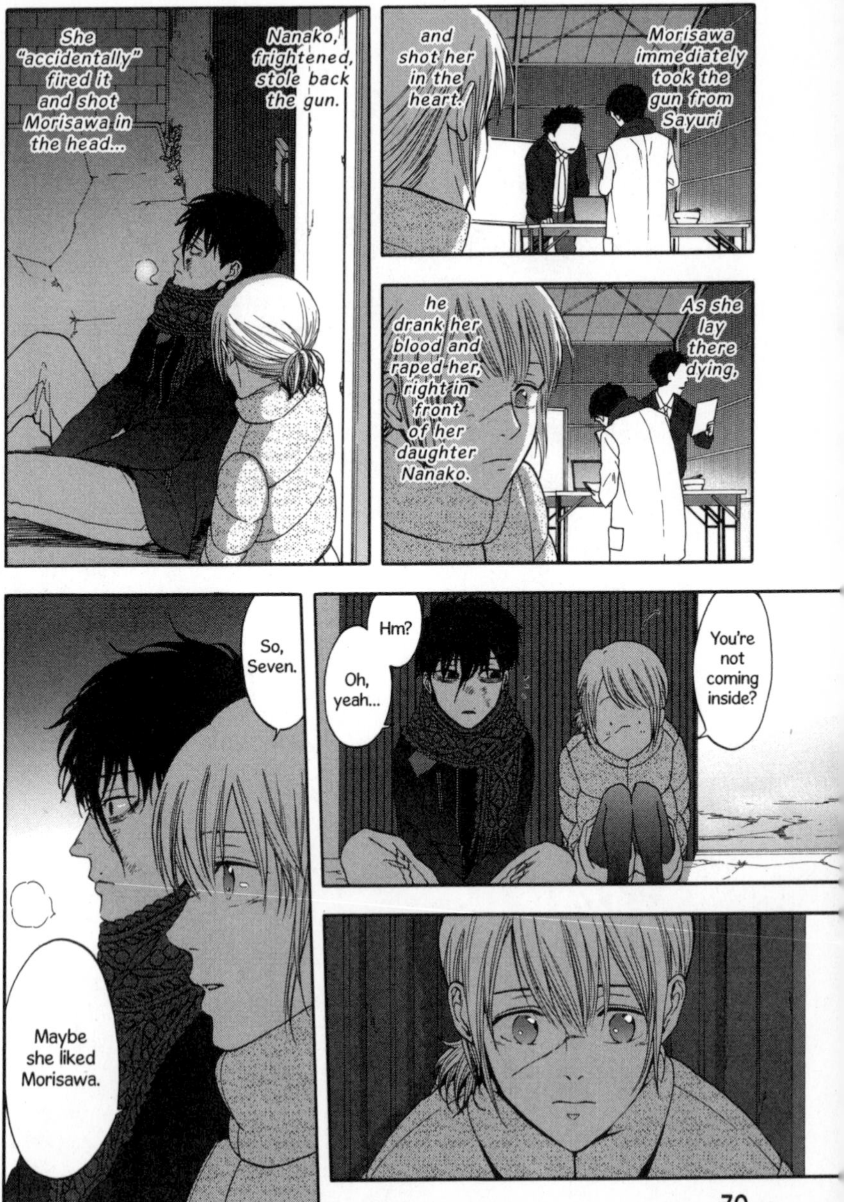
Morisawa immediately took the gun from Sayuri
and shot her in the heart.
As she lay there dying,
he drank her blood and raped her, right in front of her daughter Nanako.
Nanako, frightened, stole back the gun.
She "accidentally" fired it and shot Morisawa in the head...
You're not coming inside?
Hm?
Oh, yeah...
So, Seven.
Maybe she liked Morisawa.

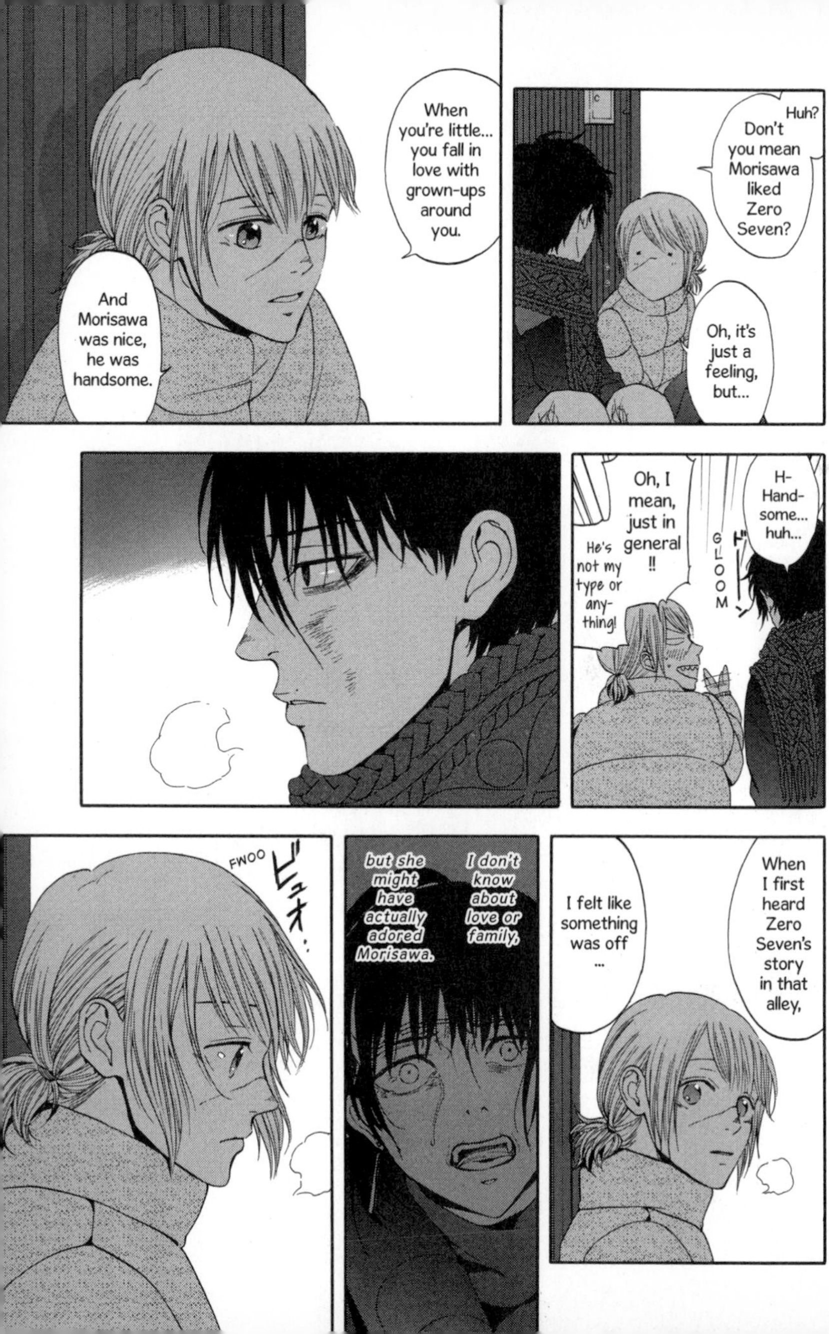
Huh? Don't you mean Morisawa liked Zero Seven?
Oh, it's just a feeling, but...
When you're little... you fall in love with grown-ups around you.
And Morisawa was nice, he was handsome.
H- Hand- some... huh...
GLOOM
Oh, I mean, just in general !!
He's not my type or any- thing!
When I first heard Zero Seven's story in that alley,
I felt like something was off ...
I don't know about love or family,
but she might have actually adored Morisawa.
FWOO

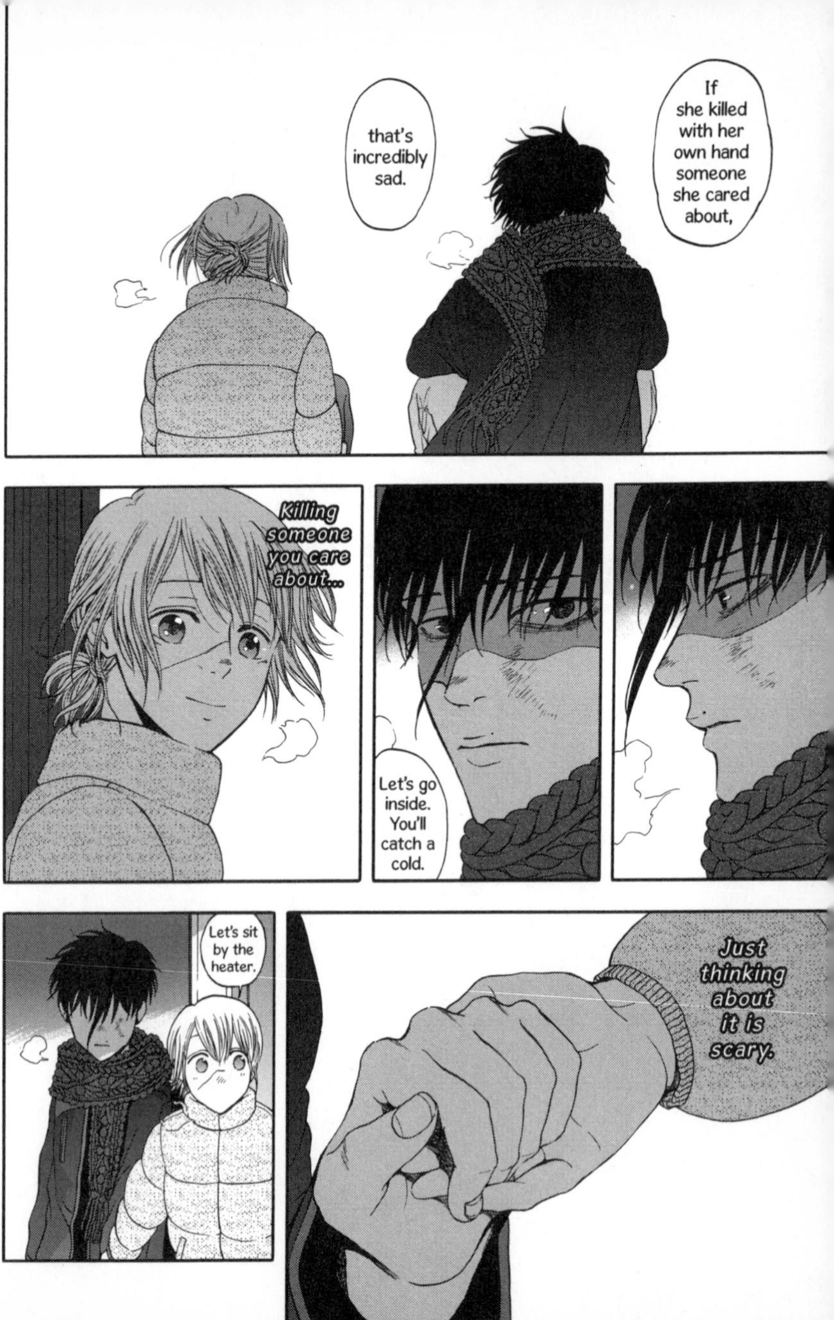
If she killed with her own hand someone she cared about,
that's incredibly sad.
Let's go inside. You'll catch a cold.
Killing someone you care about...
Just thinking about it is scary.
Let's sit by the heater.

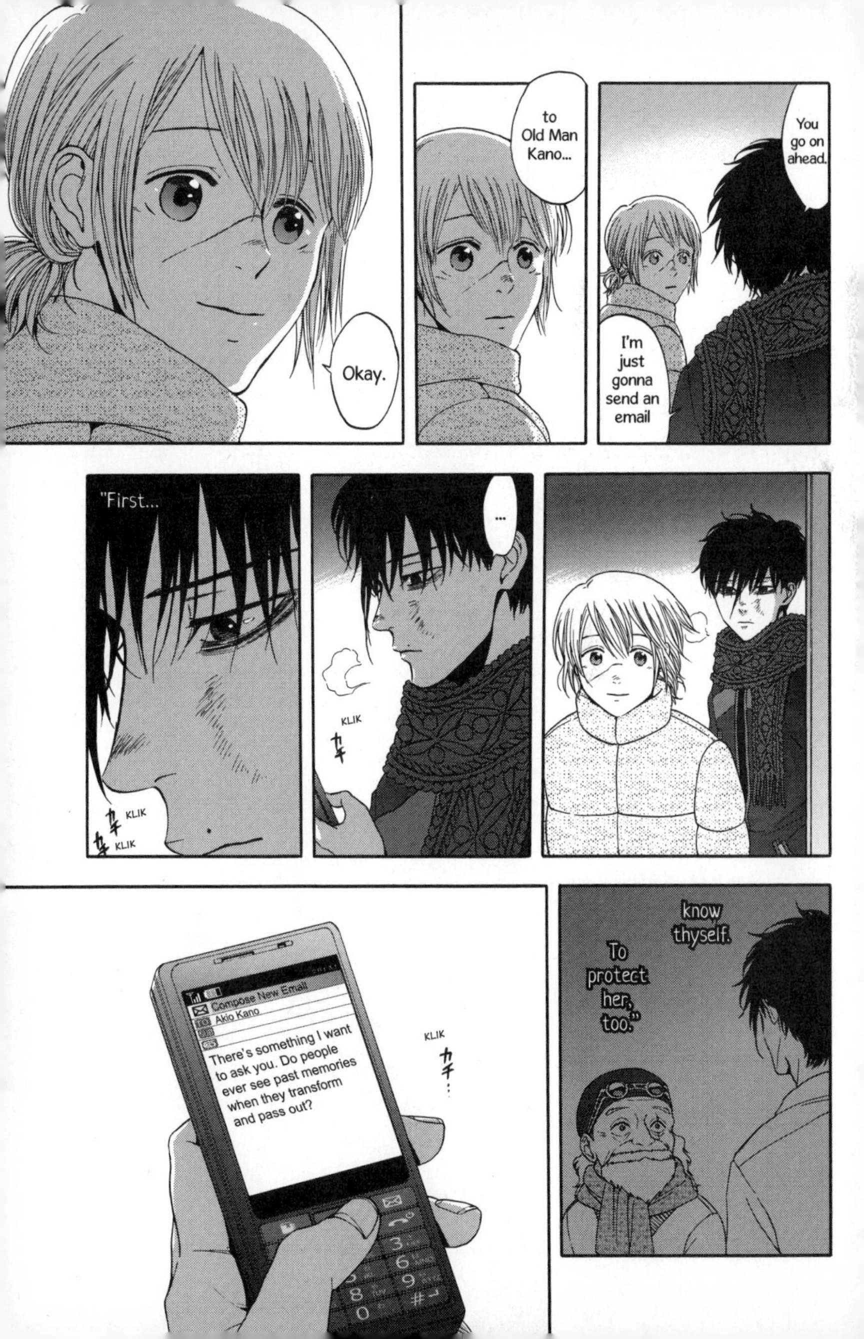
You go on ahead.
I'm just gonna send an email
to Old Man Kano...
Okay.
...
KLIK
カチ
"First...
KLIK
カチ
KLIK
カチ
know thyself.
To protect her, too."
Compose New Email
Akio Kano
There's something I want to ask you. Do people ever see past memories when they transform and pass out?
KLIK
カチ...

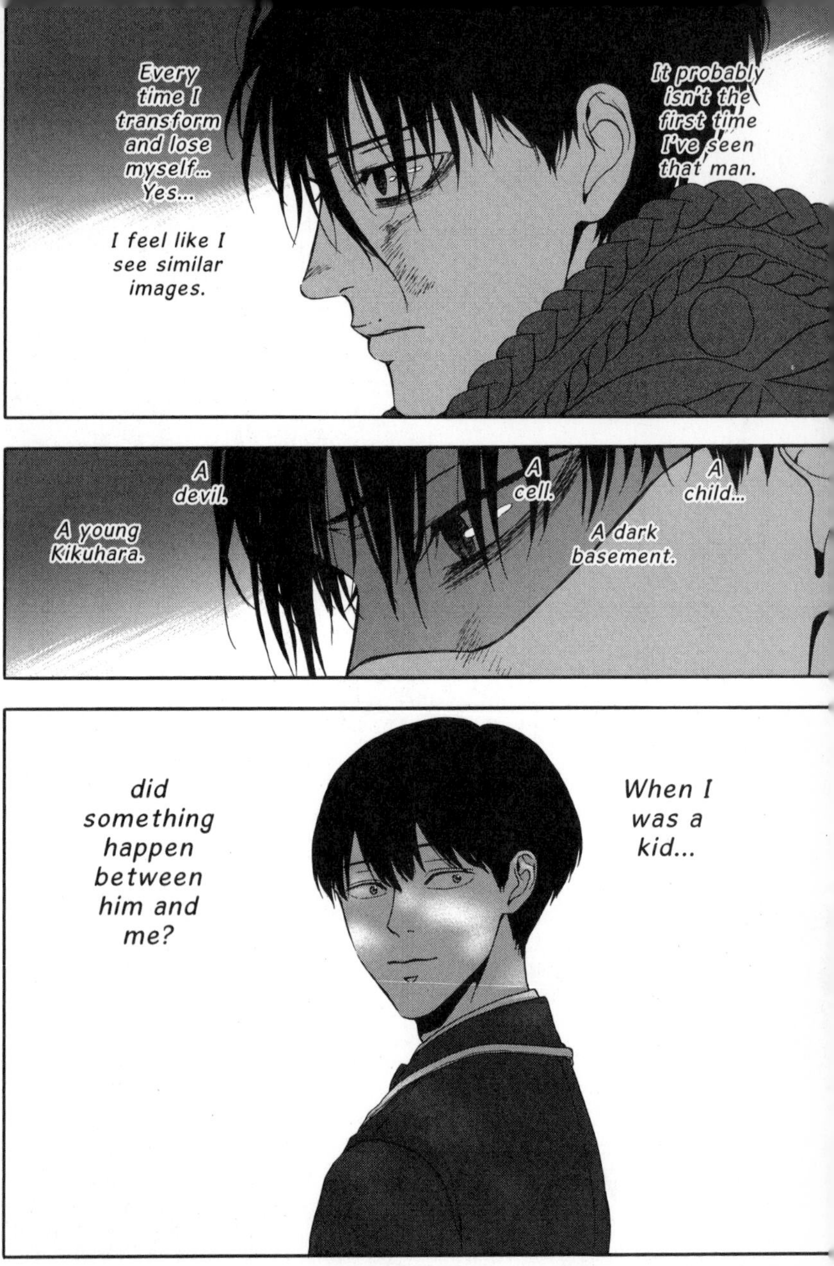
It probably isn't the first time I've seen that man.
Every time I transform and lose myself... Yes...
I feel like I see similar images.
A child...
A cell.
A dark basement.
A devil.
A young Kikuhara.
When I was a kid...
did something happen between him and me?

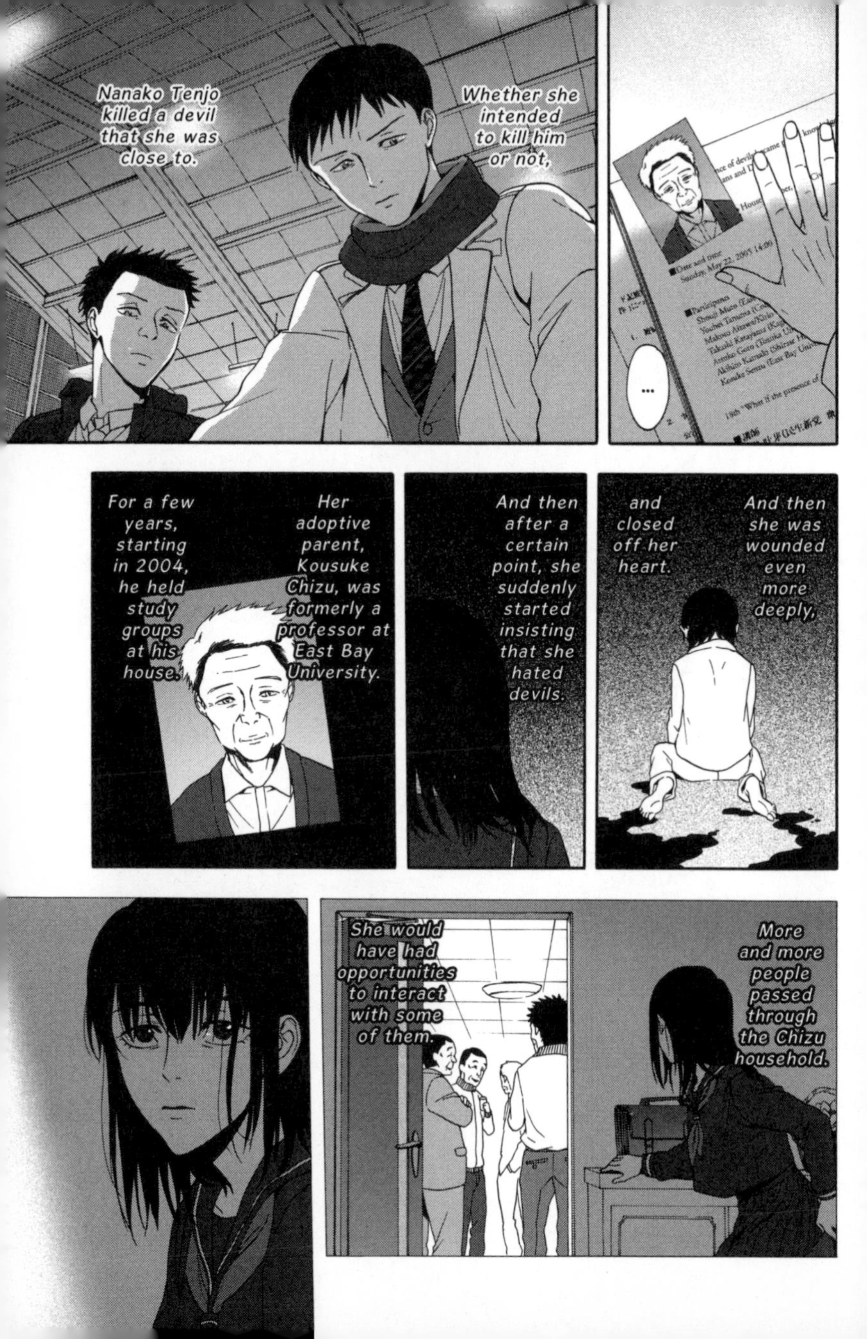
...
Whether she intended to kill him or not,
Nanako Tenjo killed a devil that she was close to.
And then she was wounded even more deeply,
and closed off her heart.
And then after a certain point, she suddenly started insisting that she hated devils.
Her adoptive parent, Kousuke Chizu, was formerly a professor at East Bay University.
For a few years, starting in 2004, he held study groups at his house.
More and more people passed through the Chizu household.
She would have had opportunities to interact with some of them.

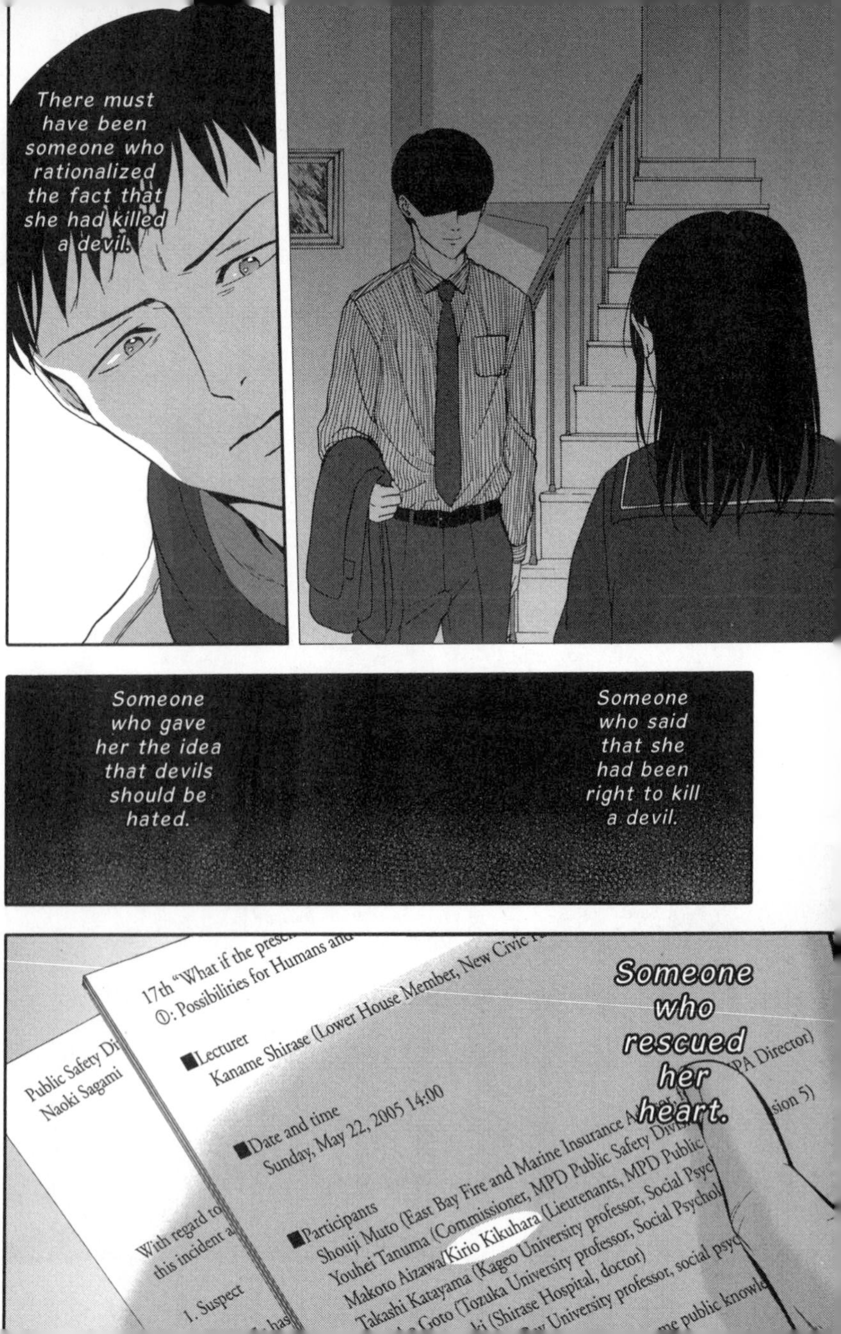
There must have been someone who rationalized the fact that she had killed a devil.
Someone who said that she had been right to kill a devil.
Someone who gave her the idea that devils should be hated.
17th "What if the pres
①: Possibilities for Humans and
■Lecturer
Kaname Shirase (Lower House Member, New Civic
■Date and time
Sunday, May 22, 2005 14:00
■Participants
Shouji Muto (East Bay Fire and Marine Insurance
Youhei Tanuma (Commissioner, MPD Public Safety Div
Makoto Aizawa/Kirio Kikuhara (Lieutenants, MPD Public
Takashi Katayama (Kageo University professor, Social Psyc
Goto (Tozuka University professor, Social Psychol
(Shirase Hospital, doctor)
University professor, social psyc
Public Safety Di
Naoki Sagami
With regard to
this incident a
1. Suspect
Someone who rescued her heart.

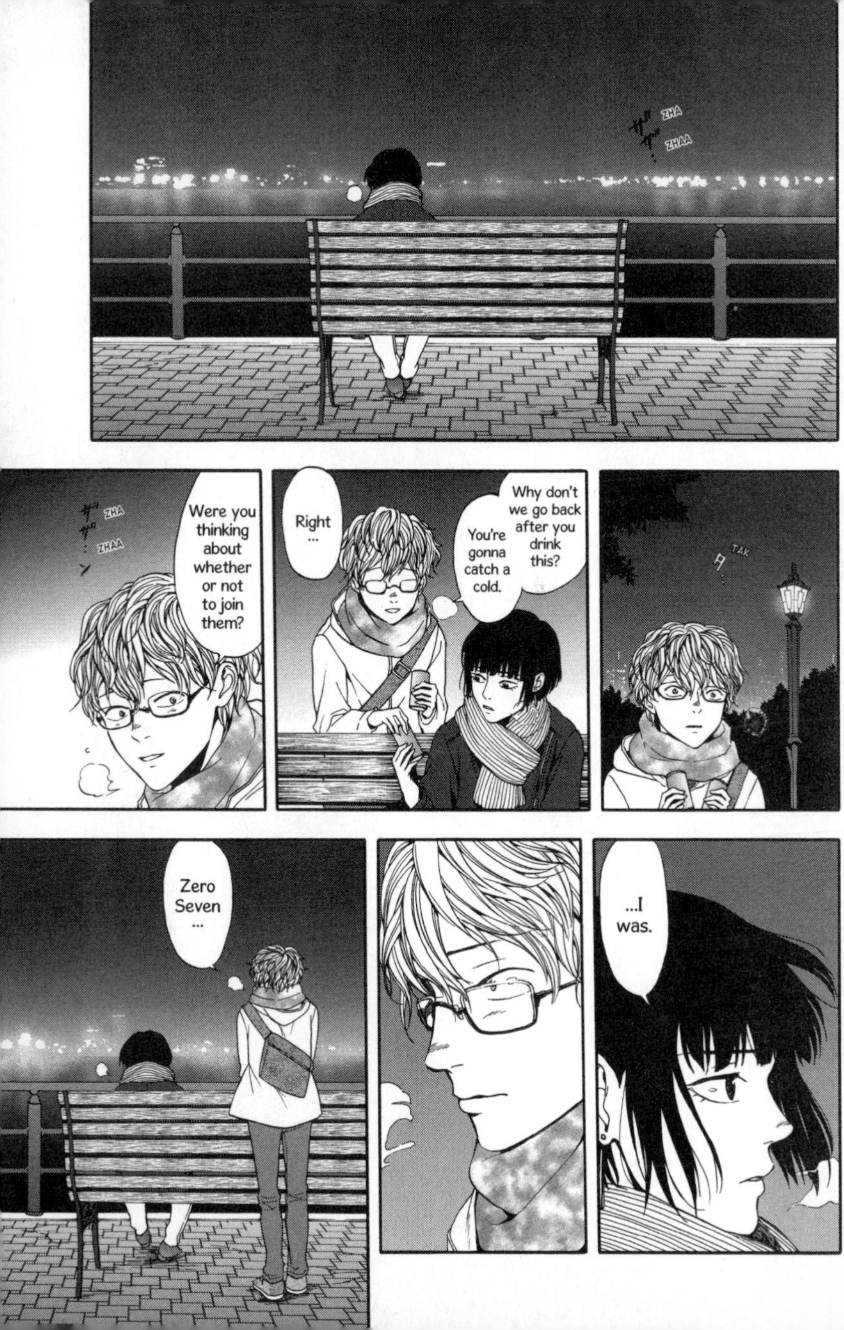
ZHA
ZHAA
TAK
Why don't we go back after you drink this?
You're gonna catch a cold.
Right ...
ZHA
ZHAA
Were you thinking about whether or not to join them?
...I was.
Zero Seven ...

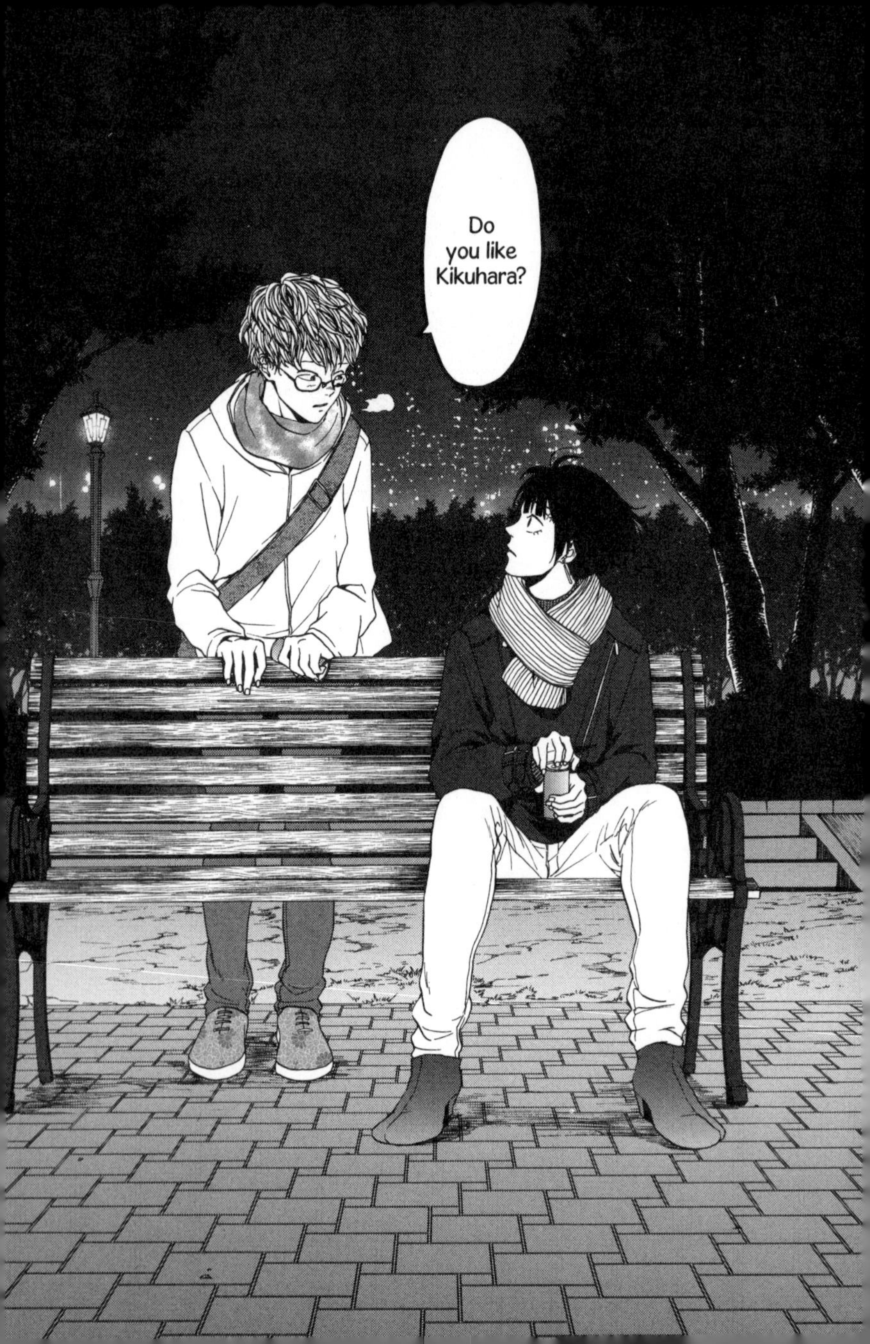
Do you like Kikuhara?

The warehouse F Squad is using
is modeled after a rental warehouse
in a certain part of the city.

The shutters make a very zestful noise
when they go up. It's a very
good warehouse.

SKREE
GREEAAH

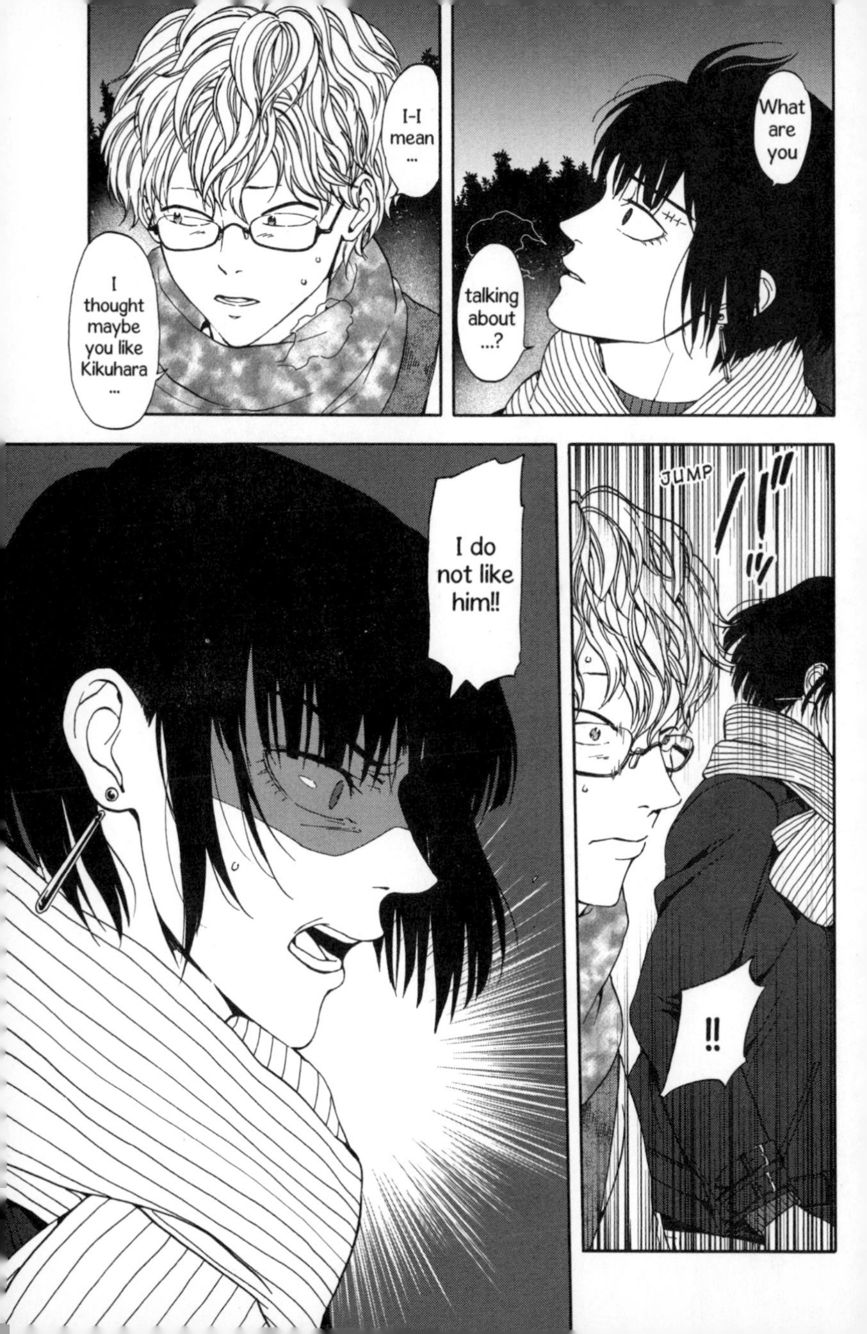

What are you
talking about ...?
I-I mean ...
I thought maybe you like Kikuhara ...
JUMP
!!
I do not like him!!

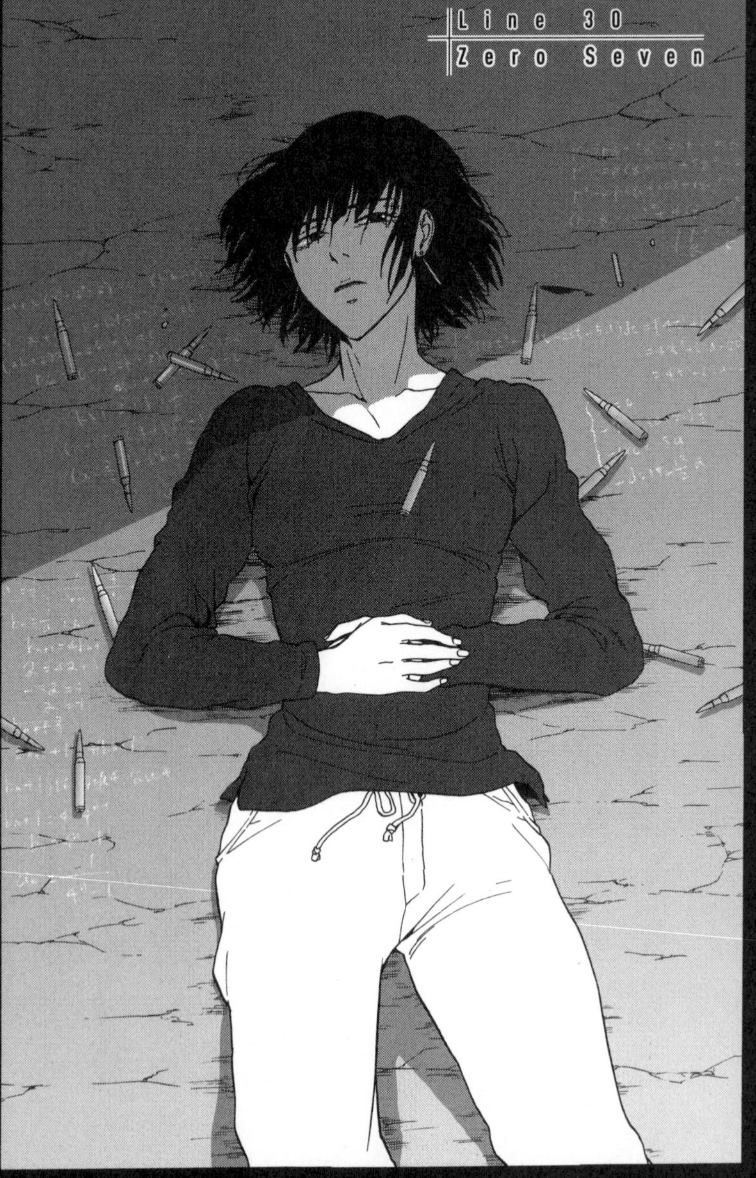
Line 30
Zero Seven

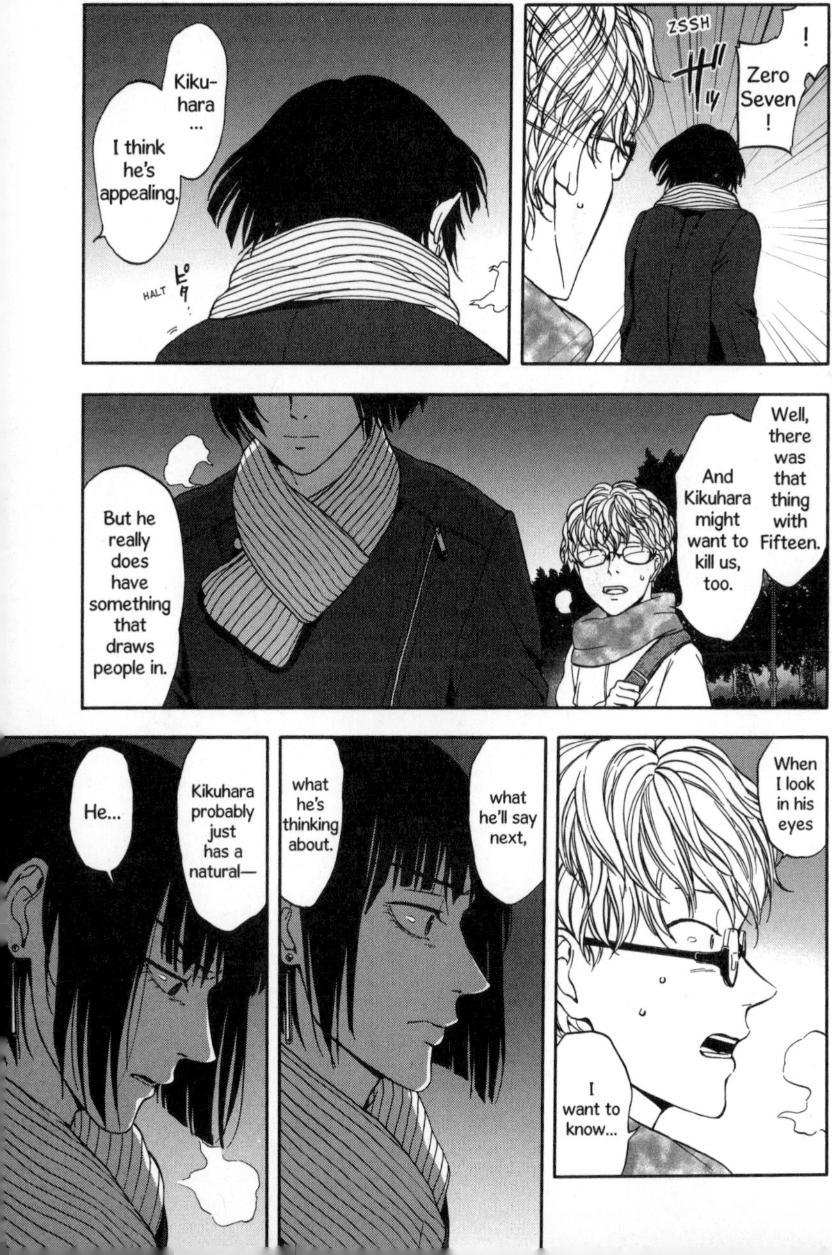
ZSSH
ザッ
! Zero Seven !
Kiku-hara ... I think he's appealing.
HALT
ピタ
Well, there was that thing with Fifteen.
And Kikuhara might want to kill us, too.
But he really does have something that draws people in.
When I look in his eyes
I want to know...
what he'll say next,
what he's thinking about.
Kikuhara probably just has a natural—
He...

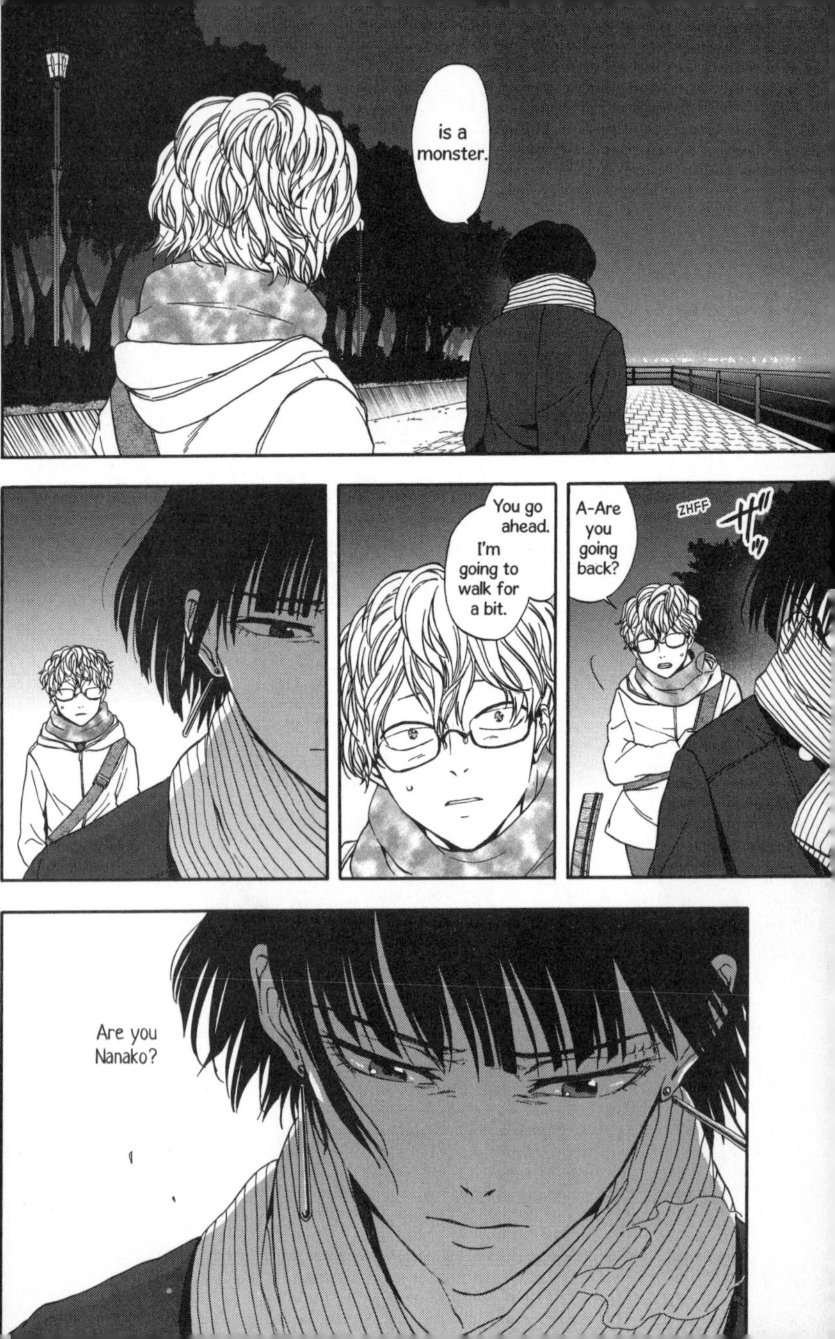
is a monster.
A-Are you going back?
ZHFF
You go ahead.
I'm going to walk for a bit.
Are you Nanako?

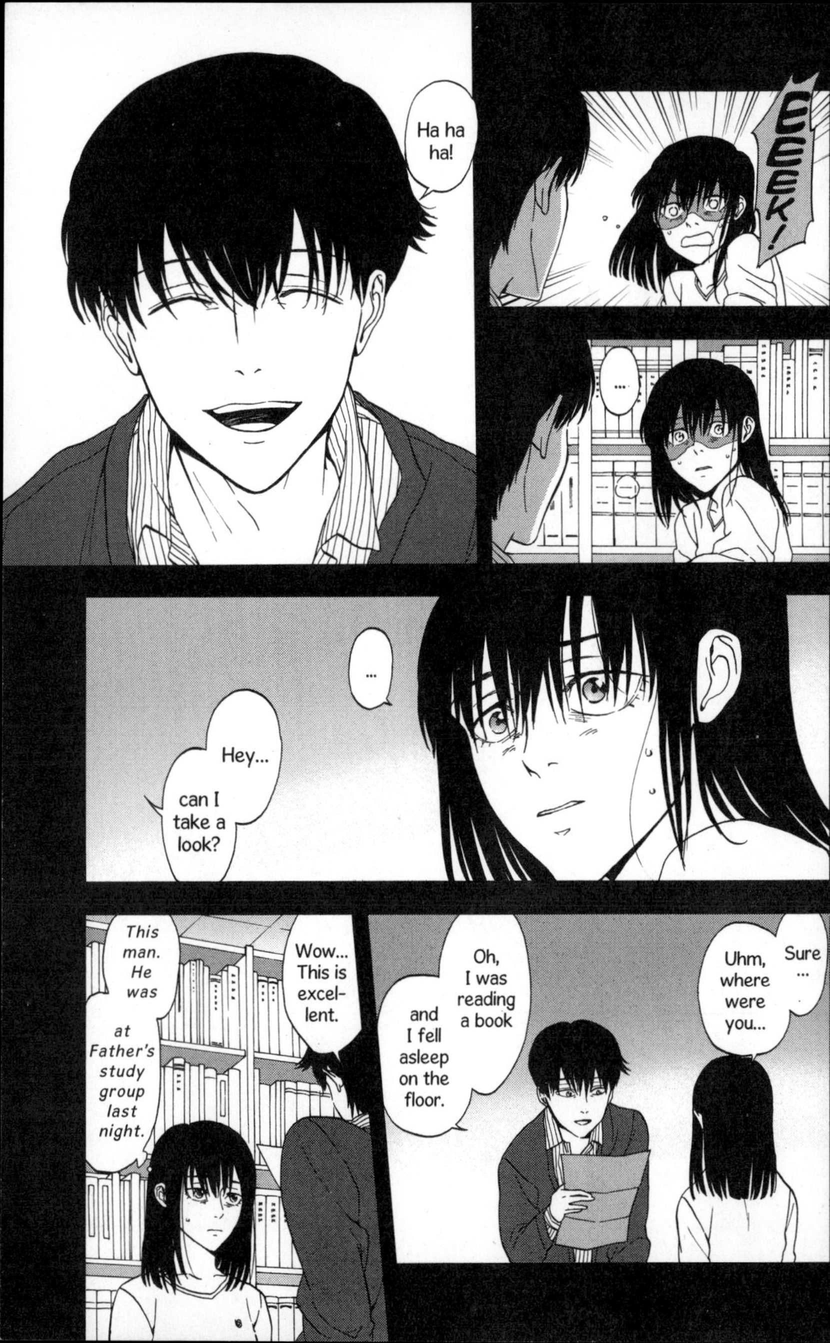
EEEEK!
...
Ha ha ha!
...
Hey... can I take a look?
Sure...
Uhm, where were you...
Oh, I was reading a book and I fell asleep on the floor.
Wow... This is excel-lent.
This man. He was at Father's study group last night.

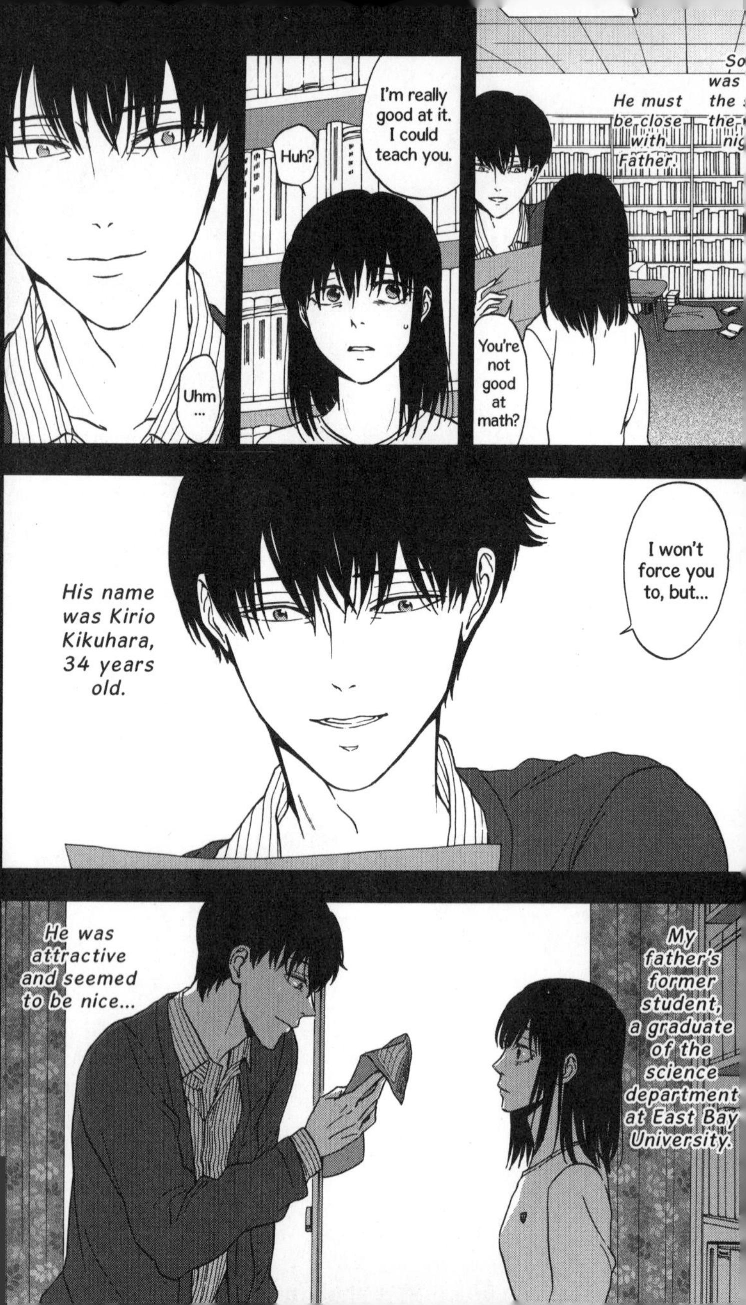
He must be close with Father.
You're not good at math?
I'm really good at it. I could teach you.
Huh?
Uhm ...
I won't force you to, but...
His name was Kirio Kikuhara, 34 years old.
My father's former student, a graduate of the science department at East Bay University.
He was attractive and seemed to be nice...

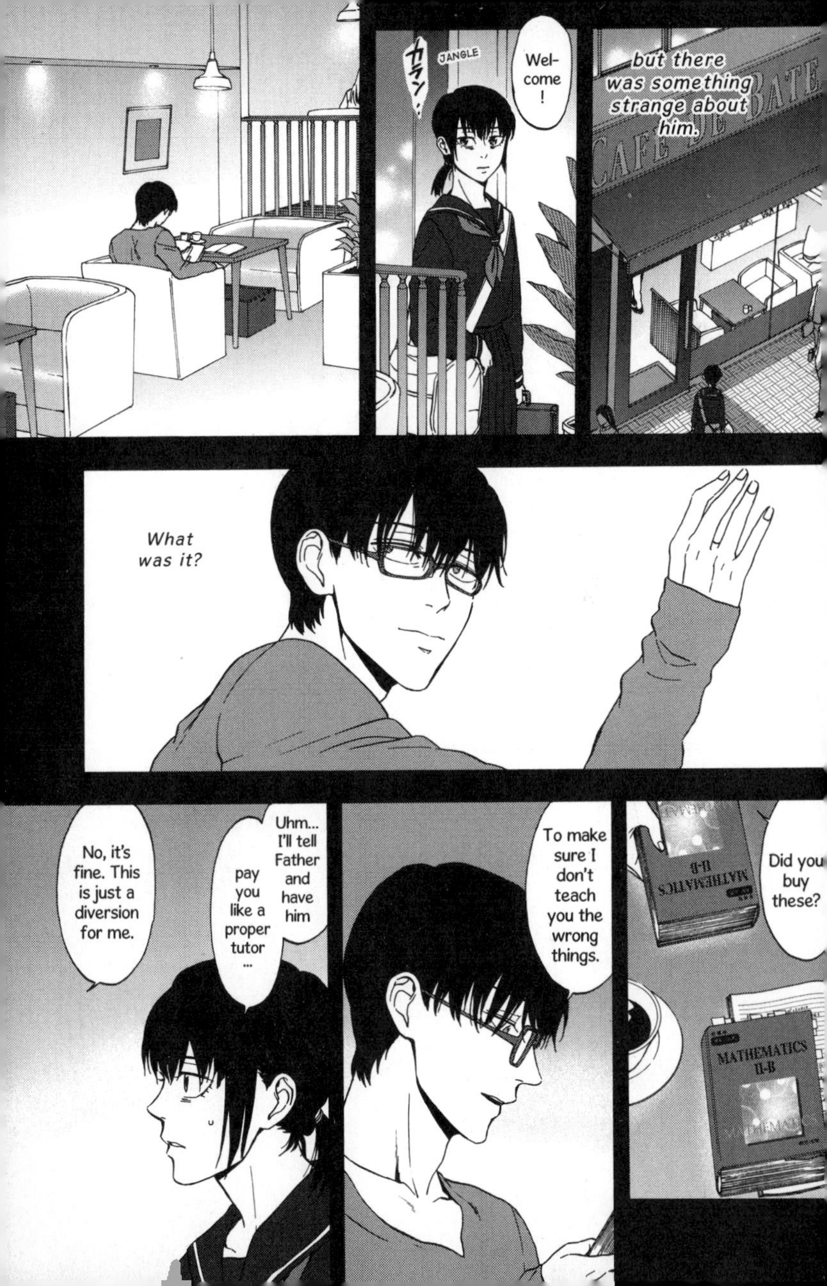
but there was something strange about him.
カラン
JANGLE
Wel-come!
What was it?
Did you buy these?
MATHEMATICS II-B
To make sure I don't teach you the wrong things.
Uhm... I'll tell Father and have him
pay you like a proper tutor...
No, it's fine. This is just a diversion for me.

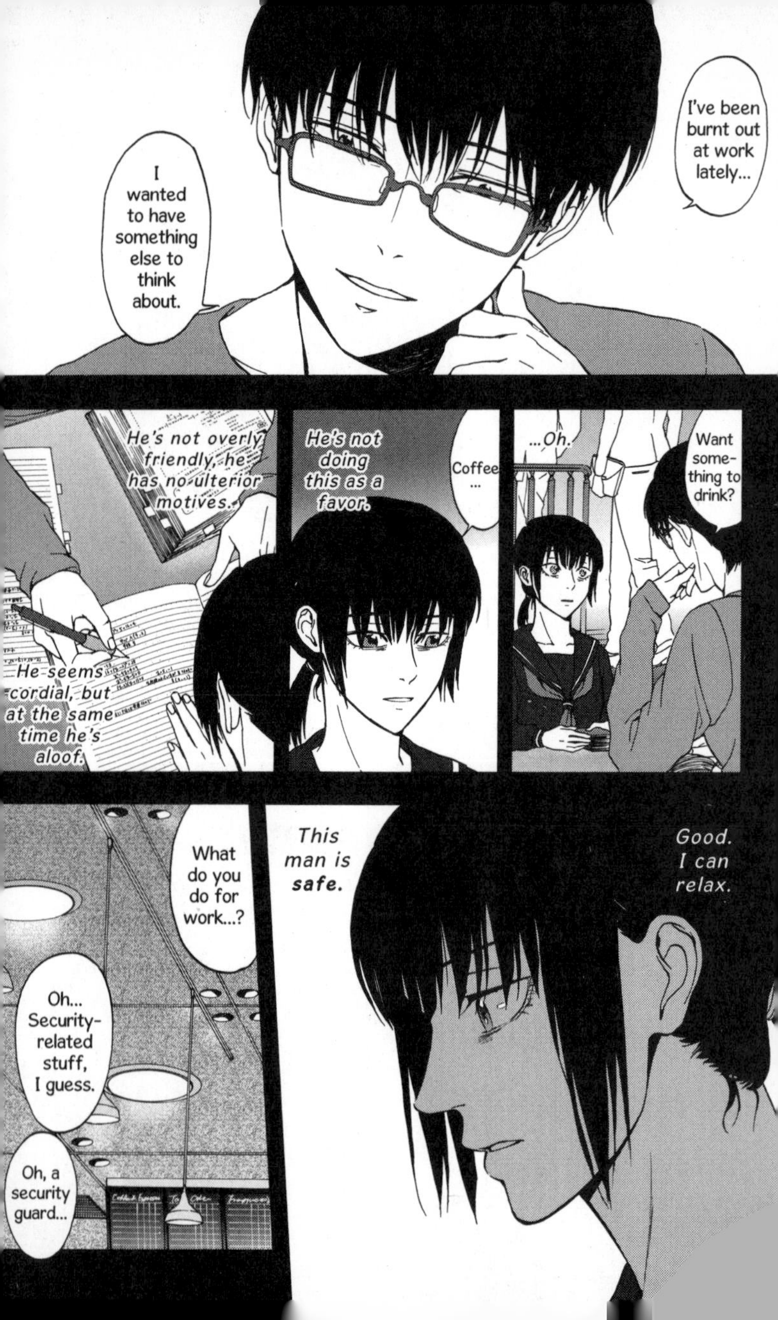
I've been burnt out at work lately...
I wanted to have something else to think about.
Want some-thing to drink?
...Oh.
Coffee...
He's not doing this as a favor.
He's not overly friendly, he has no ulterior motives.
He seems cordial, but at the same time he's aloof.
Good. I can relax.
This man is **safe.**
What do you do for work...?
Oh... Security-related stuff, I guess.
Oh, a security guard...

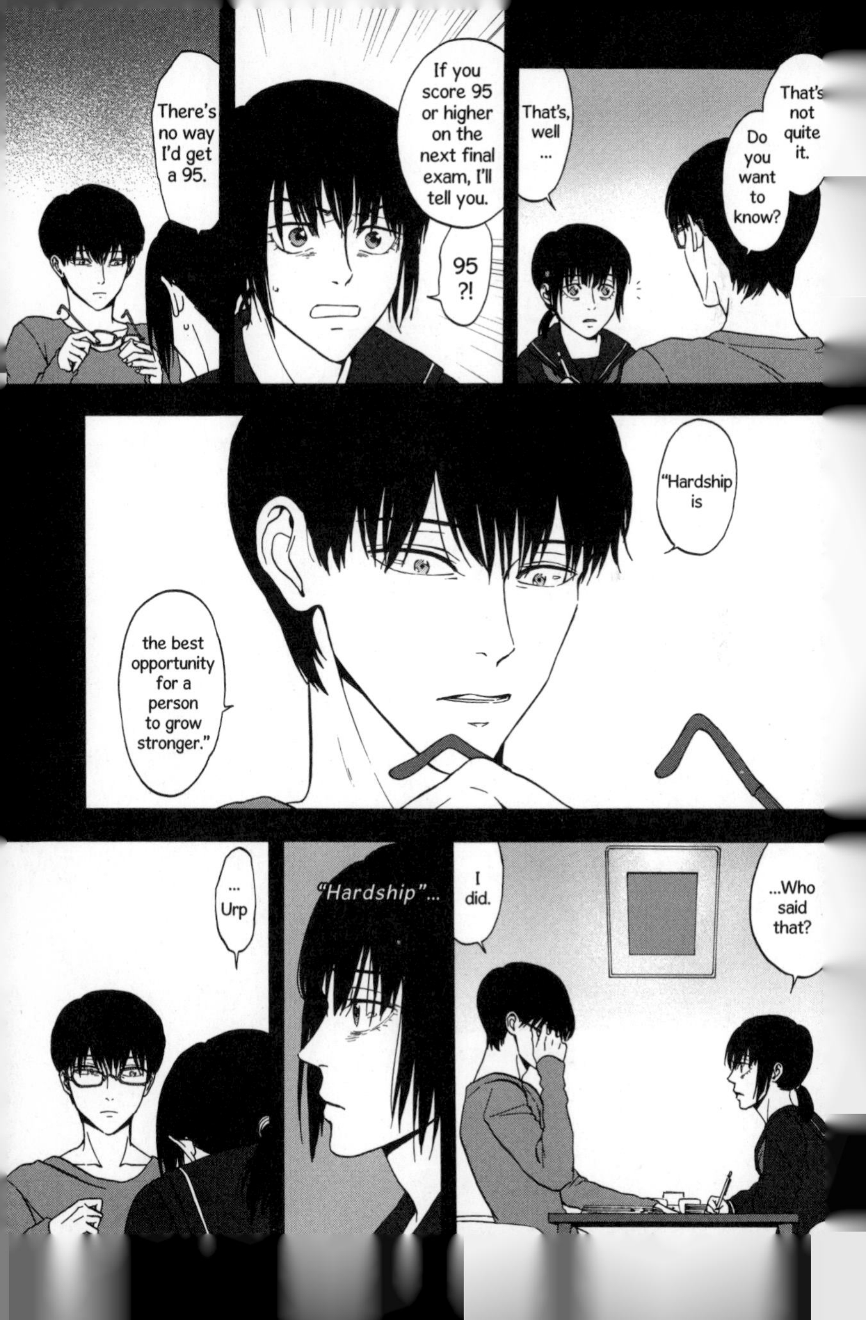
That's not quite it.
Do you want to know?
That's, well ...
If you score 95 or higher on the next final exam, I'll tell you.
95 ?!
There's no way I'd get a 95.
“Hardship is
the best opportunity for a person to grow stronger.”
...Who said that?
I did.
“Hardship”...
... Urp

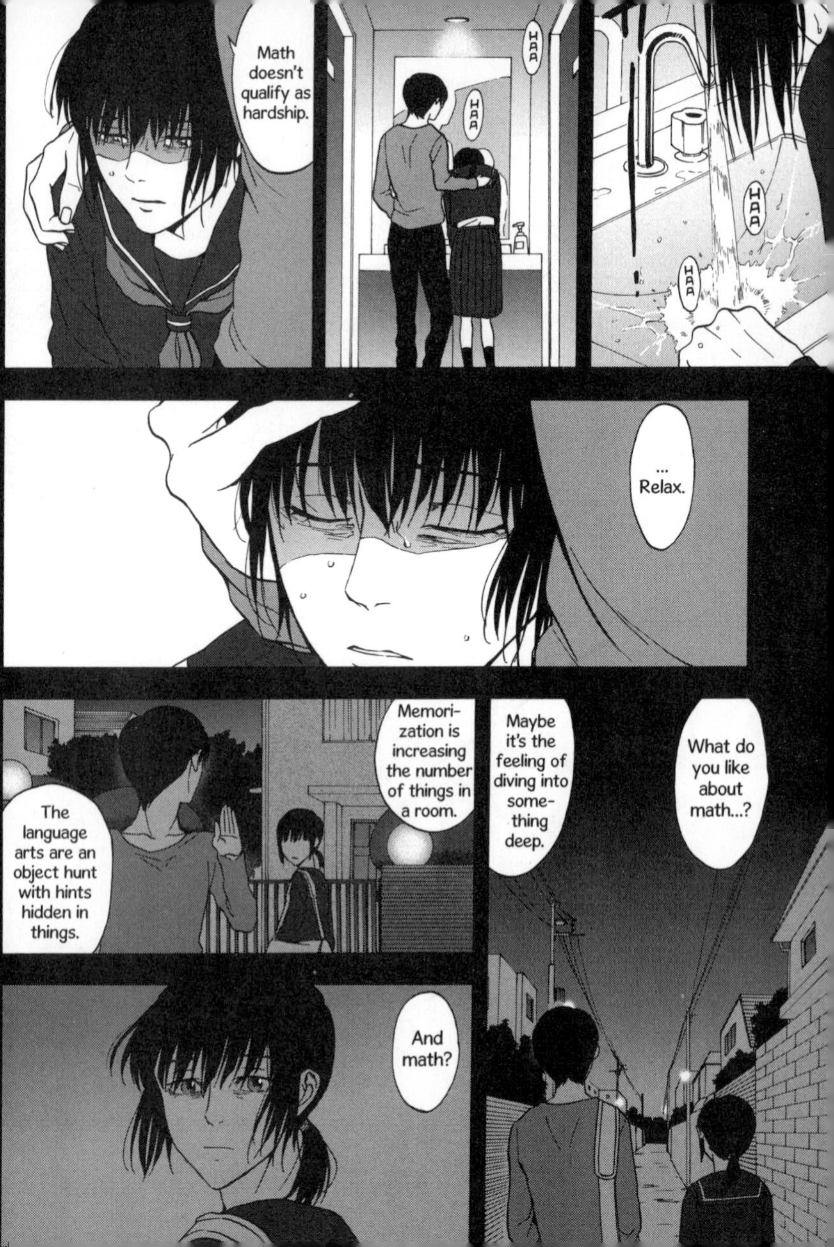
HAA
HAA
HAA
HAA
Math doesn't qualify as hardship.
... Relax.
What do you like about math...?
Maybe it's the feeling of diving into some-thing deep.
Memori-zation is increasing the number of things in a room.
The language arts are an object hunt with hints hidden in things.
And math?

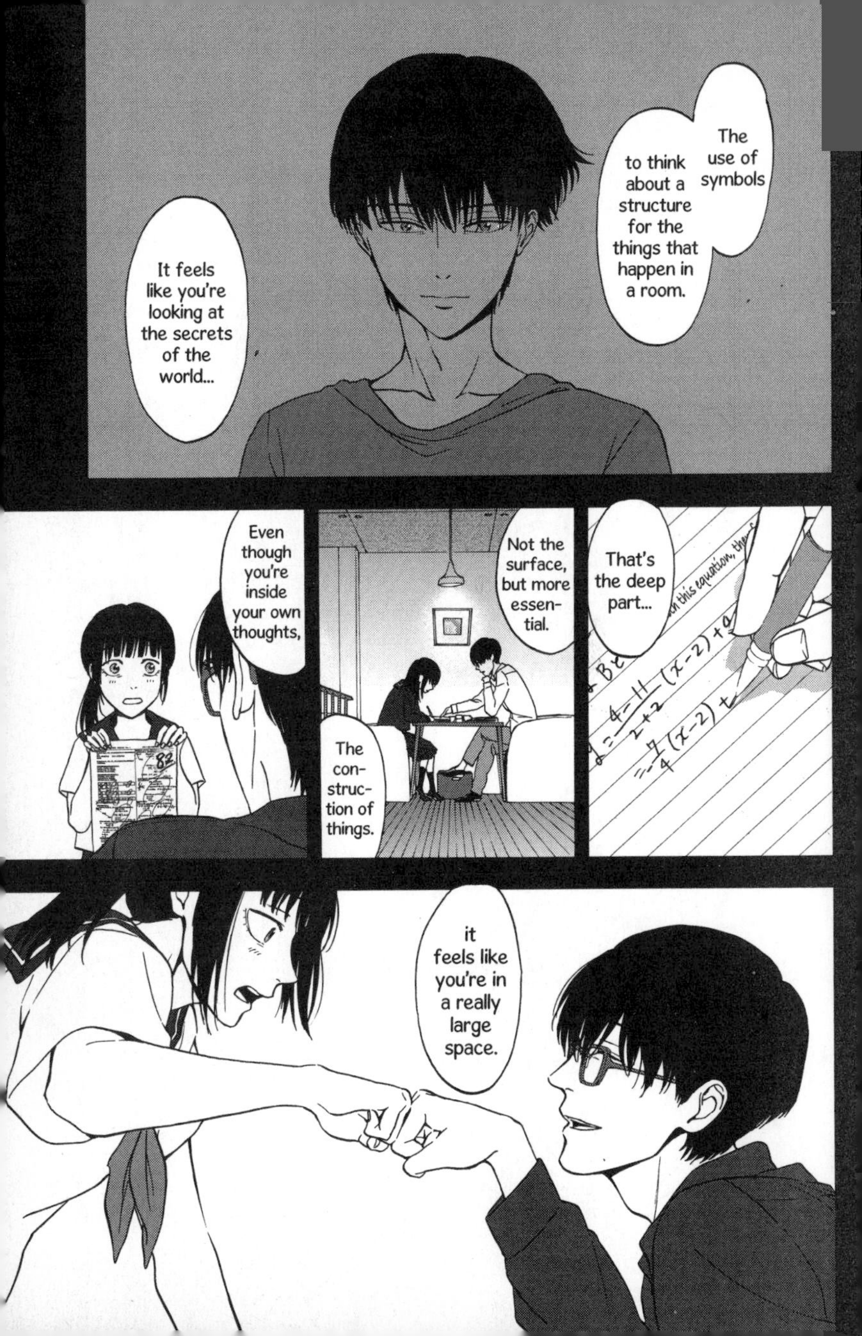
The use of symbols
to think about a structure for the things that happen in a room.
It feels like you're looking at the secrets of the world...
That's the deep part...
Not the surface, but more essential.
The construction of things.
Even though you're inside your own thoughts,
it feels like you're in a really large space.

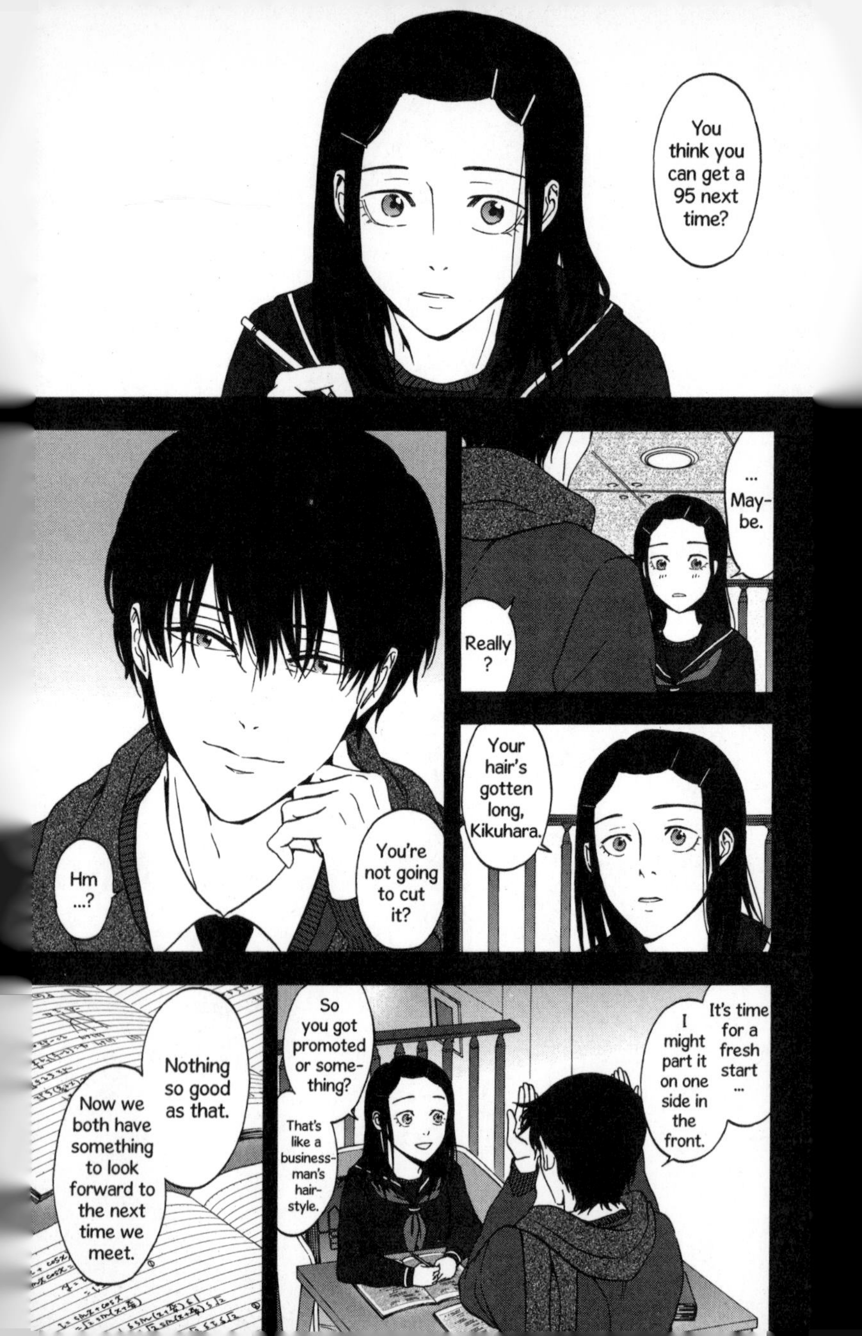
You think you can get a 95 next time?
... Maybe.
Really?
Your hair's gotten long, Kikuhara.
You're not going to cut it?
Hm ...?
It's time for a fresh start ...
I might part it on one side in the front.
So you got promoted or something?
That's like a businessman's hairstyle.
Nothing so good as that.
Now we both have something to look forward to the next time we meet.

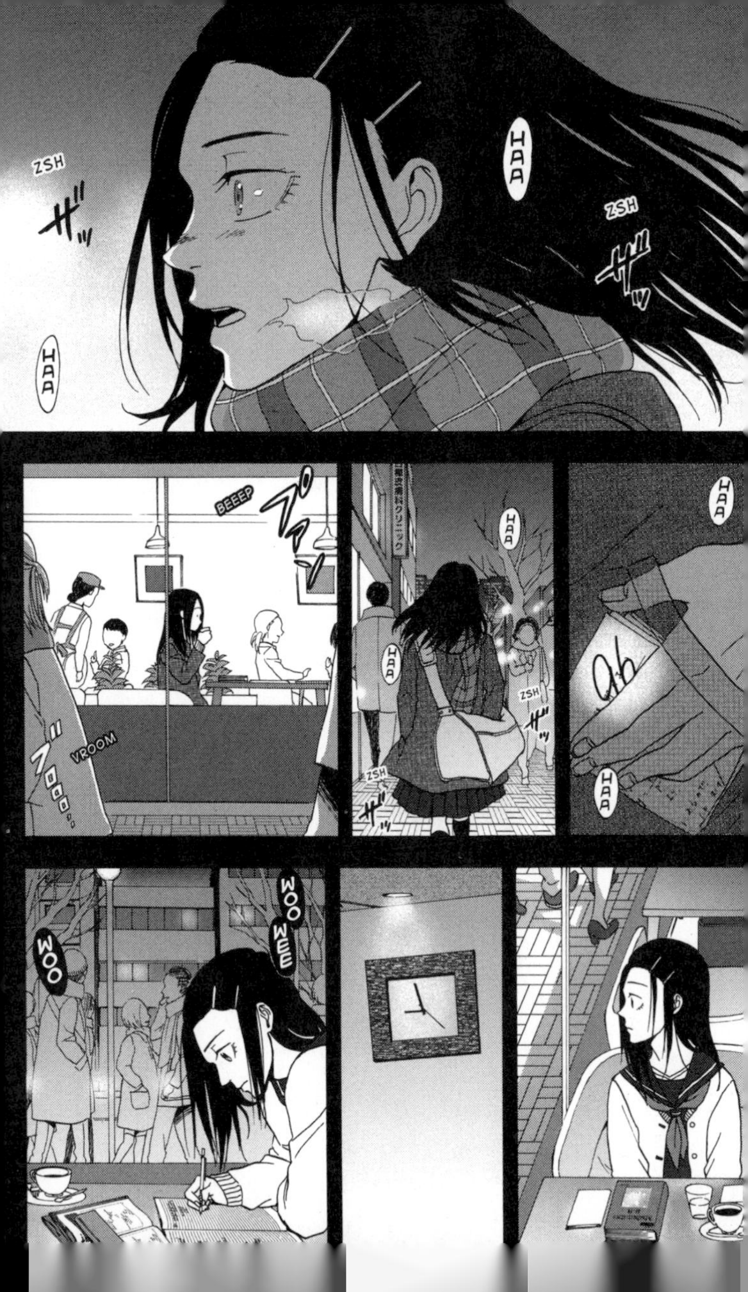
HAA
ZSH
ZSH
HAA
HAA
HAA
HAA
HAA
ZSH
ZSH
BEEEP
VROOM
WOO WEE
WOO

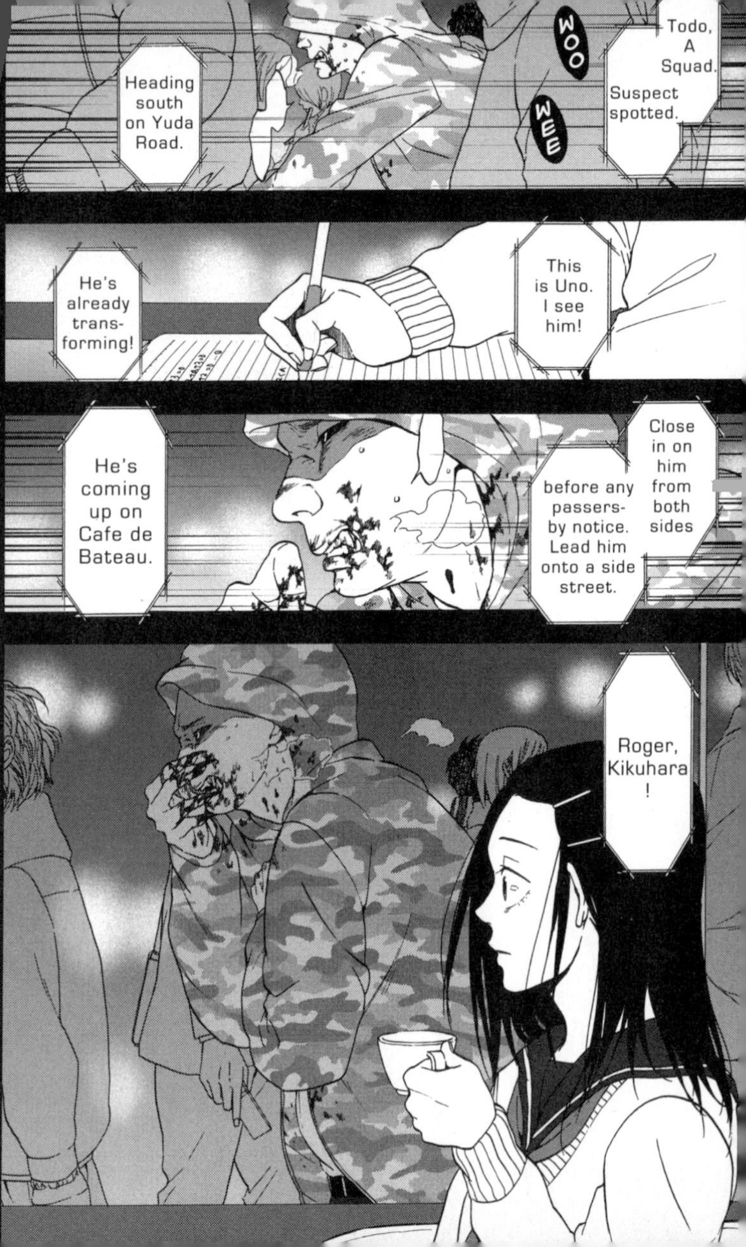
Todo, A Squad.
Suspect spotted.
WOO
WEE
Heading south on Yuda Road.
This is Uno. I see him!
He's already trans-forming!
Close in on him from both sides
before any passers-by notice. Lead him onto a side street.
He's coming up on Cafe de Bateau.
Roger, Kikuhara!

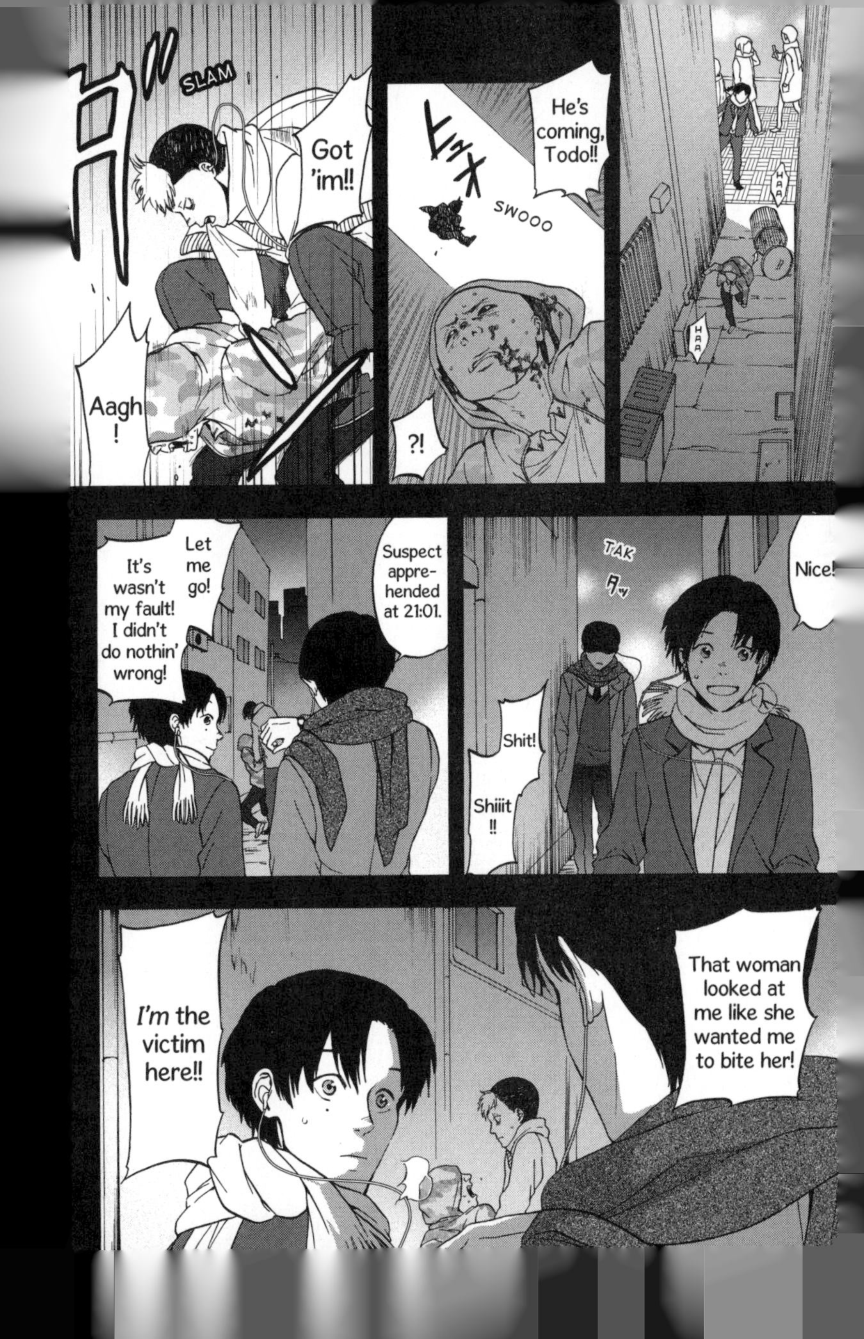
HAA
HAA
He's coming, Todo!!
SWOOO
?!
SLAM
Got 'im!!
Aagh!
Nice!
TAK
Shit!
Shiiit!!
Suspect apprehended at 21:01.
Let me go!
It's wasn't my fault! I didn't do nothin' wrong!
That woman looked at me like she wanted me to bite her!
I'm the victim here!!

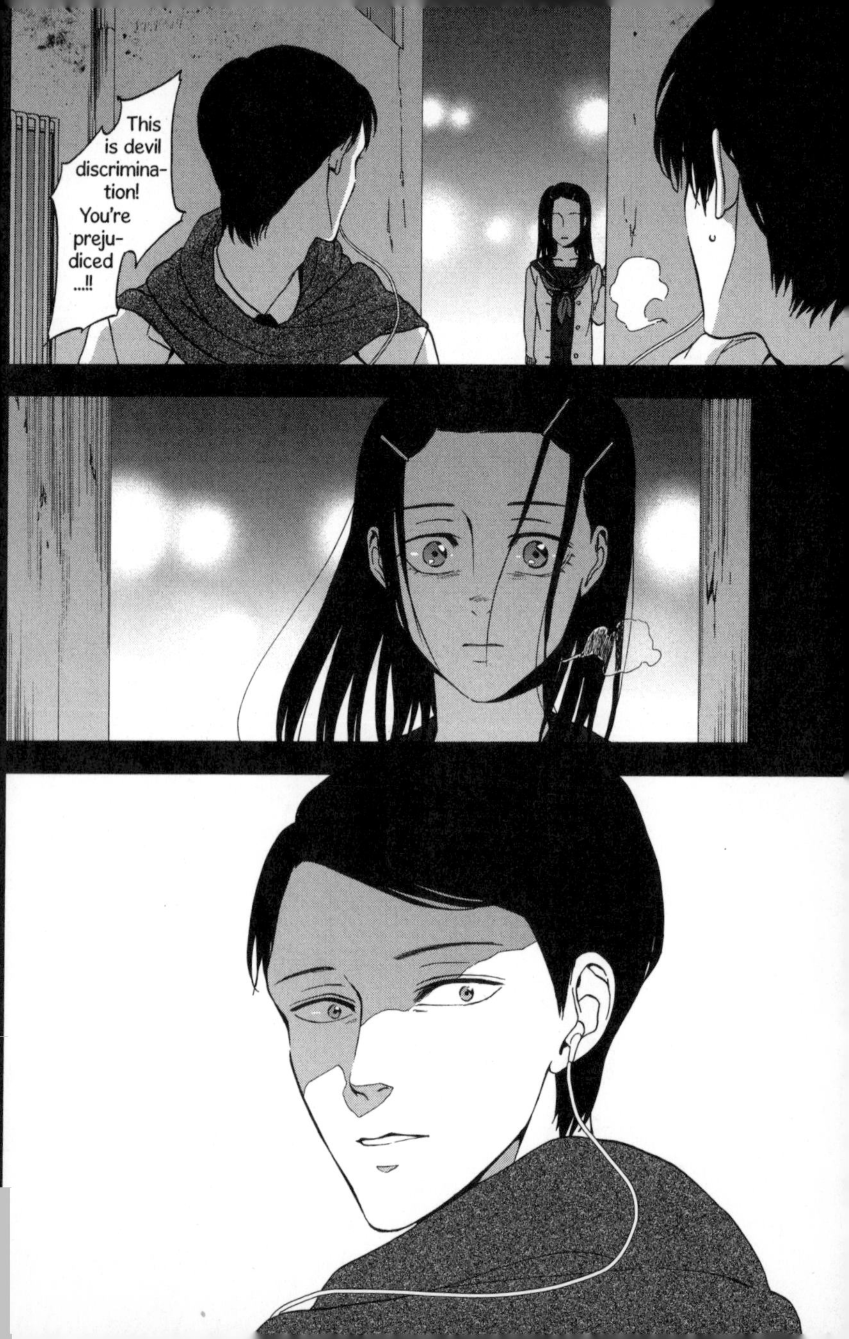
This is devil discrimina- tion! You're preju- diced ...!!

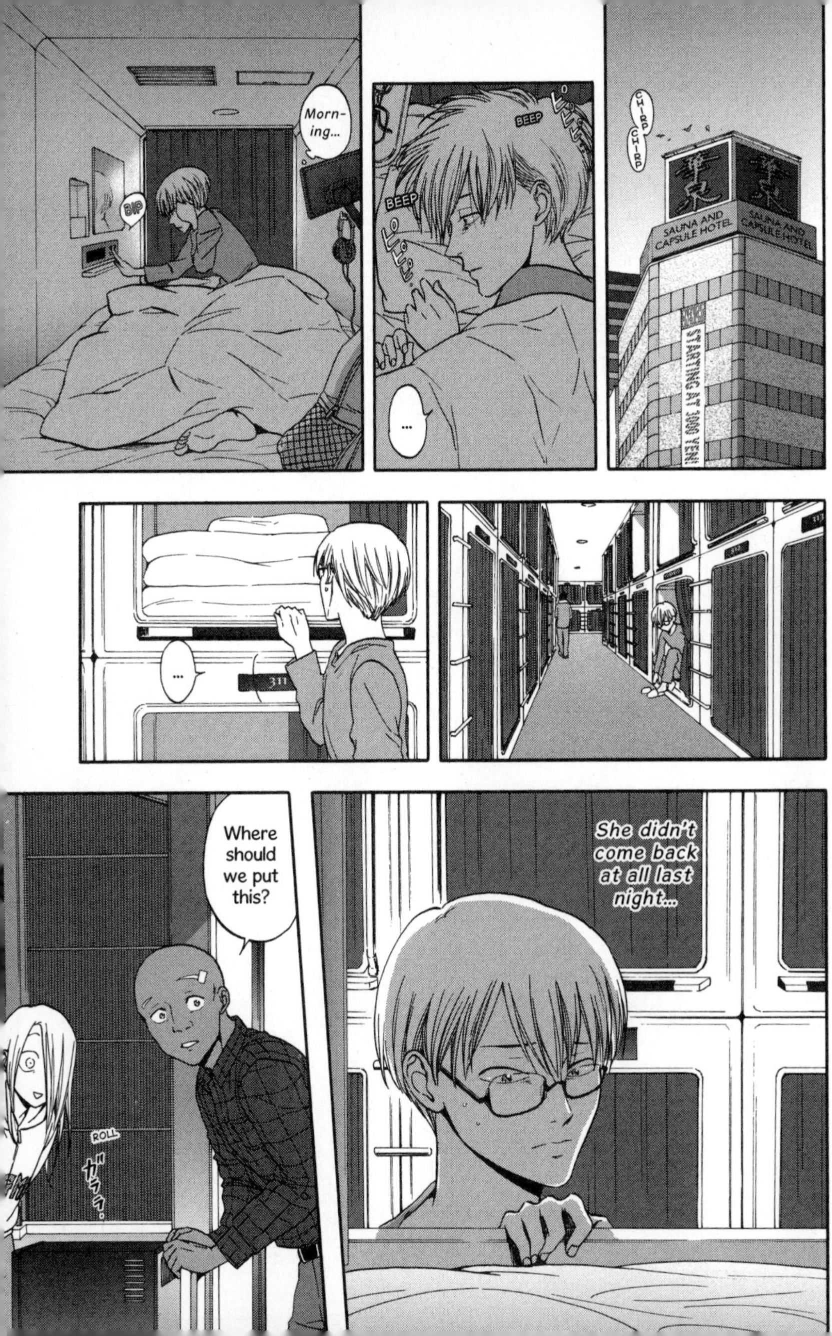
CHIRP CHIRP
SAUNA AND CAPSULE HOTEL
SAUNA AND CAPSULE HOTEL
STARTING AT 3000 YEN!
BEEP
BEEP
...
Morn-ing...
BIP
...
She didn't come back at all last night...
Where should we put this?
ROLL

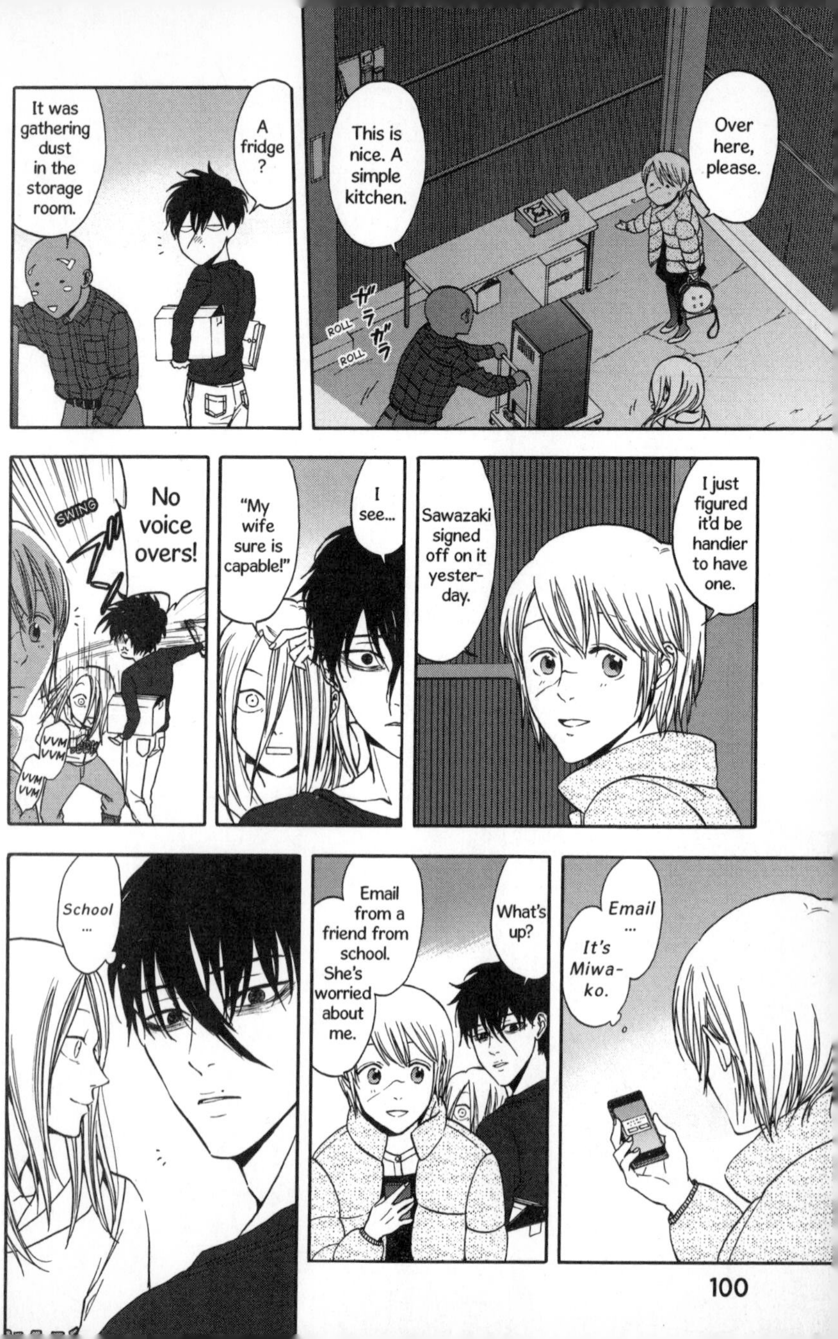
Over here, please.
This is nice. A simple kitchen.
ガラガラ
ROLL
ROLL
A fridge?
It was gathering dust in the storage room.
I just figured it'd be handier to have one.
Sawazaki signed off on it yesterday.
I see...
“My wife sure is capable!”
No voice overs!
SWING
VVM VVM
VVM VVM
Email ... It's Miwako.
What's up?
Email from a friend from school. She's worried about me.
School ...

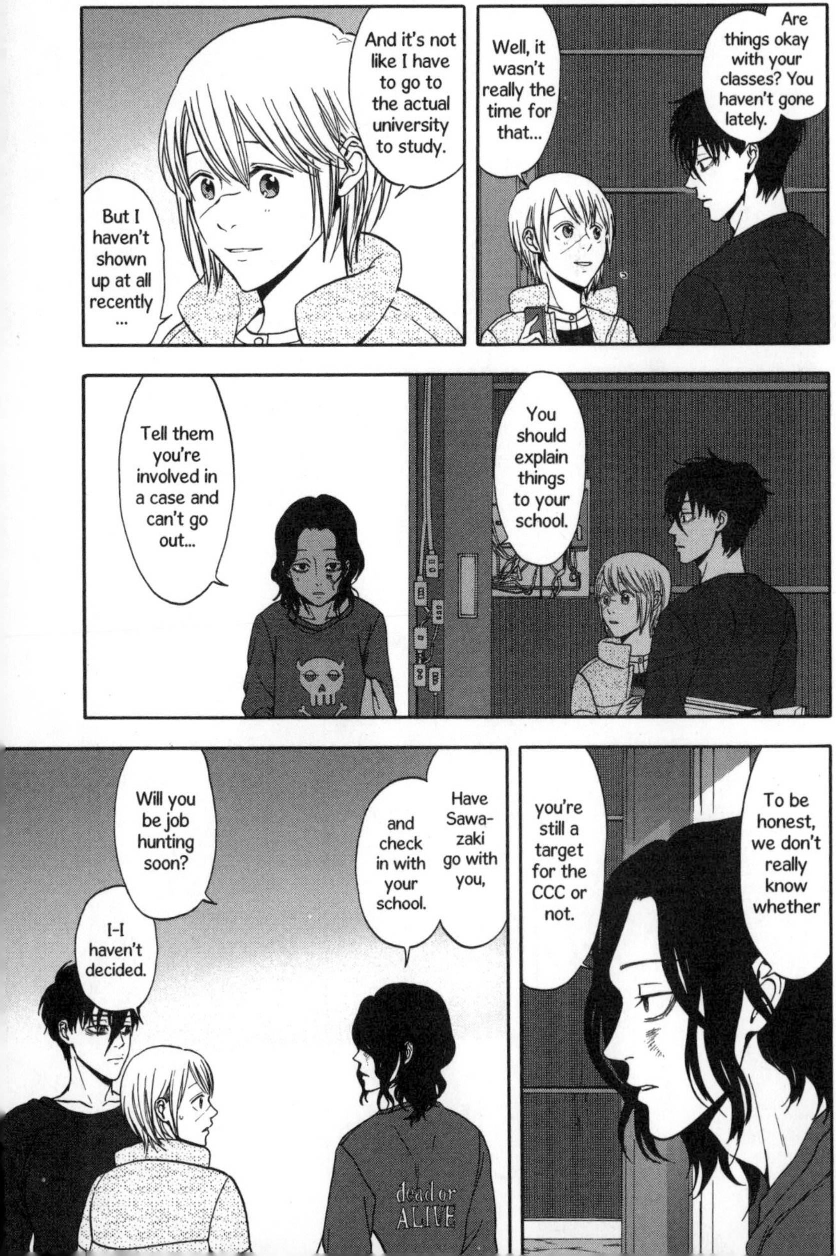
Are things okay with your classes? You haven't gone lately.
Well, it wasn't really the time for that...
And it's not like I have to go to the actual university to study.
But I haven't shown up at all recently ...
You should explain things to your school.
Tell them you're involved in a case and can't go out...
To be honest, we don't really know whether
you're still a target for the CCC or not.
Have Sawa-zaki go with you,
and check in with your school.
Will you be job hunting soon?
I-I haven't decided.
dead or ALIVE

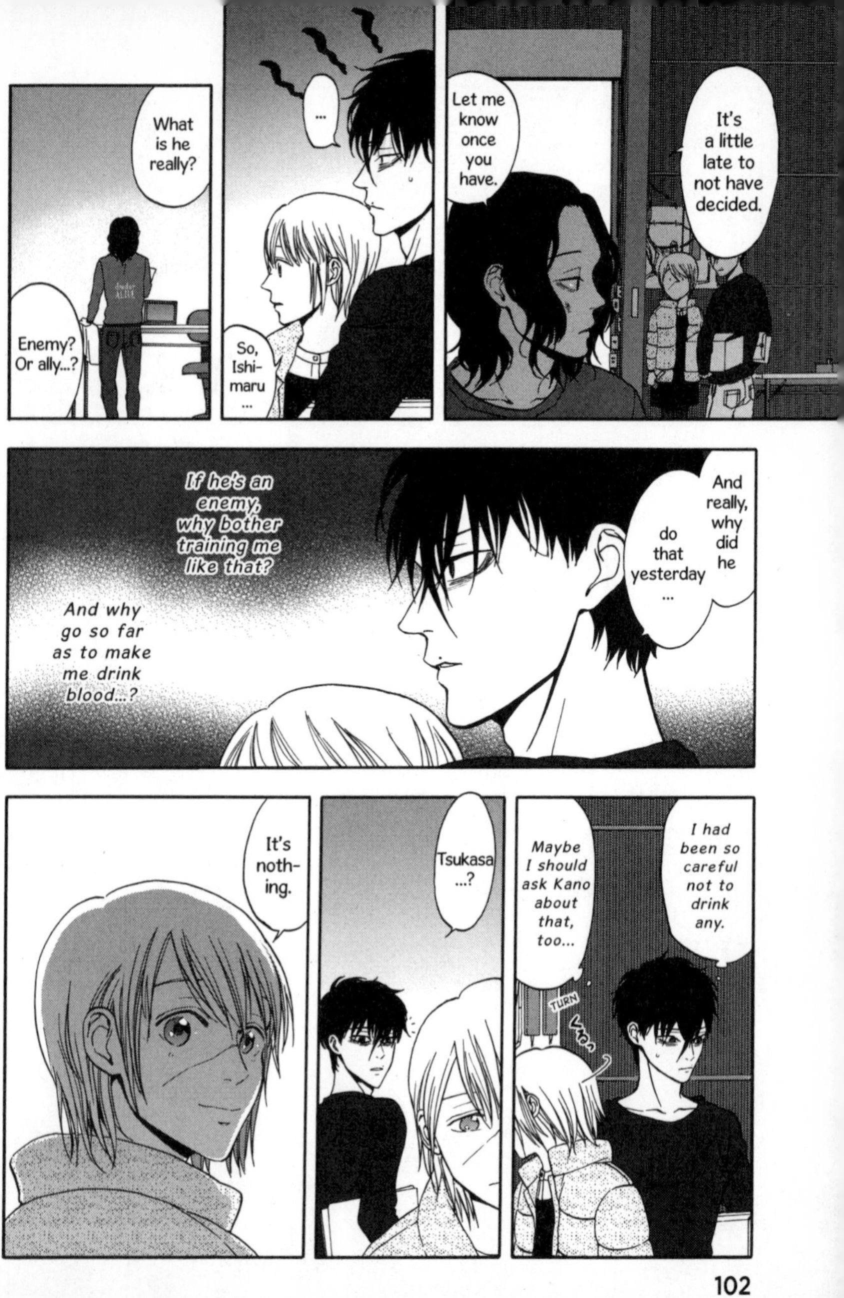
It's a little late to not have decided.
Let me know once you have.
...
So, Ishimaru...
What is he really?
Enemy? Or ally...?
And really, why did he
do that yesterday...
If he's an enemy, why bother training me like that?
And why go so far as to make me drink blood...?
I had been so careful not to drink any.
Maybe I should ask Kano about that, too...
TURN
Tsukasa...?
It's nothing.

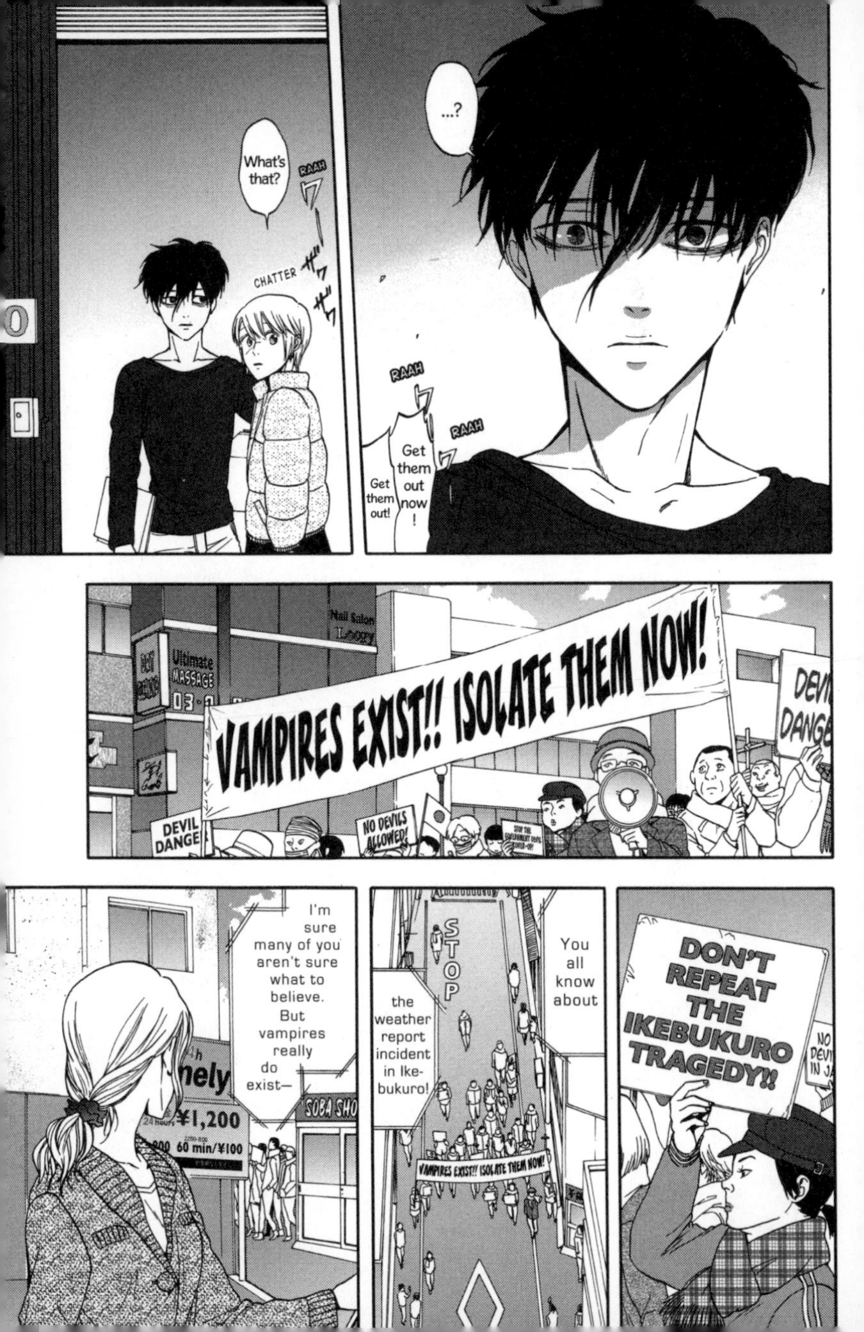

...?
RAAH
RAAH
Get them out now!
Get them out!
What's that?
RAAH
CHATTER
VAMPIRES EXIST!! ISOLATE THEM NOW!
Nail Salon
Ultimate MASSAGE
DEVIL DANGER
NO DEVILS ALLOWED!
DON'T REPEAT THE IKEBUKURO TRAGEDY!!
You all know about
the weather report incident in Ike-bukuro!
STOP
VAMPIRES EXIST!! ISOLATE THEM NOW!
I'm sure many of you aren't sure what to believe. But vampires really do exist—
¥1,200
60 min/¥100

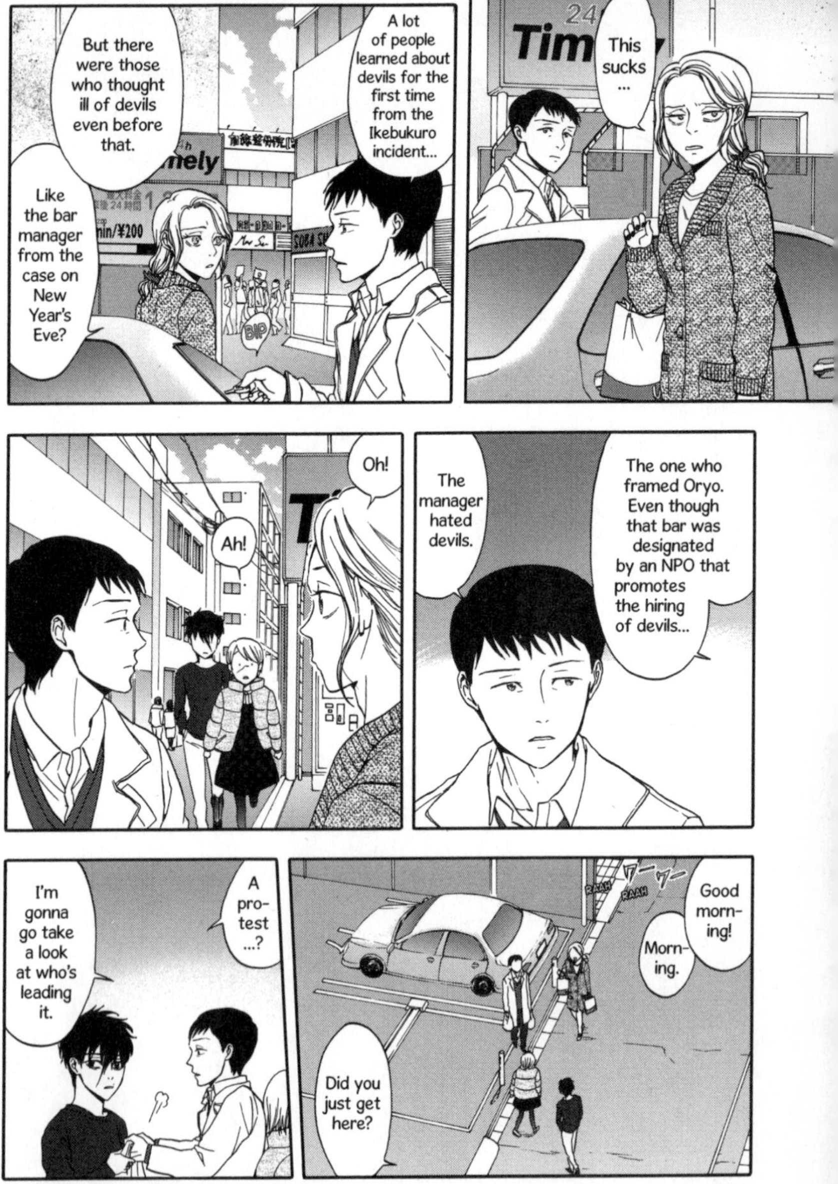
This sucks...
A lot of people learned about devils for the first time from the Ikebukuro incident...
But there were those who thought ill of devils even before that.
Like the bar manager from the case on New Year's Eve?
BIP
The one who framed Oryo. Even though that bar was designated by an NPO that promotes the hiring of devils...
The manager hated devils.
Oh!
Ah!
RAAH RAAH
Good morning!
Morn-ing.
Did you just get here?
A pro-test...?
I'm gonna go take a look at who's leading it.

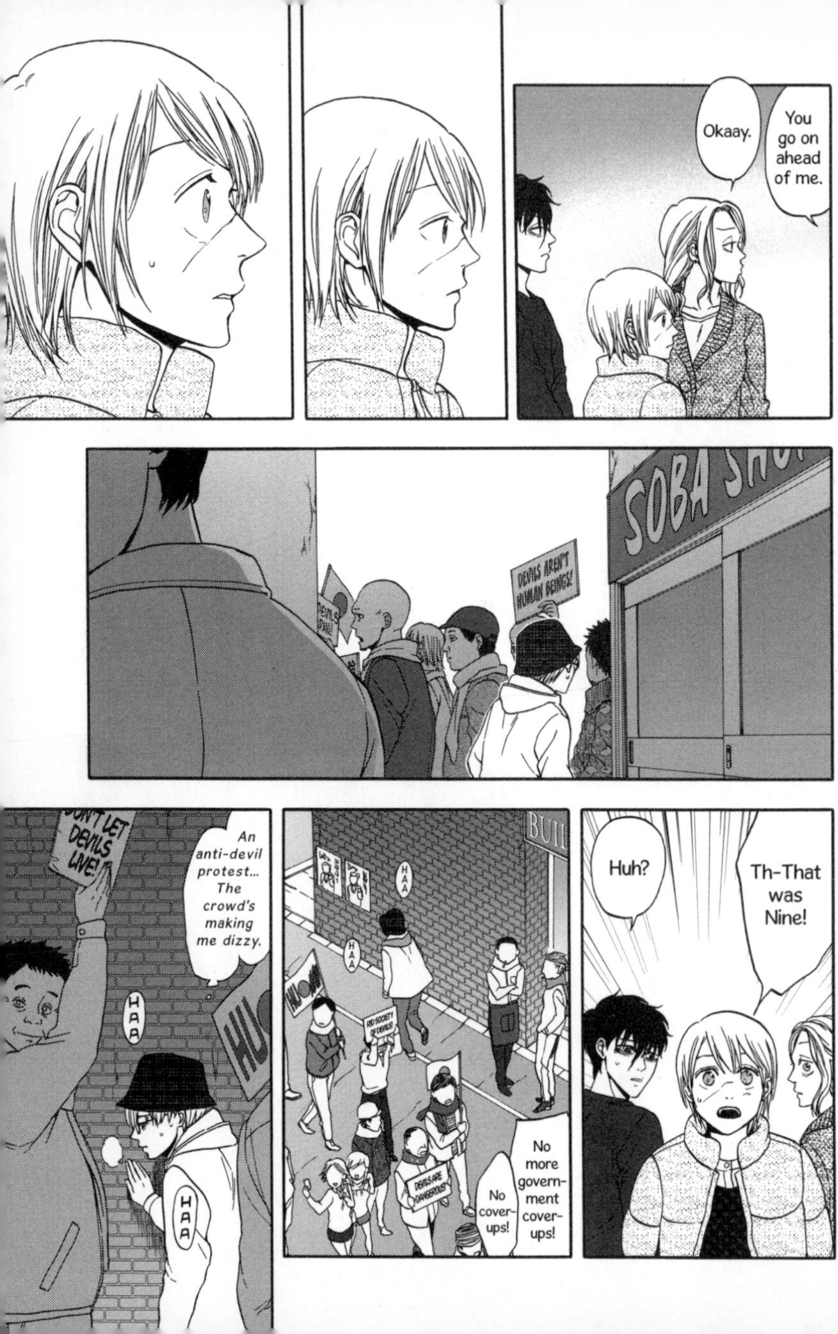
You go on ahead of me.
Okaay.
DEVILS AREN'T HUMAN BEINGS!
SOBA
Th-That was Nine!
Huh?
No more government cover-ups!
No cover-ups!
RID SOCIETY OF DEVILS!
DEVILS ARE DANGEROUS!
HAA
HAA
An anti-devil protest... The crowd's making me dizzy.
HAA
HAA

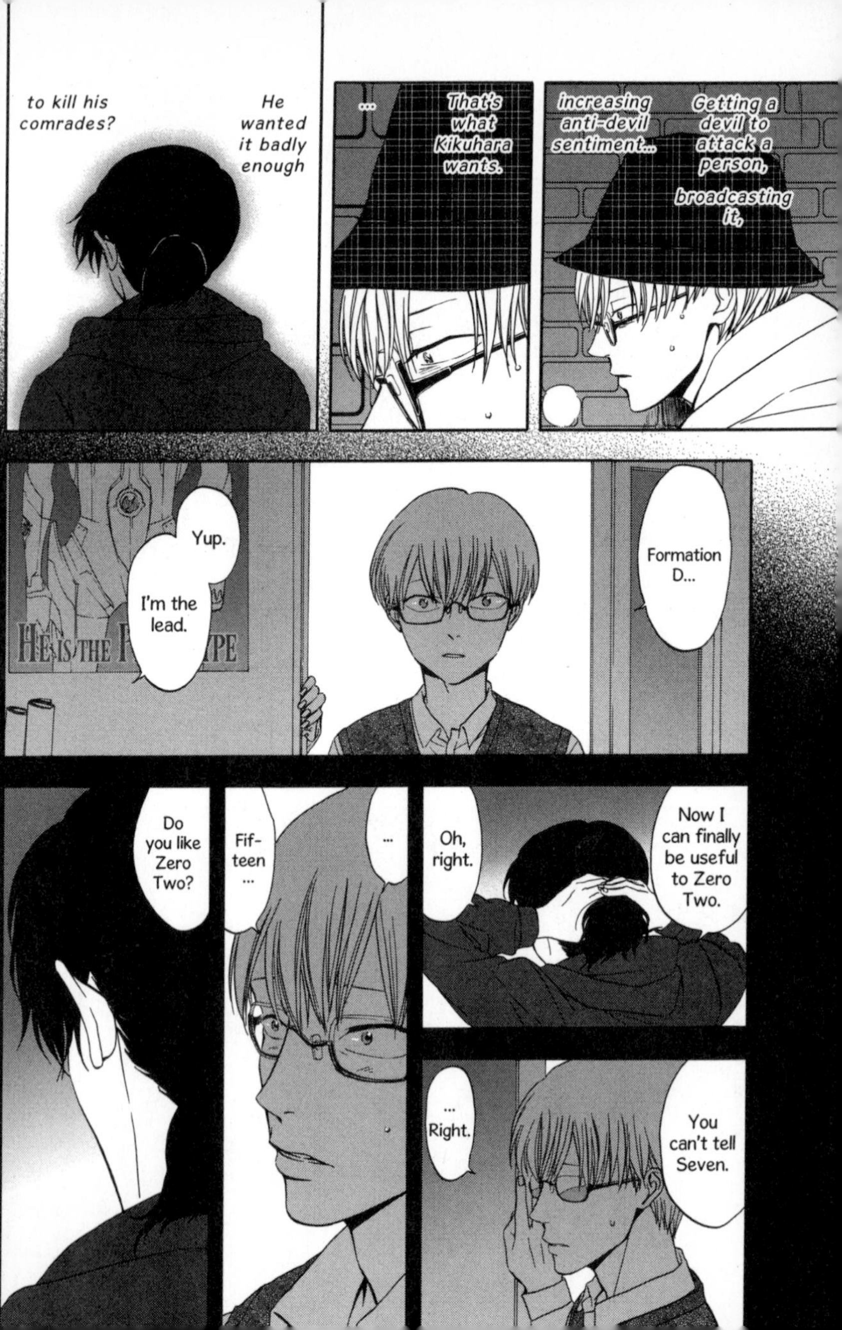
Getting a devil to attack a person,
broadcasting it,
increasing anti-devil sentiment...
That's what Kikuhara wants.
...
He wanted it badly enough
to kill his comrades?
Formation D...
Yup.
I'm the lead.
Now I can finally be useful to Zero Two.
Oh, right.
You can't tell Seven.
... Right.
...
Fif-teen ...
Do you like Zero Two?

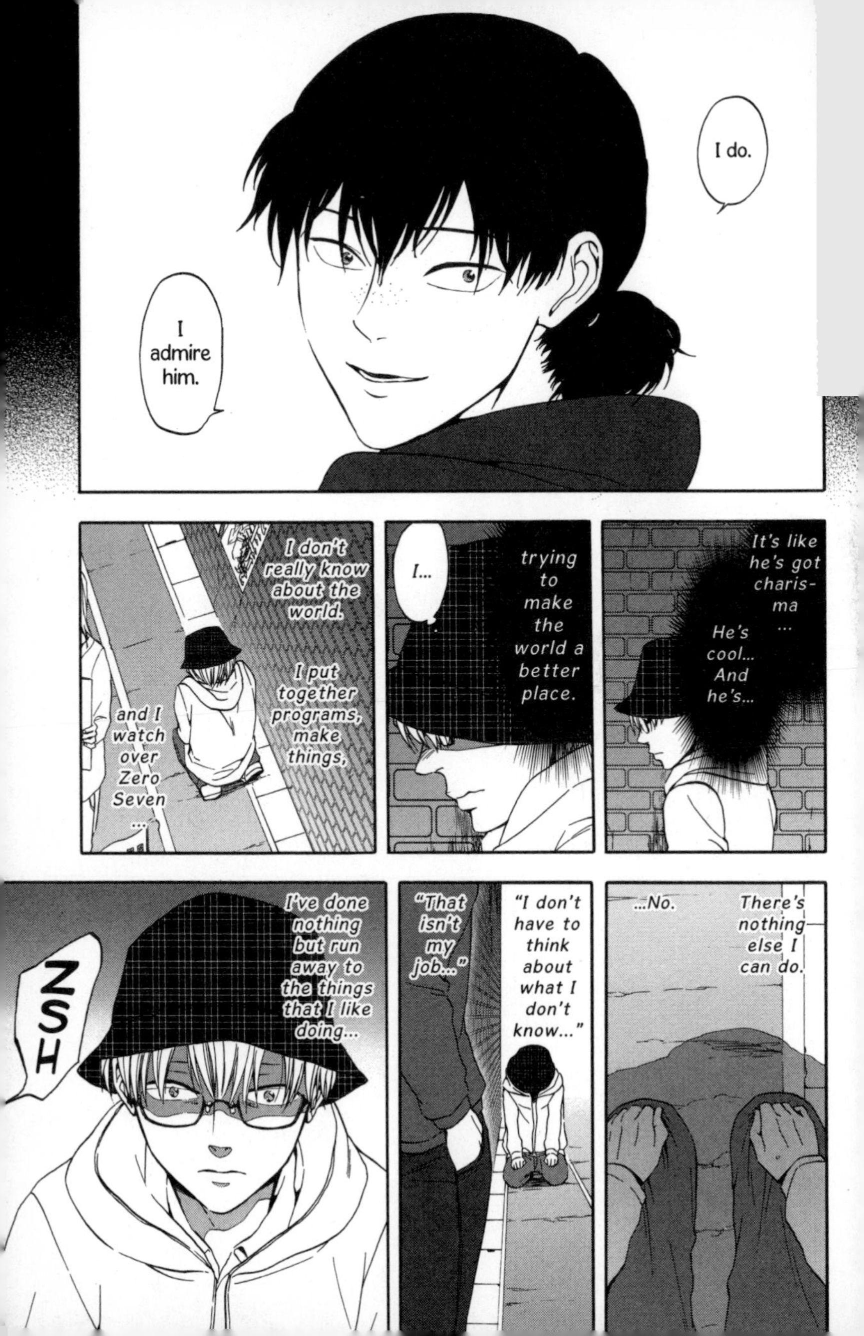
I do.
I admire him.
It's like he's got charis-ma ...
He's cool... And he's...
trying to make the world a better place.
I...
I don't really know about the world.
I put together programs, make things,
and I watch over Zero Seven ...
There's nothing else I can do.
...No.
“I don't have to think about what I don't know...”
“That isn't my job...”
I've done nothing but run away to the things that I like doing...
ZSH

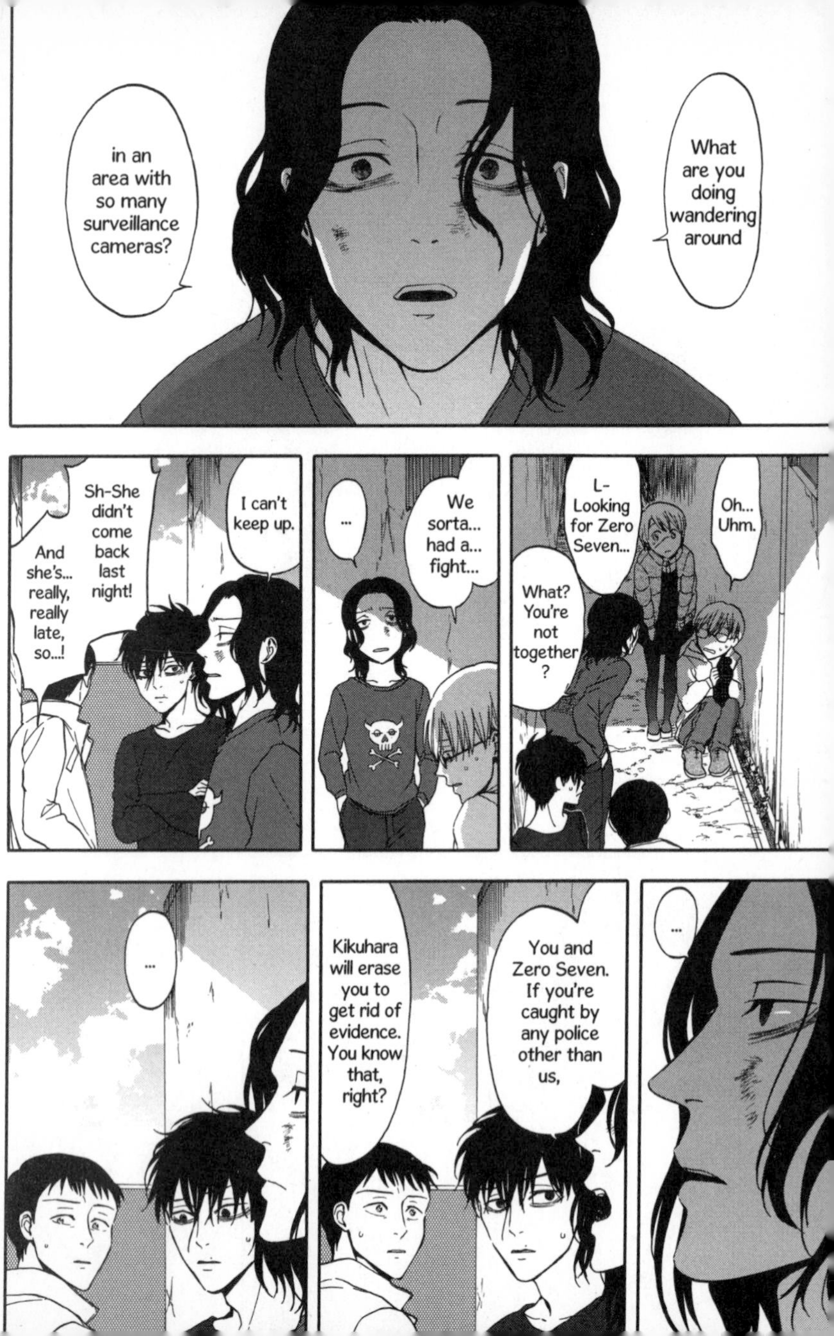
What are you doing wandering around
in an area with so many surveillance cameras?
Oh... Uhm.
L- Looking for Zero Seven...
What? You're not together?
We sorta... had a... fight...
...
I can't keep up.
Sh-She didn't come back last night!
And she's... really, really late, so...!
...
You and Zero Seven. If you're caught by any police other than us,
Kikuhara will erase you to get rid of evidence. You know that, right?
...

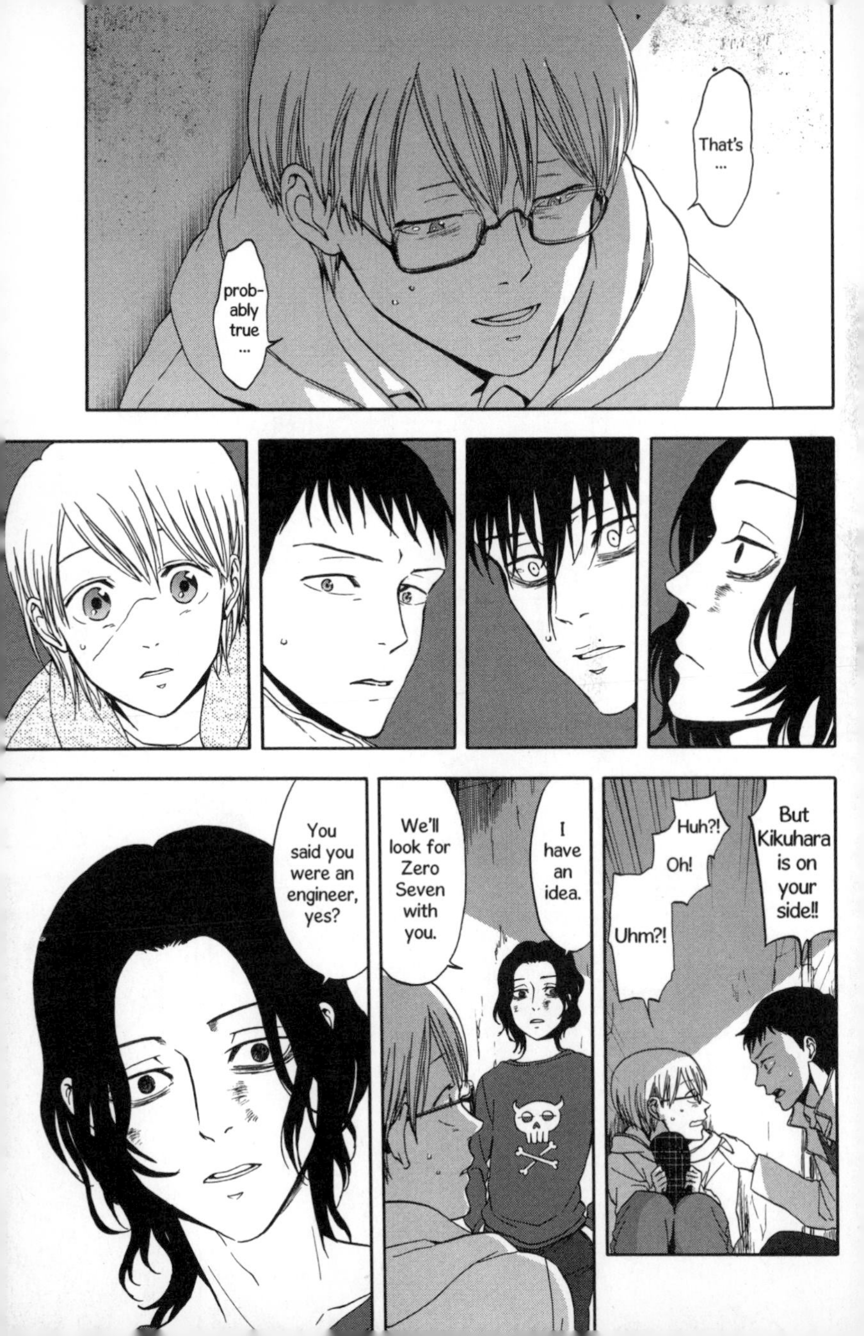
That's ...
prob-ably true ...
But Kikuhara is on your side!!
Huh?!
Oh!
Uhm?!
I have an idea.
We'll look for Zero Seven with you.
You said you were an engineer, yes?

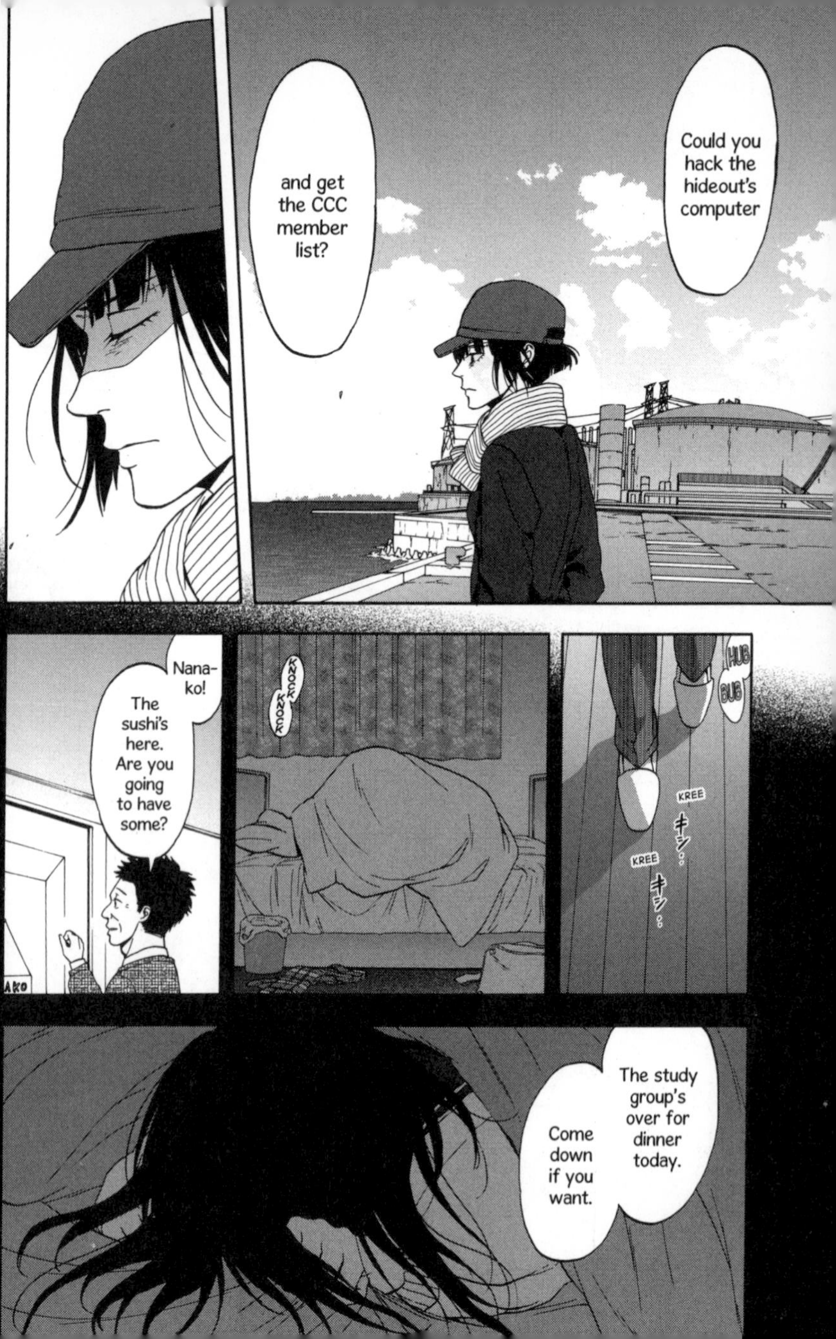
Could you hack the hideout's computer
and get the CCC member list?
HUB BUB
KREE
キシ。。
KREE
キシ。。
KNOCK KNOCK
Nana-ko!
The sushi's here. Are you going to have some?
The study group's over for dinner today.
Come down if you want.

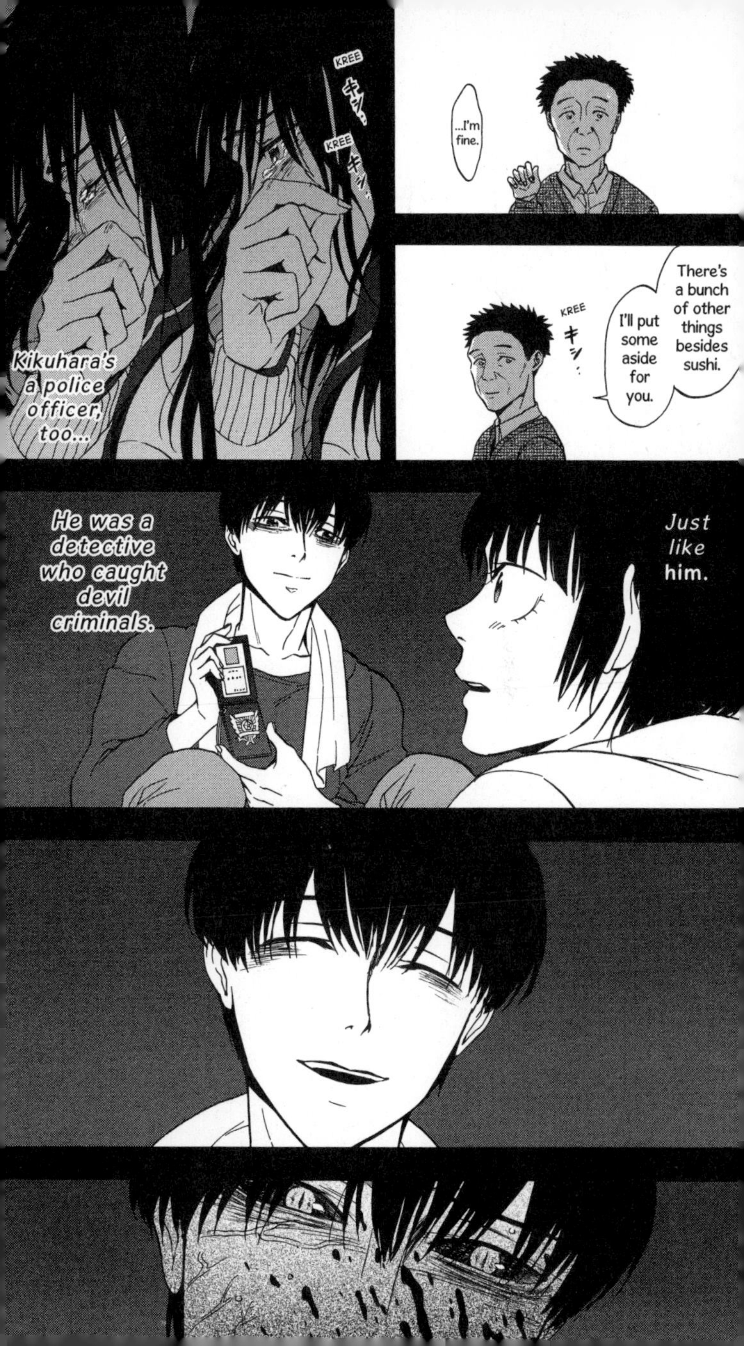
...I'm fine.
There's a bunch of other things besides sushi.
I'll put some aside for you.
KREE
キシ
KREE
キシ…
KREE
キシ
Kikuhara's a police officer, too...
Just like him.
He was a detective who caught devil criminals.

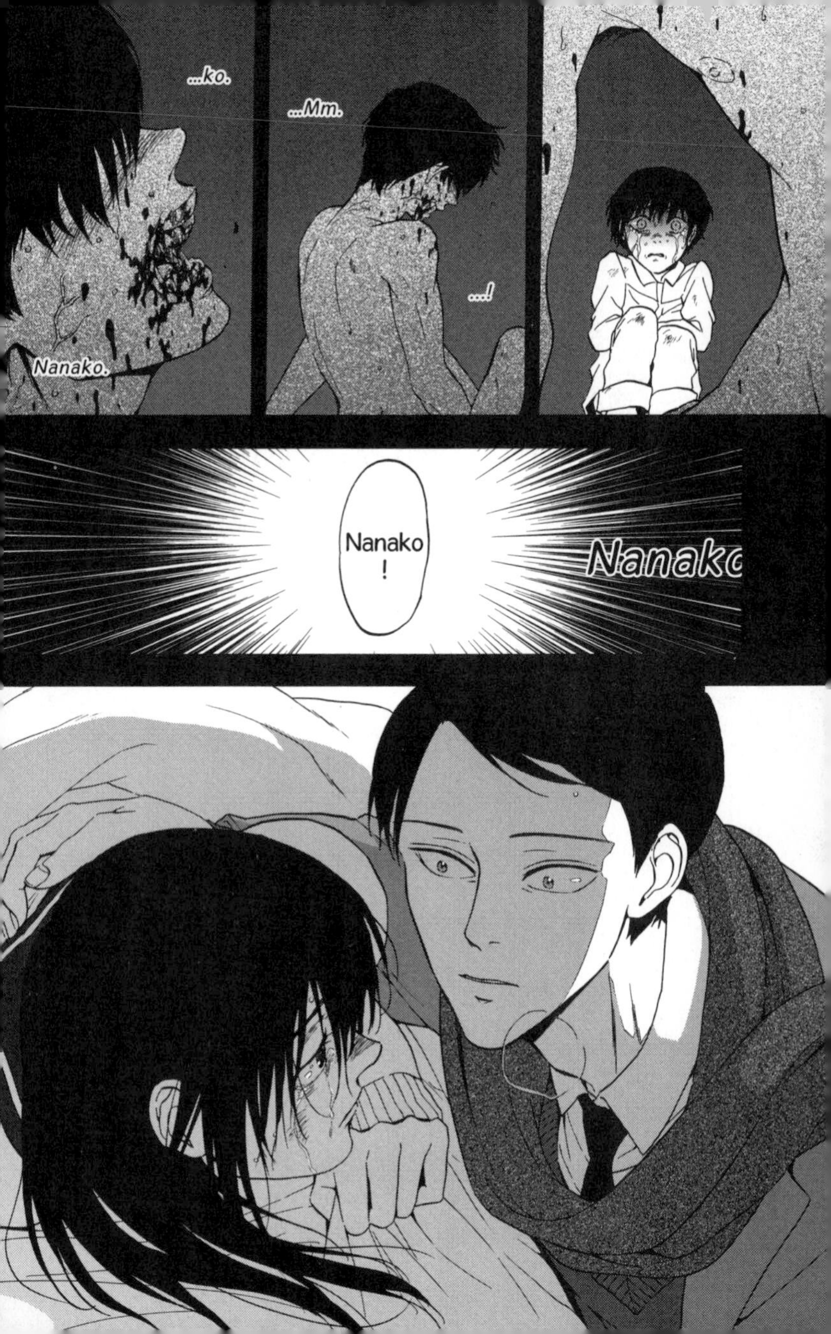
...Mm.
...!
...ko.
Nanako.
Nanako
Nanako!

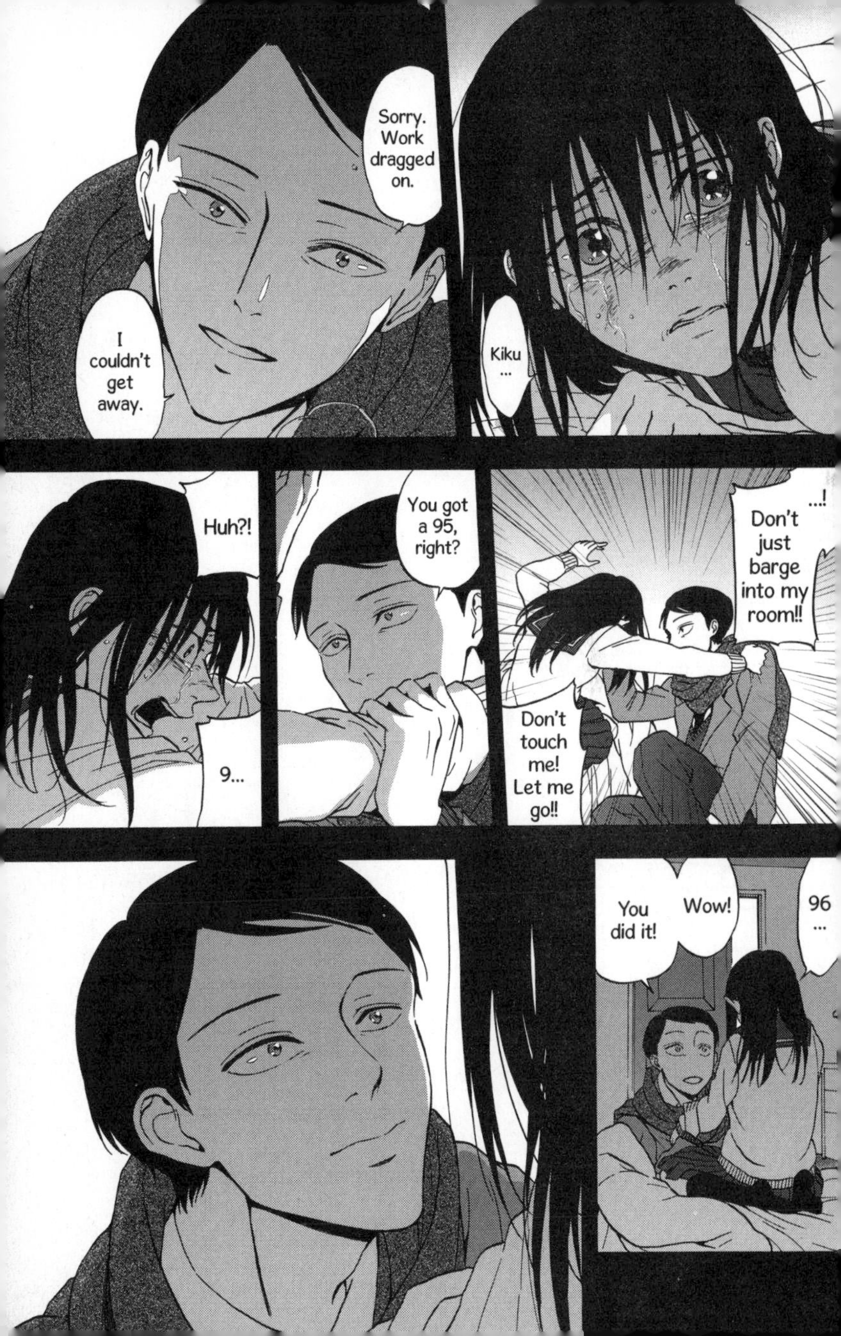
Kiku ...
Sorry. Work dragged on.
I couldn't get away.
...! Don't just barge into my room!!
Don't touch me! Let me go!!
You got a 95, right?
Huh?!
9...
96 ...
Wow!
You did it!

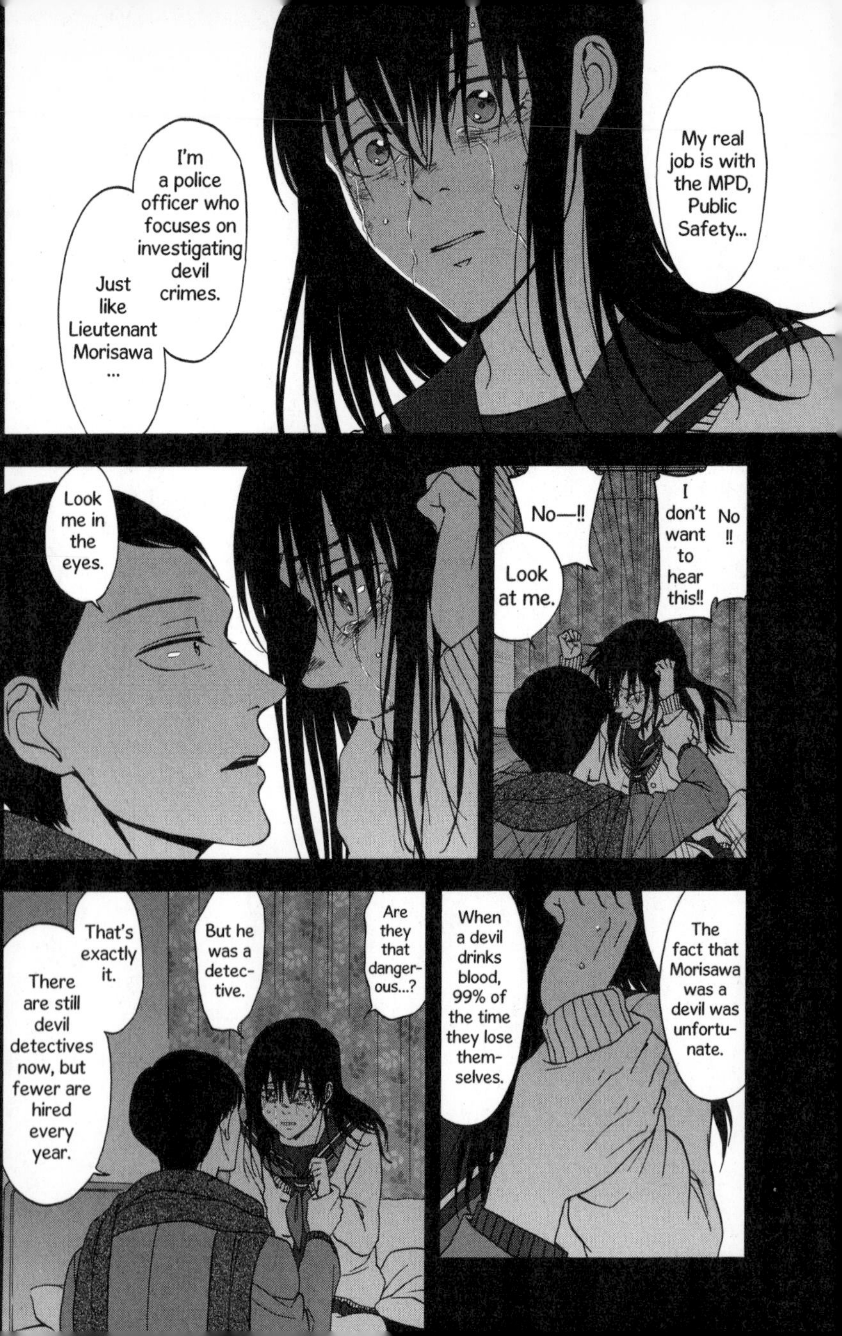
My real job is with the MPD, Public Safety...
I'm a police officer who focuses on investigating devil crimes.
Just like Lieutenant Morisawa ...
No !!
I don't want to hear this!!
No—!!
Look at me.
Look me in the eyes.
The fact that Morisawa was a devil was unfortu-nate.
When a devil drinks blood, 99% of the time they lose them-selves.
Are they that danger-ous...?
But he was a detec-tive.
That's exactly it.
There are still devil detectives now, but fewer are hired every year.

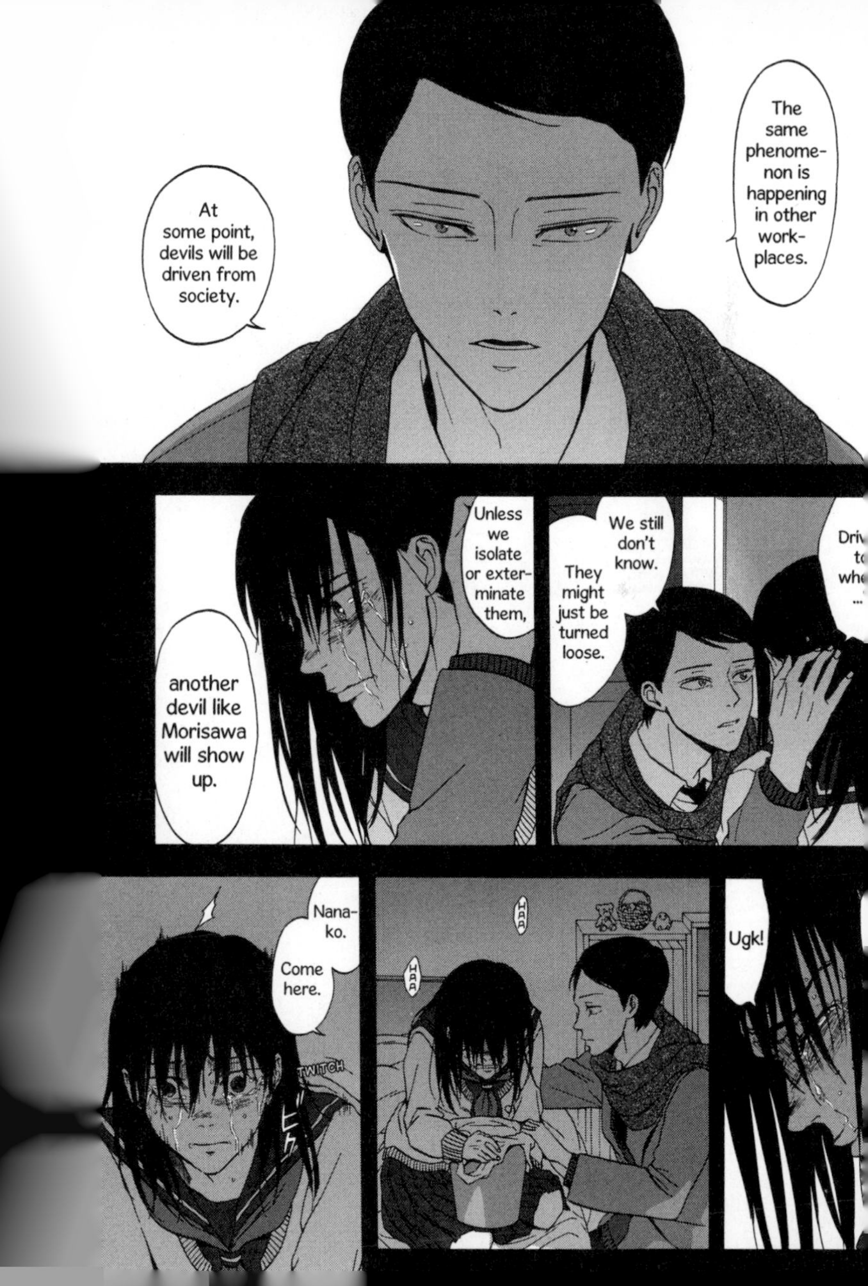
The same phenomenon is happening in other workplaces.
At some point, devils will be driven from society.
We still don't know.
They might just be turned loose.
Unless we isolate or exterminate them,
another devil like Morisawa will show up.
Ugk!
HAA
HAA
Nanako.
Come here.
TWITCH

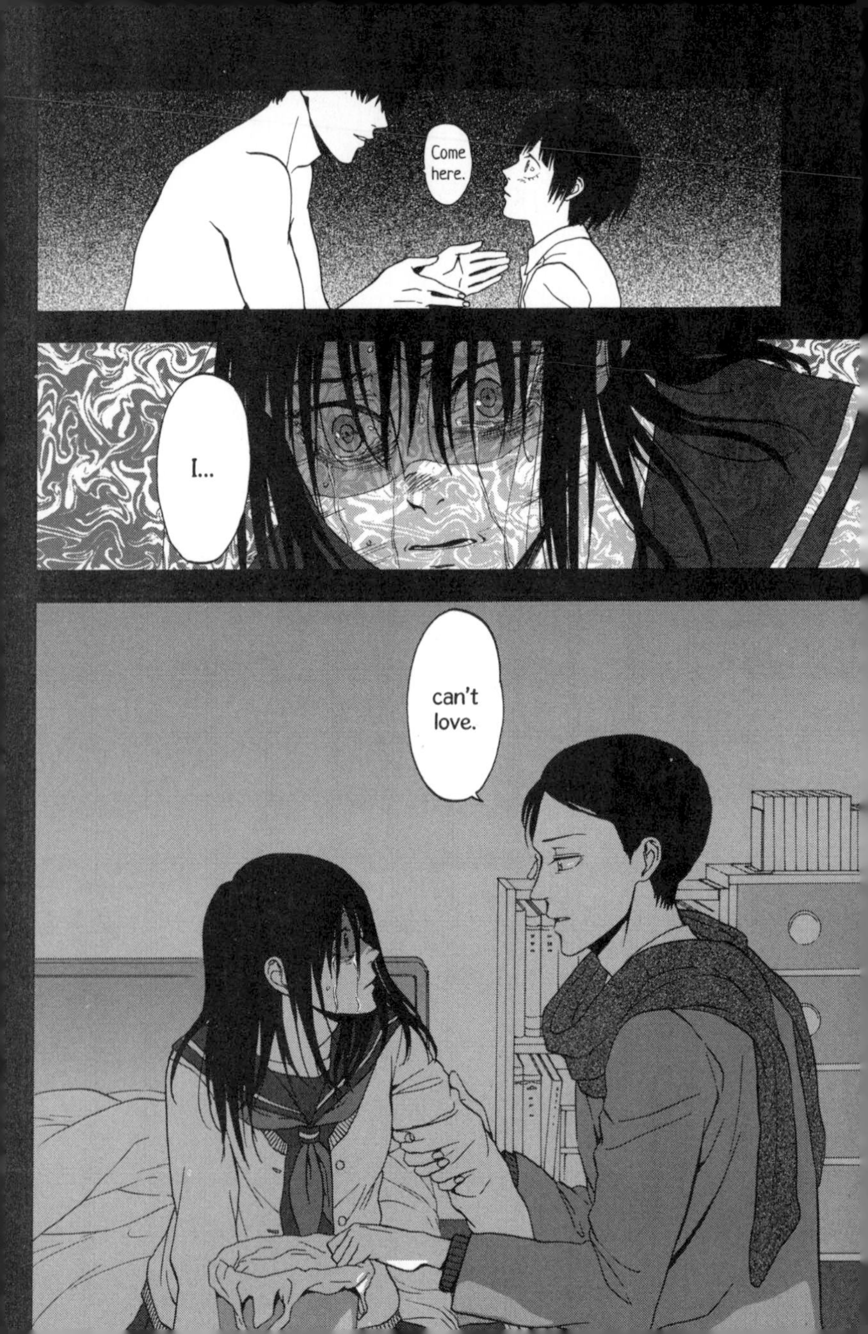
Come here.
I...
can't love.

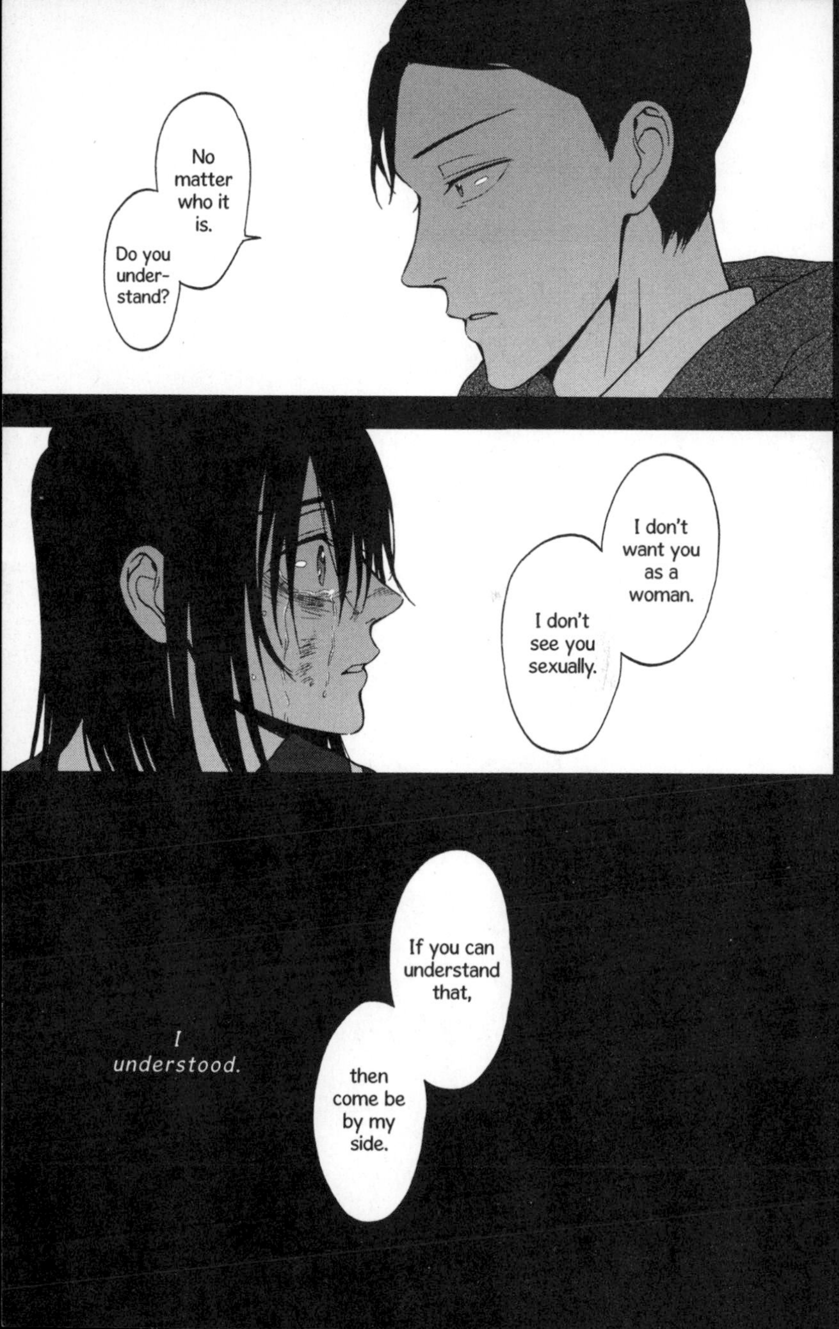
No matter who it is.
Do you under-stand?
I don't want you as a woman.
I don't see you sexually.
If you can understand that,
then come be by my side.
I understood.

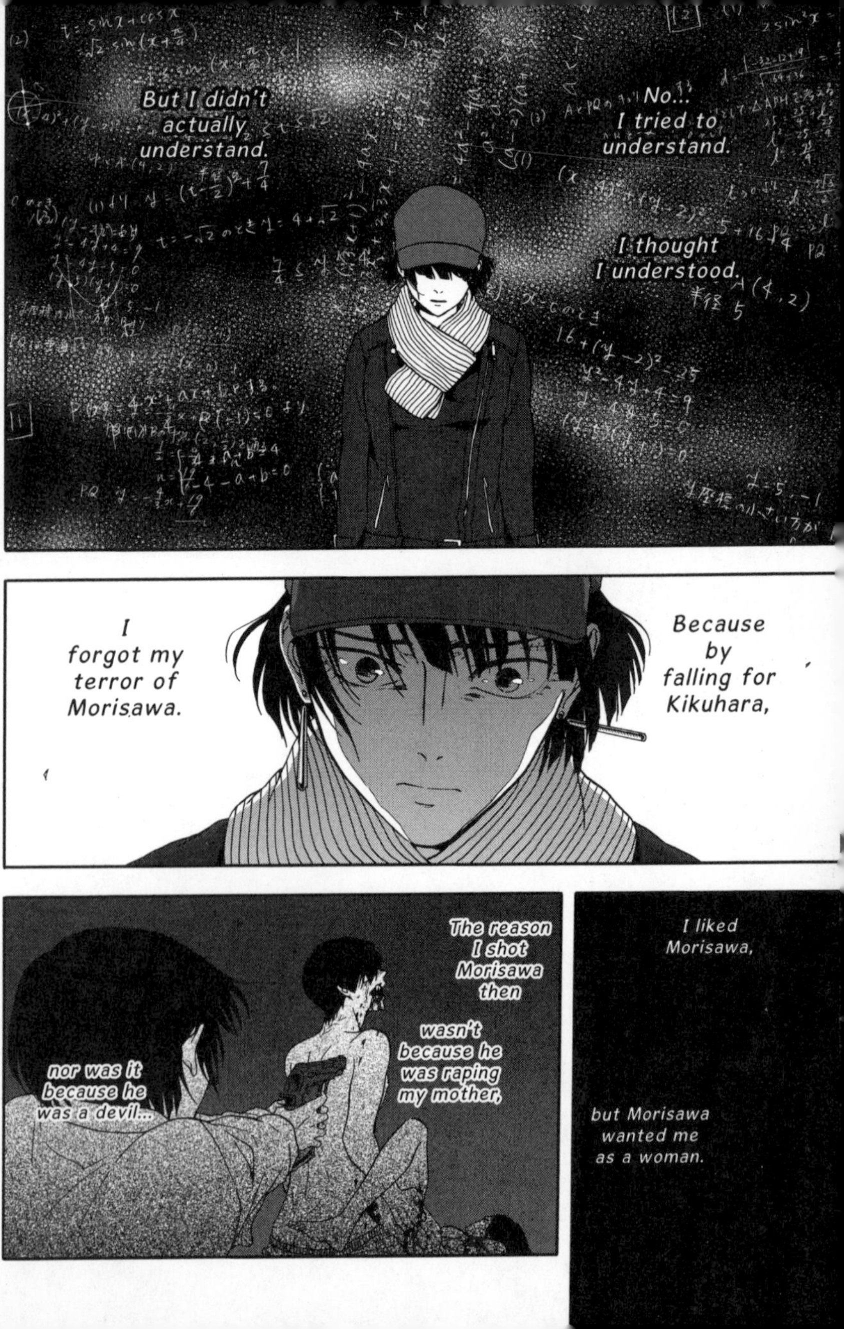
No... I tried to understand.
I thought I understood.
But I didn't actually understand.
Because by falling for Kikuhara,
I forgot my terror of Morisawa.
I liked Morisawa,
but Morisawa wanted me as a woman.
The reason I shot Morisawa then
wasn't because he was raping my mother,
nor was it because he was a devil...

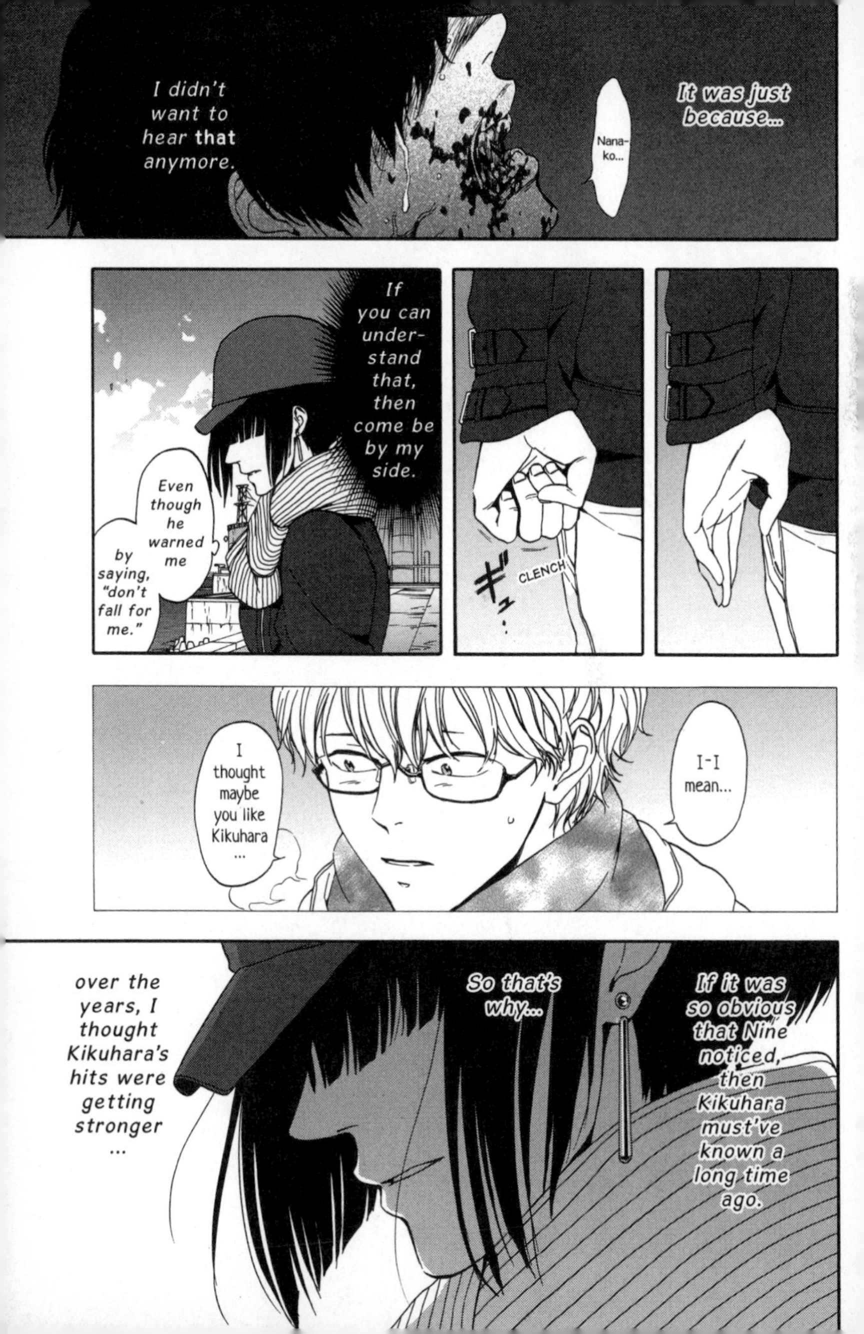

It was just because...
Nana-ko...
I didn't want to hear **that** anymore.
If you can under-stand that, then come be by my side.
Even though he warned me by saying, "don't fall for me."
ギュ
CLENCH
I-I mean...
I thought maybe you like Kikuhara ...
If it was so obvious that Nine noticed, then Kikuhara must've known a long time ago.
So that's why...
over the years, I thought Kikuhara's hits were getting stronger ...

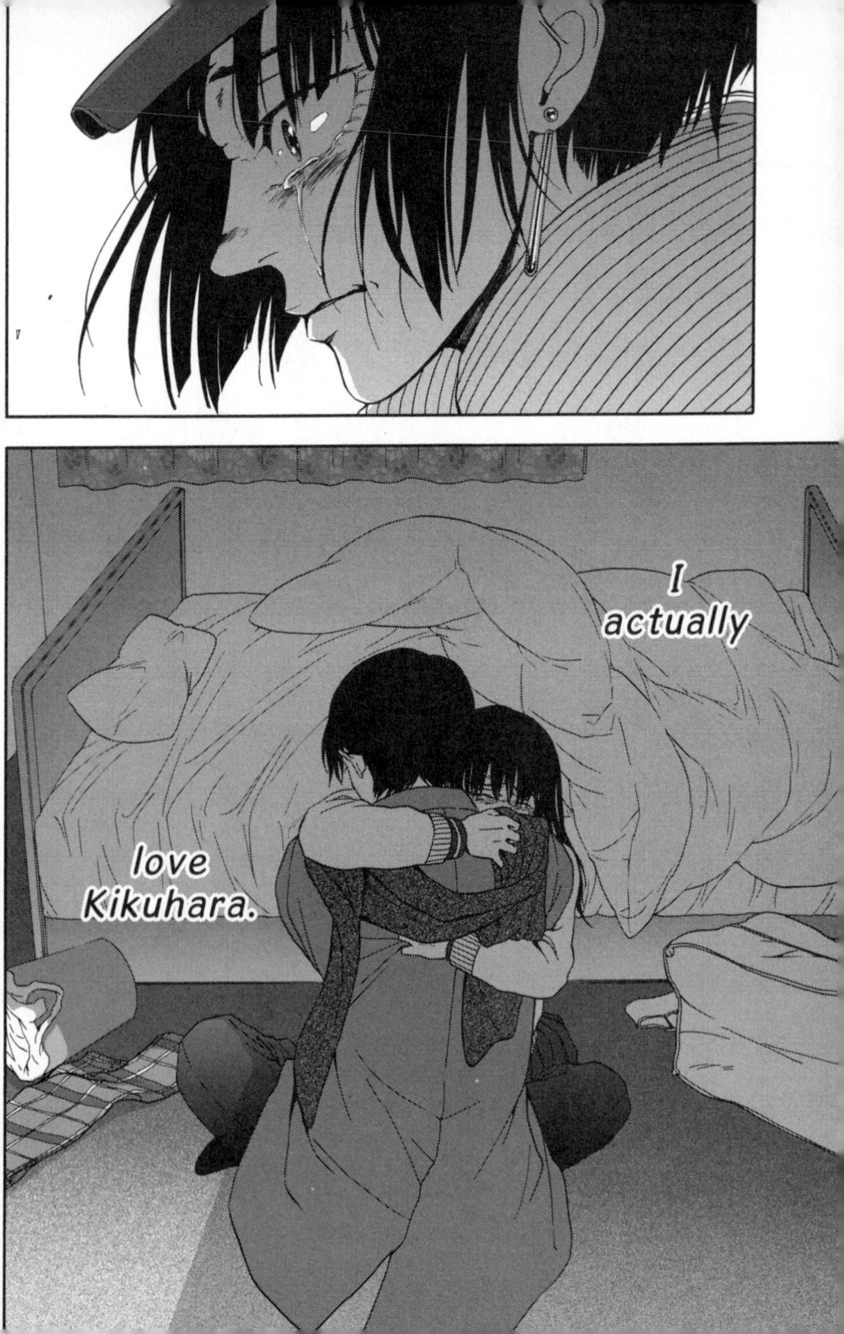
I actually
love Kikuhara.

Math book reference (blue)

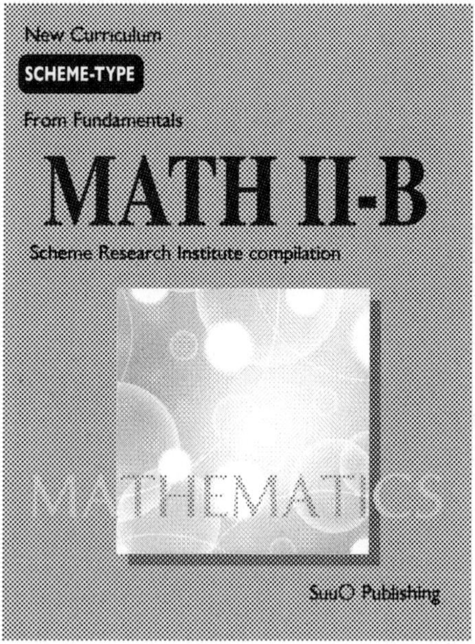
New Curriculum
SCHEME-TYPE
From Fundamentals
MATH II-B
Scheme Research Institute compilation
MATHEMATICS
SuuO Publishing

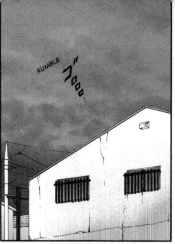

RUMBLE

PLIP
ポッ

PLIP
ポッ

カシャカシャ

I can't get in.

No good ...

...

PLIP
シト

PLIP
シト

Line 31

Isolation

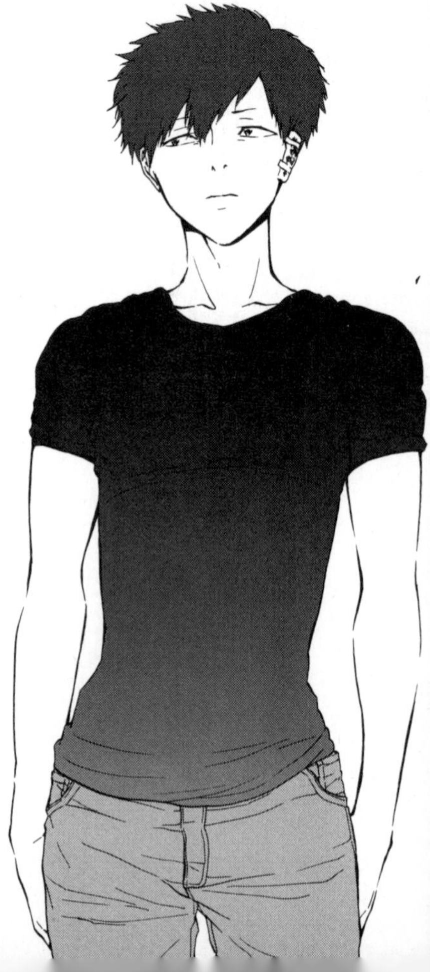

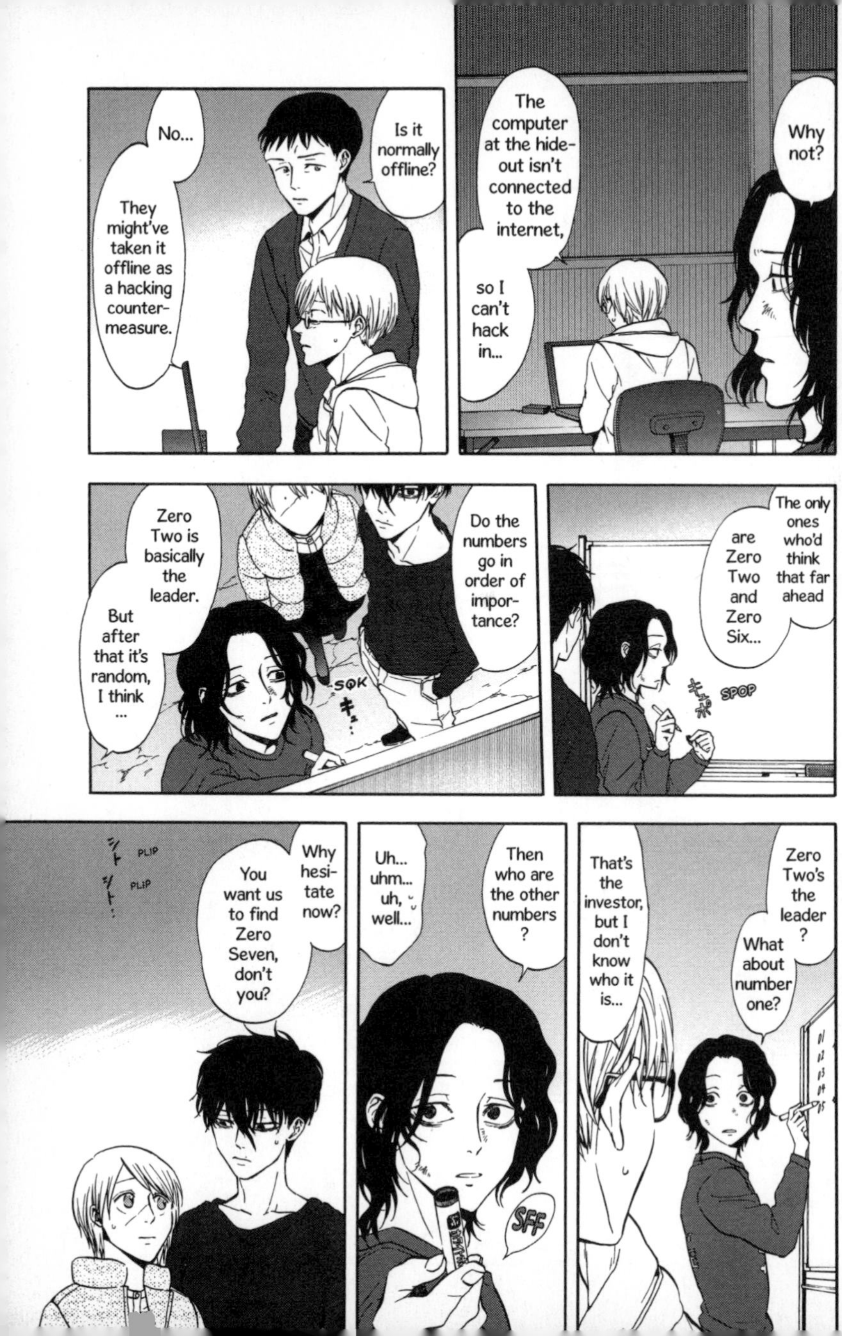
Why not?
The computer at the hide-out isn't connected to the internet,
so I can't hack in...
Is it normally offline?
No...
They might've taken it offline as a hacking counter-measure.
The only ones who'd think that far ahead
are Zero Two and Zero Six...
キュポ
SPOP
Do the numbers go in order of importance?
Zero Two is basically the leader.
But after that it's random, I think ...
SQK
キュ
Zero Two's the leader?
What about number one?
01
02
03
04
05
That's the investor, but I don't know who it is...
Then who are the other numbers?
Uh... uhm... uh, well...
SFF
Why hesitate now?
You want us to find Zero Seven, don't you?
シト
PLIP
シト
PLIP

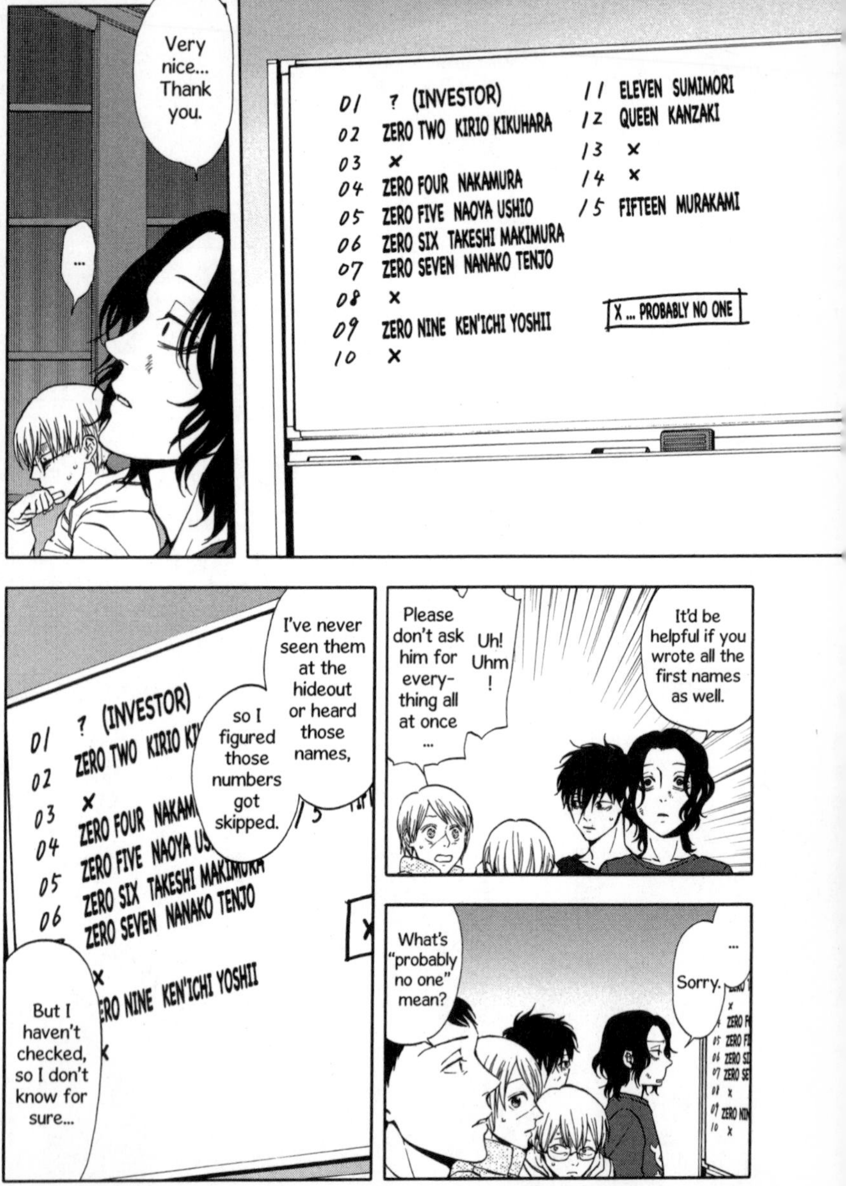
01 ? (INVESTOR)
02 ZERO TWO KIRIO KIKUHARA
03 ×
04 ZERO FOUR NAKAMURA
05 ZERO FIVE NAOYA USHIO
06 ZERO SIX TAKESHI MAKIMURA
07 ZERO SEVEN NANAKO TENJO
08 ×
09 ZERO NINE KEN'ICHI YOSHII
10 ×
11 ELEVEN SUMIMORI
12 QUEEN KANZAKI
13 ×
14 ×
15 FIFTEEN MURAKAMI
X ... PROBABLY NO ONE
Very nice... Thank you.
...
It'd be helpful if you wrote all the first names as well.
Uh! Uhm!
Please don't ask him for every-thing all at once ...
... Sorry.
What's "probably no one" mean?
I've never seen them at the hideout or heard those names,
so I figured those numbers got skipped.
But I haven't checked, so I don't know for sure...

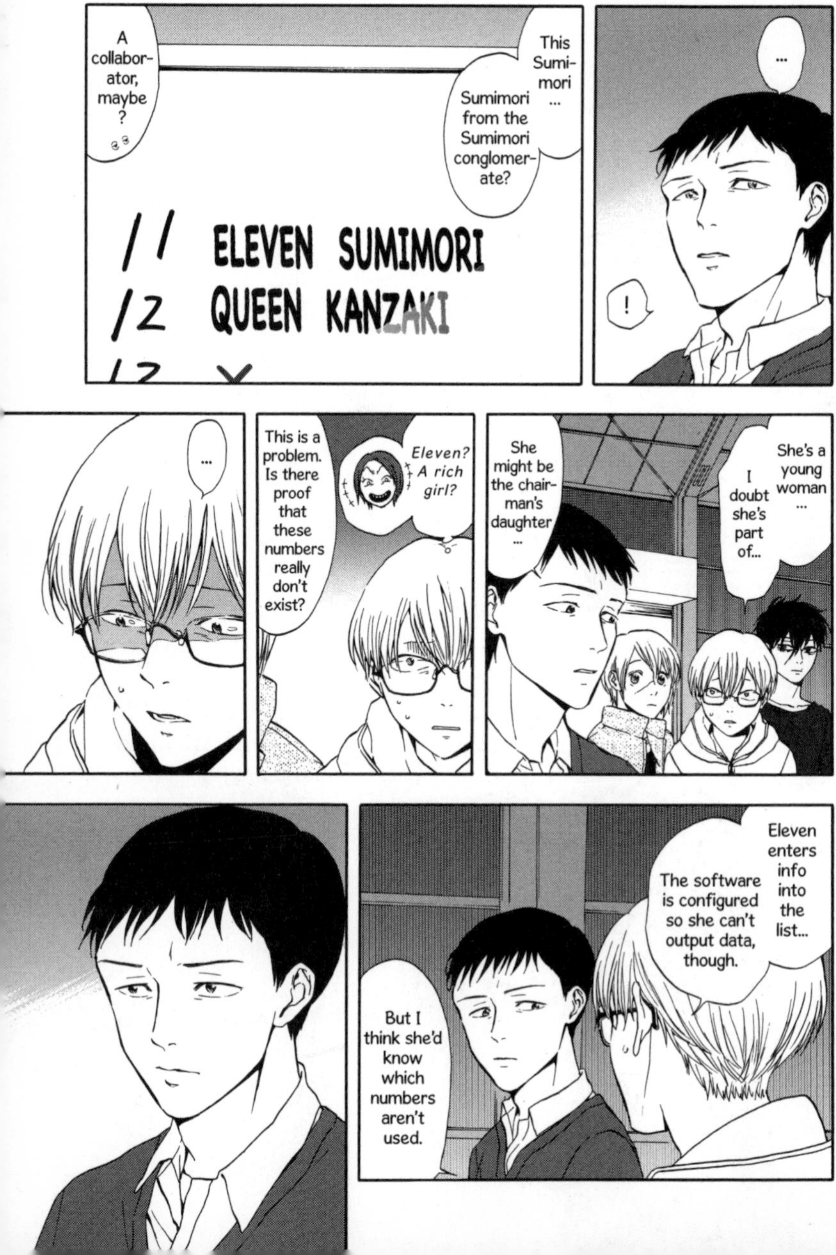
...
!
This Sumimori...
Sumimori from the Sumimori conglomerate?
A collaborator, maybe?
11 ELEVEN SUMIMORI
12 QUEEN KANZAKI
She's a young woman...
I doubt she's part of...
She might be the chairman's daughter...
Eleven? A rich girl?
This is a problem. Is there proof that these numbers really don't exist?
...
Eleven enters info into the list...
The software is configured so she can't output data, though.
But I think she'd know which numbers aren't used.

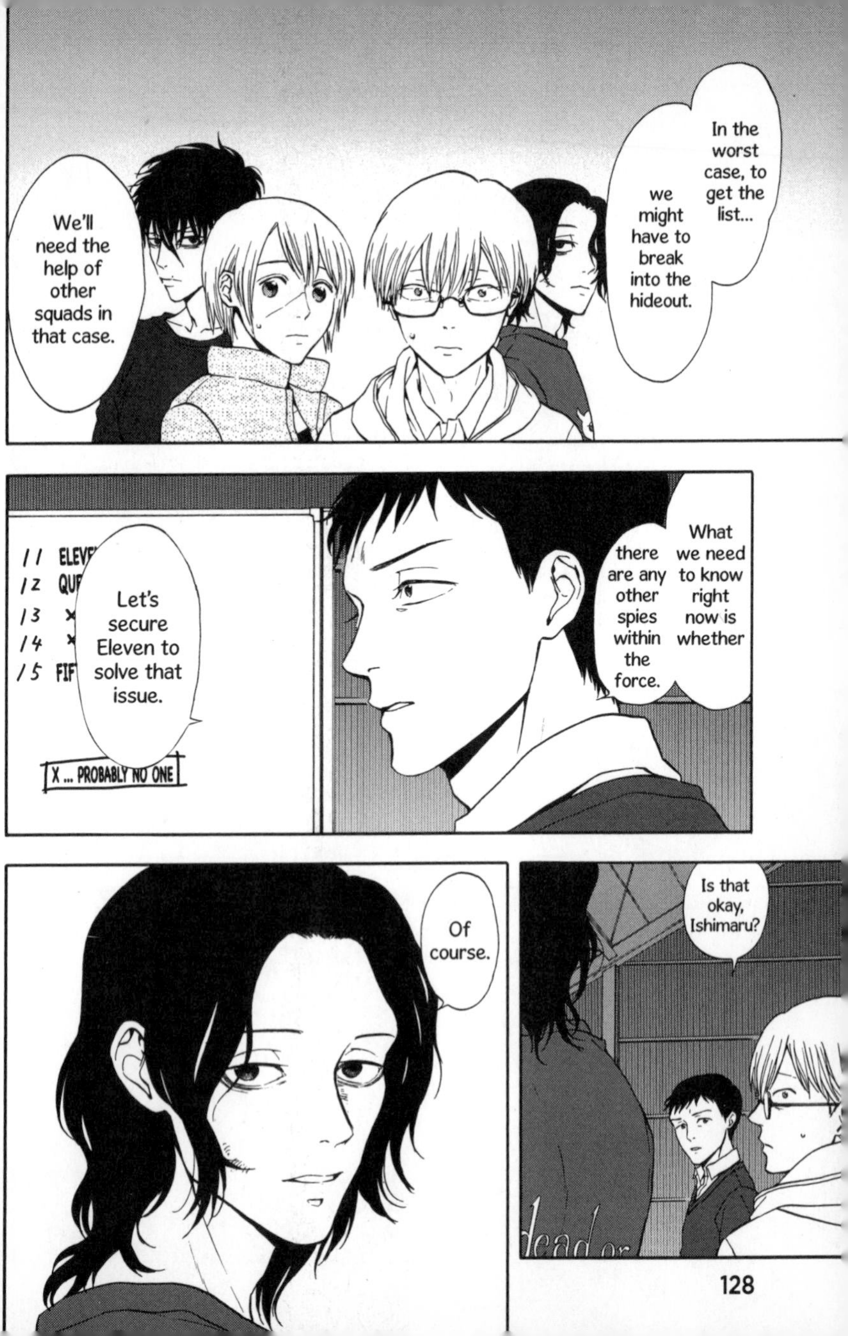
In the worst case, to get the list... we might have to break into the hideout.
We'll need the help of other squads in that case.
What we need to know right now is whether there are any other spies within the force.
Let's secure Eleven to solve that issue.
X ... PROBABLY NO ONE
Is that okay, Ishimaru?
Of course.

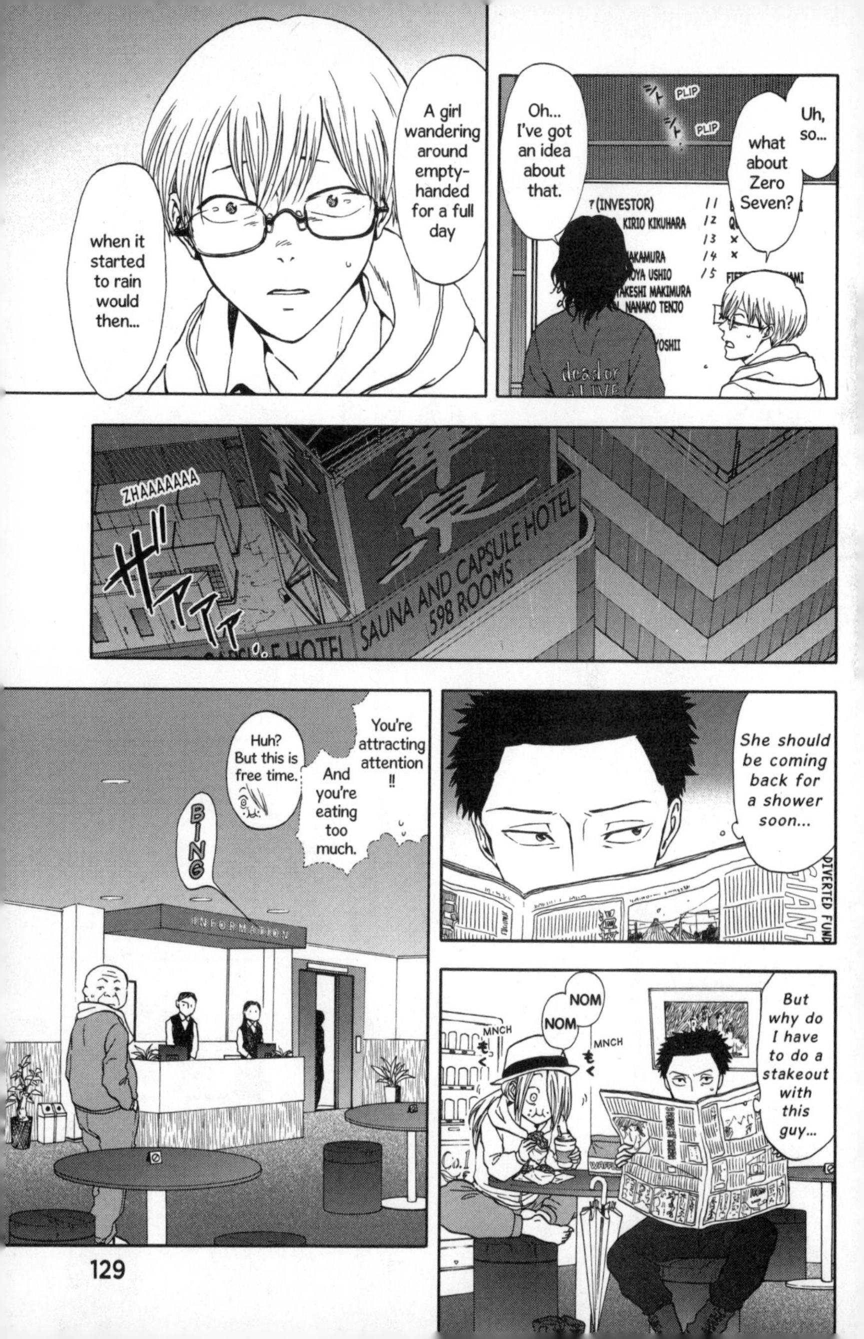
PLIP
PLIP
Uh, so... what about Zero Seven?
Oh... I've got an idea about that.
(INVESTOR)
KIRIO KIKUHARA
TAKESHI MAKIMURA
NANAKO TENJO
A girl wandering around empty-handed for a full day
when it started to rain would then...
ZHAAAAAAA
SAUNA AND CAPSULE HOTEL 598 ROOMS
She should be coming back for a shower soon...
DIVERTED FUND
But why do I have to do a stakeout with this guy...
NOM
NOM
MNCH
MNCH
You're attracting attention!!
Huh? But this is free time.
And you're eating too much.
BING
INFORMATION

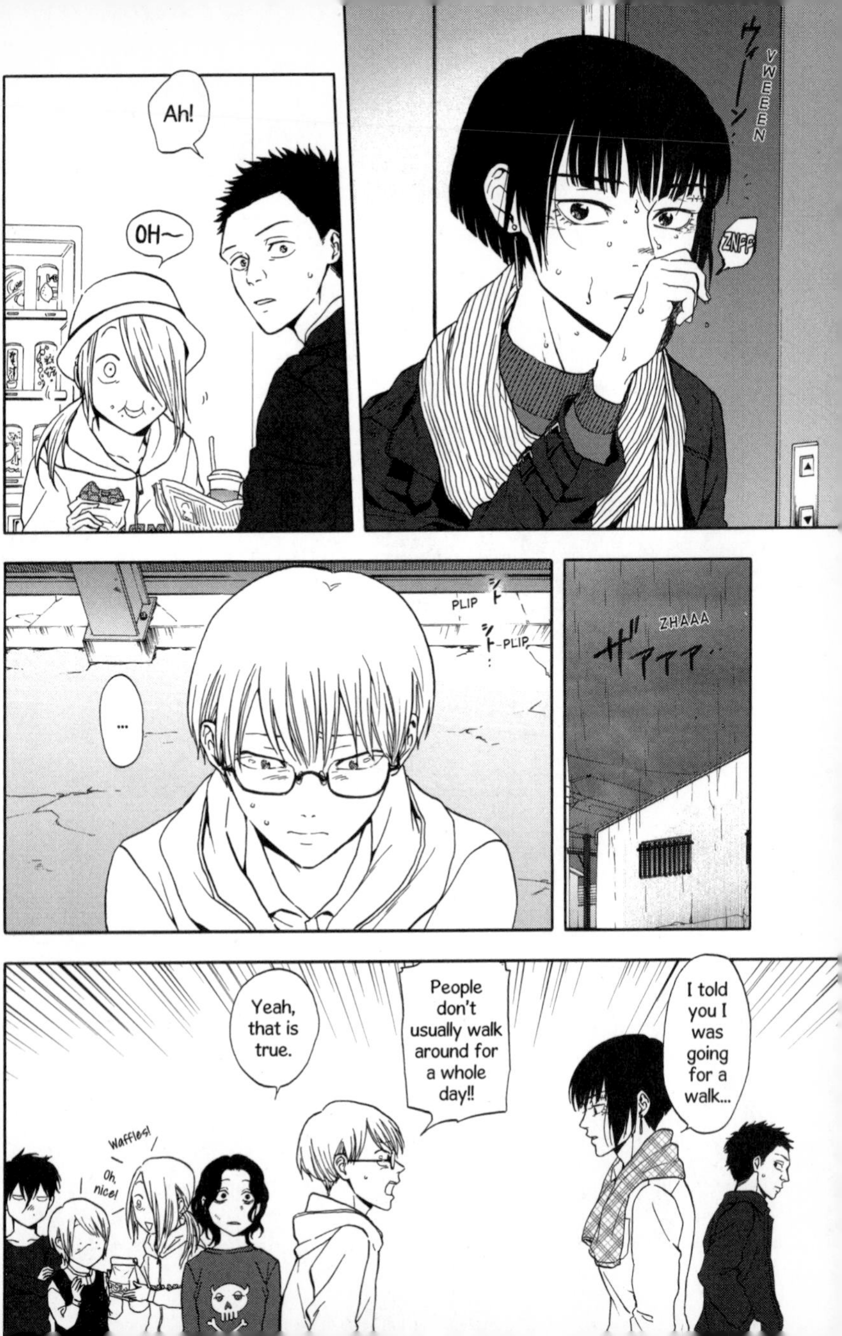
VWEEEN
ZNFF
Ah!
OH~
ザアア…
ZHAAA
PLIP
PLIP
...
I told you I was going for a walk...
People don't usually walk around for a whole day!!
Yeah, that is true.
Waffles!
Oh, nice!

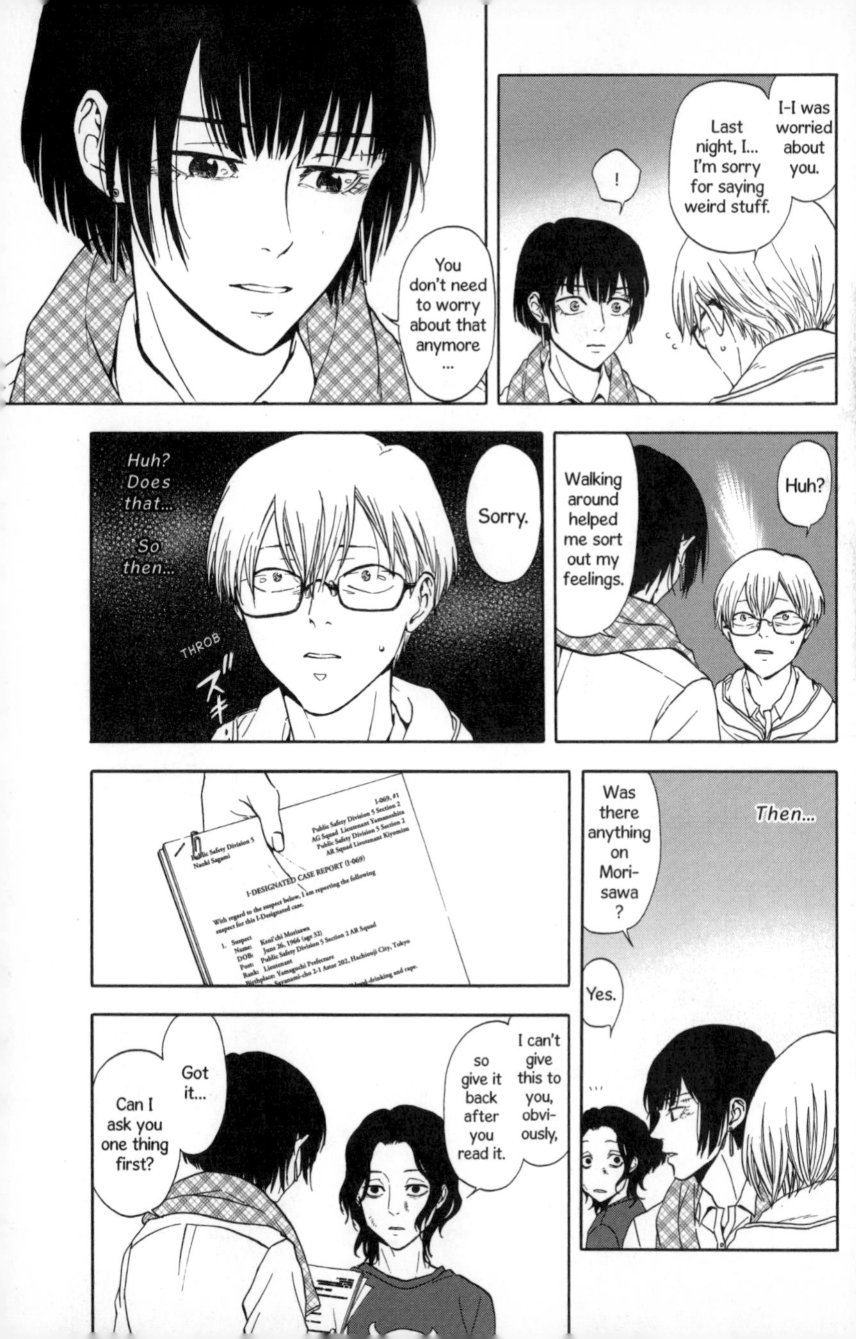
I-I was worried about you.
Last night, I... I'm sorry for saying weird stuff.
!
You don't need to worry about that anymore ...
Huh?
Walking around helped me sort out my feelings.
Sorry.
Huh? Does that...
So then...
THROB
ズキ
Then...
Was there anything on Mori-sawa?
Yes.
I-069, #1
Public Safety Division 5 Section 2
AG Squad Lieutenant Yamanoshita
Public Safety Division 5 Section 2
AR Squad Lieutenant Kiyomizu
Public Safety Division 5
Naoki Sagami
I-DESIGNATED CASE REPORT (I-069)
With regard to the suspect below, I am reporting the following suspect for this I-Designated case.
1. Suspect
Name: Keni'chi Morisawa
DOB: June 26, 1966 (age 32)
Post: Public Safety Division 5 Section 2 AR Squad
Rank: Lieutenant
Birthplace: Yamaguchi Prefecture
Sayanami-cho 2-1 Astor 202, Hachiouji City, Tokyo
drinking and rape.
I can't give this to you, obviously,
so give it back after you read it.
Got it...
Can I ask you one thing first?

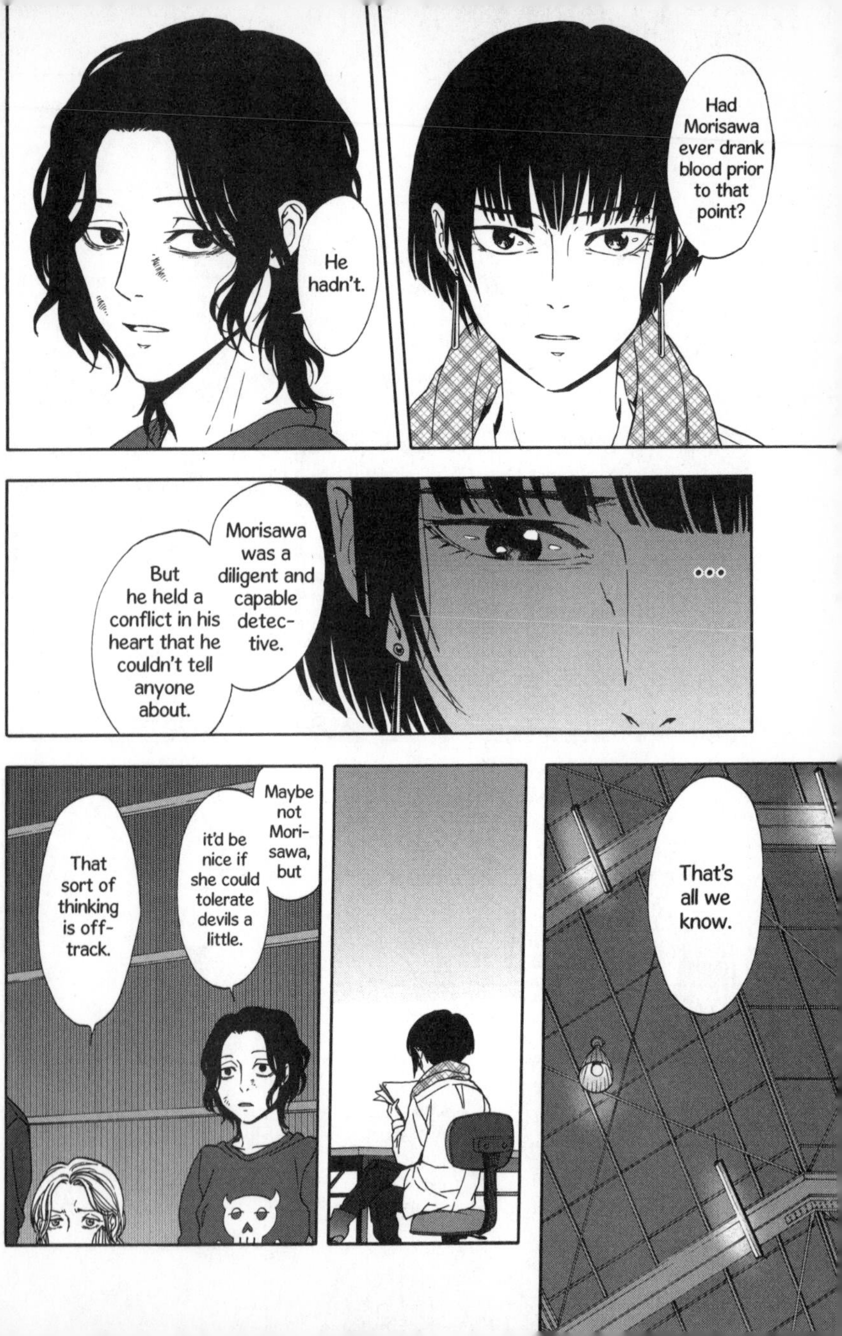
Had Morisawa ever drank blood prior to that point?
He hadn't.
•••
Morisawa was a diligent and capable detective.
But he held a conflict in his heart that he couldn't tell anyone about.
That's all we know.
Maybe not Morisawa, but
it'd be nice if she could tolerate devils a little.
That sort of thinking is off-track.

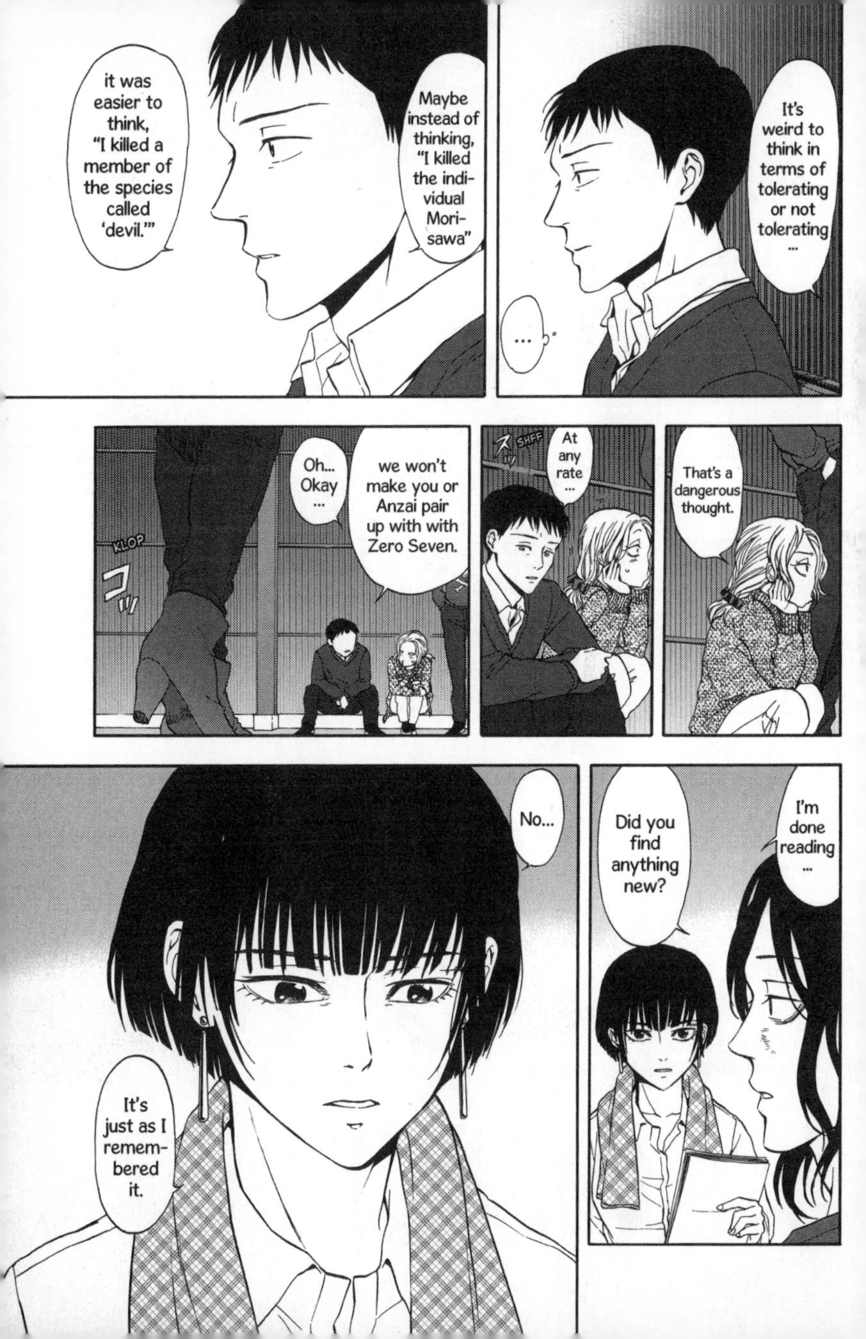
It's weird to think in terms of tolerating or not tolerating ...
...
Maybe instead of thinking, "I killed the indi-vidual Mori-sawa"
it was easier to think, "I killed a member of the species called 'devil.'"
That's a dangerous thought.
SHFF
At any rate ...
we won't make you or Anzai pair up with with Zero Seven.
Oh... Okay ...
KLOP
I'm done reading ...
Did you find anything new?
No...
It's just as I remembered it.

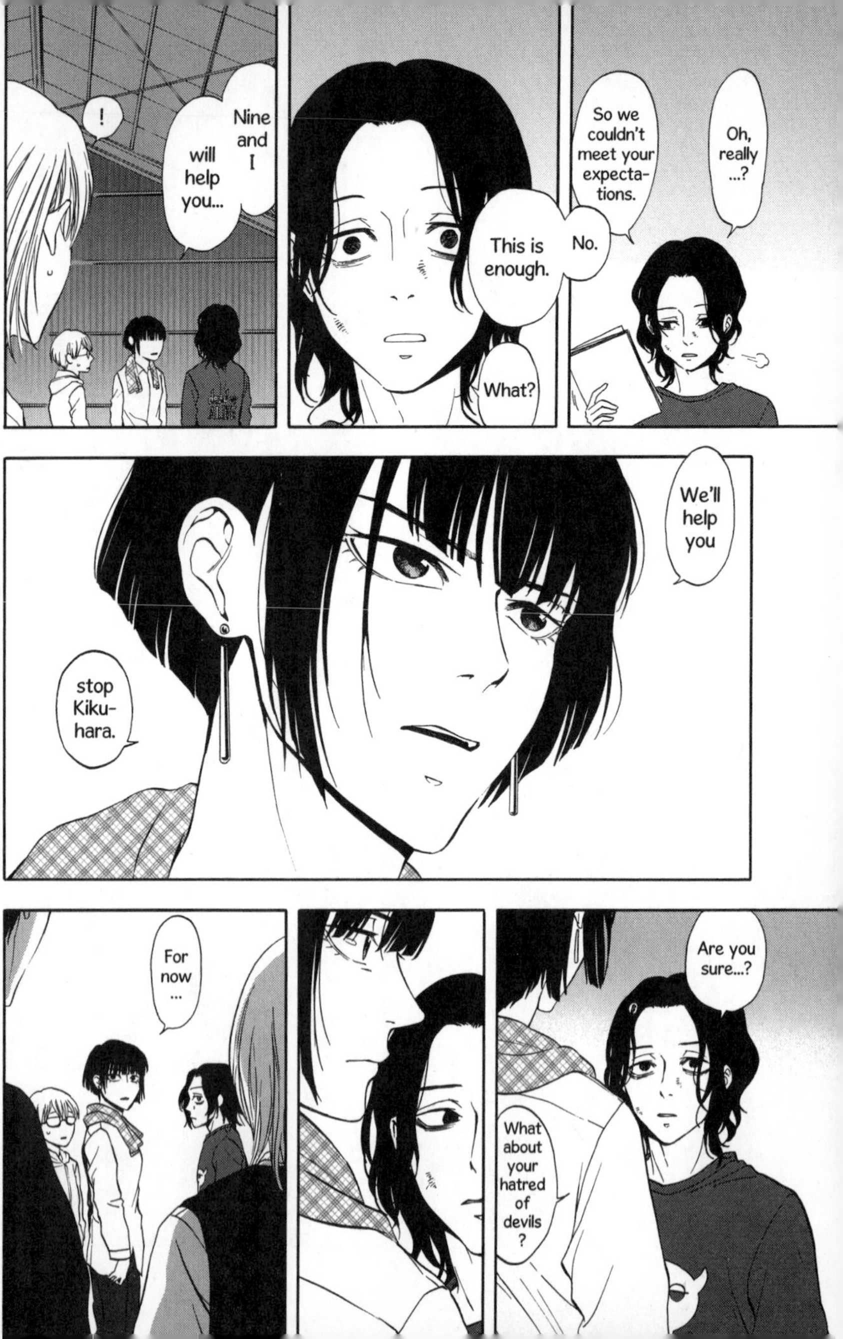
Oh, really ...?
So we couldn't meet your expectations.
No.
This is enough.
What?
Nine and I
will help you...
!
We'll help you
stop Kiku-hara.
Are you sure...?
What about your hatred of devils?
For now ...

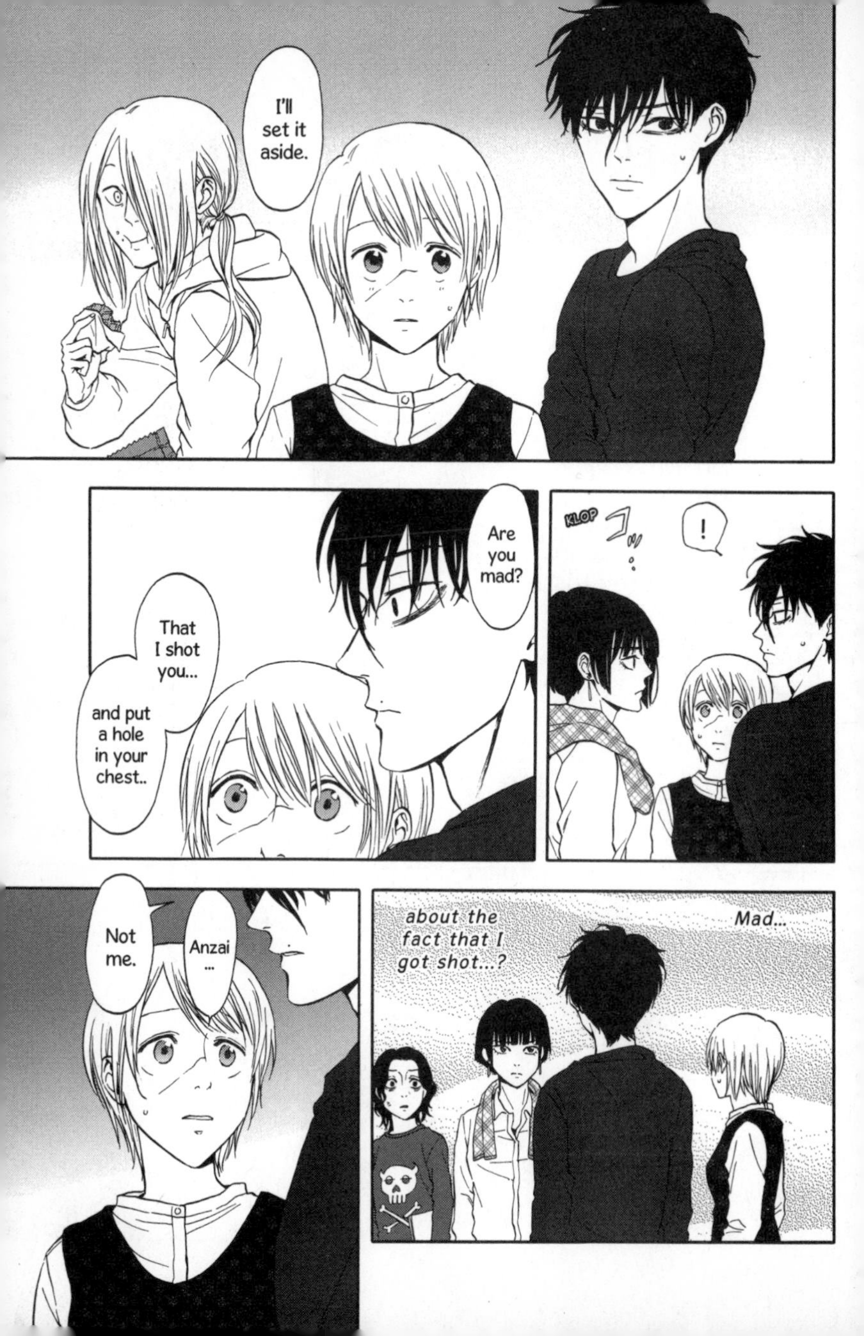
I'll set it aside.
KLOP
!
Are you mad?
That I shot you...
and put a hole in your chest..
Mad...
about the fact that I got shot...?
Anzai ...
Not me.

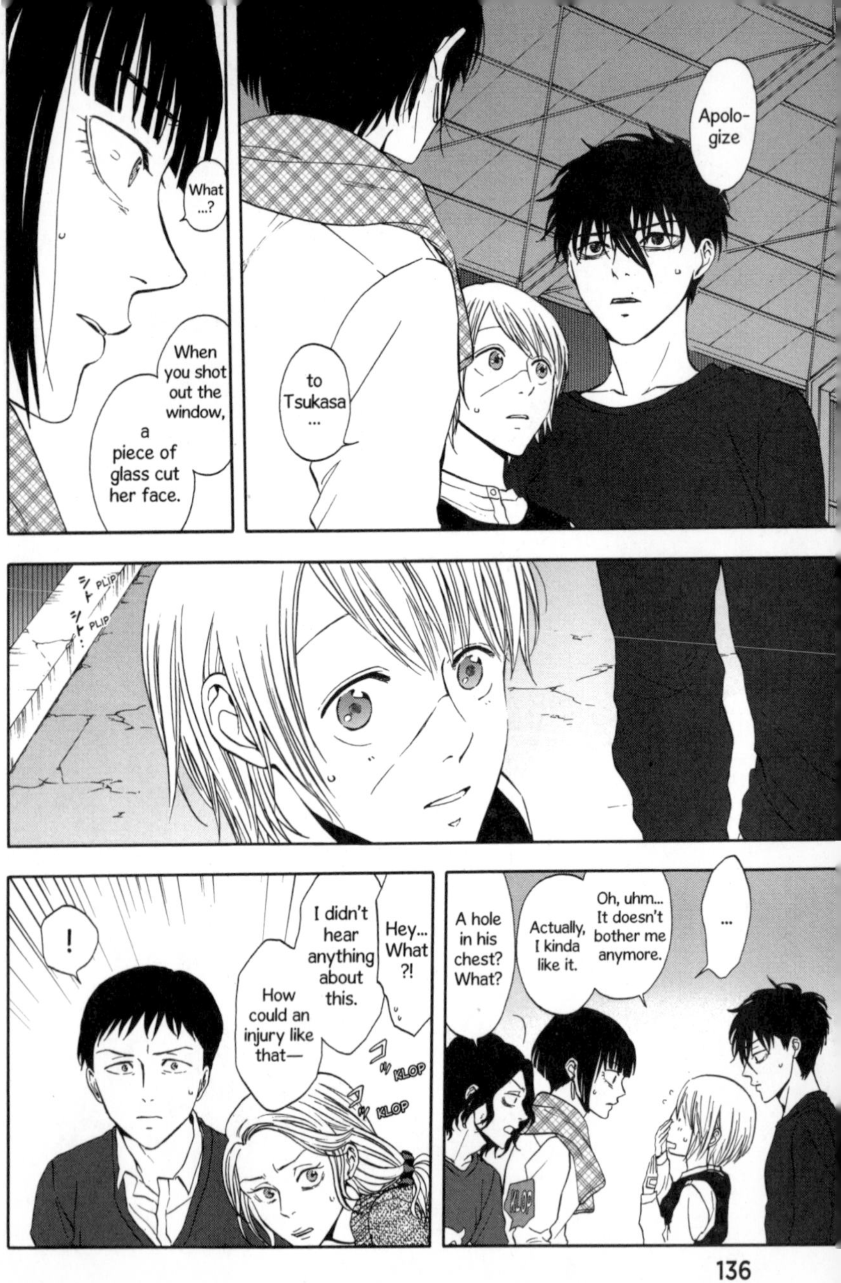
Apolo-gize
to Tsukasa ...
What ...?
When you shot out the window, a piece of glass cut her face.
PLIP
PLIP
...
Oh, uhm... It doesn't bother me anymore.
Actually, I kinda like it.
A hole in his chest? What?
KLOP
Hey... What ?!
I didn't hear anything about this.
How could an injury like that—
KLOP
KLOP
!

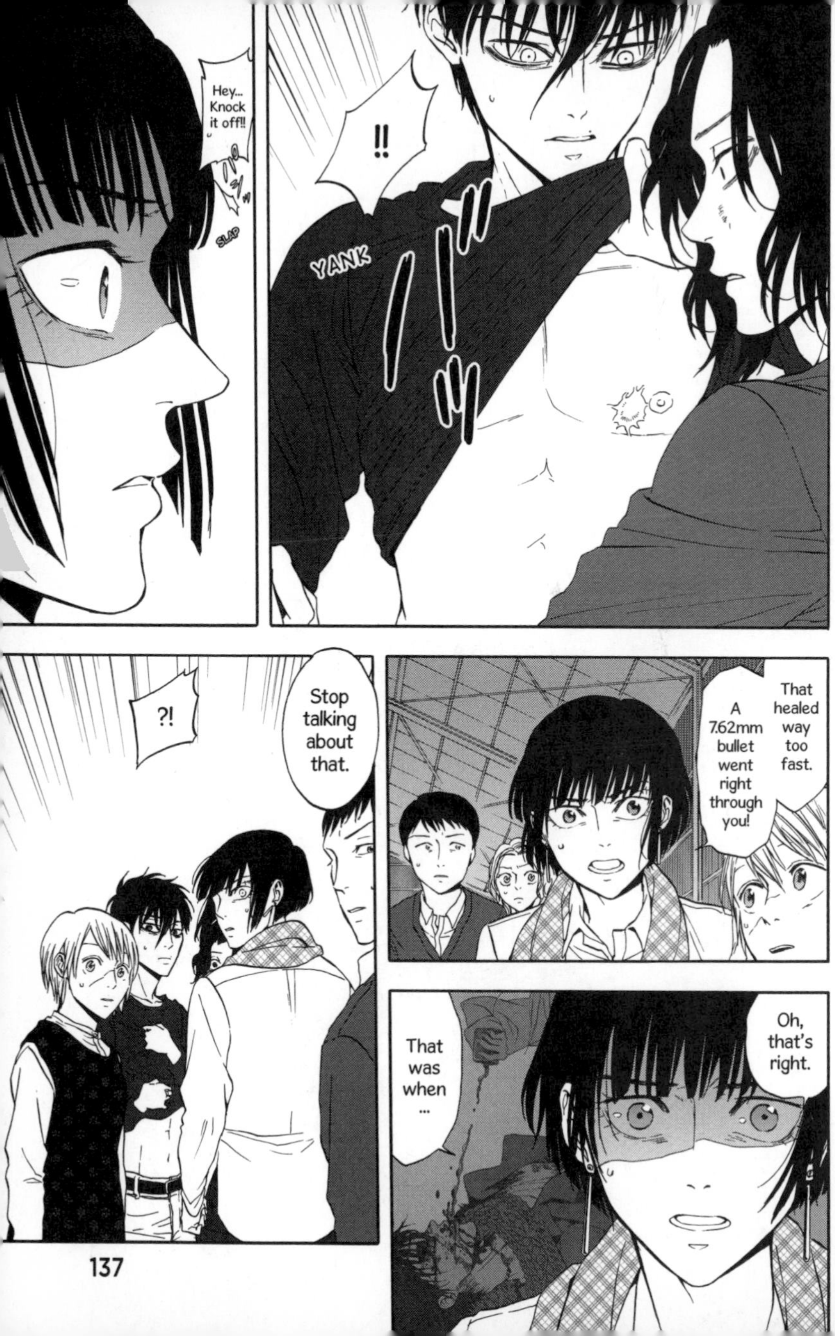
!!
YANK
Hey... Knock it off!!
SLAP
That healed way too fast.
A 7.62mm bullet went right through you!
Oh, that's right.
That was when ...
Stop talking about that.
?!

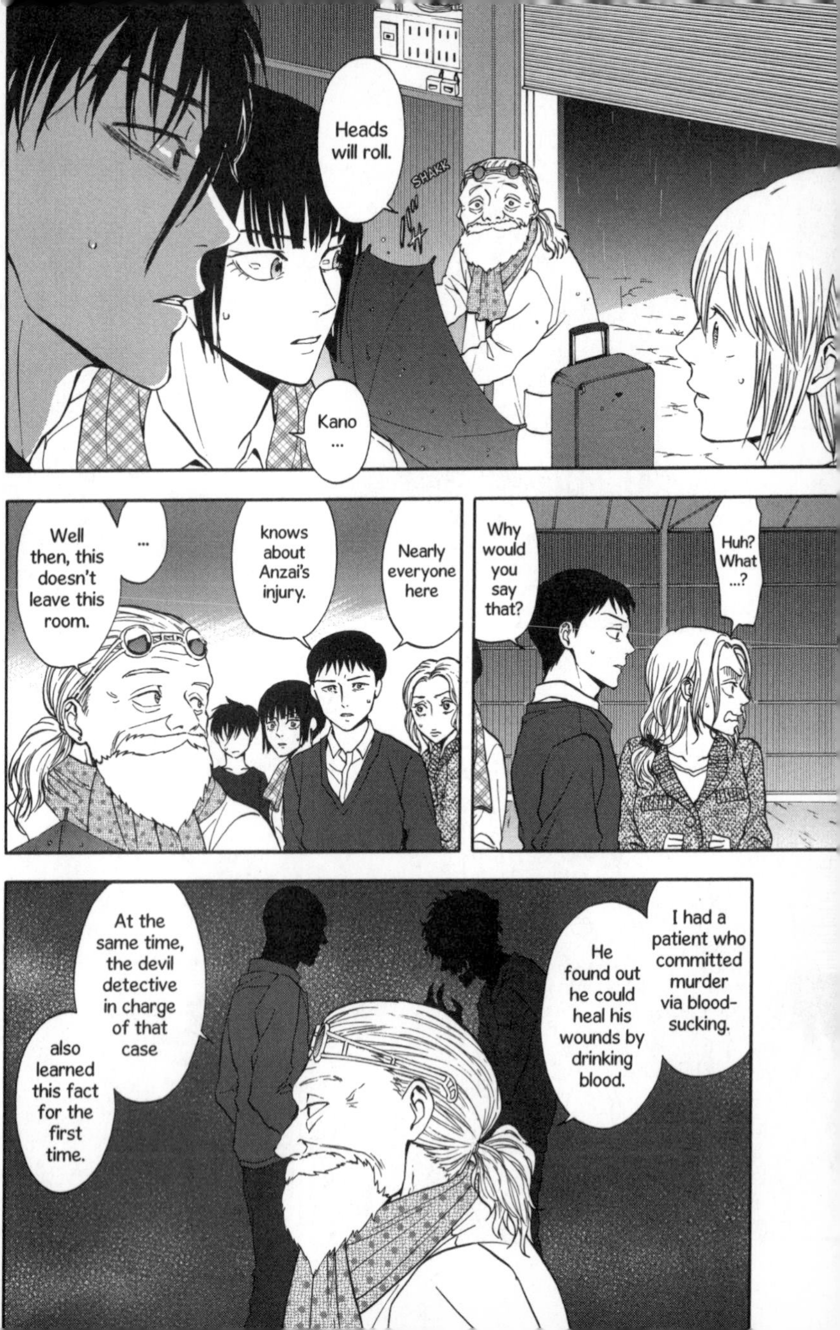
Heads will roll.
SHAKK
Kano ...
Huh? What ...?
Why would you say that?
Nearly everyone here
knows about Anzai's injury.
...
Well then, this doesn't leave this room.
I had a patient who committed murder via blood-sucking.
He found out he could heal his wounds by drinking blood.
At the same time, the devil detective in charge of that case
also learned this fact for the first time.

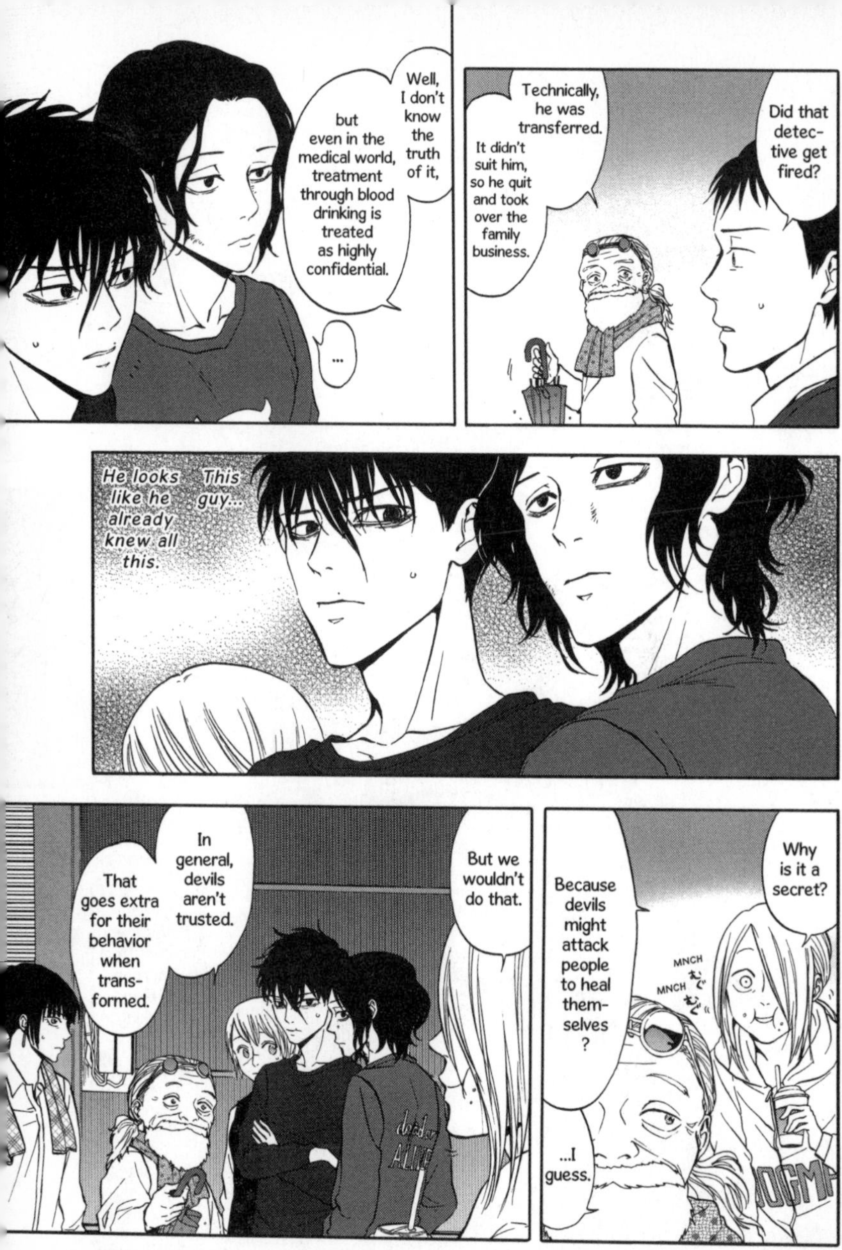
Did that detective get fired?
Technically, he was transferred.
It didn't suit him, so he quit and took over the family business.
Well, I don't know the truth of it,
but even in the medical world, treatment through blood drinking is treated as highly confidential.
...
This guy...
He looks like he already knew all this.
Why is it a secret?
MNCH MNCH むぐ むぐ
Because devils might attack people to heal themselves?
...I guess.
But we wouldn't do that.
In general, devils aren't trusted.
That goes extra for their behavior when transformed.

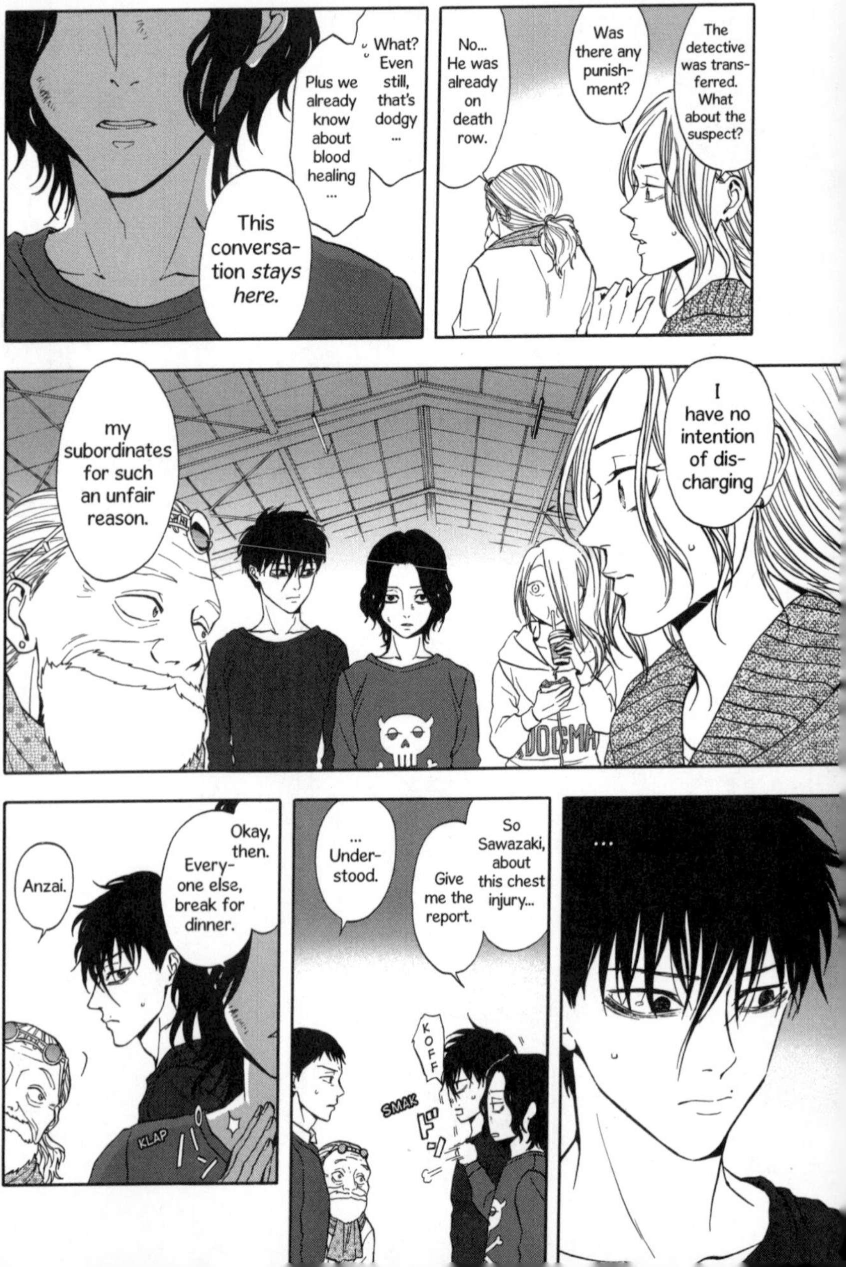
The detective was transferred. What about the suspect?
Was there any punishment?
No... He was already on death row.
What? Even still, that's dodgy...
Plus we already know about blood healing...
This conversation *stays here.*
I have no intention of discharging
my subordinates for such an unfair reason.
...
So Sawazaki, about this chest injury...
Give me the report.
KOFF
SMAK
... Understood.
Okay, then. Everyone else, break for dinner.
Anzai.
KLAP

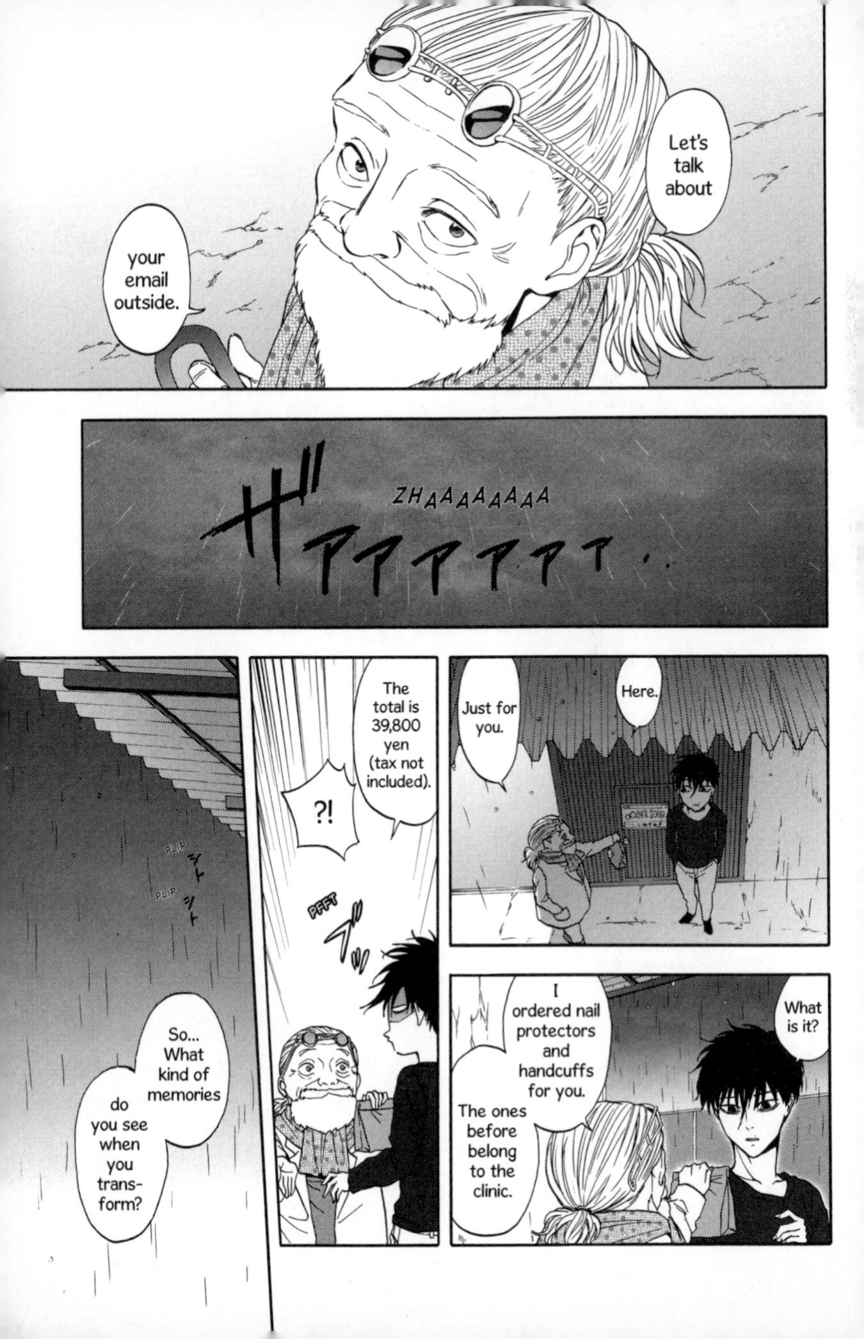
Let's talk about
your email outside.
ザアアアアアア
ZHAAAAAAAA
Here.
Just for you.
What is it?
I ordered nail protectors and handcuffs for you.
The ones before belong to the clinic.
The total is 39,800 yen (tax not included).
?!
PFFT
So... What kind of memories
do you see when you transform?
PLIP
PLIP

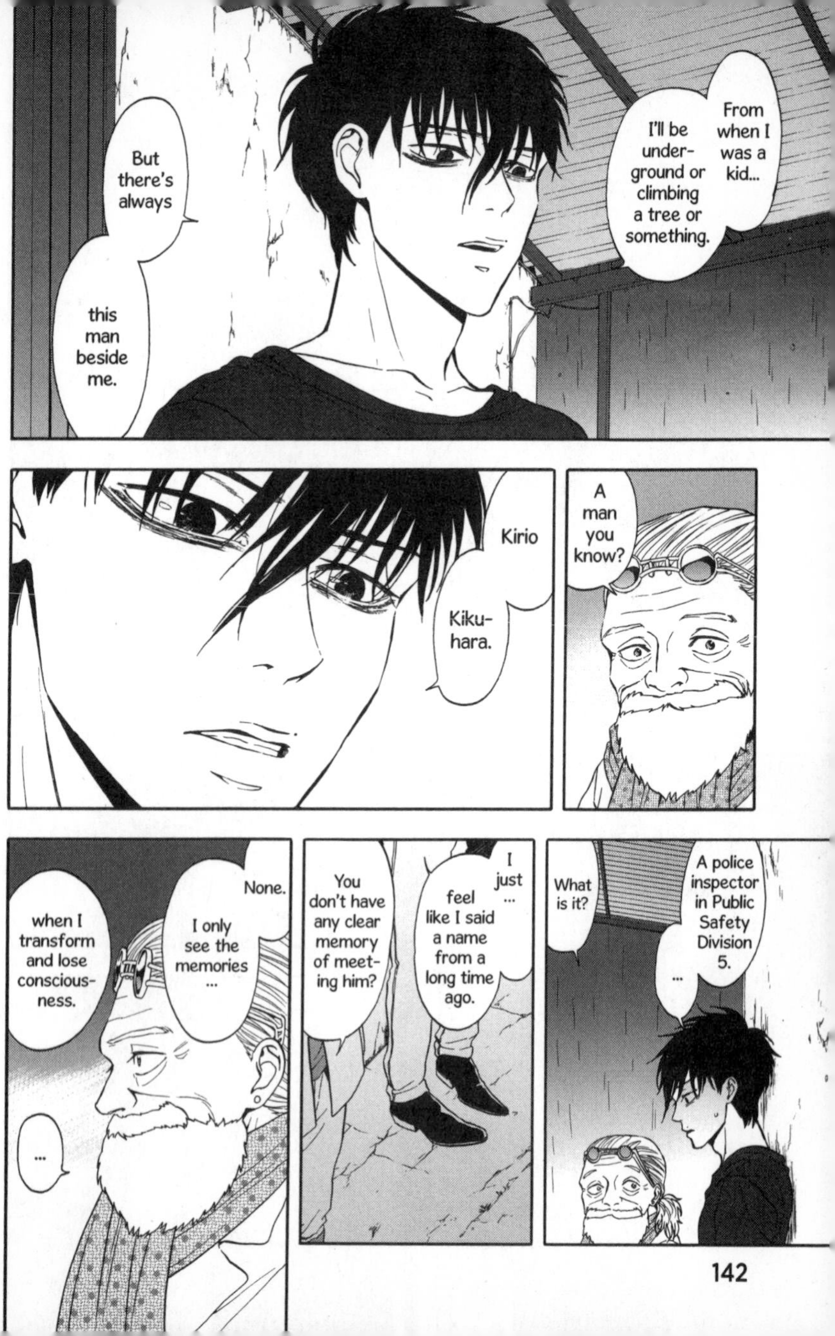
From when I was a kid...
I'll be underground or climbing a tree or something.
But there's always
this man beside me.
A man you know?
Kirio
Kikuhara.
A police inspector in Public Safety Division 5.
...
What is it?
I just ...
feel like I said a name from a long time ago.
You don't have any clear memory of meeting him?
None.
I only see the memories ...
when I transform and lose consciousness.
...

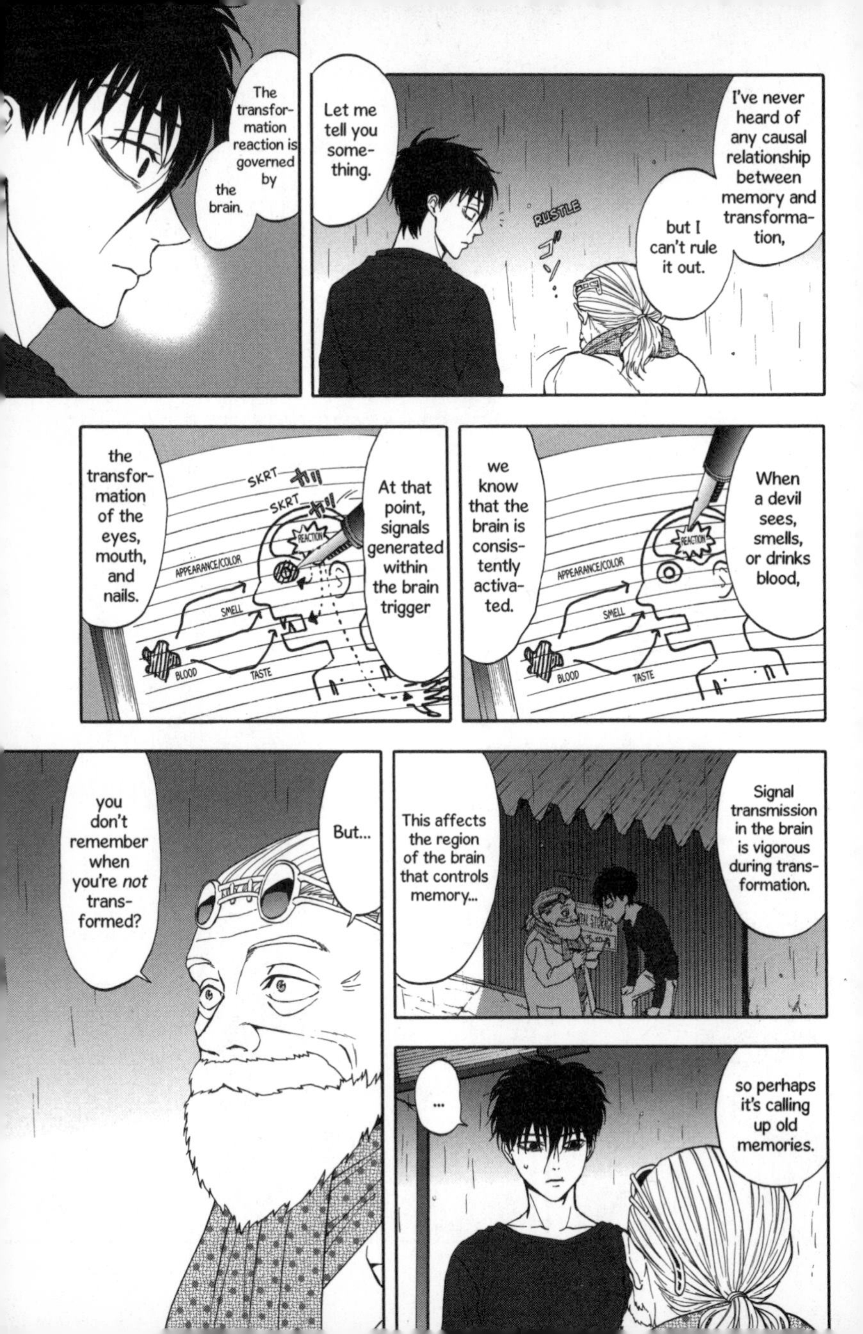
I've never heard of any causal relationship between memory and transformation,
but I can't rule it out.
RUSTLE
Let me tell you something.
The transformation reaction is governed by the brain.
When a devil sees, smells, or drinks blood,
REACTION
APPEARANCE/COLOR
SMELL
BLOOD
TASTE
we know that the brain is consistently activated.
At that point, signals generated within the brain trigger
SKRT
SKRT
REACTION
APPEARANCE/COLOR
SMELL
BLOOD
TASTE
the transformation of the eyes, mouth, and nails.
Signal transmission in the brain is vigorous during transformation.
This affects the region of the brain that controls memory...
so perhaps it's calling up old memories.
...
But...
you don't remember when you're *not* transformed?

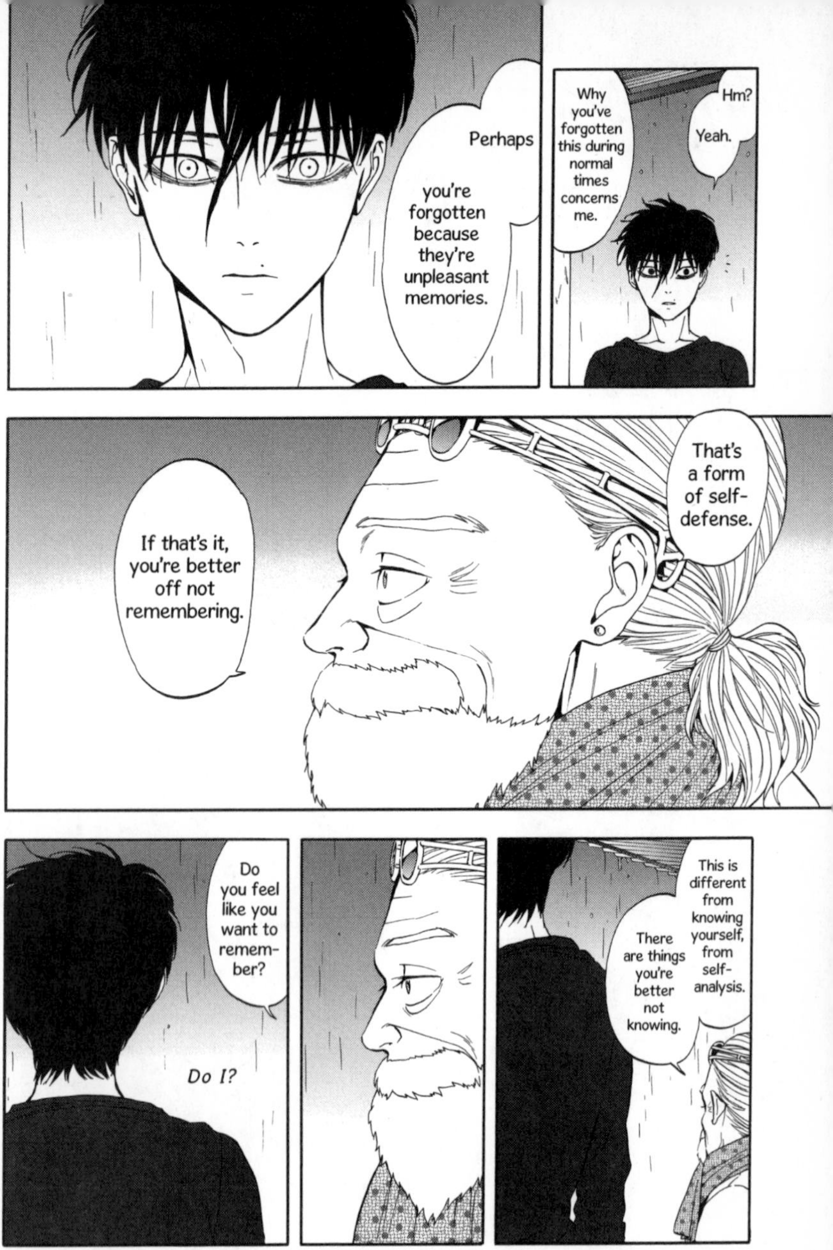
Hm?
Yeah.
Why you've forgotten this during normal times concerns me.
Perhaps
you're forgotten because they're unpleasant memories.
That's a form of self-defense.
If that's it, you're better off not remembering.
This is different from knowing yourself, from self-analysis.
There are things you're better not knowing.
Do you feel like you want to remember?
Do I?

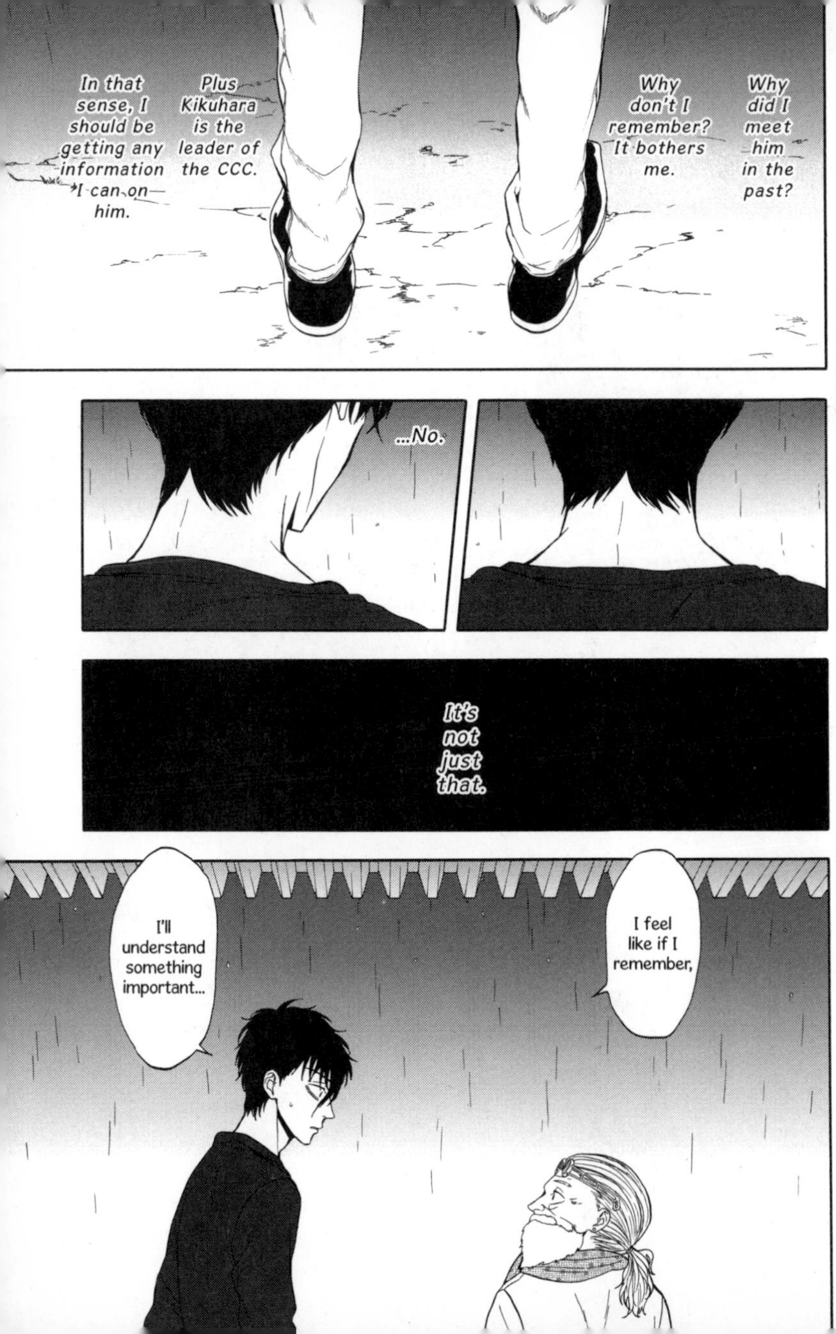
Why did I meet him in the past?
Why don't I remember? It bothers me.
Plus Kikuhara is the leader of the CCC.
In that sense, I should be getting any information I can on him.
...No.
It's not just that.
I feel like if I remember,
I'll understand something important...

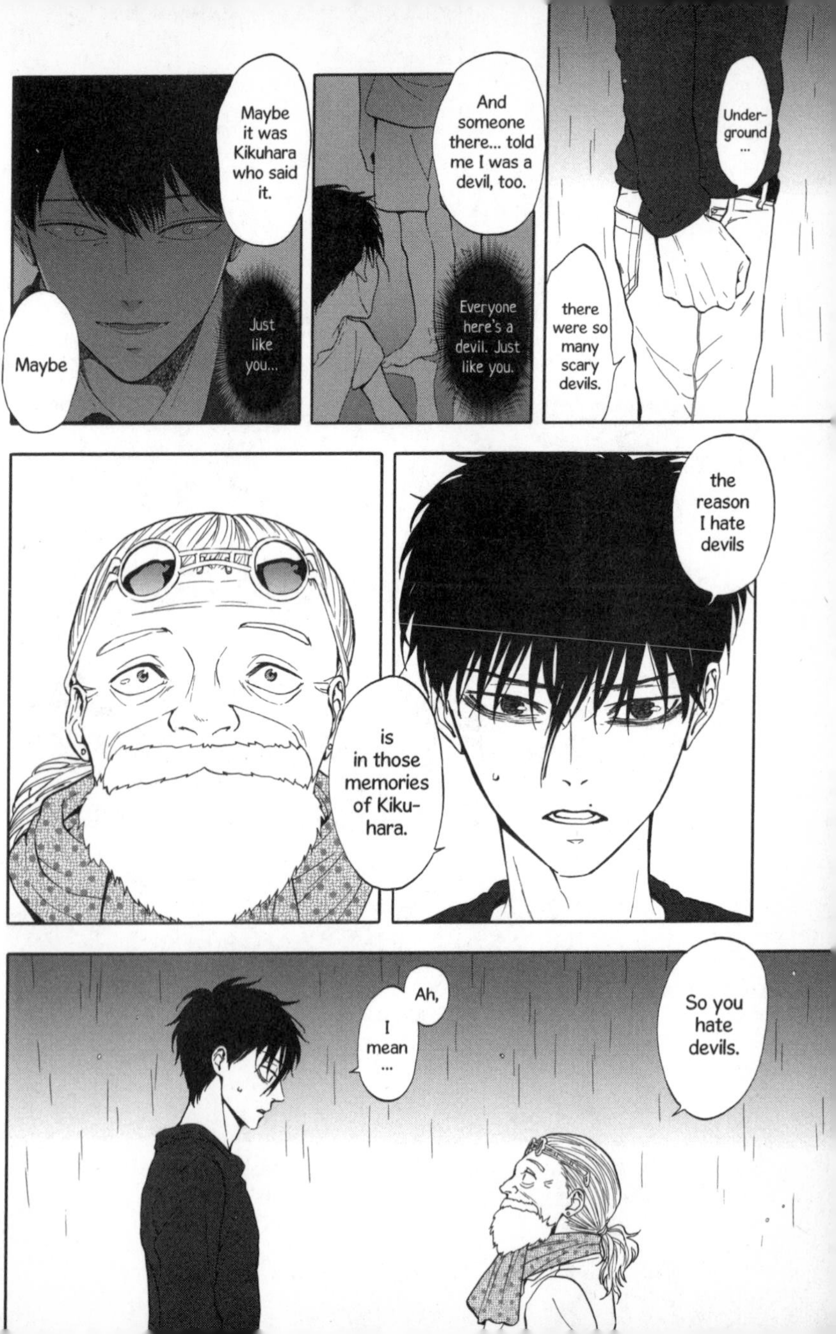
Under-ground ...
there were so many scary devils.
And someone there... told me I was a devil, too.
Everyone here's a devil. Just like you.
Maybe it was Kikuhara who said it.
Just like you...
Maybe
the reason I hate devils
is in those memories of Kiku-hara.
So you hate devils.
Ah, I mean ...

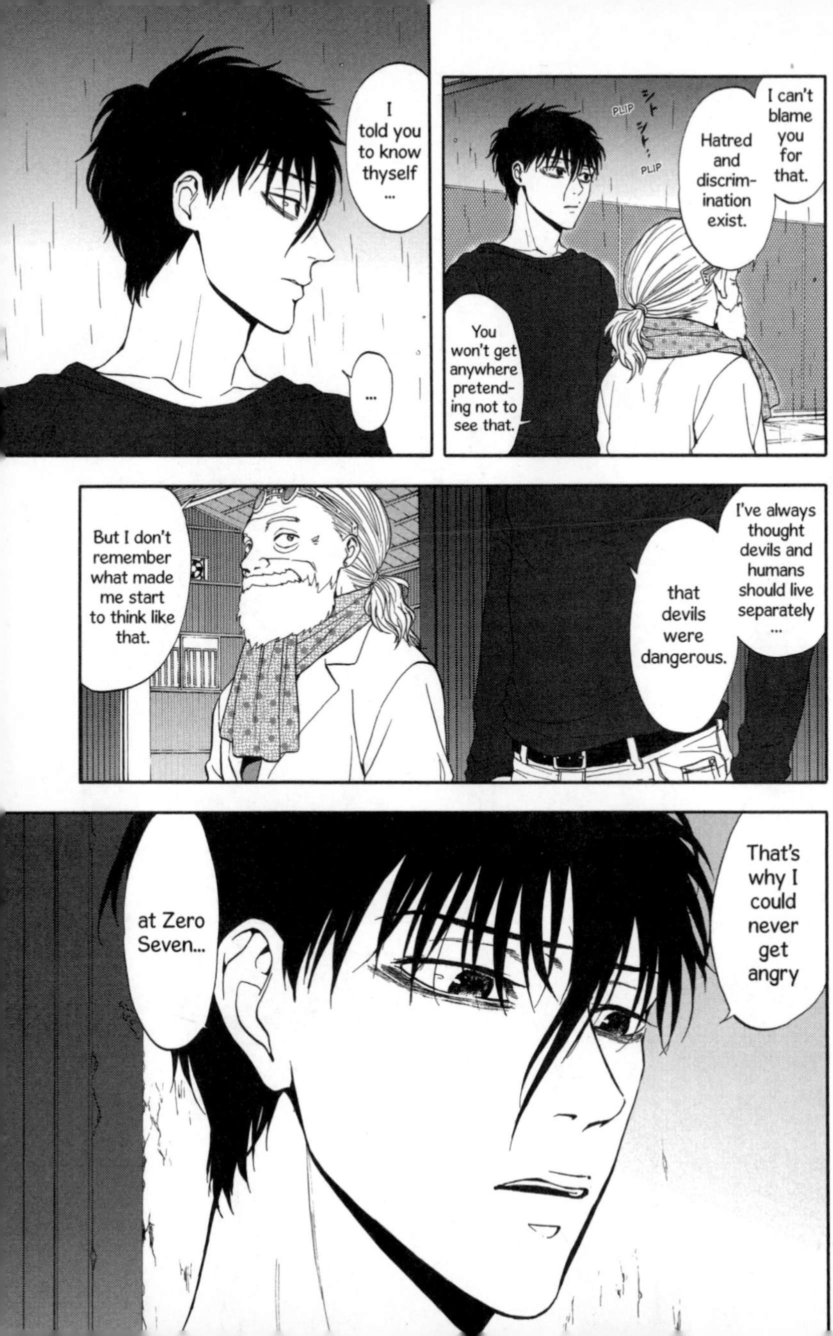
I can't blame you for that.
Hatred and discrimination exist.
PLIP
PLIP
You won't get anywhere pretending not to see that.
I told you to know thyself ...
...
I've always thought devils and humans should live separately ...
that devils were dangerous.
But I don't remember what made me start to think like that.
That's why I could never get angry
at Zero Seven...

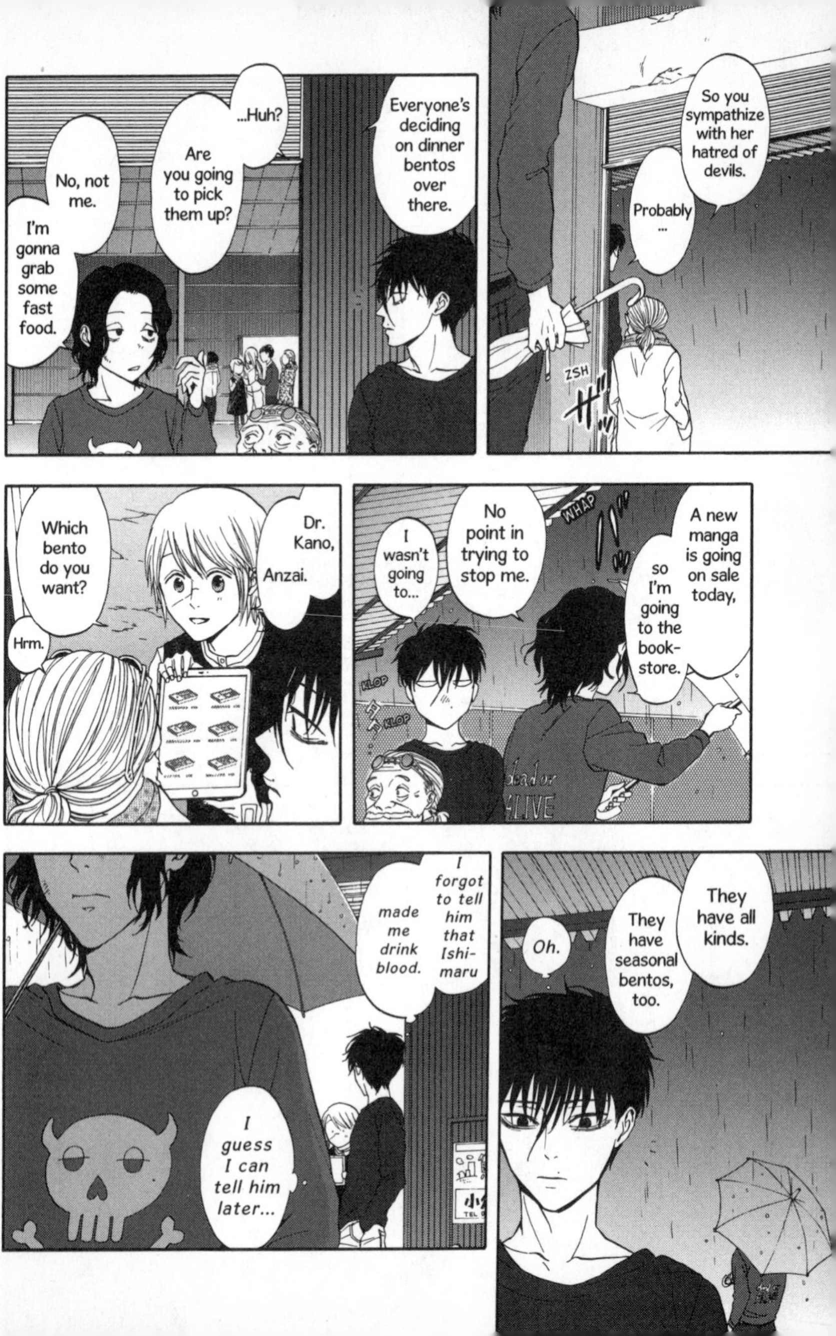
So you sympathize with her hatred of devils.
Probably...
ZSH
Everyone's deciding on dinner bentos over there.
...Huh?
Are you going to pick them up?
No, not me.
I'm gonna grab some fast food.
A new manga is going on sale today,
so I'm going to the book-store.
WHAP
No point in trying to stop me.
I wasn't going to...
KLOP
KLOP
Dr. Kano, Anzai.
Which bento do you want?
Hrm.
They have all kinds.
They have seasonal bentos, too.
Oh.
I forgot to tell him that Ishi-maru
made me drink blood.
I guess I can tell him later...

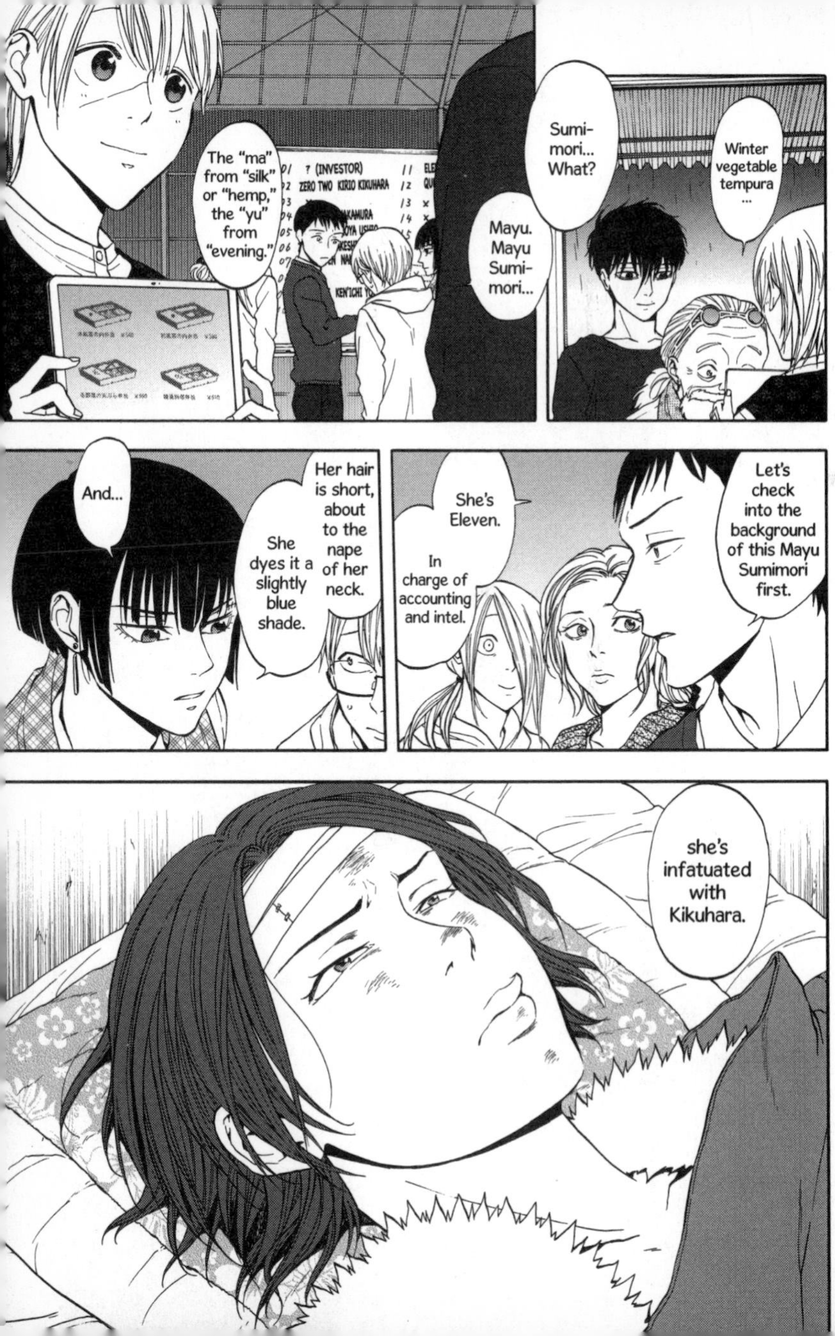
Winter vegetable tempura ...
Sumi-mori... What?
Mayu. Mayu Sumi-mori...
The "ma" from "silk" or "hemp," the "yu" from "evening."
01 ? (INVESTOR)
02 ZERO TWO KIRIO KIKUHARA
Let's check into the background of this Mayu Sumimori first.
She's Eleven.
In charge of accounting and intel.
Her hair is short, about to the nape of her neck.
She dyes it a slightly blue shade.
And...
she's infatuated with Kikuhara.

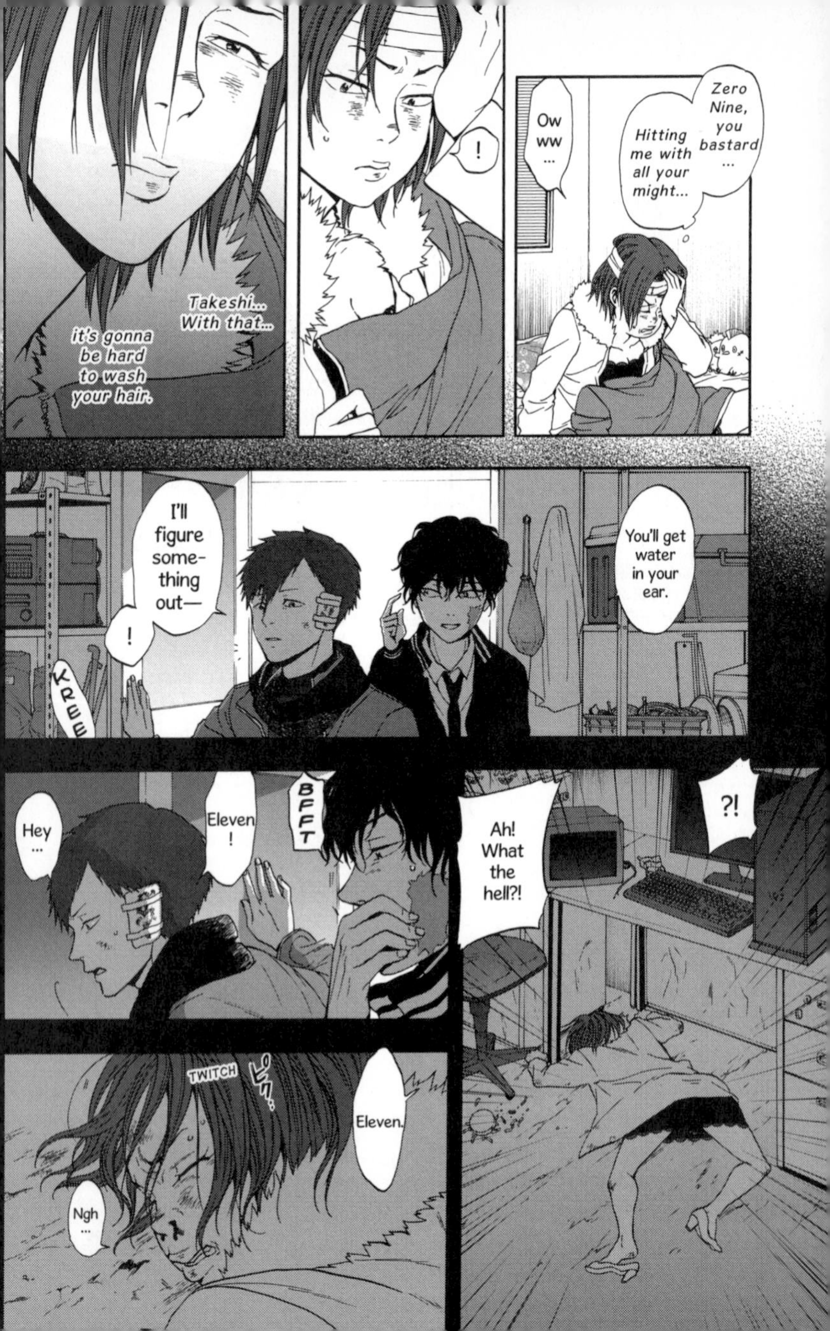
Zero Nine, you bastard...
Hitting me with all your might...
Ow ww...
!
Takeshi... With that...
it's gonna be hard to wash your hair.
You'll get water in your ear.
I'll figure some-thing out—
!
KREE
?!
Ah! What the hell?!
BFFT
Eleven!
Hey...
TWITCH
Eleven.
Ngh...

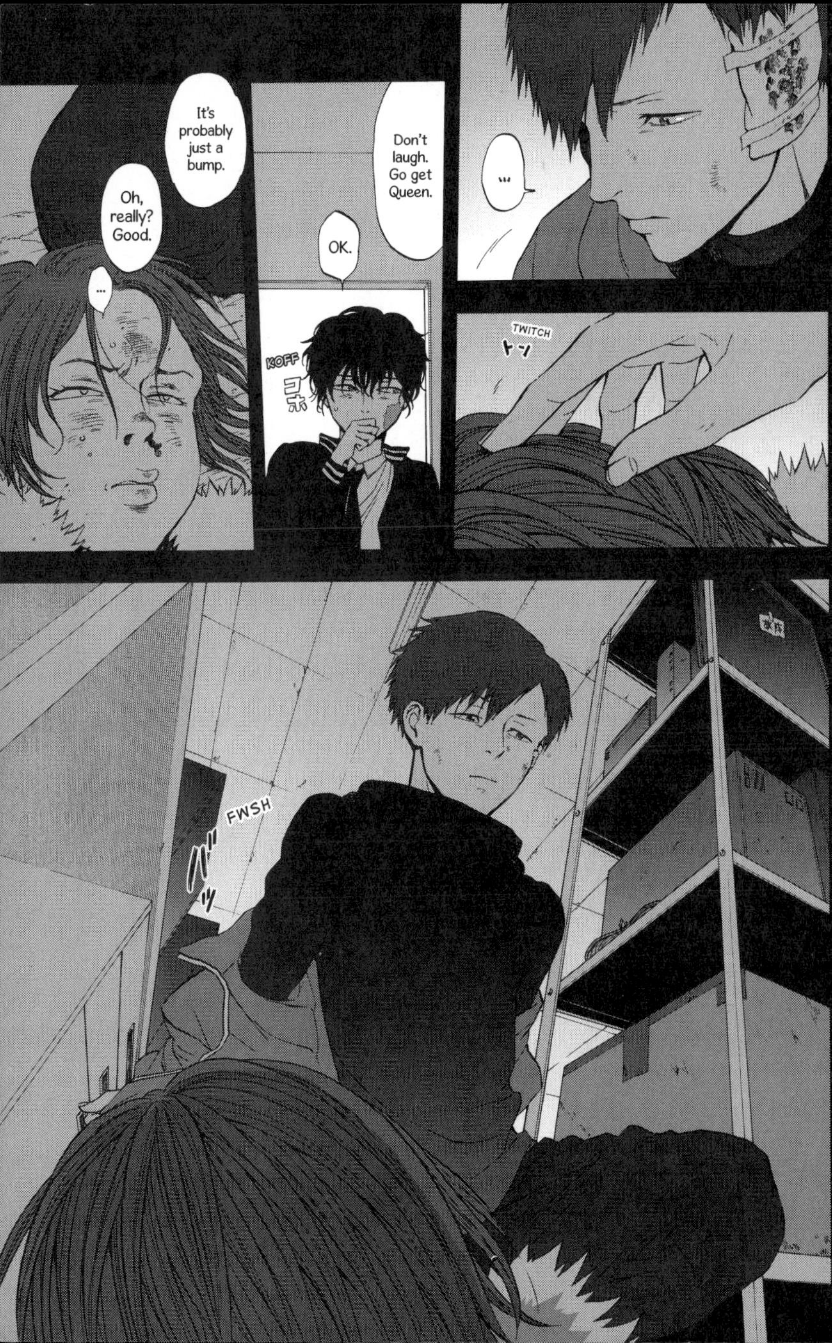
…
TWITCH
トン
Don't laugh. Go get Queen.
OK.
KOFF
コホ
It's probably just a bump.
Oh, really? Good.
…
FWSH
バッ

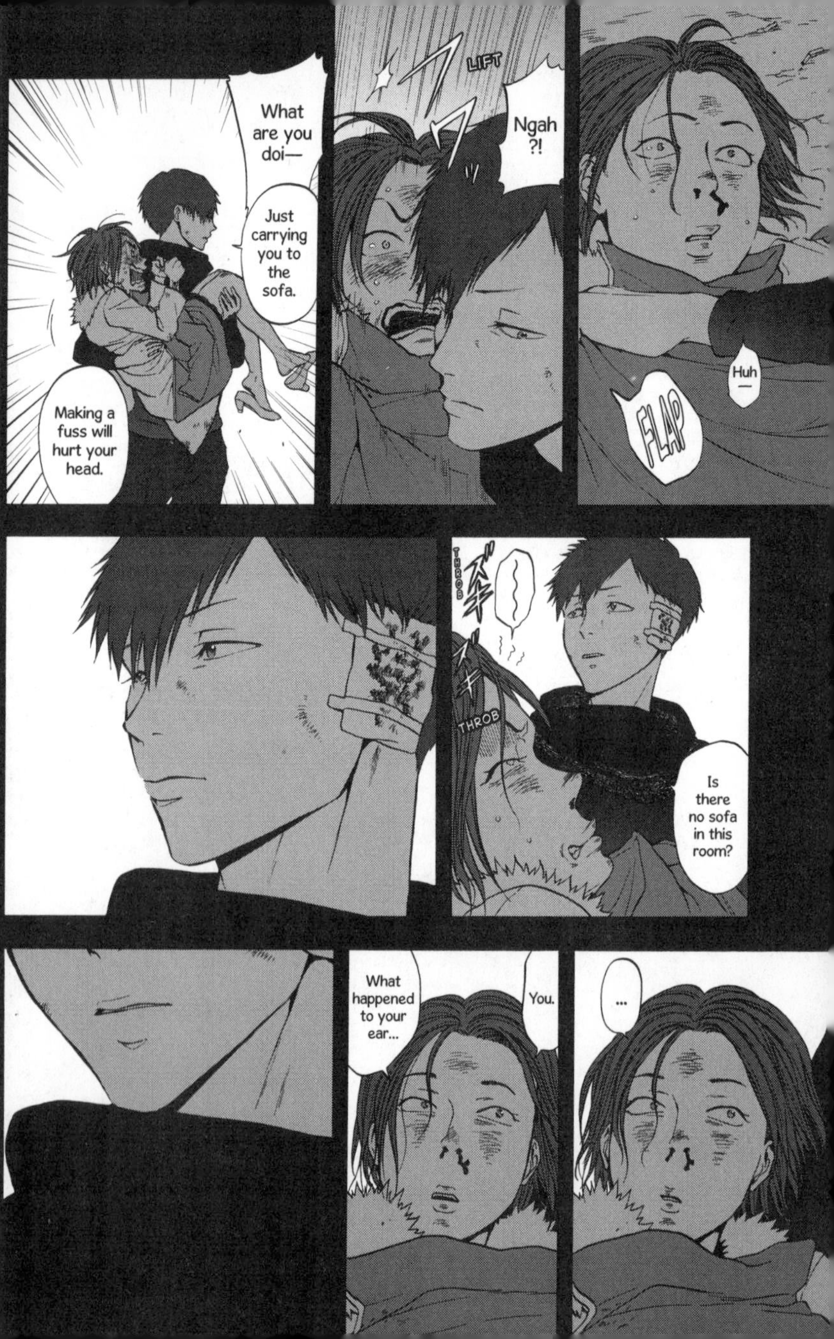
Huh—
FLAP
LIFT
Ngah ?!
What are you doi—
Just carrying you to the sofa.
Making a fuss will hurt your head.
THROB
...
THROB
Is there no sofa in this room?
...
You.
What happened to your ear...

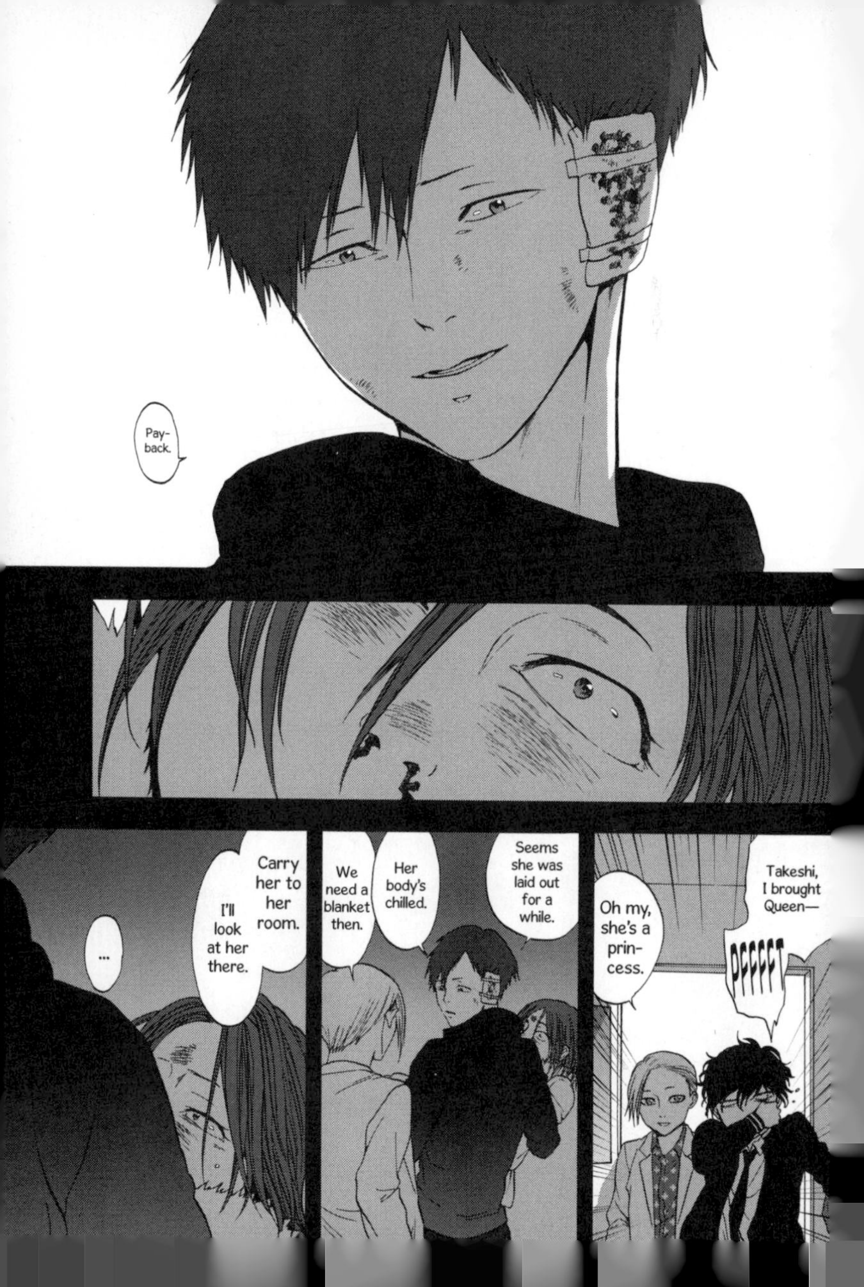
Pay-back.
Takeshi, I brought Queen—
PFFFFT
Oh my, she's a princess.
Seems she was laid out for a while.
Her body's chilled.
We need a blanket then.
Carry her to her room.
I'll look at her there.
...

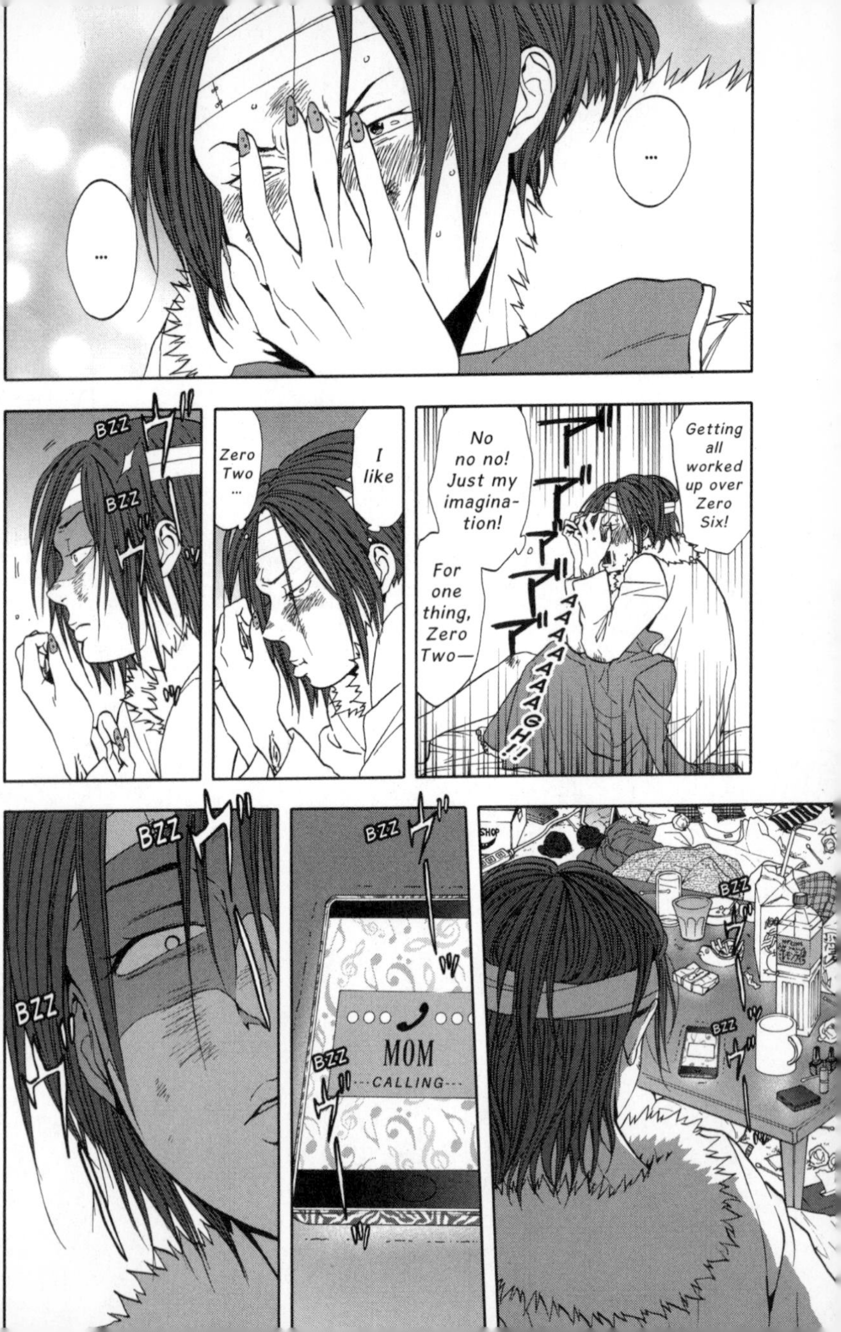
...
...
Getting all worked up over Zero Six!
No no no! Just my imagination!
For one thing, Zero Two—
AAAAAAAAGH!!
I like
Zero Two ...
BZZ
BZZ
BZZ
BZZ
BZZ
BZZ
MOM
CALLING
BZZ
BZZ
BZZ

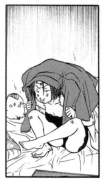

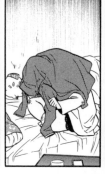

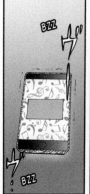

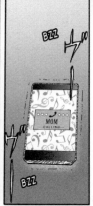

BZZ
MOM
CALLING
BZZ
BZZ
BZZ
Aah ...
Tired ...
FWAP
!
Blood ...
...
Have to give this coat back
to Zero Six...
Plan B's gone off the rails...
It wasn't as perfect as Zero Two thought.
I got hit on the head by that little jerk-off.
And I get meaningless phone calls. But like...

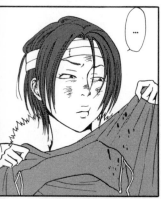

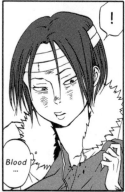

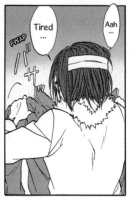

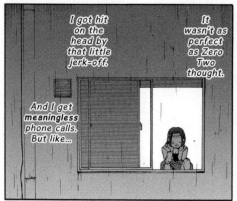

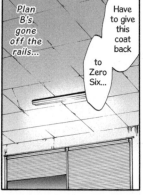

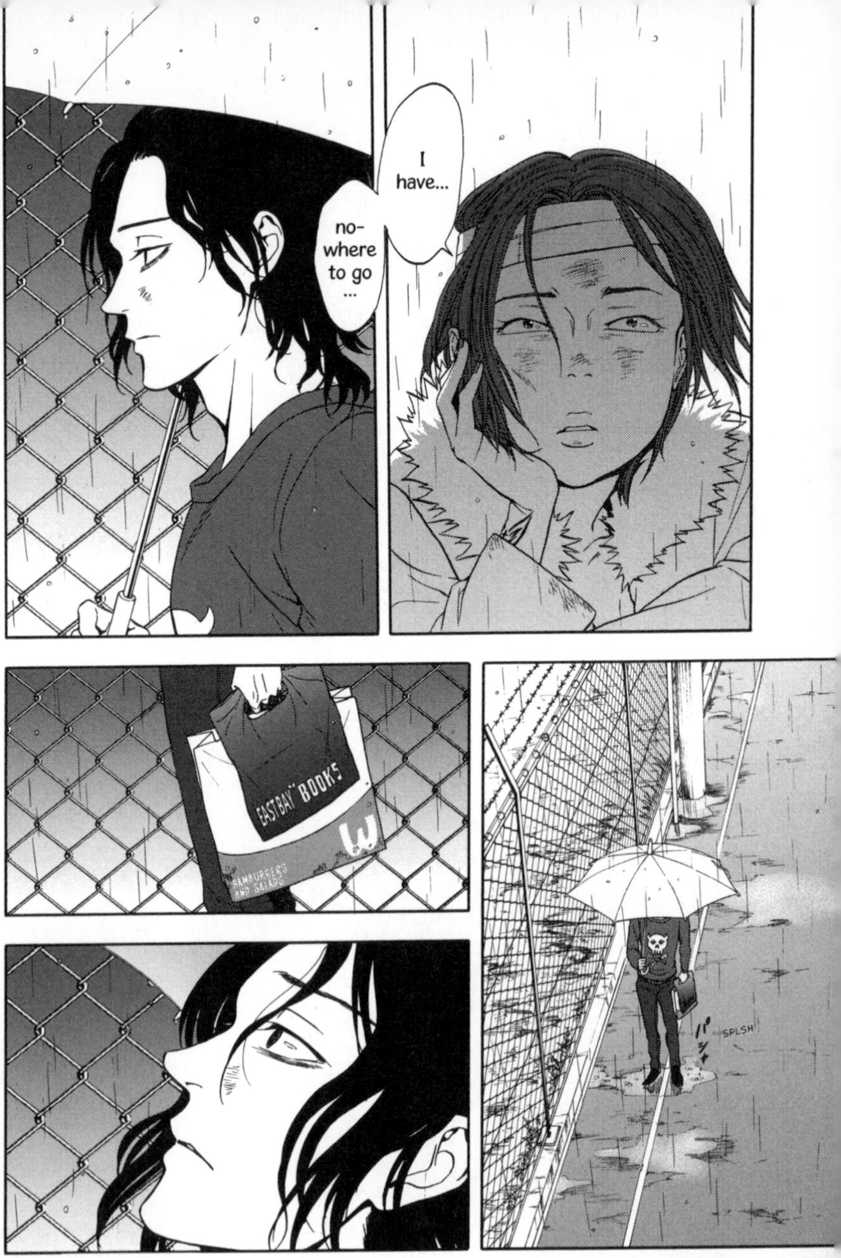
I have...
no-where to go ...
パシャ
SPLSH
EASTBAY BOOKS
HAMBURGERS AND SALADS

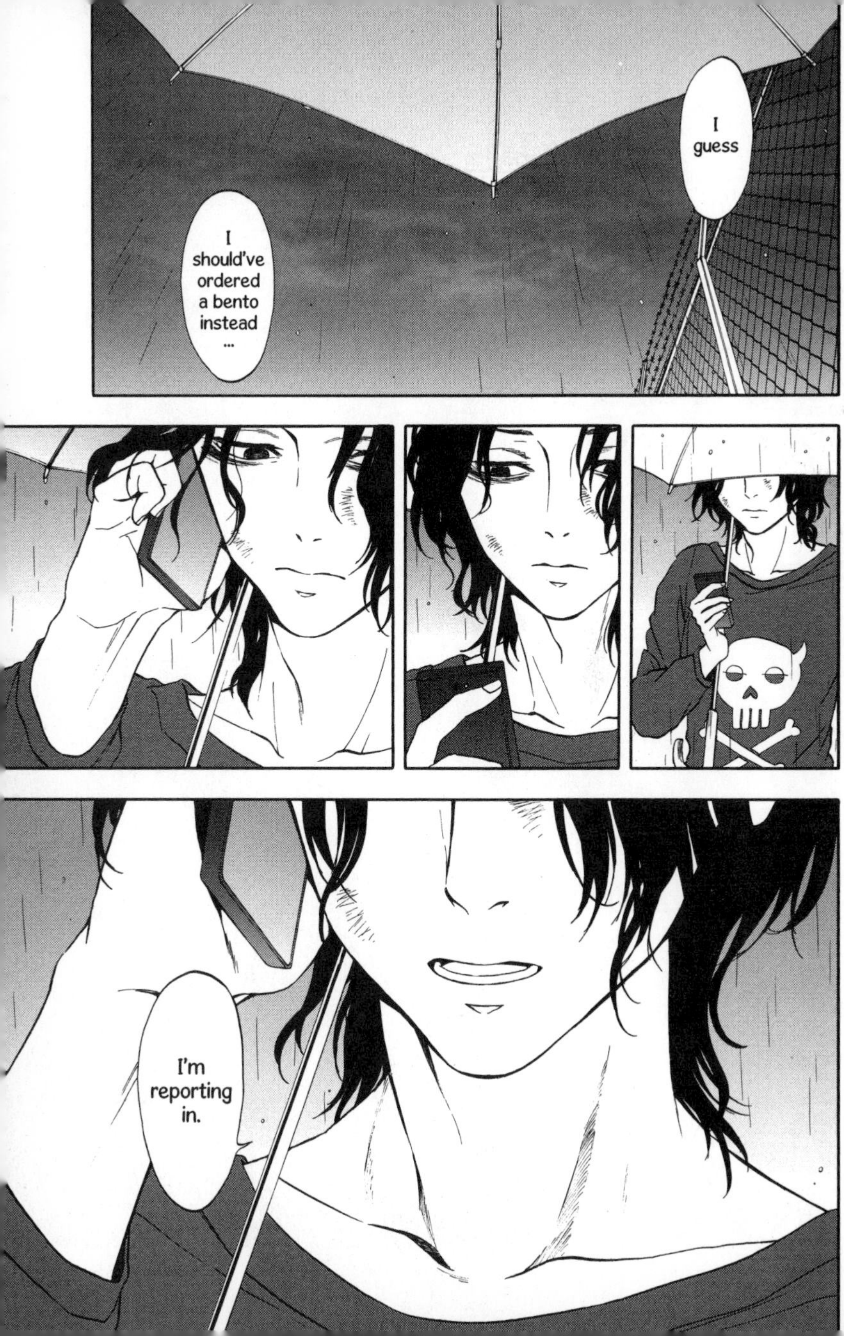
I guess
I should've ordered a bento instead ...
I'm reporting in.

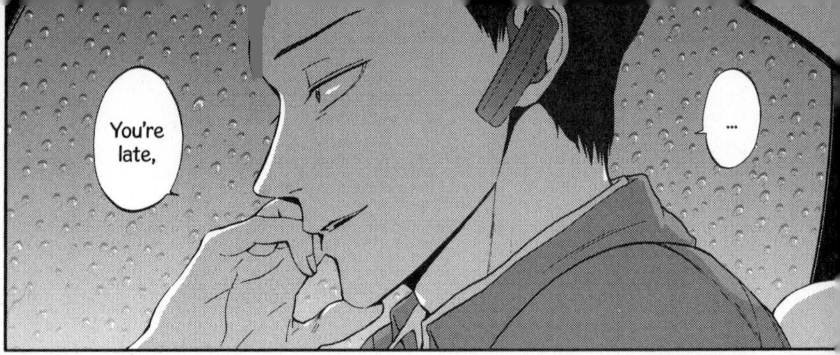
…
You're late,
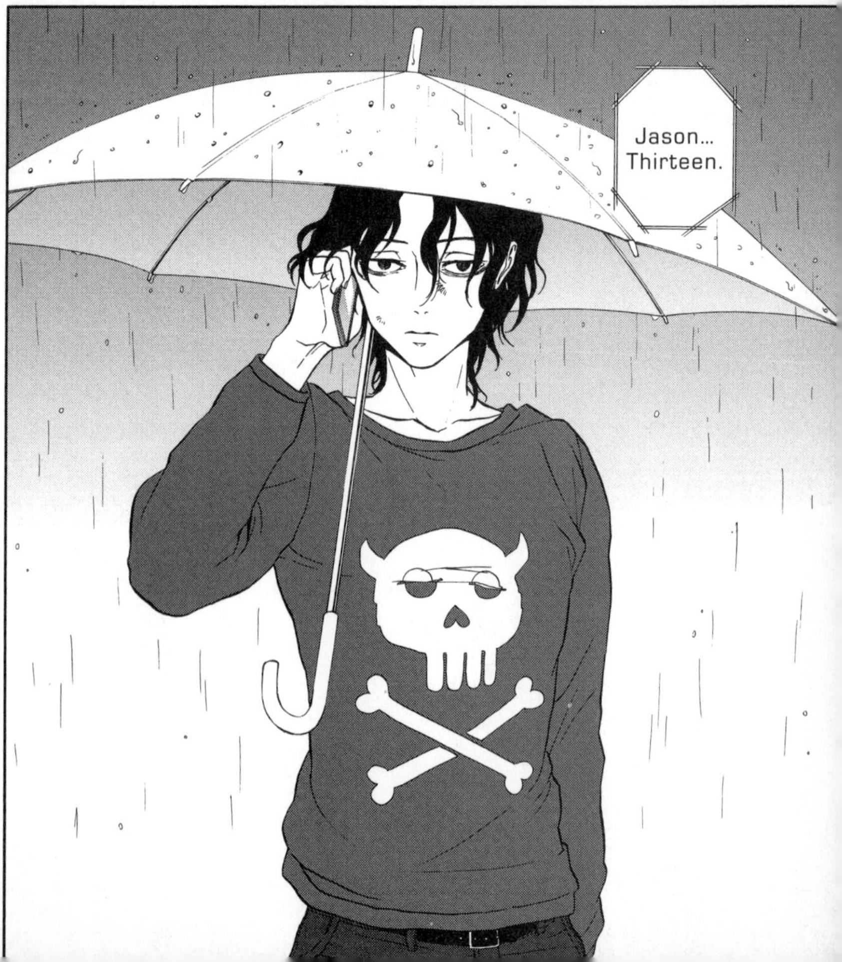
Jason… Thirteen.

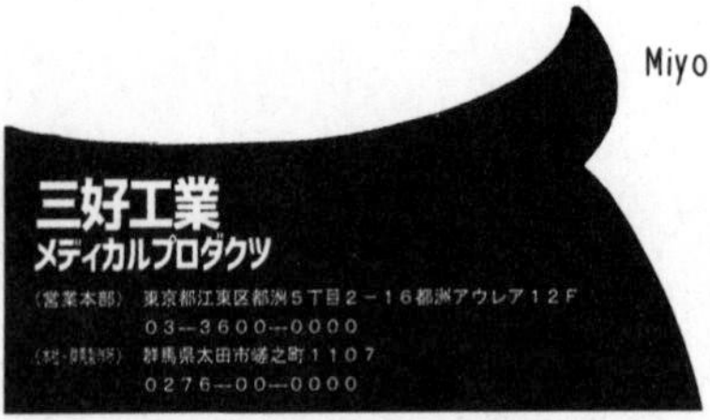
三好工業
メディカルプロダクツ
（営業本部）　東京都江東区豊洲５丁目２－１６豊洲アウレア１２Ｆ
０３－３６００－００００
０２７６－００－００００

Miyoshi Industries Medical Products, Inc.

The company, introduced in Chapter 28, is where the grandfather of the boy Miyoshi works.

They produce handcuffs and nail protectors for devils. Their head office is in Gunma.

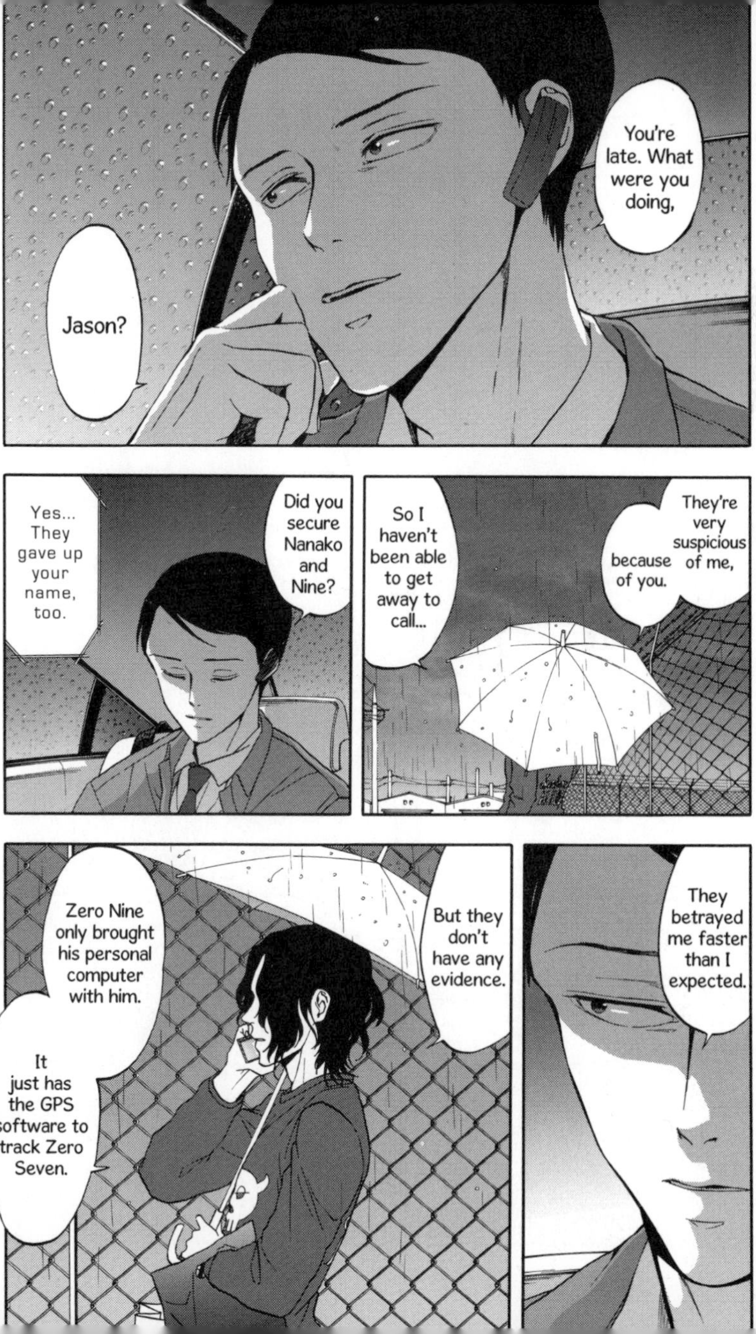
You're late. What were you doing,
Jason?
They're very suspicious of me,
because of you.
So I haven't been able to get away to call...
Did you secure Nanako and Nine?
Yes... They gave up your name, too.
They betrayed me faster than I expected.
But they don't have any evidence.
Zero Nine only brought his personal computer with him.
It just has the GPS software to track Zero Seven.

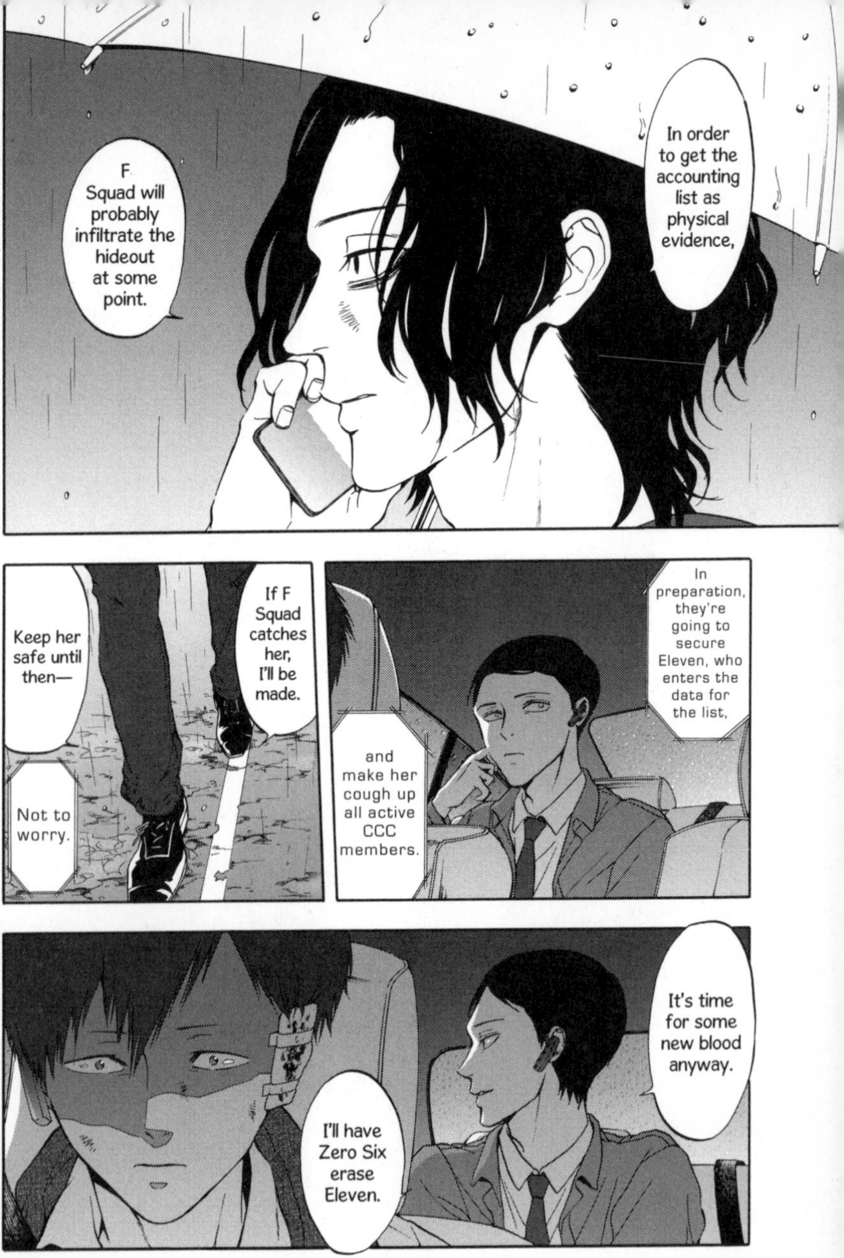
In order to get the accounting list as physical evidence,
F Squad will probably infiltrate the hideout at some point.
In preparation, they're going to secure Eleven, who enters the data for the list,
and make her cough up all active CCC members.
If F Squad catches her, I'll be made.
Keep her safe until then—
Not to worry.
It's time for some new blood anyway.
I'll have Zero Six erase Eleven.

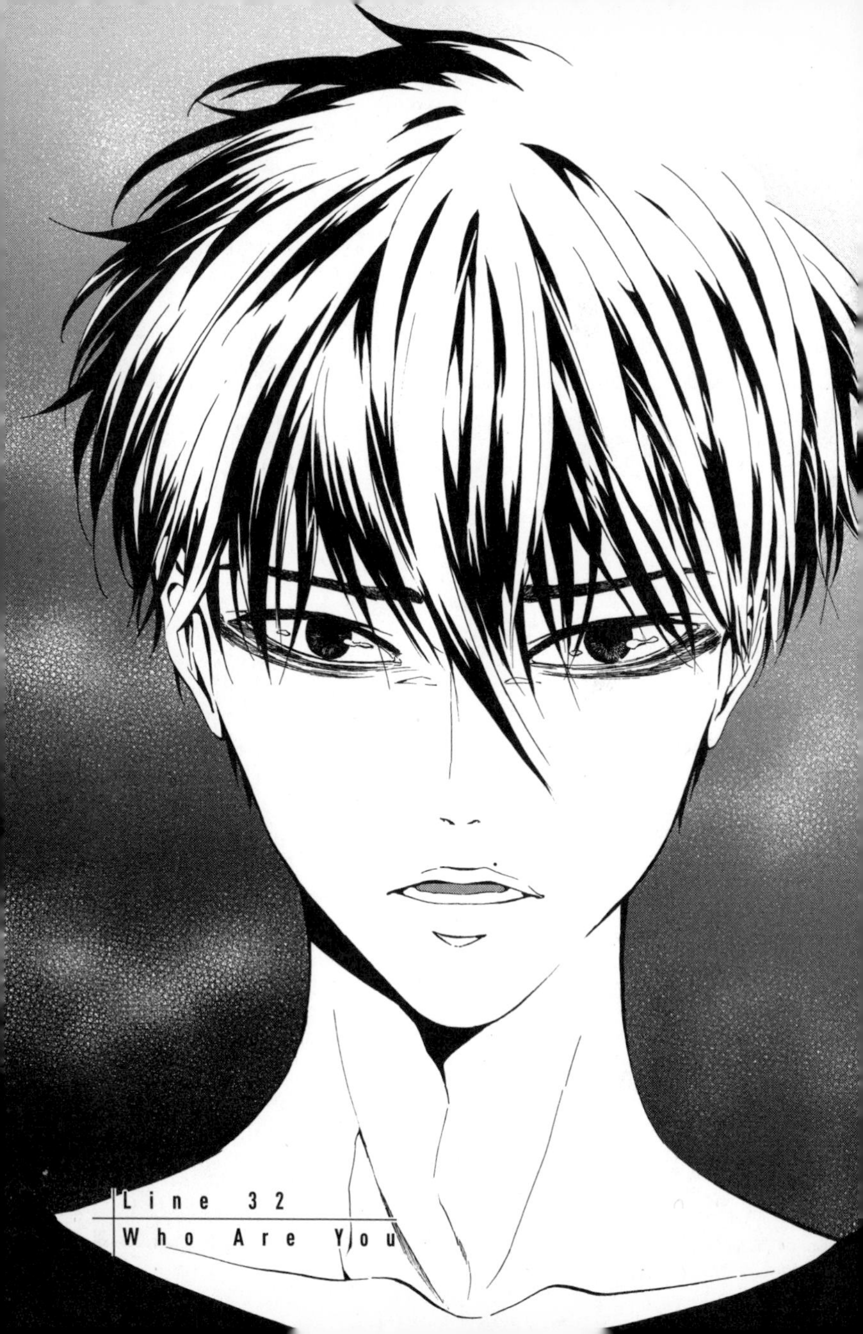
Line 32
Who Are You

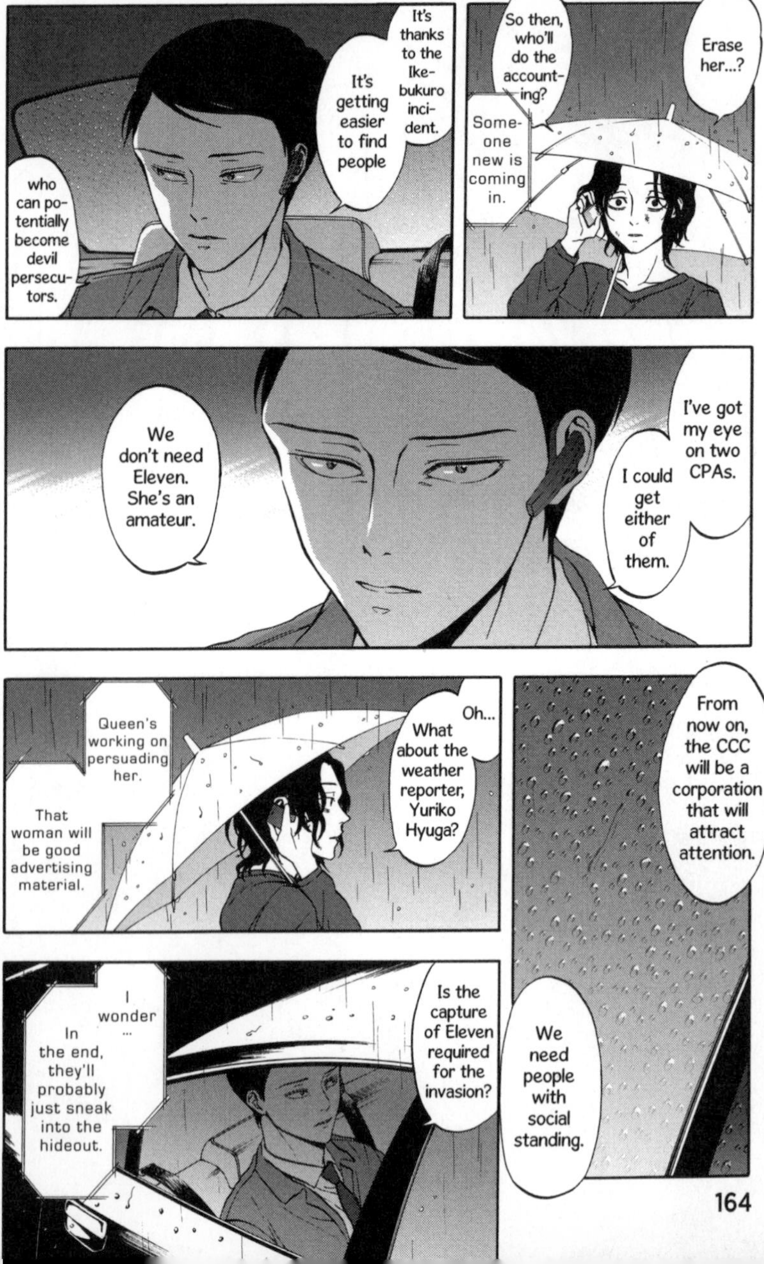
Erase her...?
So then, who'll do the accounting?
Someone new is coming in.
It's thanks to the Ikebukuro incident.
It's getting easier to find people
who can potentially become devil persecutors.
I've got my eye on two CPAs.
I could get either of them.
We don't need Eleven. She's an amateur.
From now on, the CCC will be a corporation that will attract attention.
We need people with social standing.
Oh... What about the weather reporter, Yuriko Hyuga?
Queen's working on persuading her.
That woman will be good advertising material.
Is the capture of Eleven required for the invasion?
I wonder...
In the end, they'll probably just sneak into the hideout.

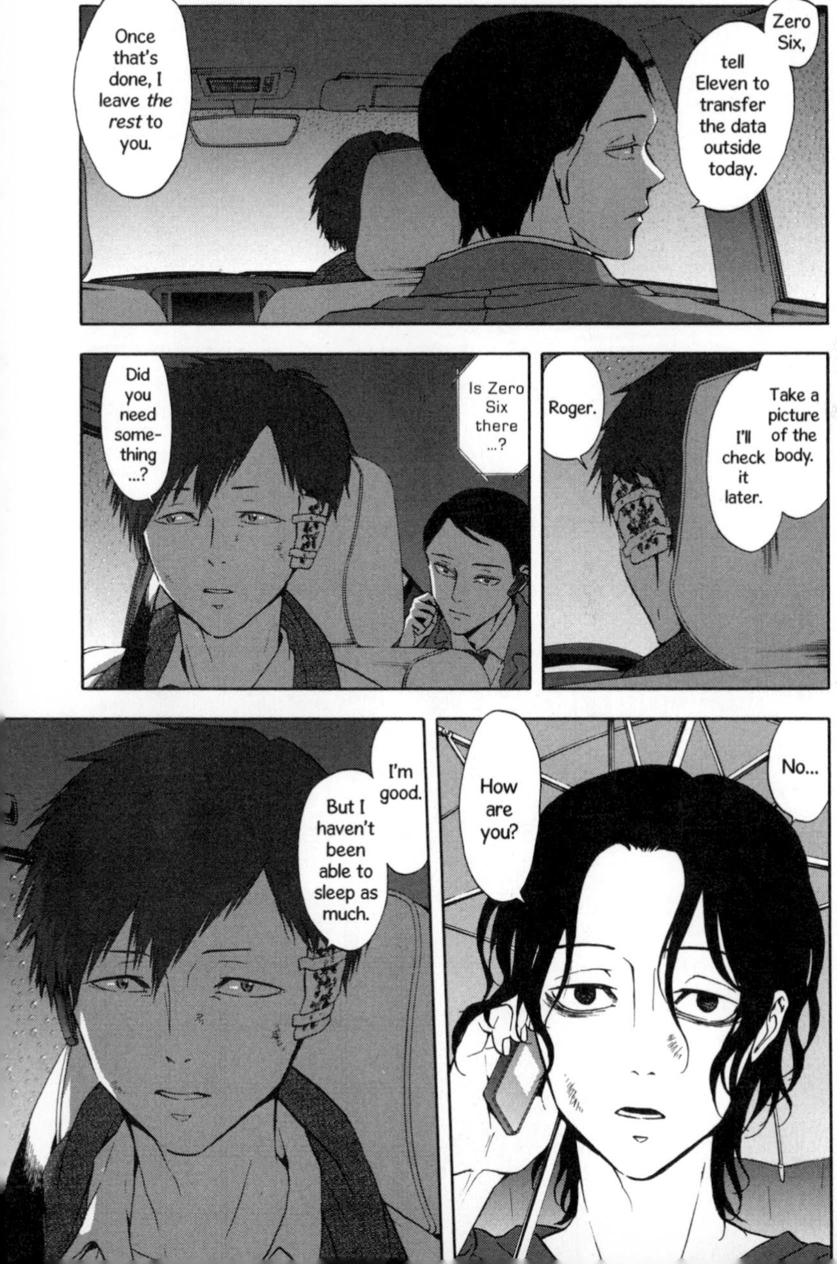

Zero Six, tell Eleven to transfer the data outside today.
Once that's done, I leave *the rest* to you.
Take a picture of the body.
I'll check it later.
Roger.
Is Zero Six there ...?
Did you need something ...?
No...
How are you?
I'm good.
But I haven't been able to sleep as much.

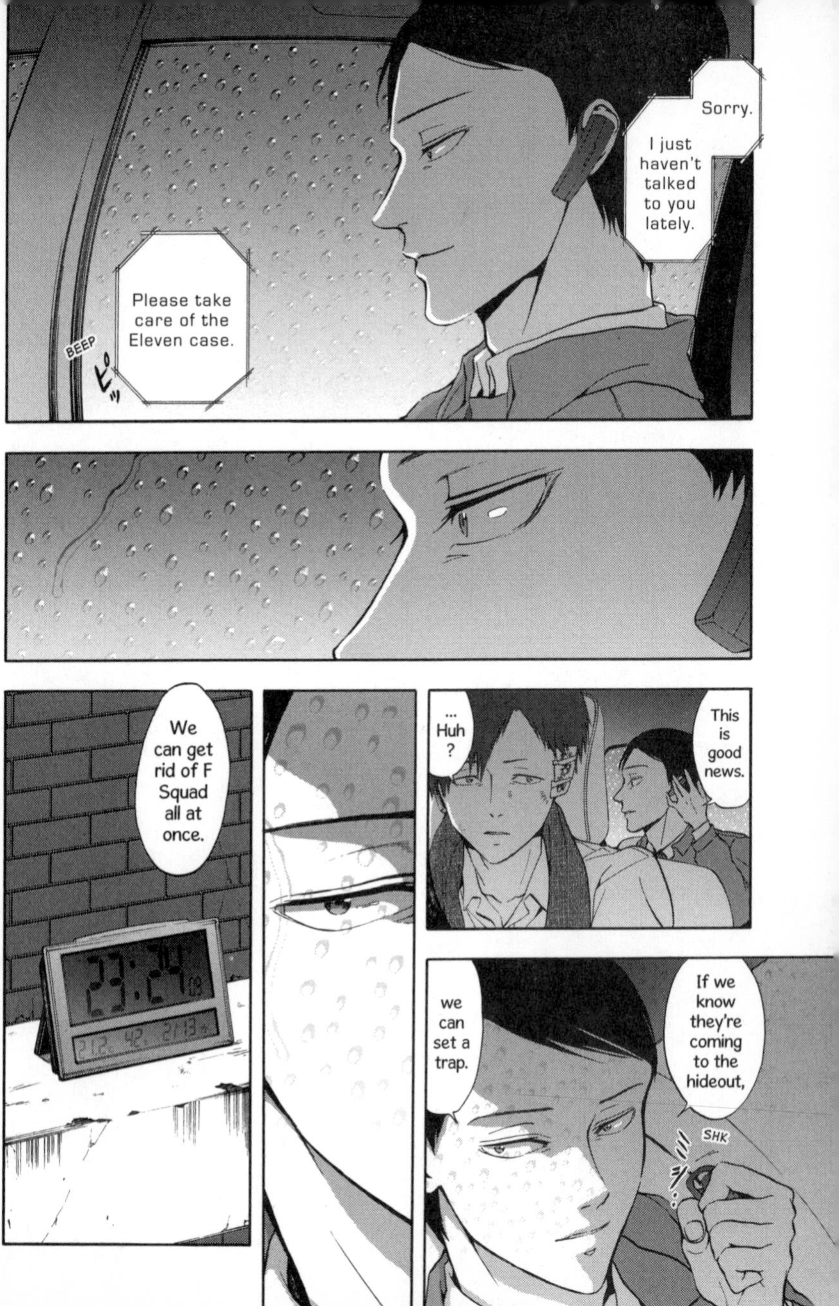
Sorry.
I just haven't talked to you lately.
Please take care of the Eleven case.
BEEP
This is good news.
...Huh?
If we know they're coming to the hideout,
we can set a trap.
SHK
We can get rid of F Squad all at once.

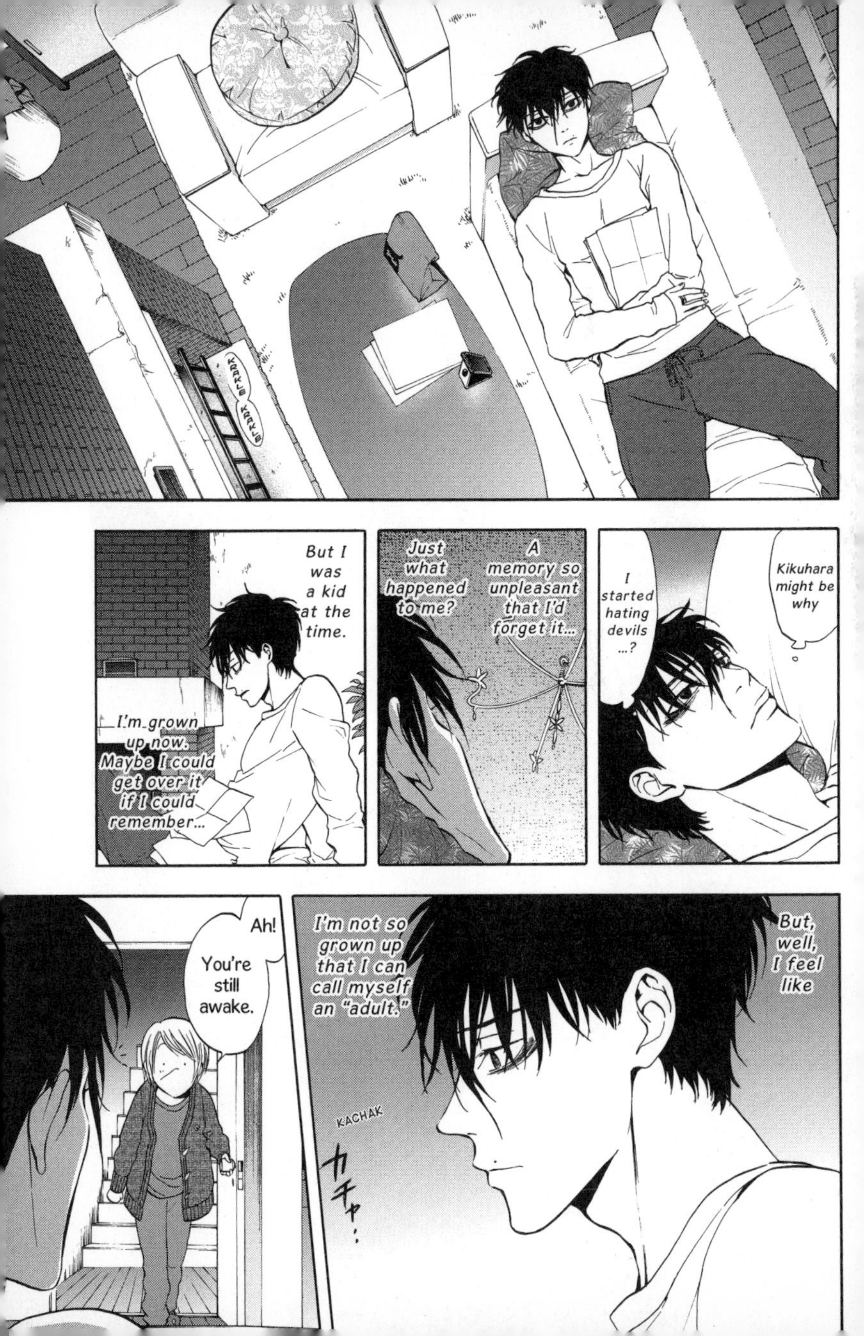
KRAKLE KRAKLE
Kikuhara might be why
I started hating devils ...?
A memory so unpleasant that I'd forget it...
Just what happened to me?
But I was a kid at the time.
I'm grown up now. Maybe I could get over it if I could remember...
But, well, I feel like
I'm not so grown up that I can call myself an "adult."
Ah!
You're still awake.
KACHAK
カチャ…

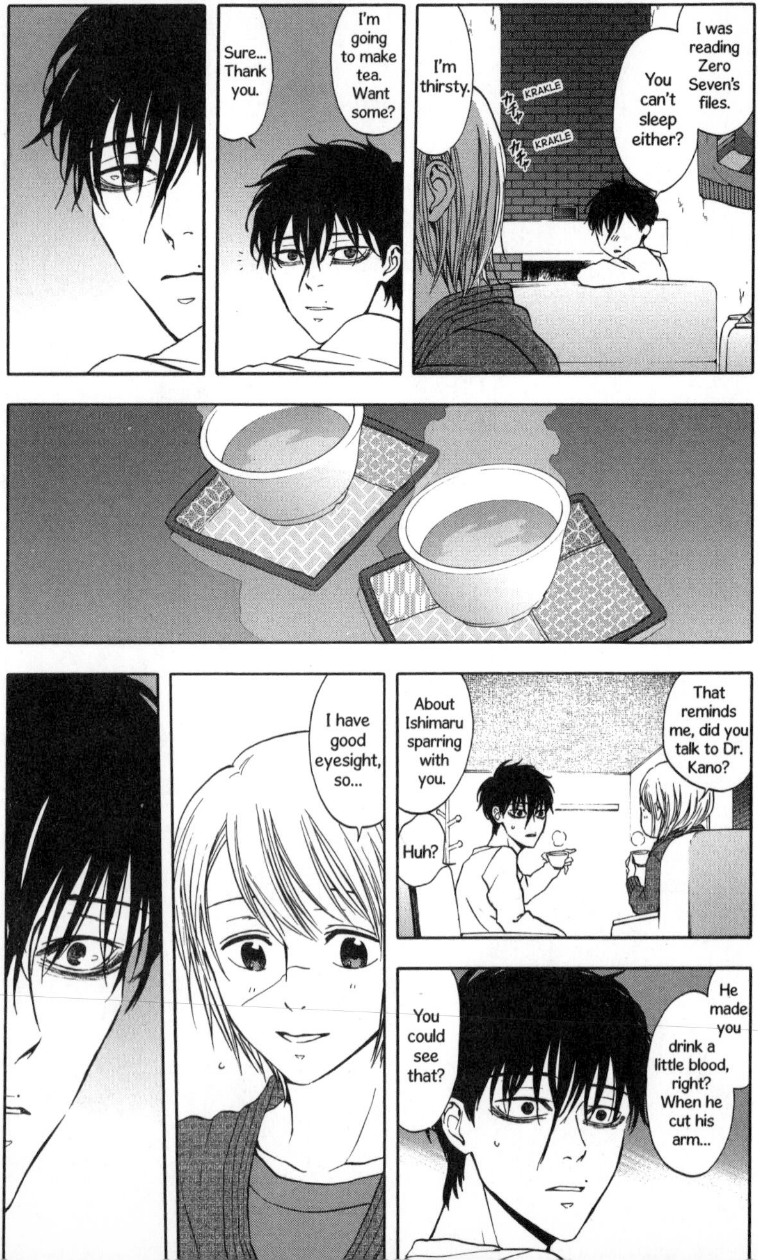
I was reading Zero Seven's files.
You can't sleep either?
KRAKLE
KRAKLE
I'm thirsty.
I'm going to make tea. Want some?
Sure... Thank you.
That reminds me, did you talk to Dr. Kano?
About Ishimaru sparring with you.
Huh?
He made you drink a little blood, right? When he cut his arm...
You could see that?
I have good eyesight, so...

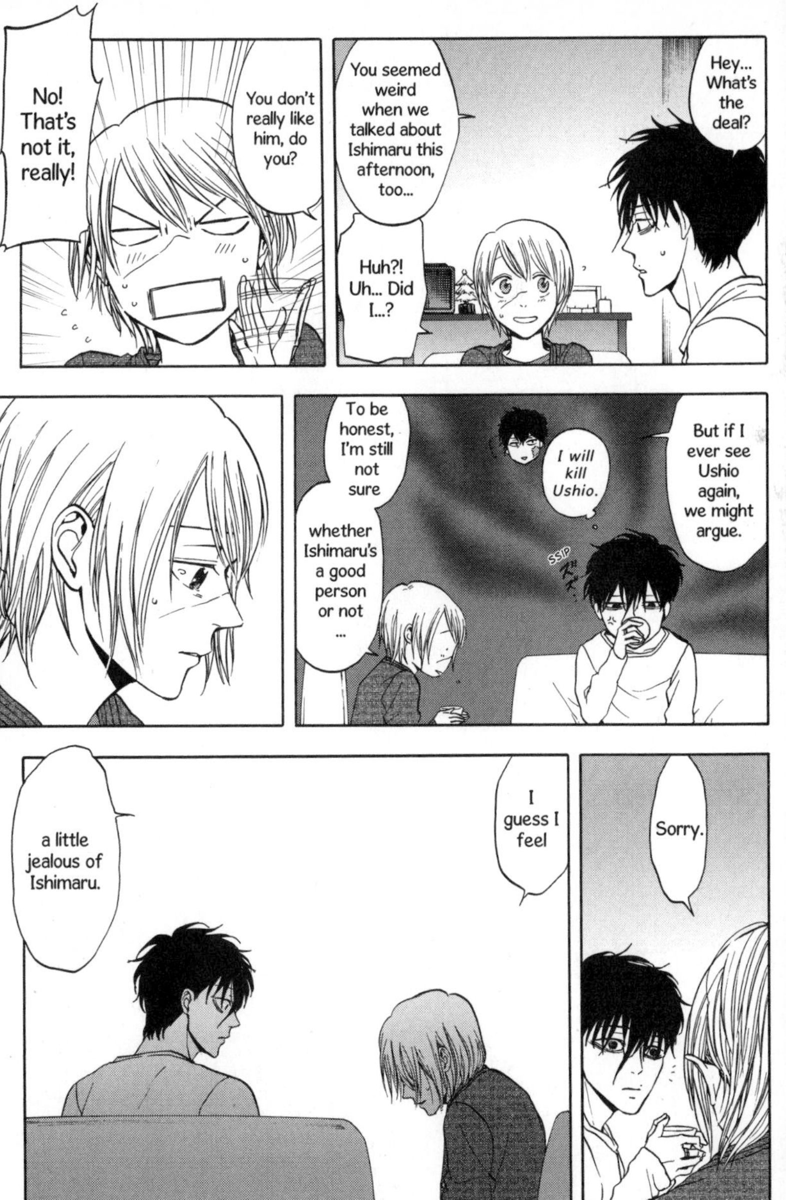
Hey... What's the deal?
You seemed weird when we talked about Ishimaru this afternoon, too...
Huh?! Uh... Did I...?
You don't really like him, do you?
No! That's not it, really!
But if I ever see Ushio again, we might argue.
I will kill Ushio.
SSIP
To be honest, I'm still not sure
whether Ishimaru's a good person or not
...
Sorry.
I guess I feel
a little jealous of Ishimaru.

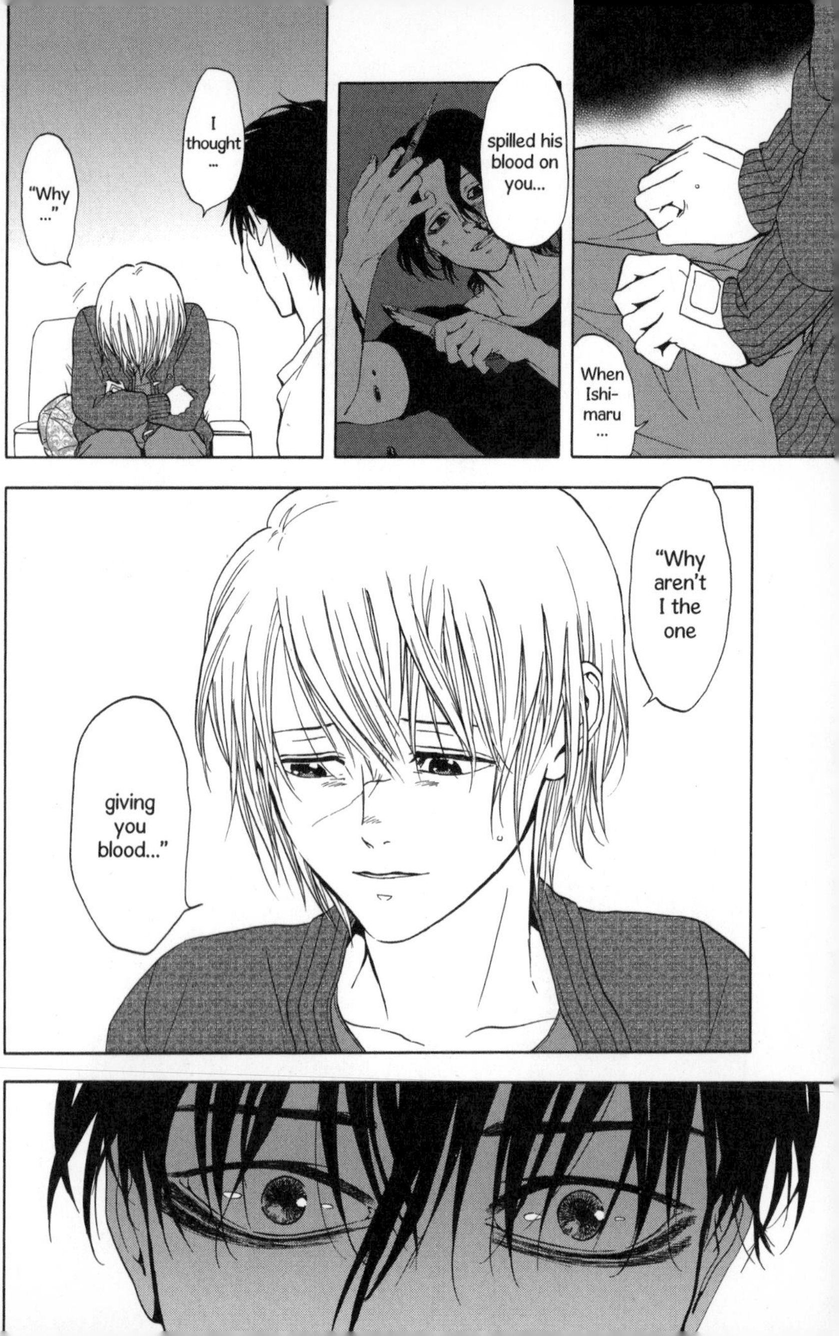
When Ishi-maru ...
spilled his blood on you...
I thought ...
"Why ..."
"Why aren't I the one
giving you blood..."

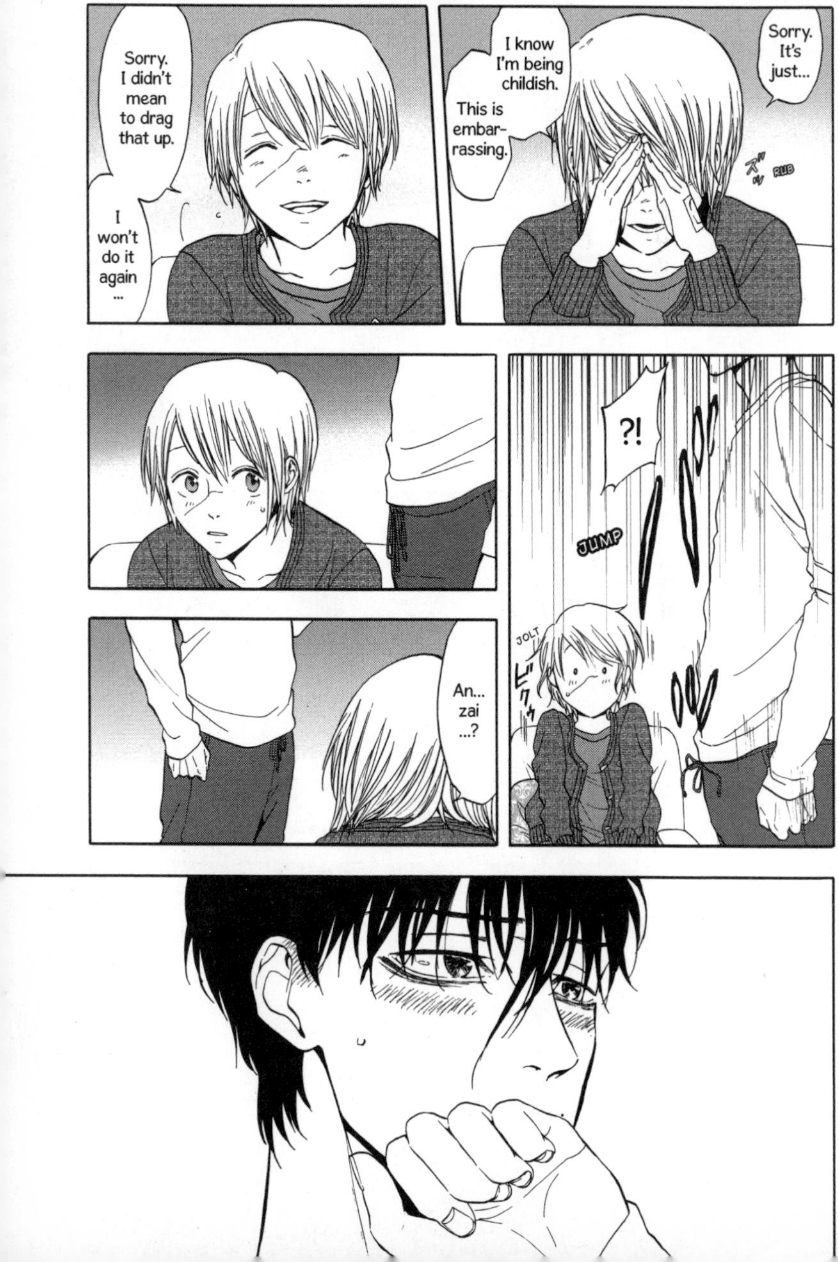
Sorry. It's just...
RUB
I know I'm being childish.
This is embarrassing.
Sorry. I didn't mean to drag that up.
I won't do it again...
?!
JUMP
JOLT
An... zai ...?

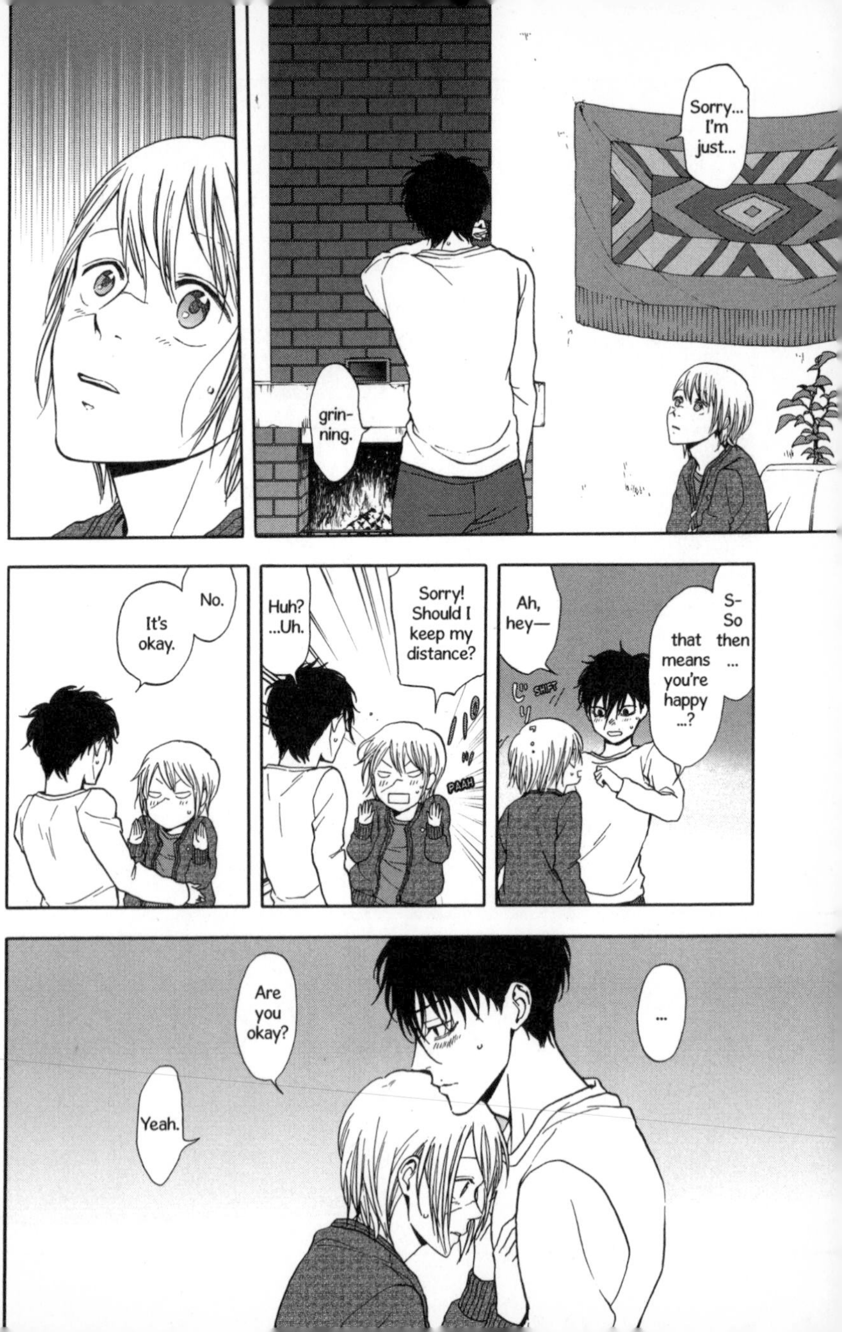

Sorry... I'm just...
grin-ning.
S-So then that means you're happy ...?
Ah, hey—
SHIFT
Sorry! Should I keep my distance?
Huh? ...Uh.
PAAH
No.
It's okay.
...
Are you okay?
Yeah.

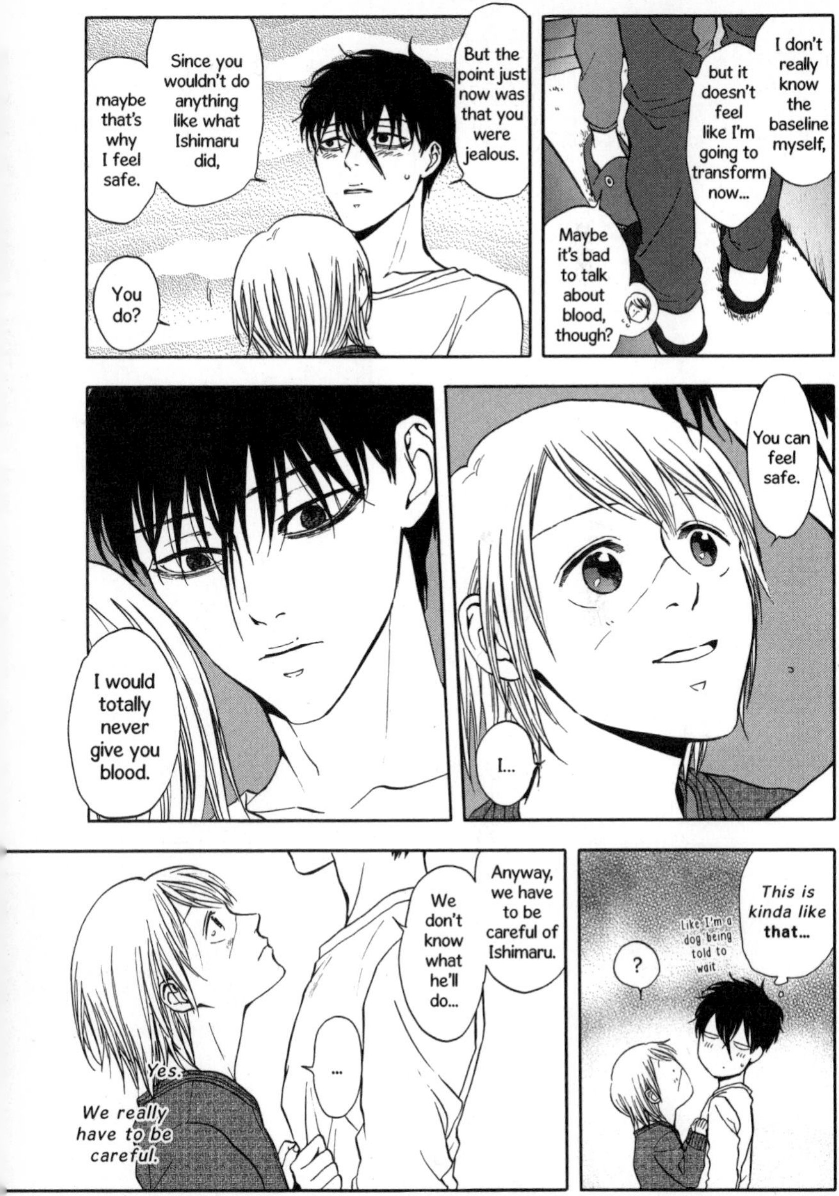
I don't really know the baseline myself,
but it doesn't feel like I'm going to transform now...
Maybe it's bad to talk about blood, though?
But the point just now was that you were jealous.
Since you wouldn't do anything like what Ishimaru did,
maybe that's why I feel safe.
You do?
You can feel safe.
I...
I would totally never give you blood.
This is kinda like **that...**
Like I'm a dog being told to wait
?
Anyway, we have to be careful of Ishimaru.
We don't know what he'll do...
...
Yes.
We really have to be careful.

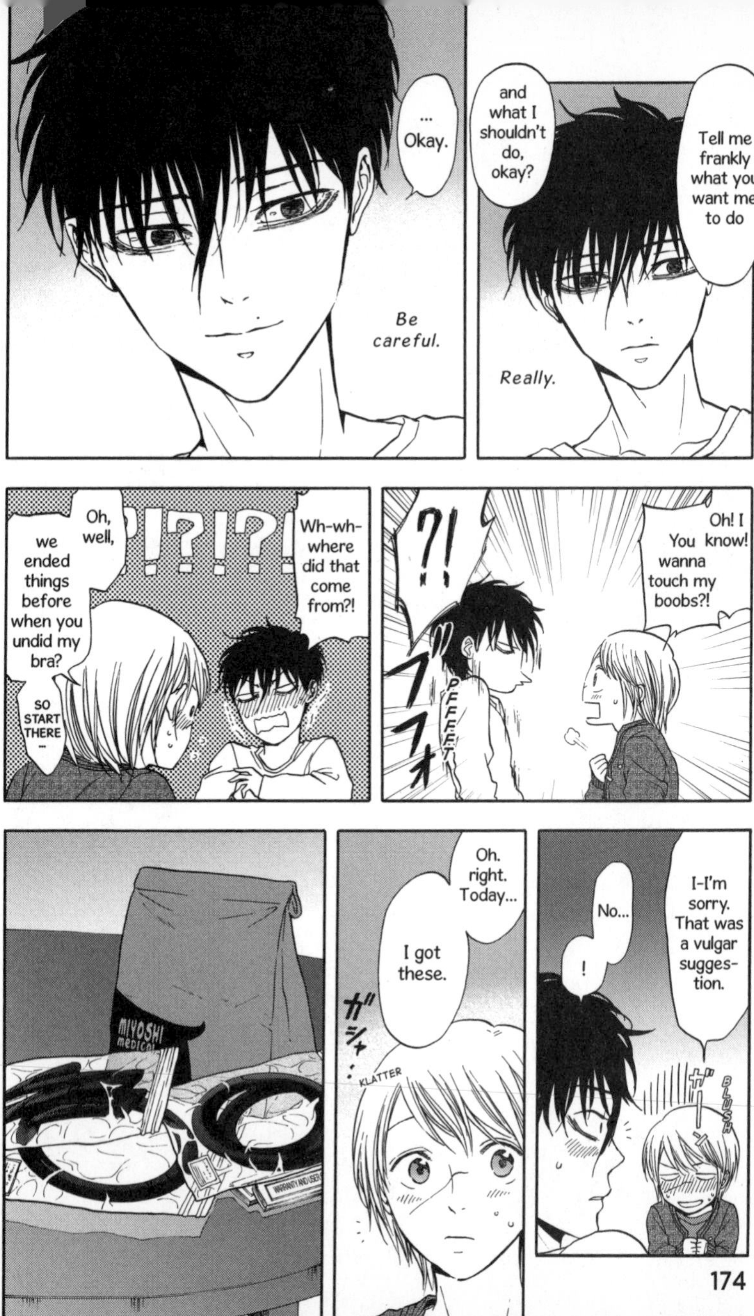
Tell me frankly what you want me to do
and what I shouldn't do, okay?
Really.
... Okay.
Be careful.
?!
Oh! You know! I wanna touch my boobs?!
PFFFFT
Wh-wh-where did that come from?!
?!?!?!
Oh, well, we ended things before when you undid my bra?
SO START THERE ...
I-I'm sorry. That was a vulgar suggestion.
No...
!
BLUSH
Oh. right. Today...
I got these.
KLATTER
MIYOSHI MEDICAL

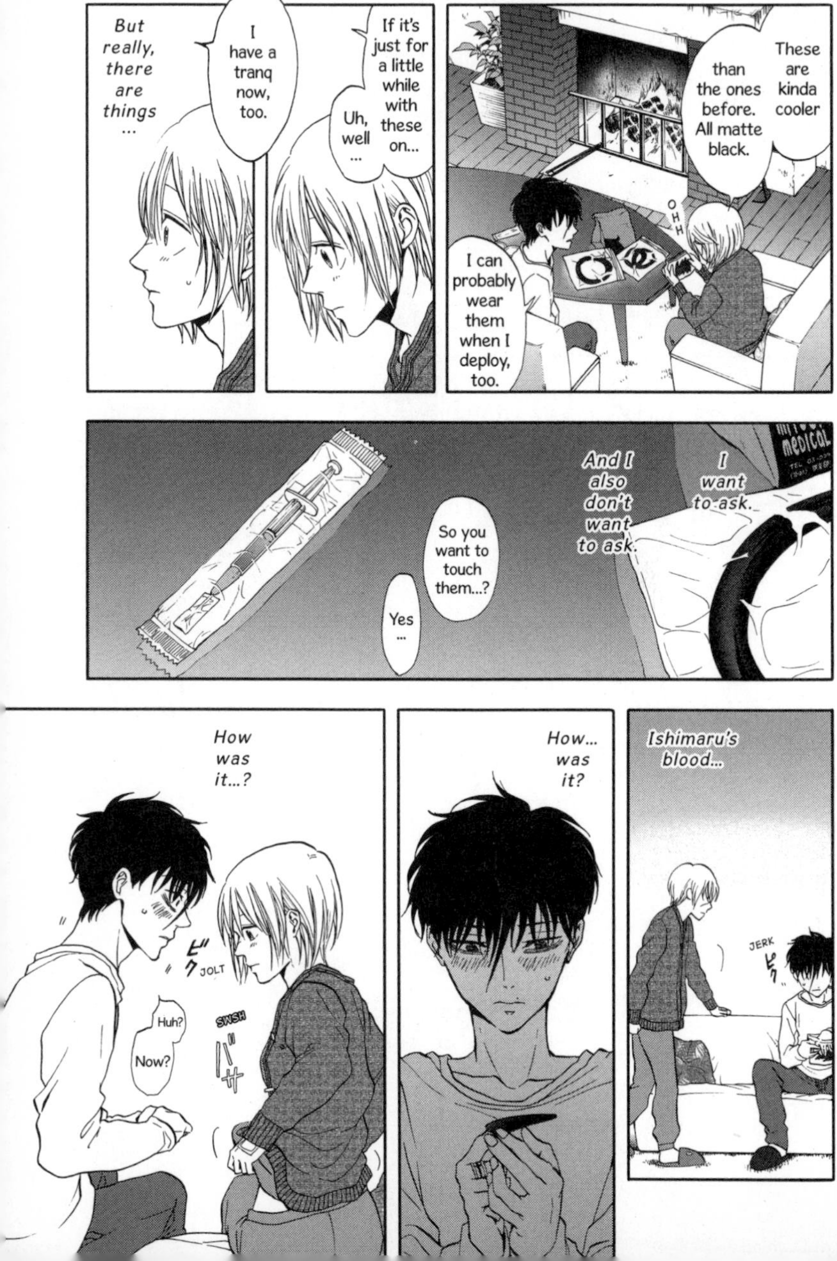
These are kinda cooler
than the ones before. All matte black.
OHH
I can probably wear them when I deploy, too.
If it's just for a little while with these on...
Uh, well...
I have a tranq now, too.
But really, there are things...
I want to ask.
And I also don't want to ask.
So you want to touch them...?
Yes...
Ishimaru's blood...
JERK
How... was it?
How was it...?
JOLT
SWSH
Huh?
Now?

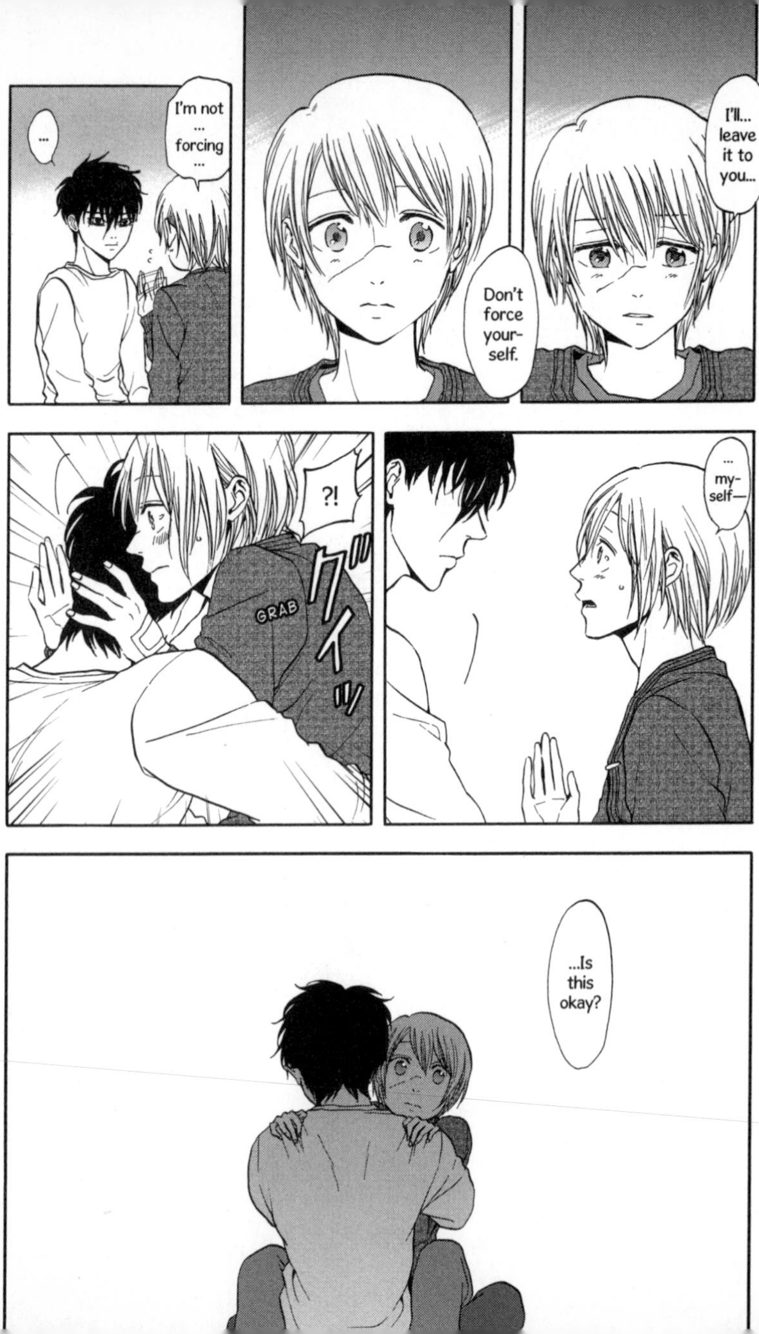
I'll... leave it to you...
Don't force your-self.
I'm not ... forcing ...
...
... my-self—
?!
GRAB
グイッ
...Is this okay?

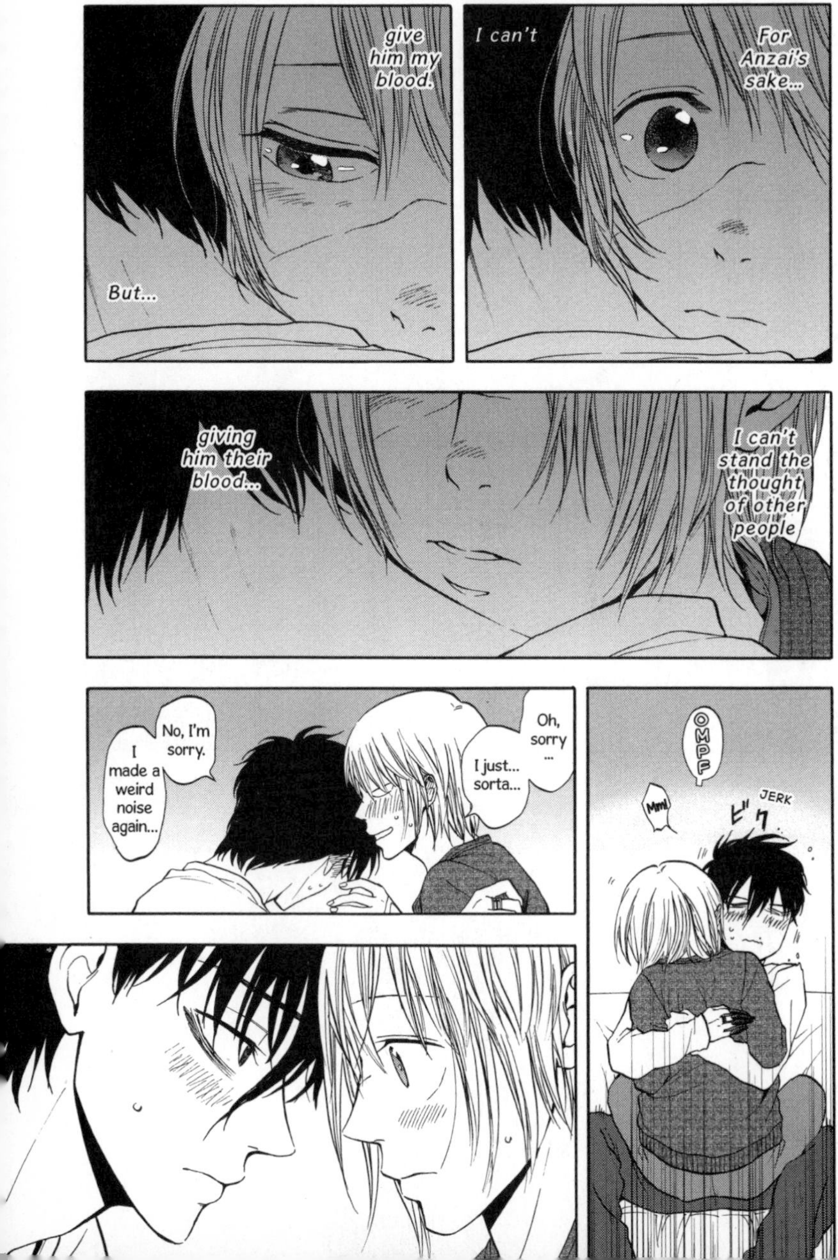
For Anzai's sake...
I can't
give him my blood.
But...
I can't stand the thought of other people
giving him their blood...
OMPF
JERK
Mm!
Oh, sorry ...
I just... sorta...
No, I'm sorry.
I made a weird noise again...

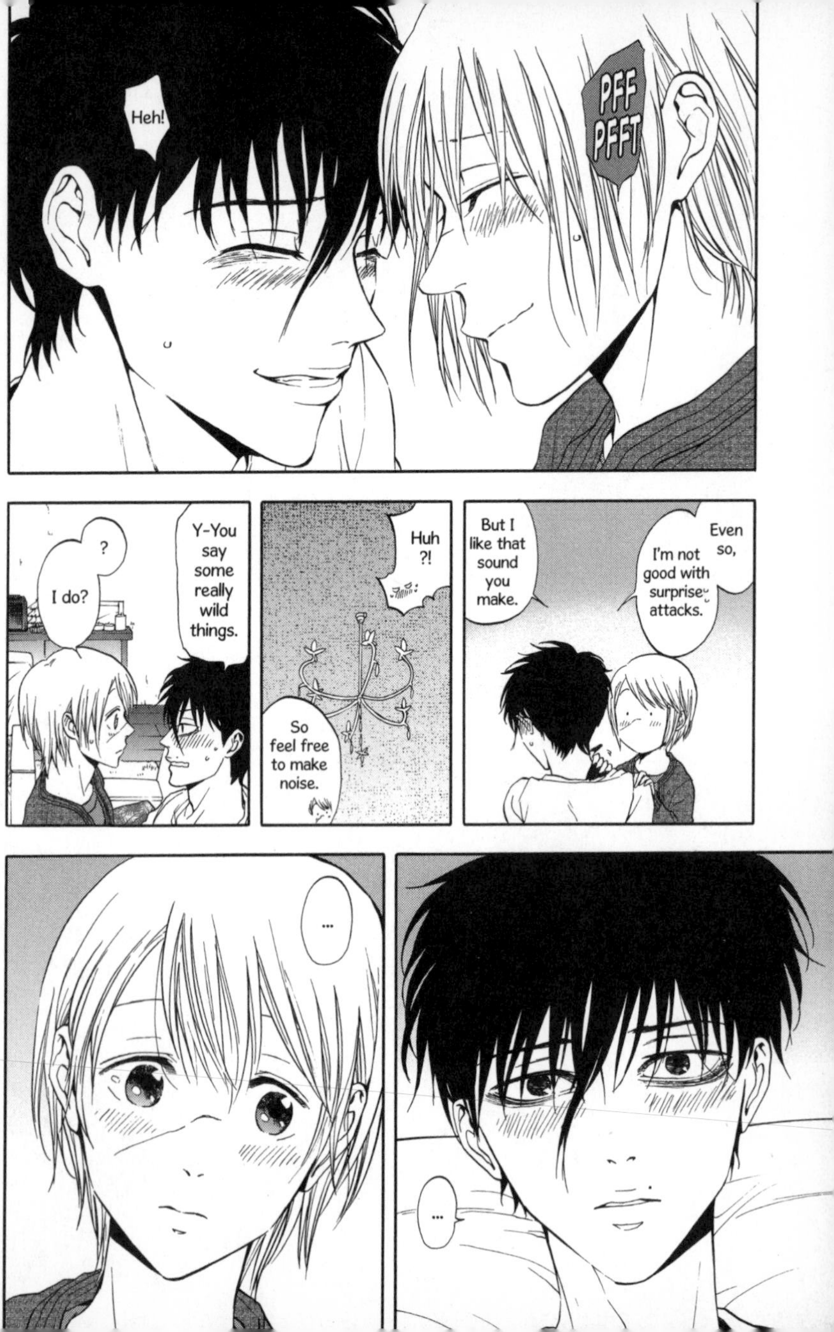
PFF PFFT
Heh!
Even so, I'm not good with surprise attacks.
But I like that sound you make.
Huh?!
So feel free to make noise.
Y-You say some really wild things.
? I do?
...
...

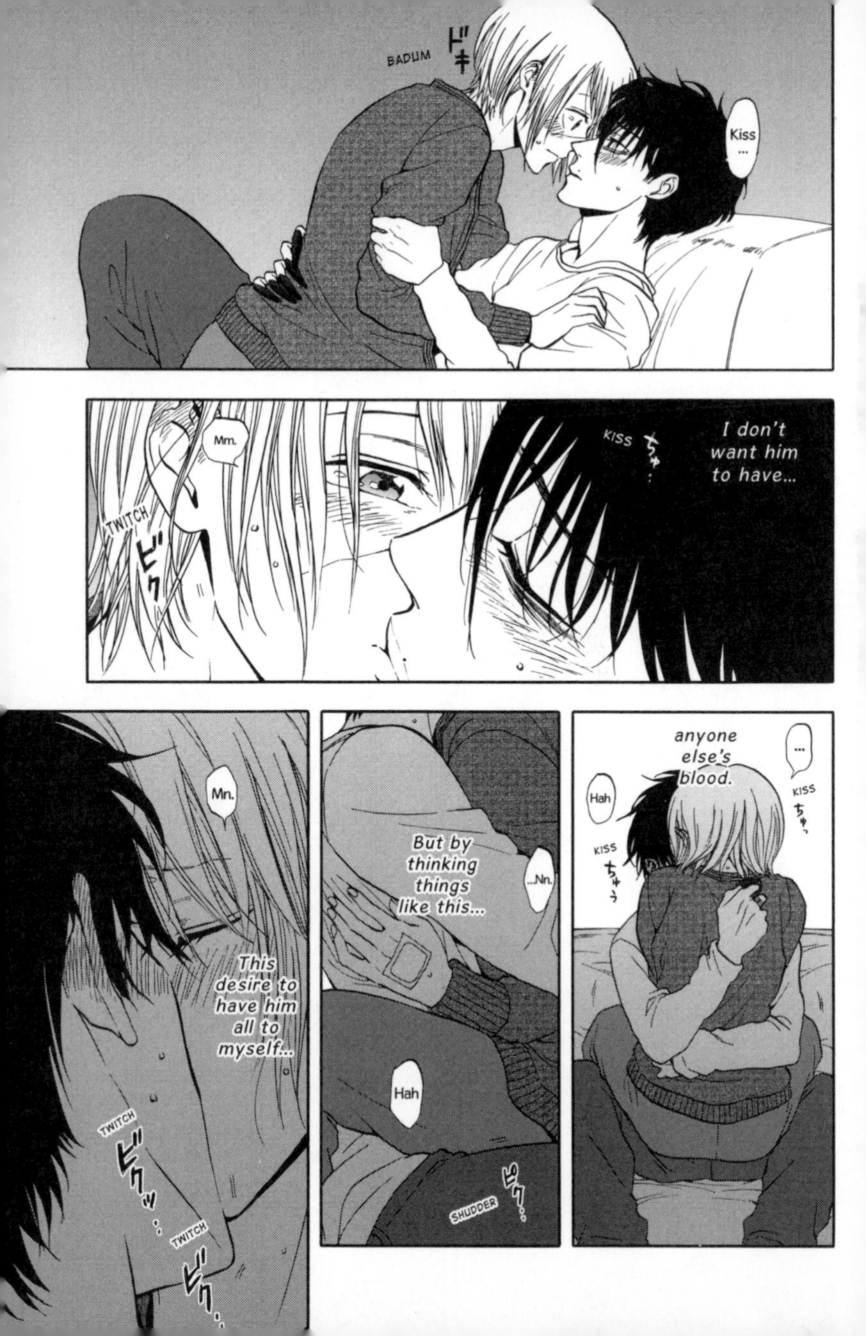
Kiss...
BADUM ドキ
I don't want him to have...
KISS ちゃ
Mm.
TWITCH ビク
anyone else's blood.
...
KISS ちゅっ
Hah
KISS ちゅう
But by thinking things like this...
...Nn.
Hah
SHUDDER ビク..
Mn.
This desire to have him all to myself...
TWITCH ビクッ..
TWITCH ビク..

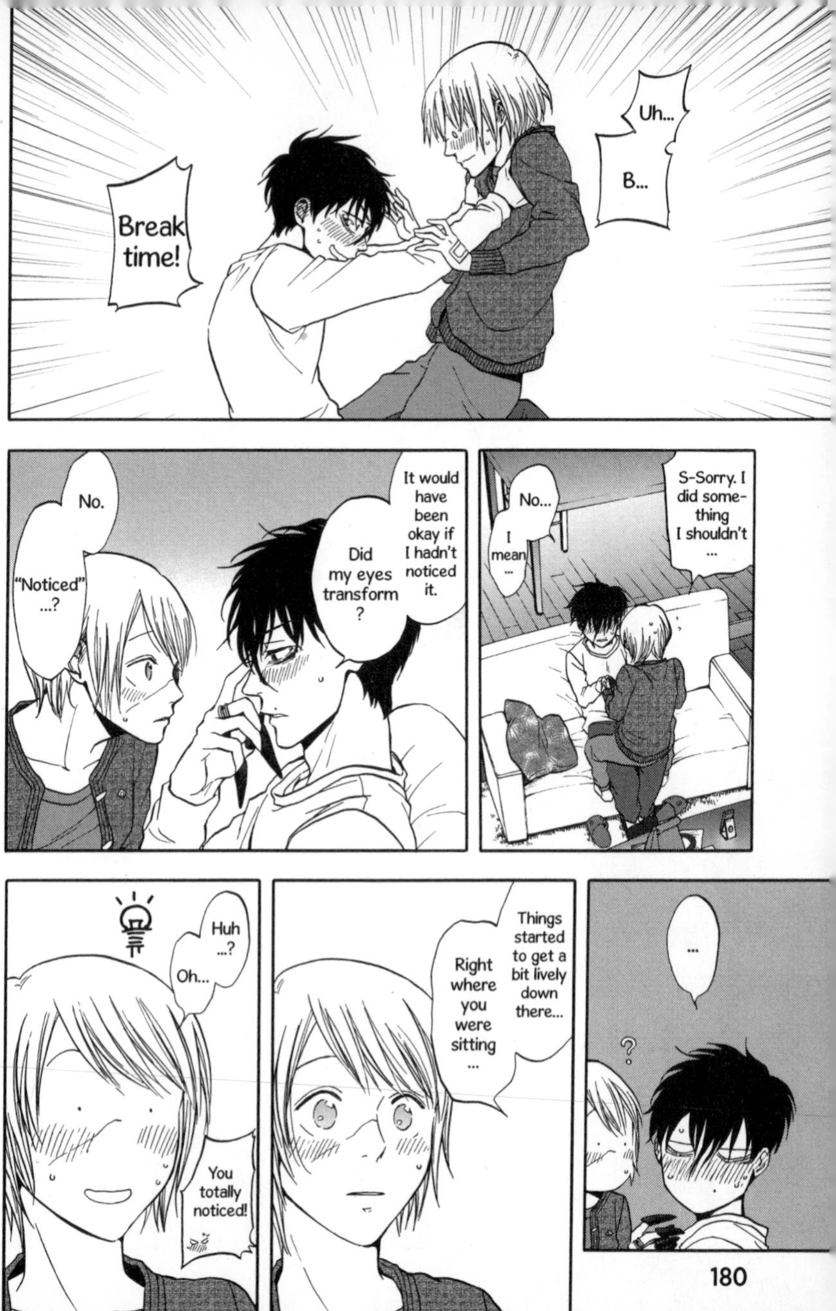
Uh...
B...
Break time!
S-Sorry. I did something I shouldn't ...
No...
I mean ...
It would have been okay if I hadn't noticed it.
Did my eyes transform ?
No.
"Noticed" ...?
...
Things started to get a bit lively down there...
Right where you were sitting ...
Huh ...?
Oh...
You totally noticed!

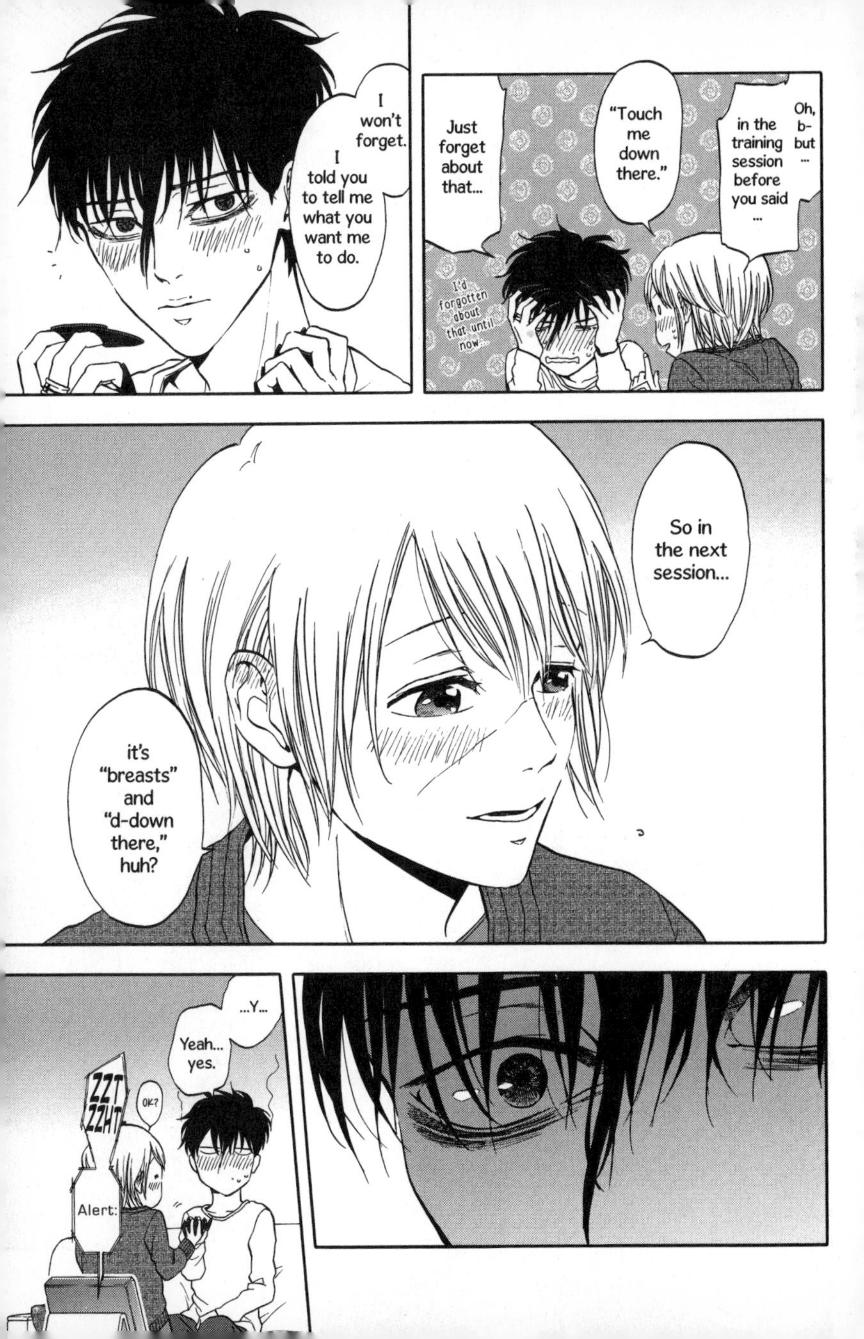
Oh, b-but...
in the training session before you said...
"Touch me down there."
Just forget about that...
I'd forgotten about that until now...
I won't forget.
I told you to tell me what you want me to do.
So in the next session...
it's "breasts" and "d-down there," huh?
...Y...
Yeah... yes.
OK?
ZZT ZZHT
Alert:

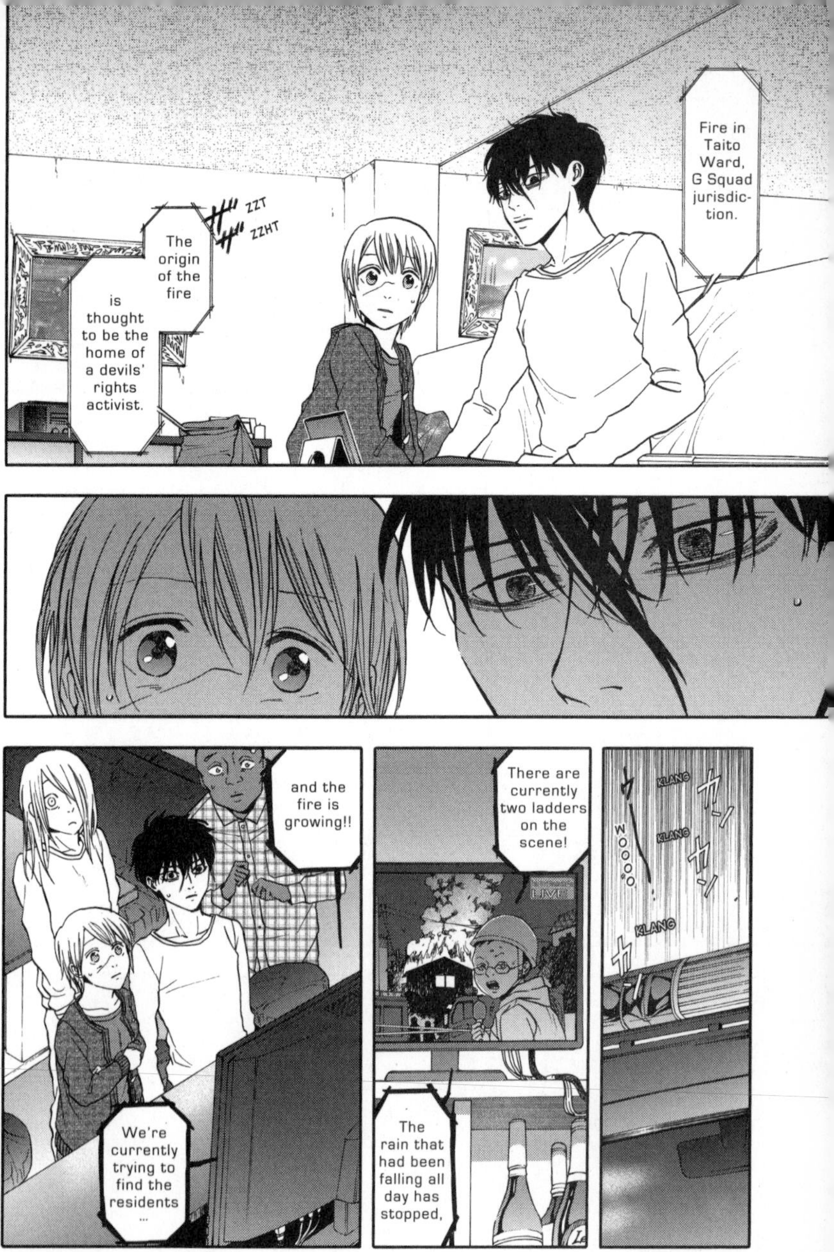
Fire in Taito Ward, G Squad jurisdic- tion.
ZZT
ZZHT
The origin of the fire
is thought to be the home of a devils' rights activist.
KLANG
KLANG
WOOOO
KLANG
There are currently two ladders on the scene!
LIVE
The rain that had been falling all day has stopped,
and the fire is growing!!
We're currently trying to find the residents ...

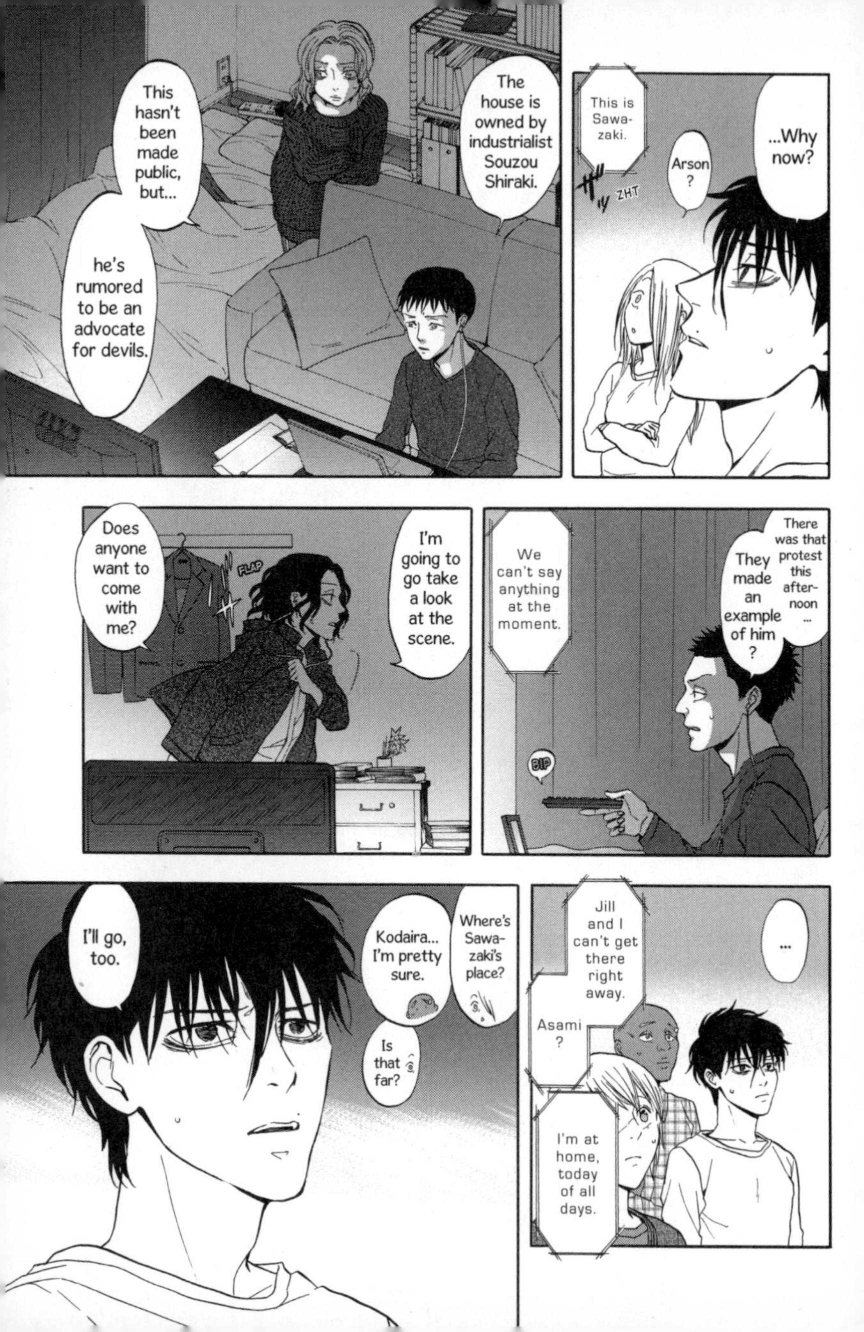
...Why now?
Arson?
This is Sawa-zaki.
ZHT
The house is owned by industrialist Souzou Shiraki.
This hasn't been made public, but...
he's rumored to be an advocate for devils.
There was that protest this after-noon ...
They made an example of him?
We can't say anything at the moment.
BIP
I'm going to go take a look at the scene.
FLAP
Does anyone want to come with me?
...
Jill and I can't get there right away.
Asami?
I'm at home, today of all days.
Where's Sawa-zaki's place?
Kodaira... I'm pretty sure.
Is that far?
I'll go, too.

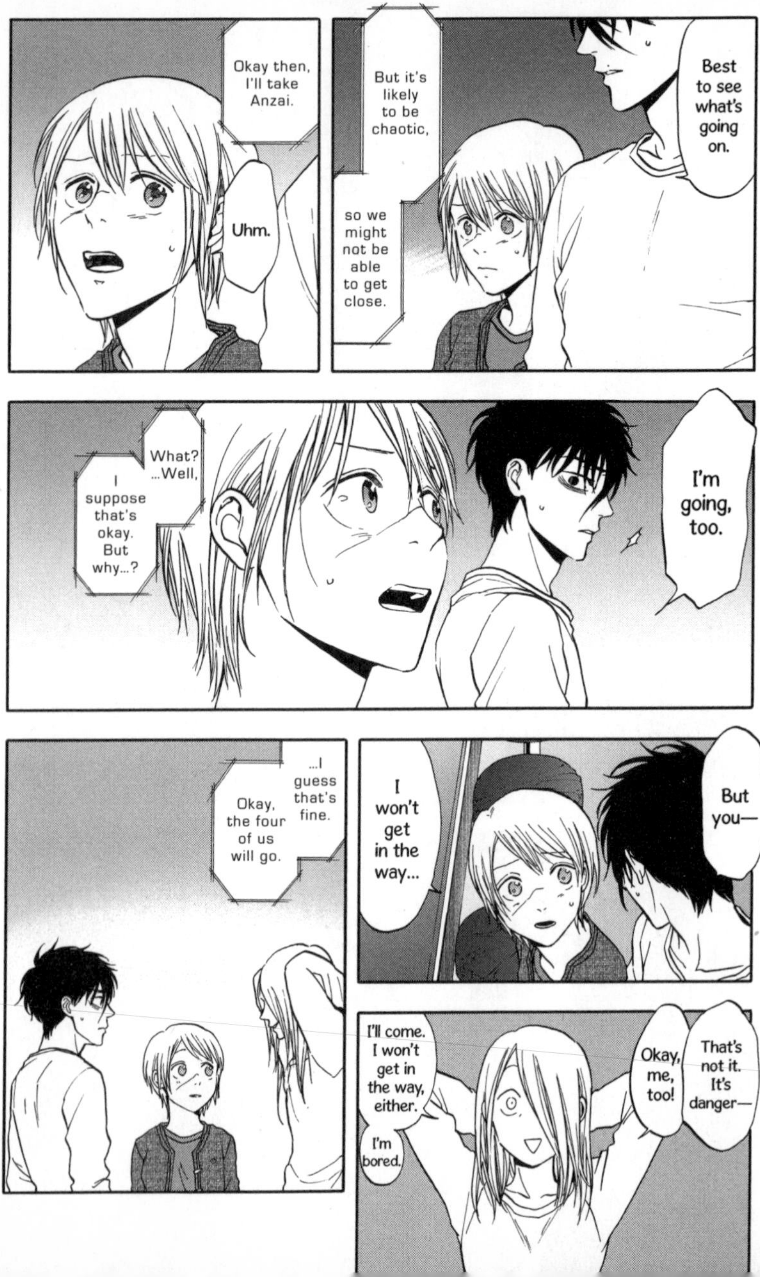
Best to see what's going on.
But it's likely to be chaotic,
so we might not be able to get close.
Okay then, I'll take Anzai.
Uhm.
I'm going, too.
What? ...Well,
I suppose that's okay. But why...?
But you—
I won't get in the way...
That's not it. It's danger—
Okay, me, too!
I'll come. I won't get in the way, either.
I'm bored.
...I guess that's fine.
Okay, the four of us will go.

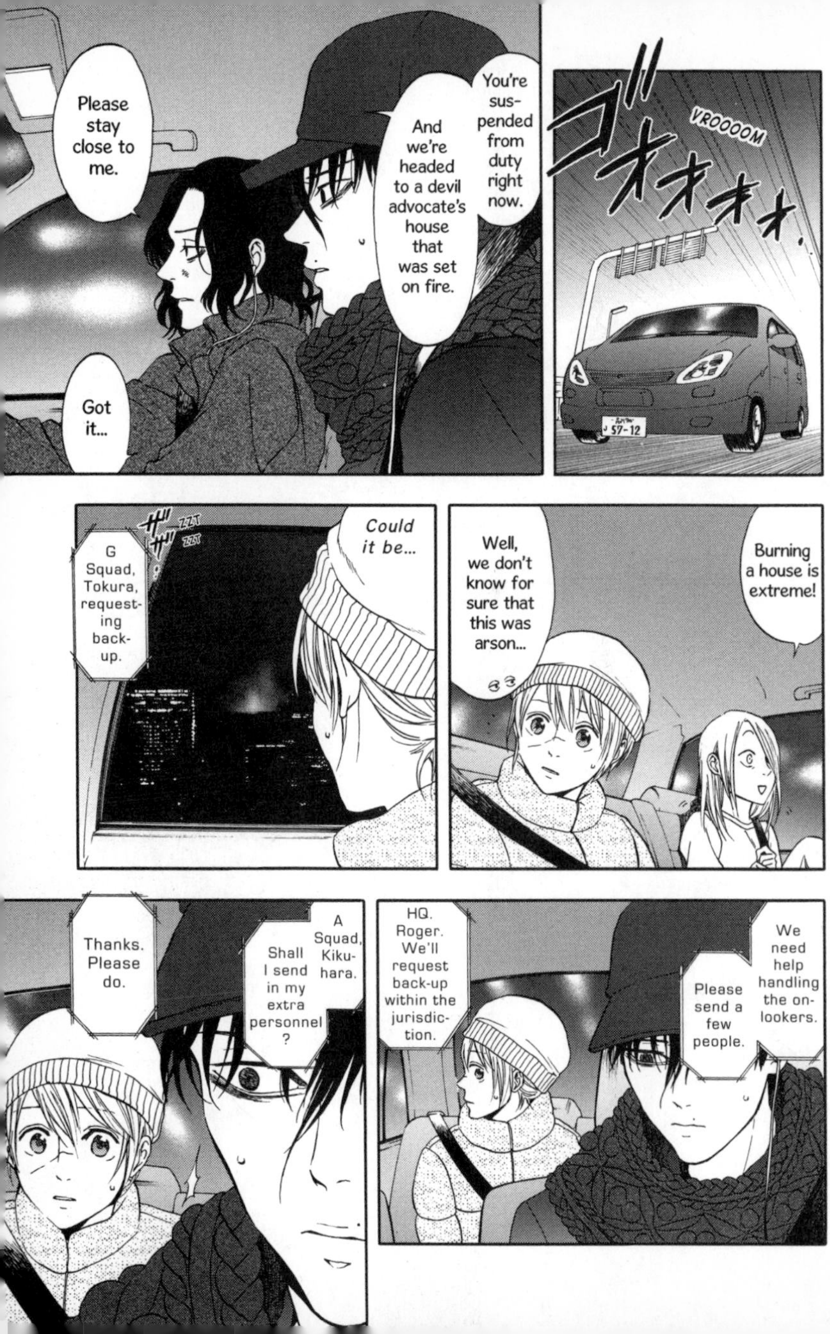
ゴオオオオ
VROOOOM
You're suspended from duty right now.
And we're headed to a devil advocate's house that was set on fire.
Please stay close to me.
Got it...
Burning a house is extreme!
Well, we don't know for sure that this was arson...
Could it be...
ZZT ZZT
G Squad, Tokura, requesting back-up.
We need help handling the onlookers.
Please send a few people.
HQ. Roger. We'll request back-up within the jurisdiction.
A Squad, Kikuhara.
Shall I send in my extra personnel?
Thanks. Please do.

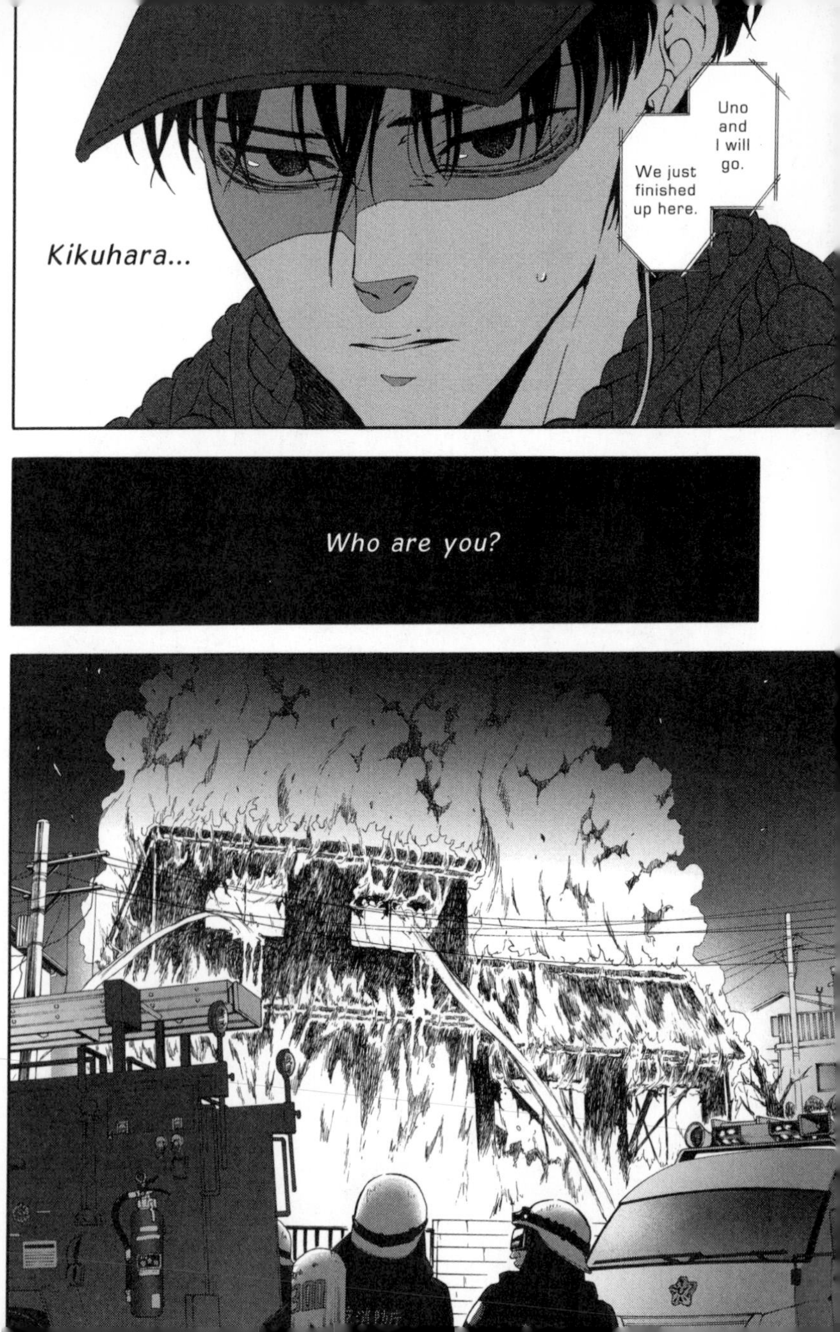
Uno and I will go.
We just finished up here.
Kikuhara...
Who are you?

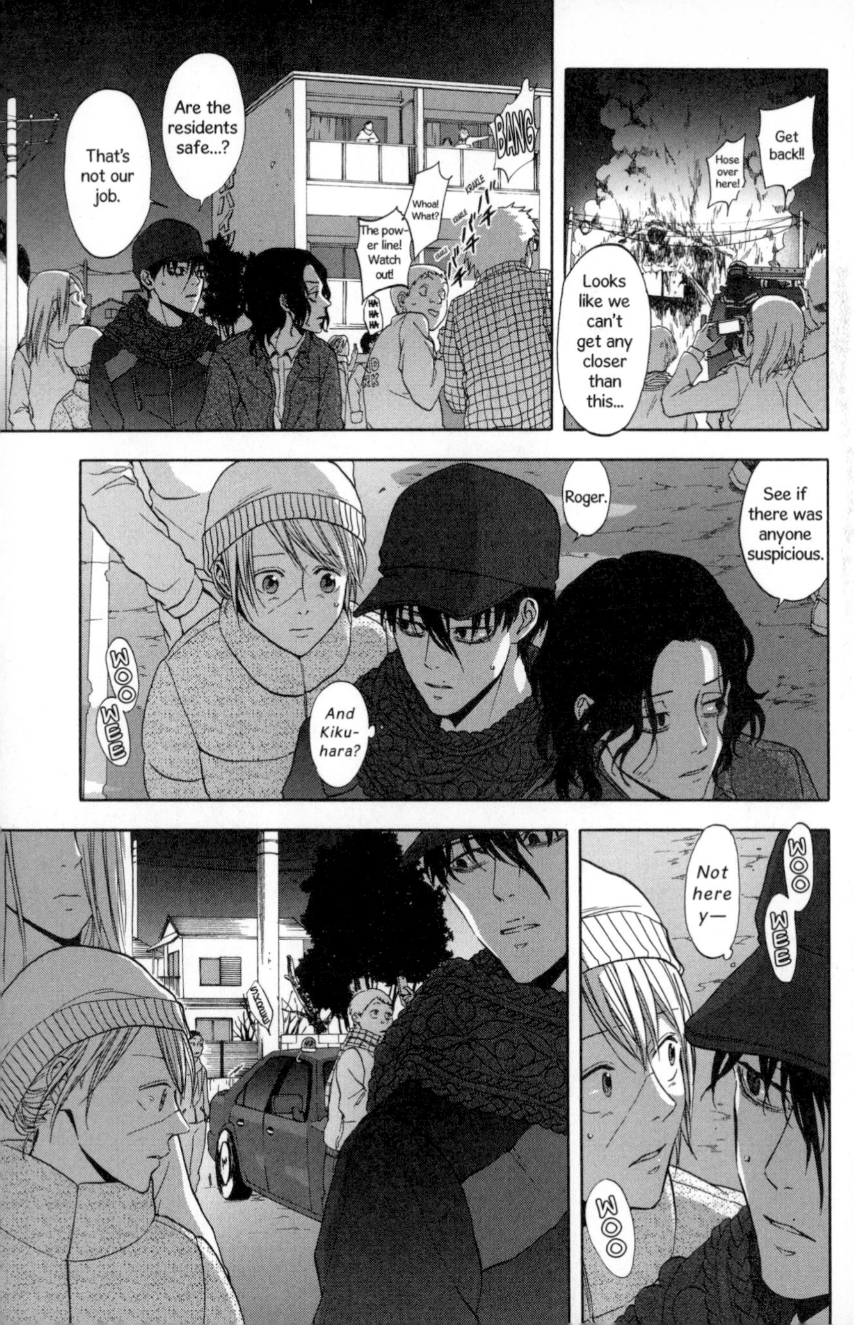
Get back!!
Hose over here!
Looks like we can't get any closer than this...
Are the residents safe...?
That's not our job.
BANG
KRACKLE
Whoa! What?
The power line! Watch out!
See if there was anyone suspicious.
Roger.
And Kiku-hara?
WOO WEE
WOO WEE
Not here y—
WOO

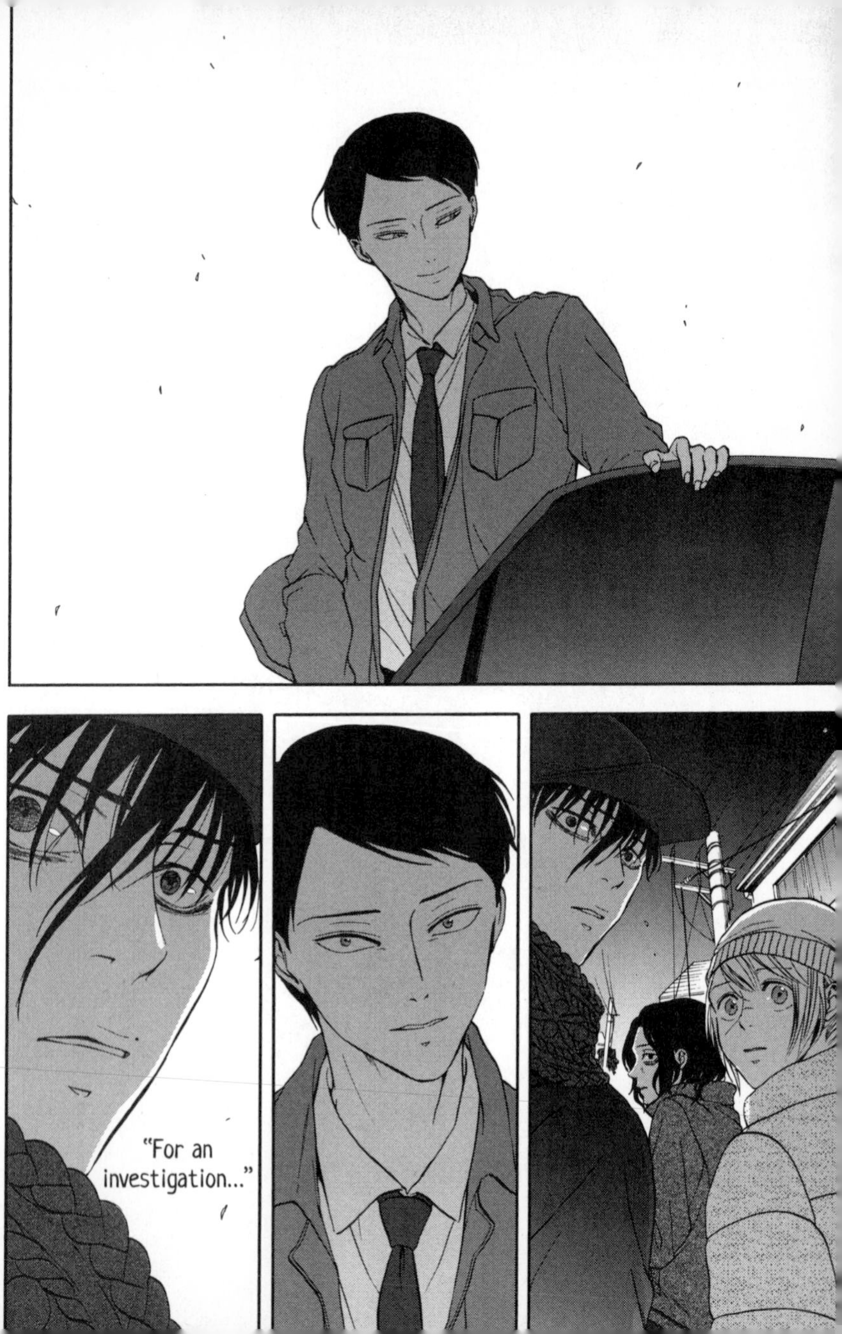
"For an investigation..."

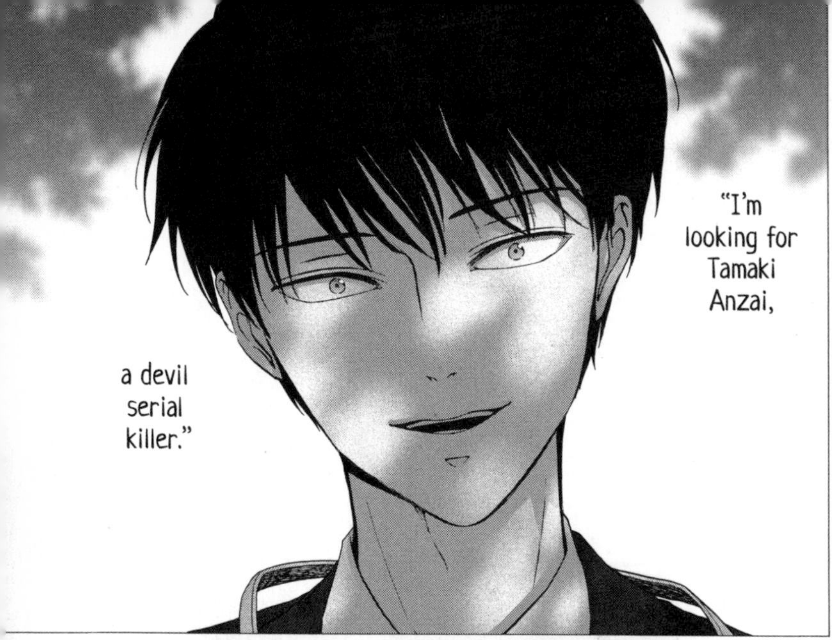
"I'm looking for Tamaki Anzai,
a devil serial killer."

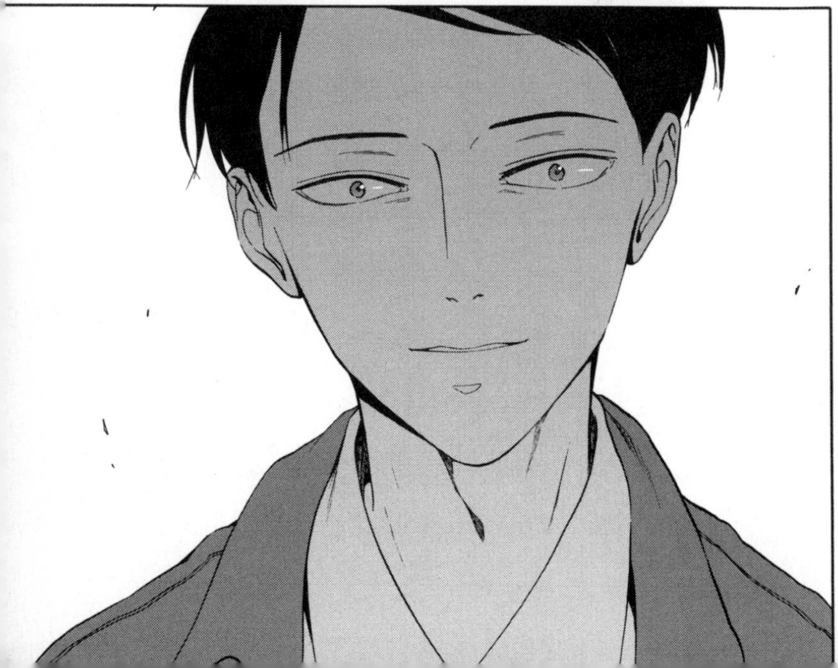

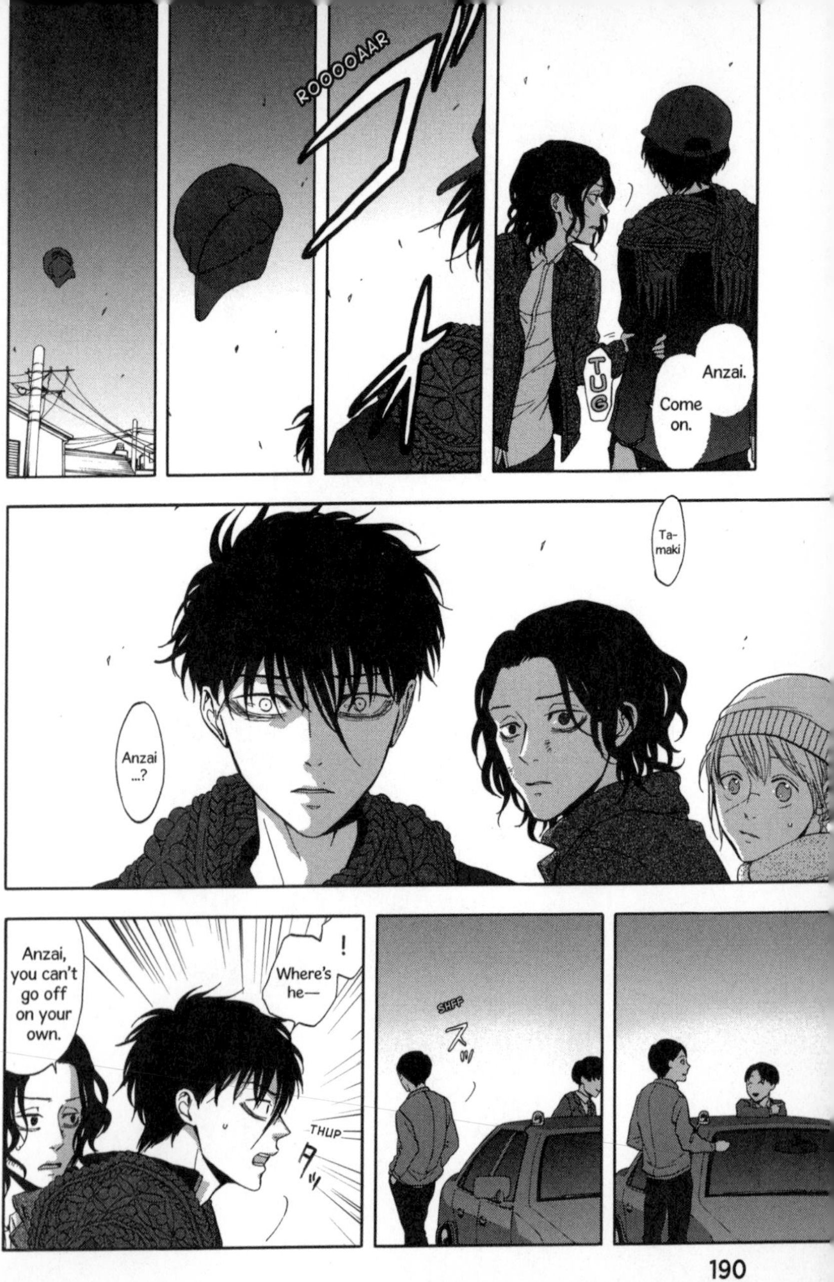
Anzai.
Come on.
TUG
ROOOOAAR
Ta-
maki
Anzai
...?
SHFF
!
Where's
he—
Anzai,
you can't
go off
on your
own.
THUP

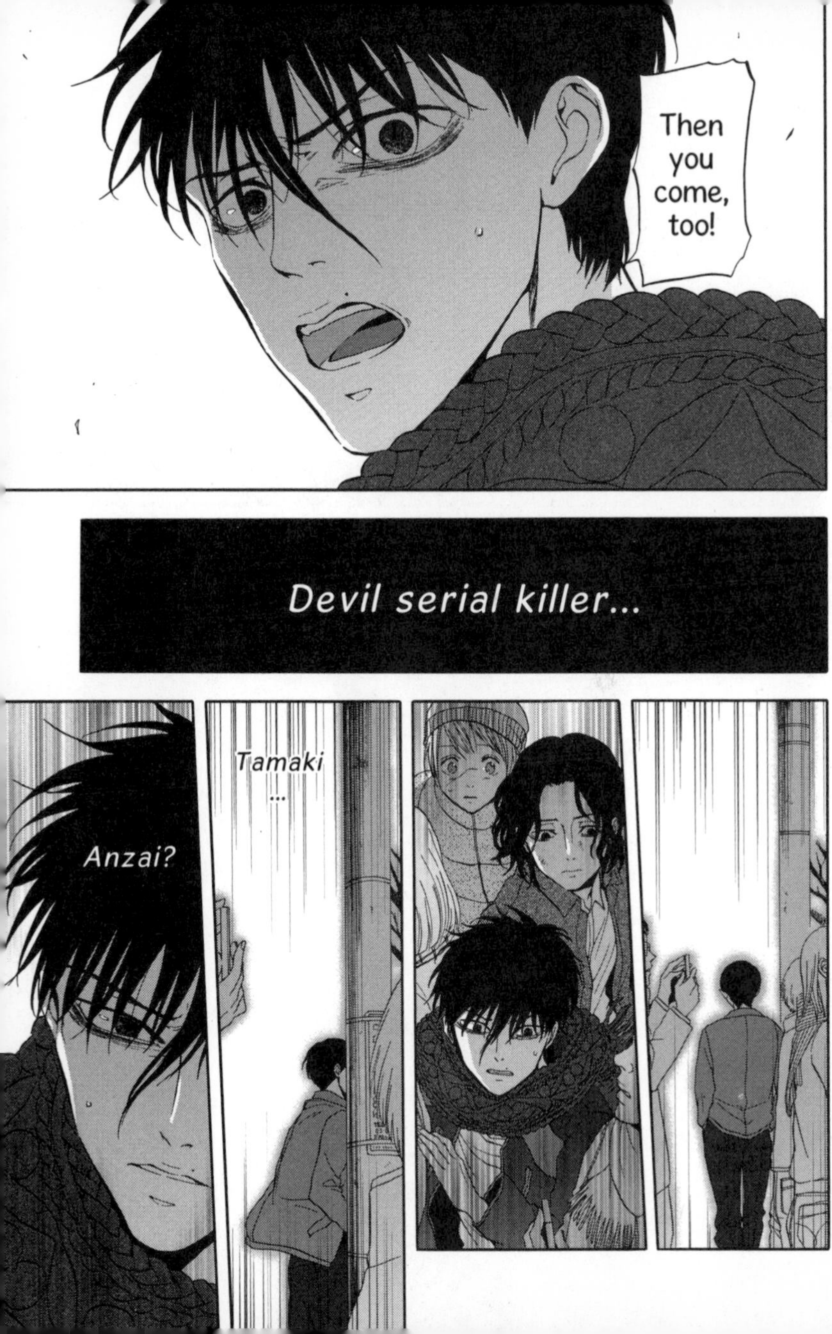
Then you come, too!
Devil serial killer...
Tamaki ...
Anzai?

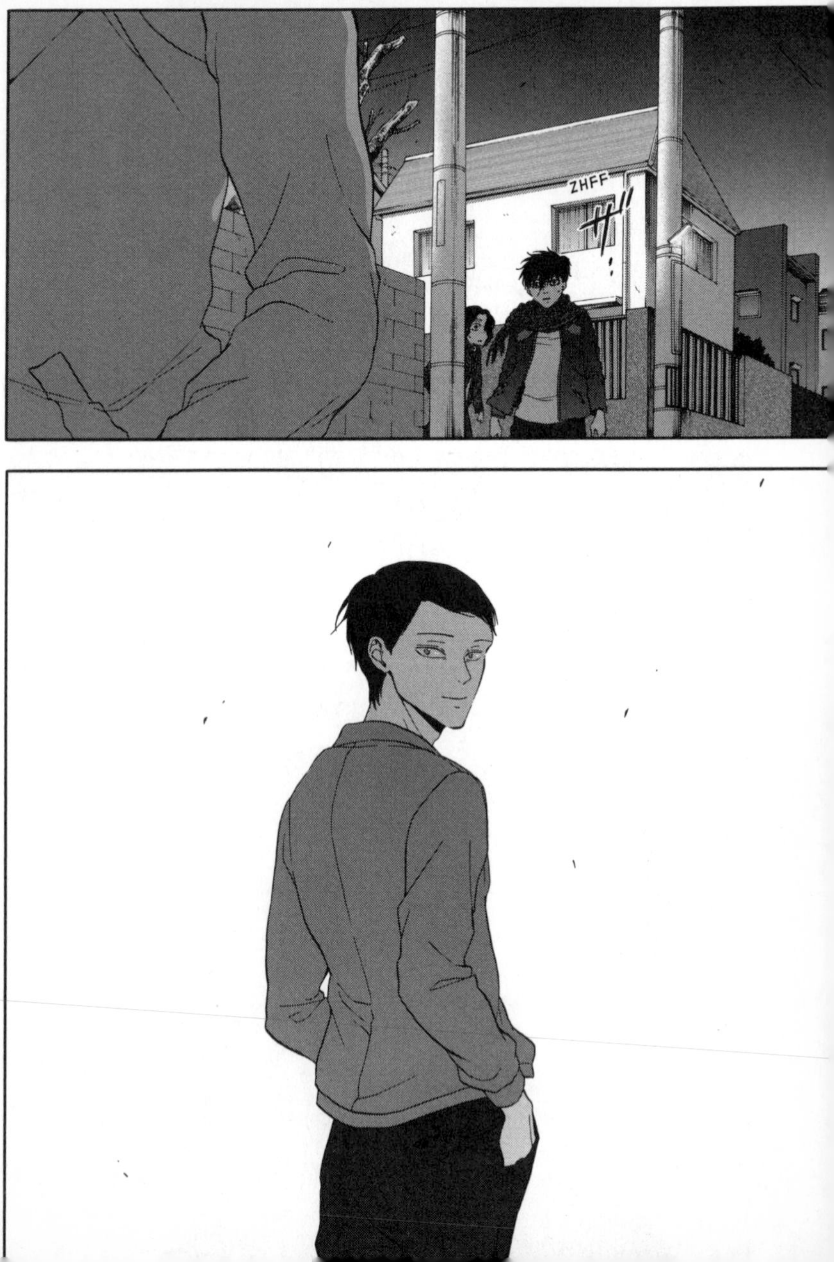
ZHFF

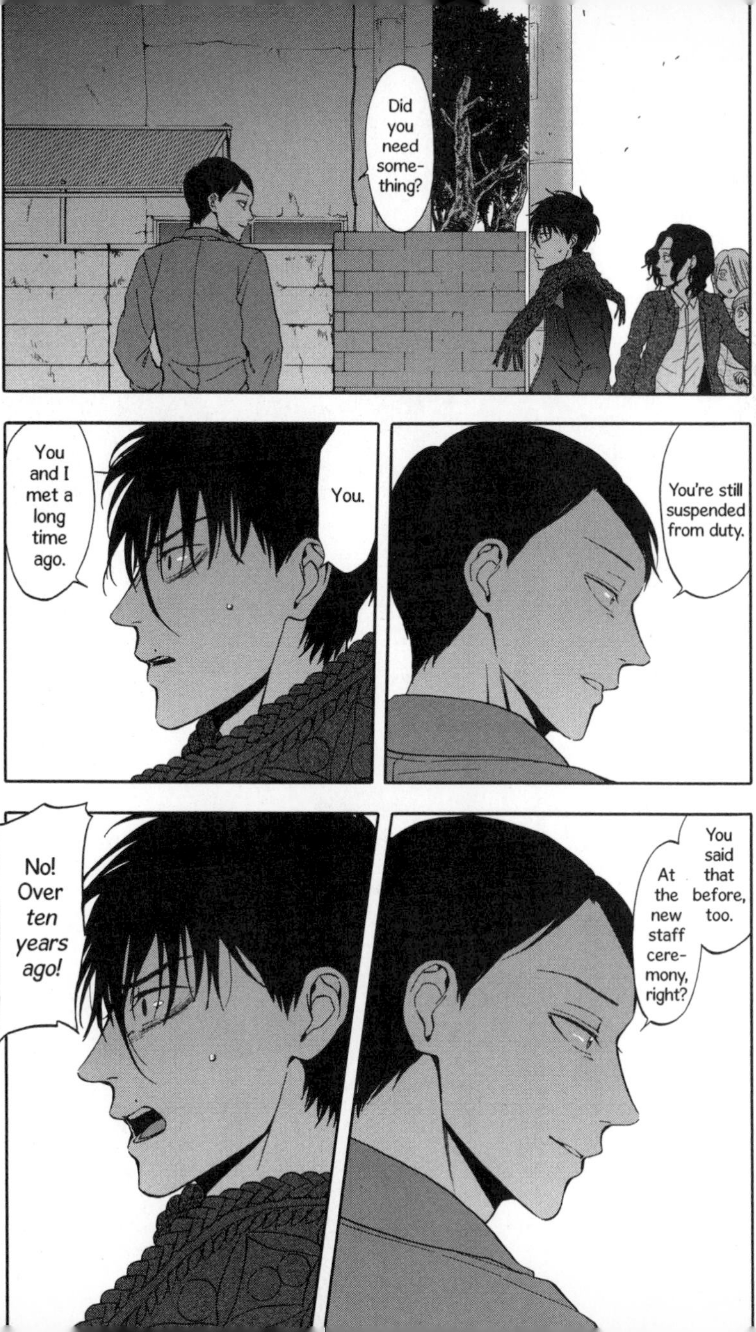
Did you need some-thing?
You're still suspended from duty.
You.
You and I met a long time ago.
You said that before, too.
At the new staff cere-mony, right?
No! Over *ten years ago!*

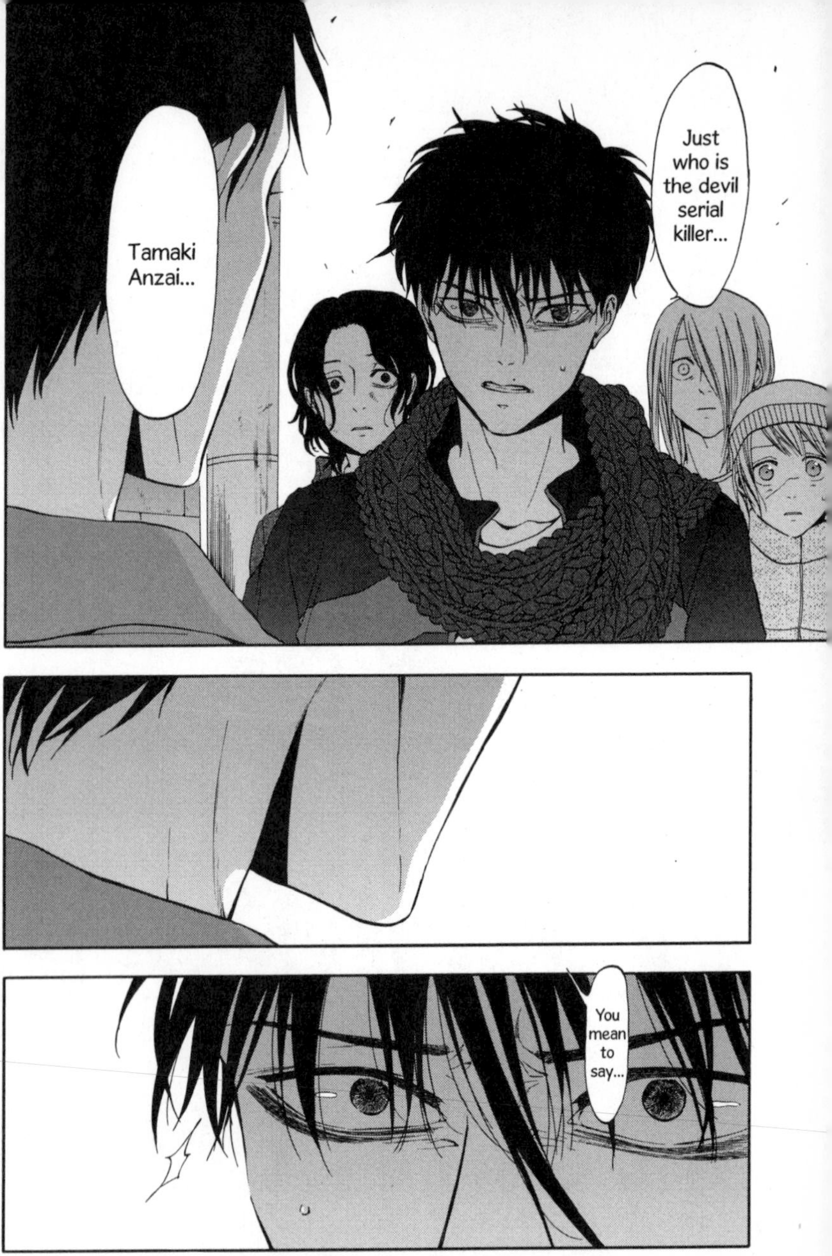
Just who is the devil serial killer...
Tamaki Anzai...
You mean to say...

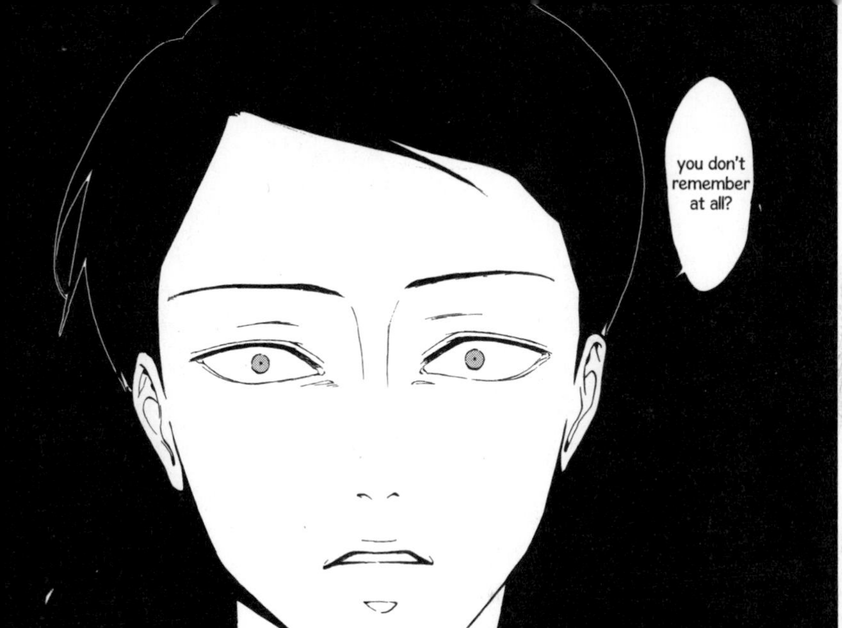
you don't remember at all?

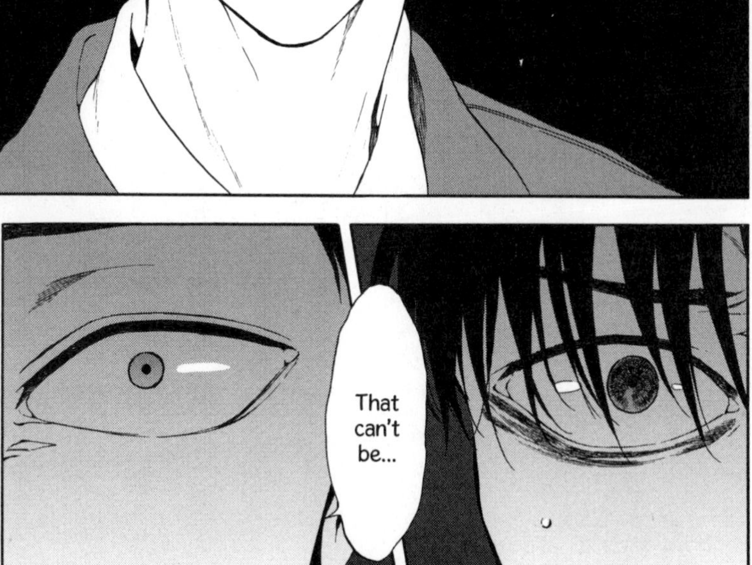
That can't be...

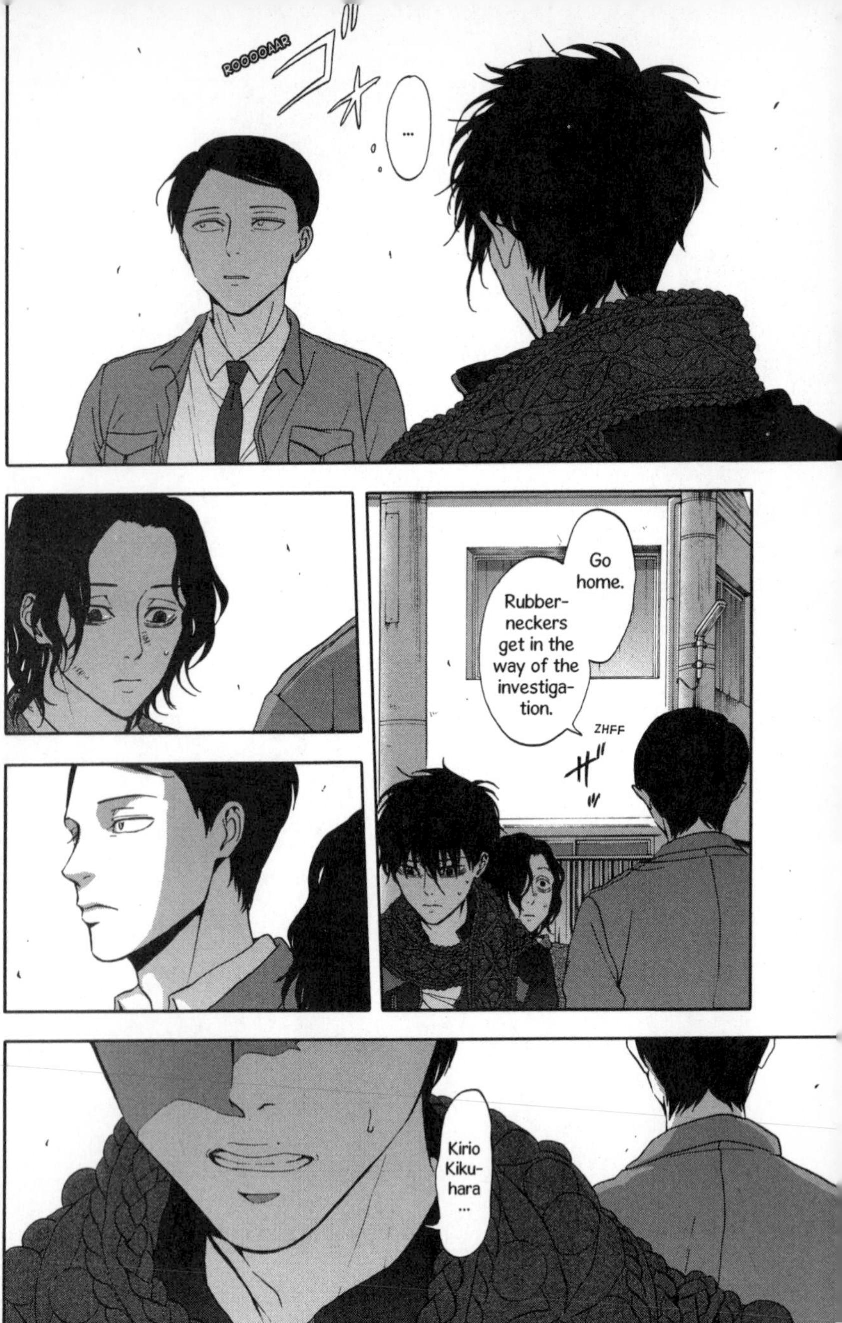
ROOOOAAR
...
Go home. Rubber-neckers get in the way of the investiga-tion.
ZHFF
Kirio Kiku-hara ...

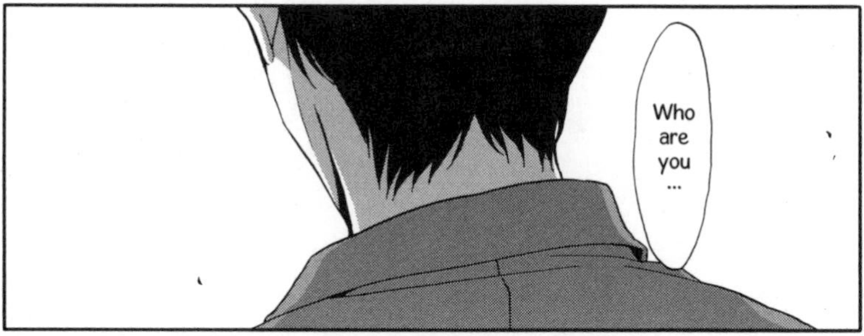
Who are you ...

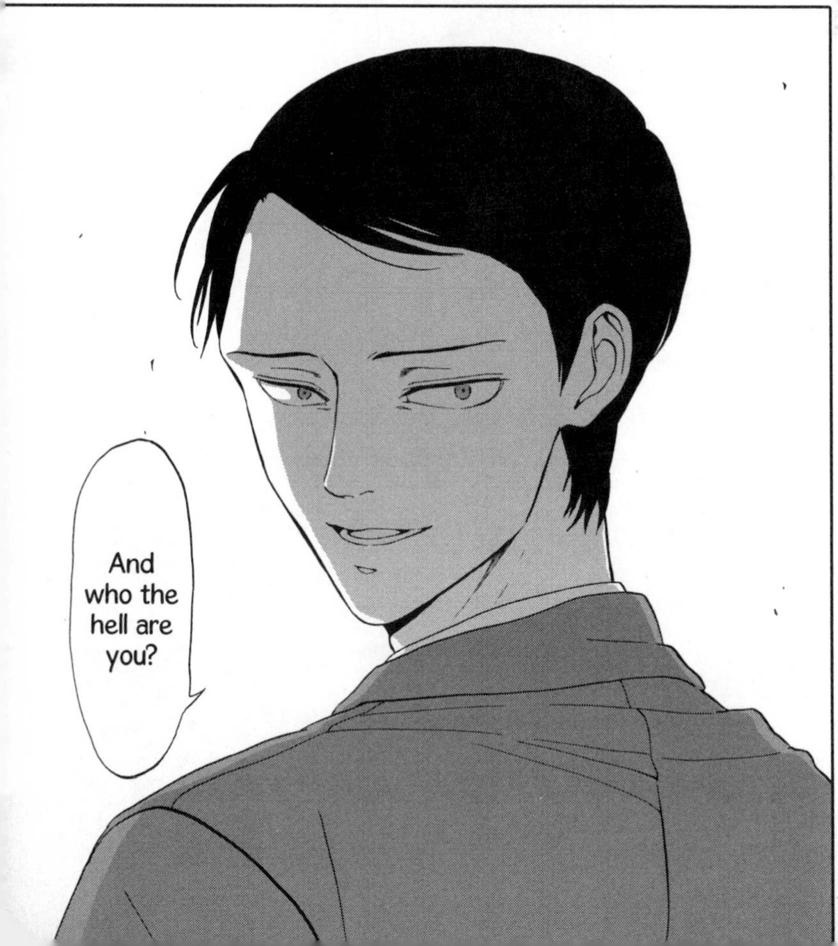
And who the hell are you?

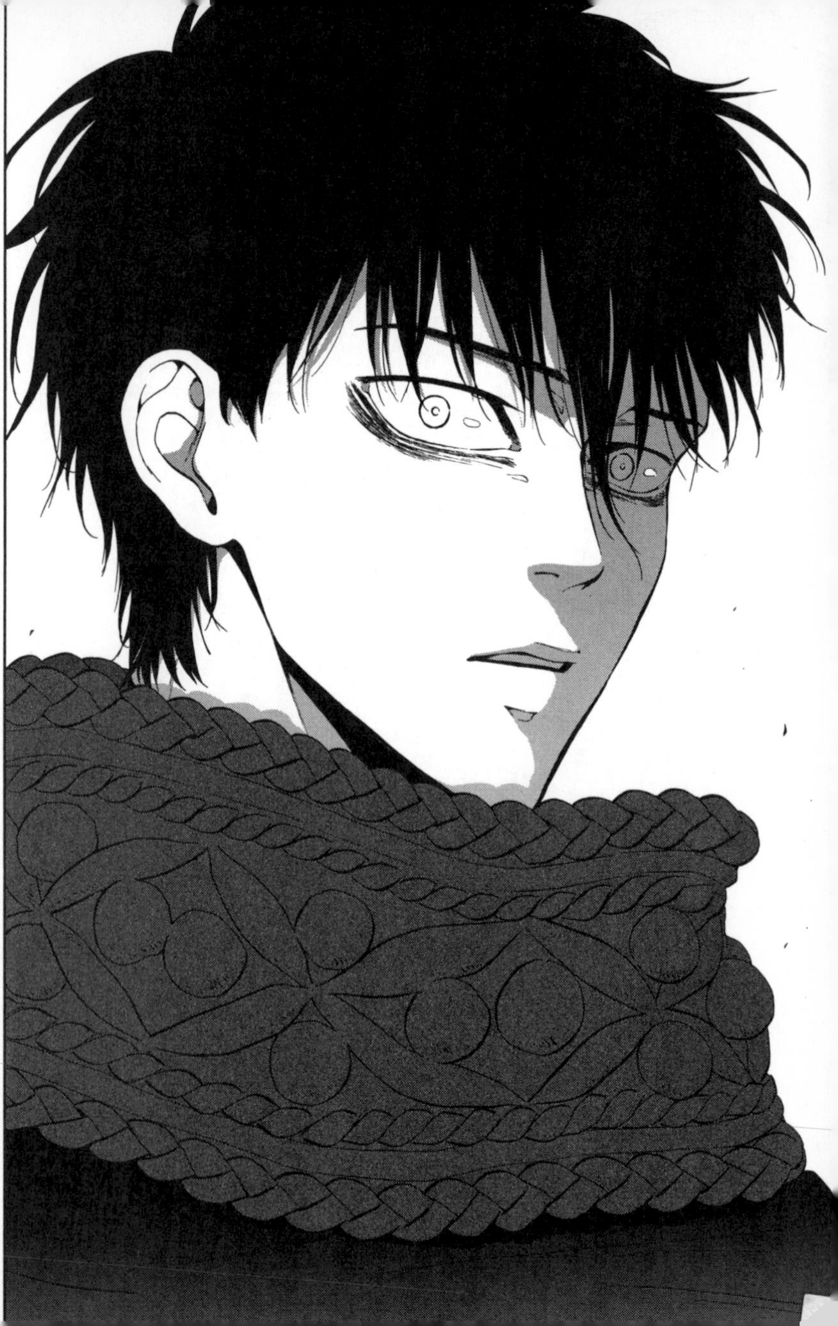

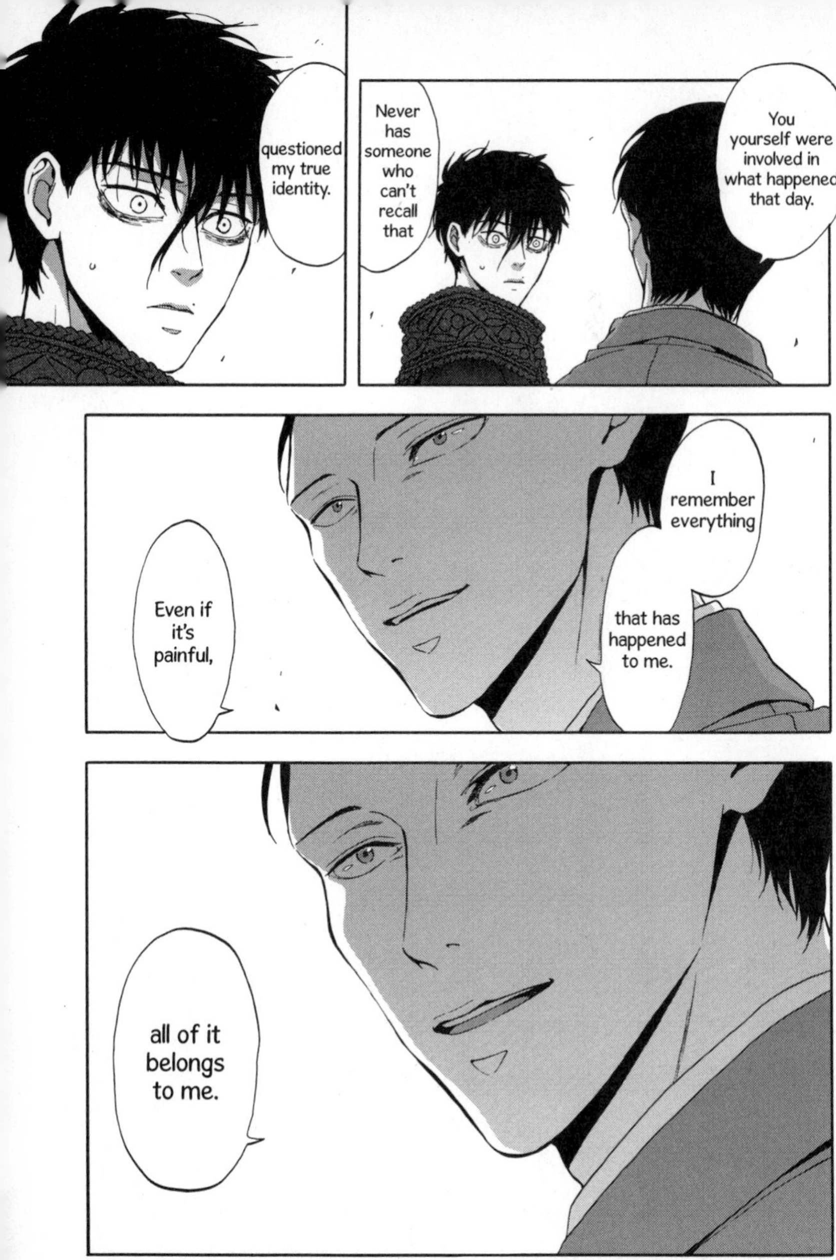
You yourself were involved in what happened that day.
Never has someone who can't recall that
questioned my true identity.
I remember everything
that has happened to me.
Even if it's painful,
all of it belongs to me.

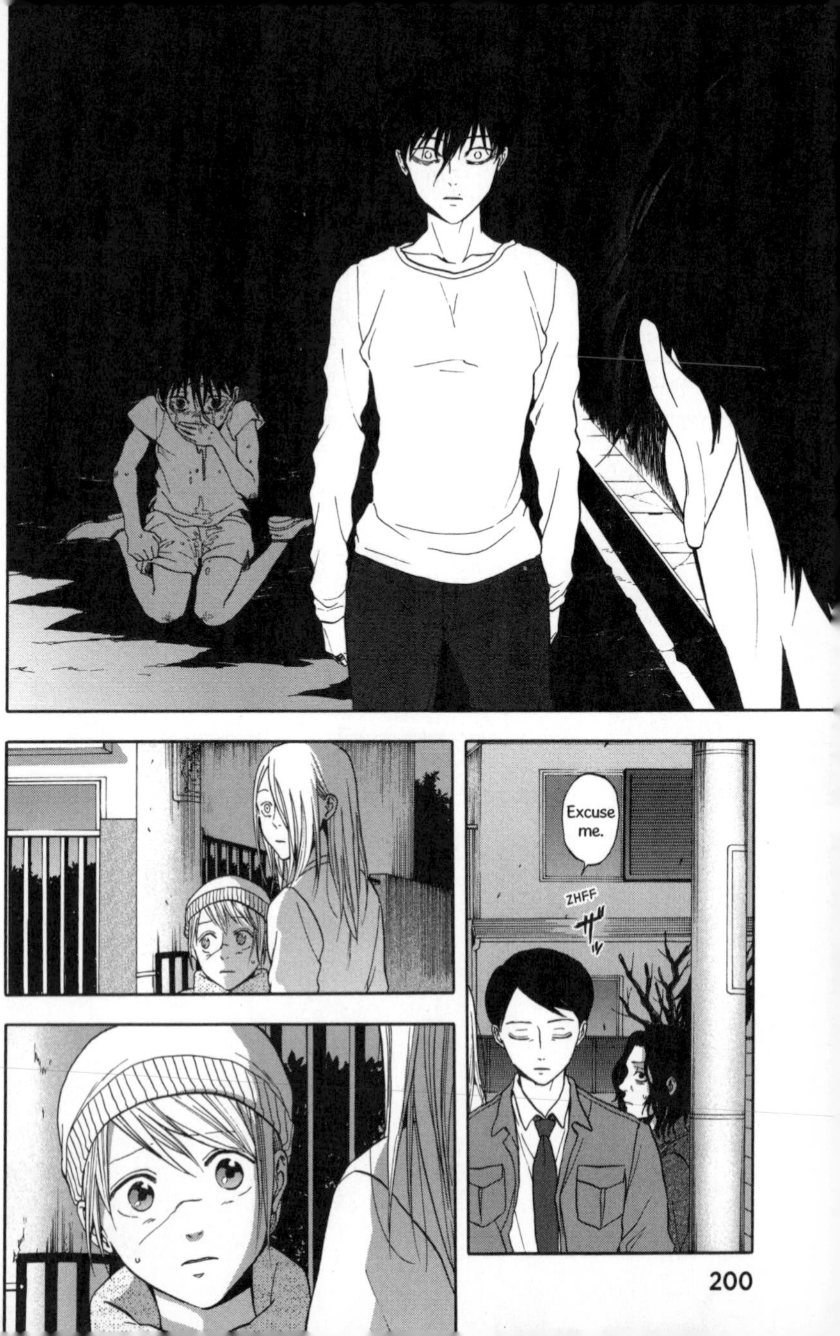
Excuse me.
ZHFF

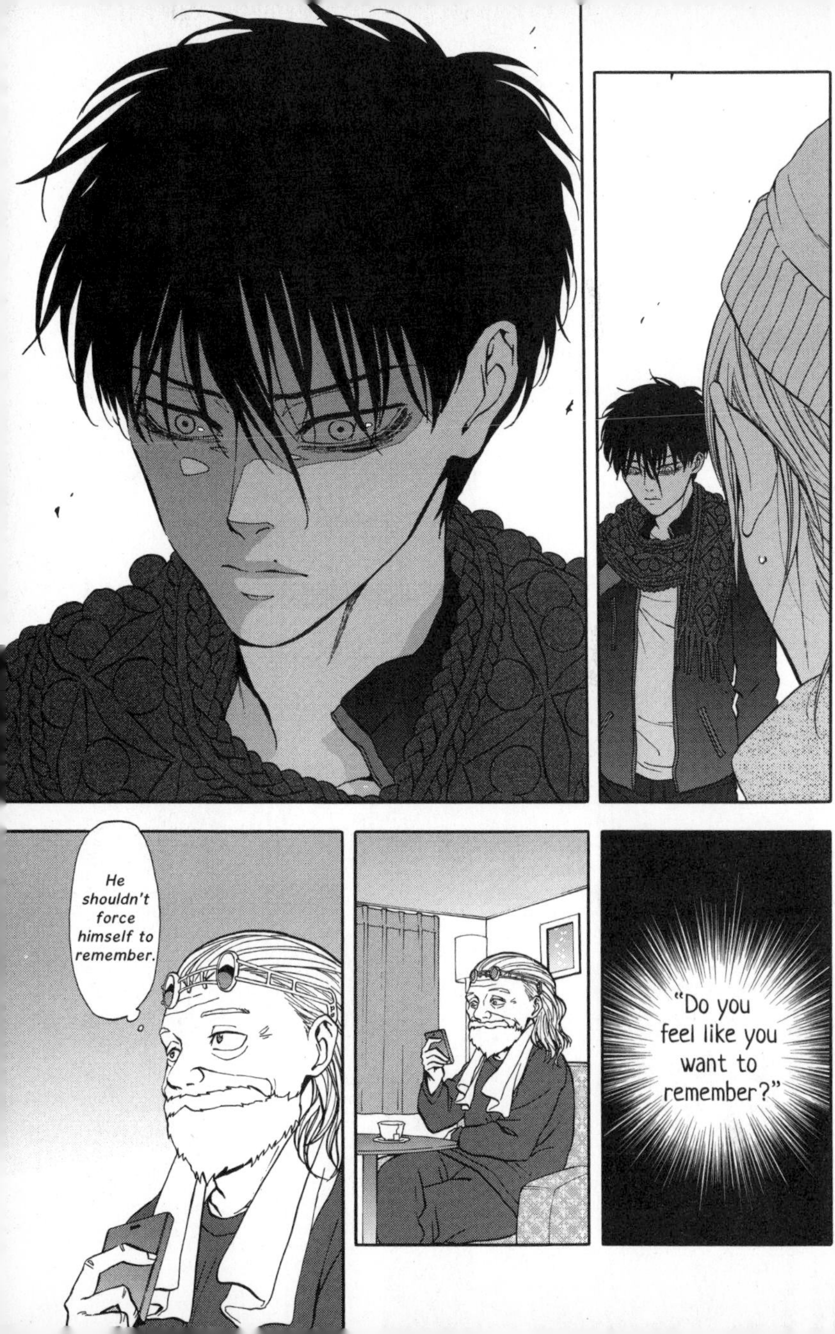
"Do you feel like you want to remember?"
He shouldn't force himself to remember.

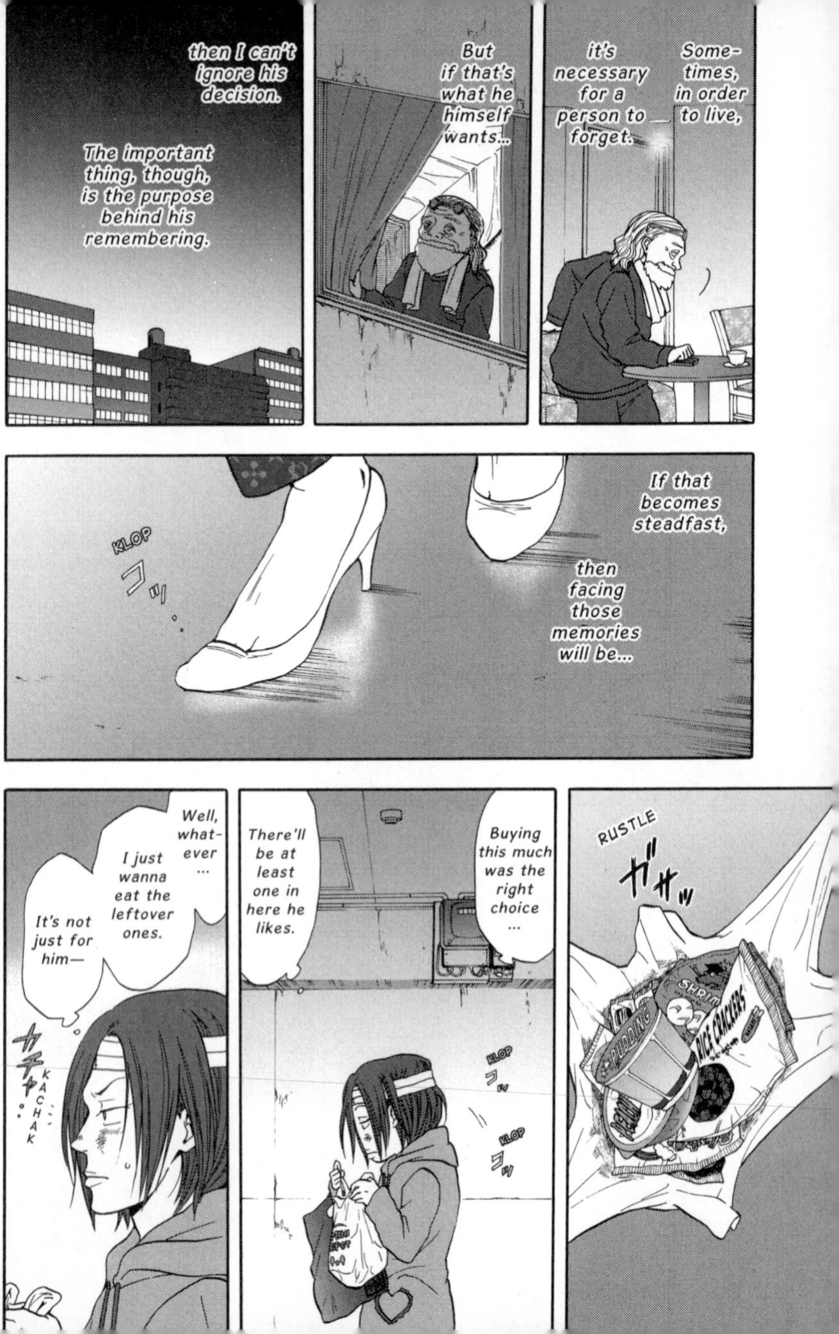
Sometimes, in order to live,
it's necessary for a person to forget.
But if that's what he himself wants...
then I can't ignore his decision.
The important thing, though, is the purpose behind his remembering.
If that becomes steadfast,
KLOP
then facing those memories will be...
RUSTLE
PUDDING
RICE CRACKERS
Buying this much was the right choice ...
There'll be at least one in here he likes.
KLOP
KLOP
Well, whatever ...
I just wanna eat the leftover ones.
It's not just for him—
KACHAK

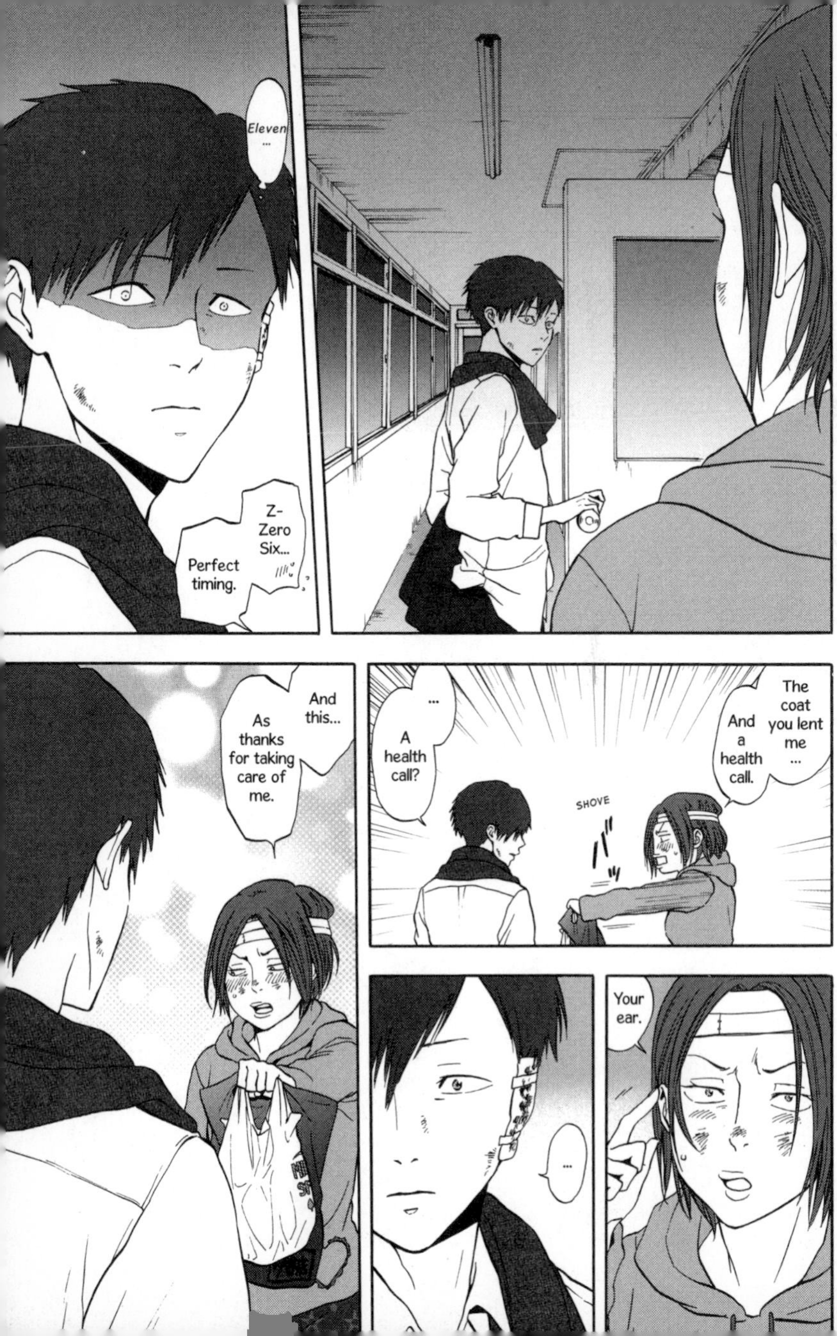
Eleven...
Z- Zero Six...
Perfect timing.
The coat you lent me...
And a health call.
SHOVE
... A health call?
Your ear.
...
And this...
As thanks for taking care of me.

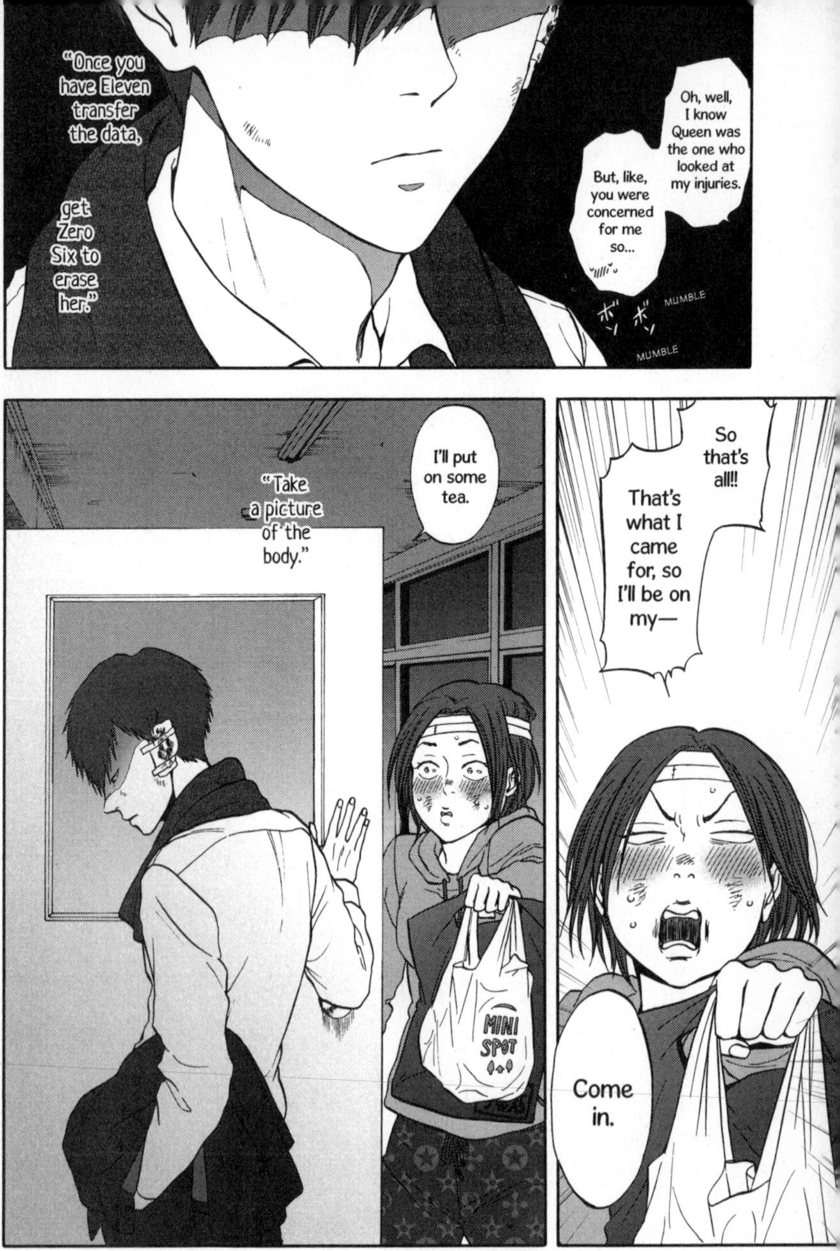
Oh, well, I know Queen was the one who looked at my injuries.
But, like, you were concerned for me so...
ボソ ボソ
MUMBLE
MUMBLE
"Once you have Eleven transfer the data,
get Zero Six to erase her."
So that's all!!
That's what I came for, so I'll be on my—
Come in.
I'll put on some tea.
"Take a picture of the body."

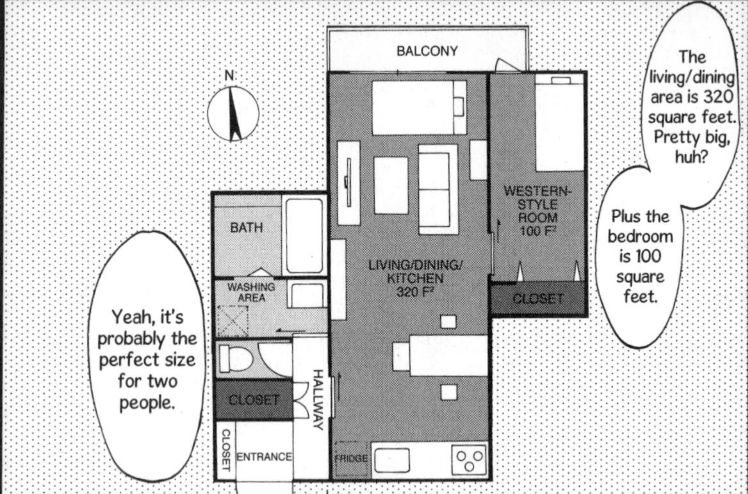
The living/dining area is 320 square feet. Pretty big, huh?
Plus the bedroom is 100 square feet.
Yeah, it's probably the perfect size for two people.
BALCONY
N
WESTERN-STYLE ROOM 100 F²
CLOSET
LIVING/DINING/KITCHEN 320 F²
BATH
WASHING AREA
HALLWAY
CLOSET
CLOSET
ENTRANCE
FRIDGE

Previously unpublished Line 29.5

Go Nowhere

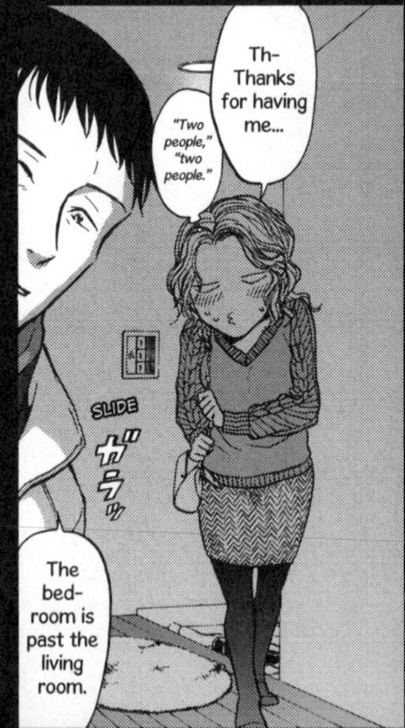
Th- Thanks for having me...
"Two people," "two people."
SLIDE
The bed-room is past the living room.

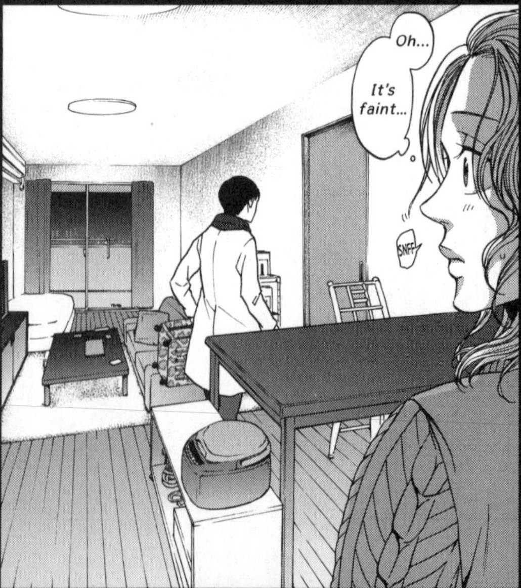
Oh...
It's faint...
SNFF

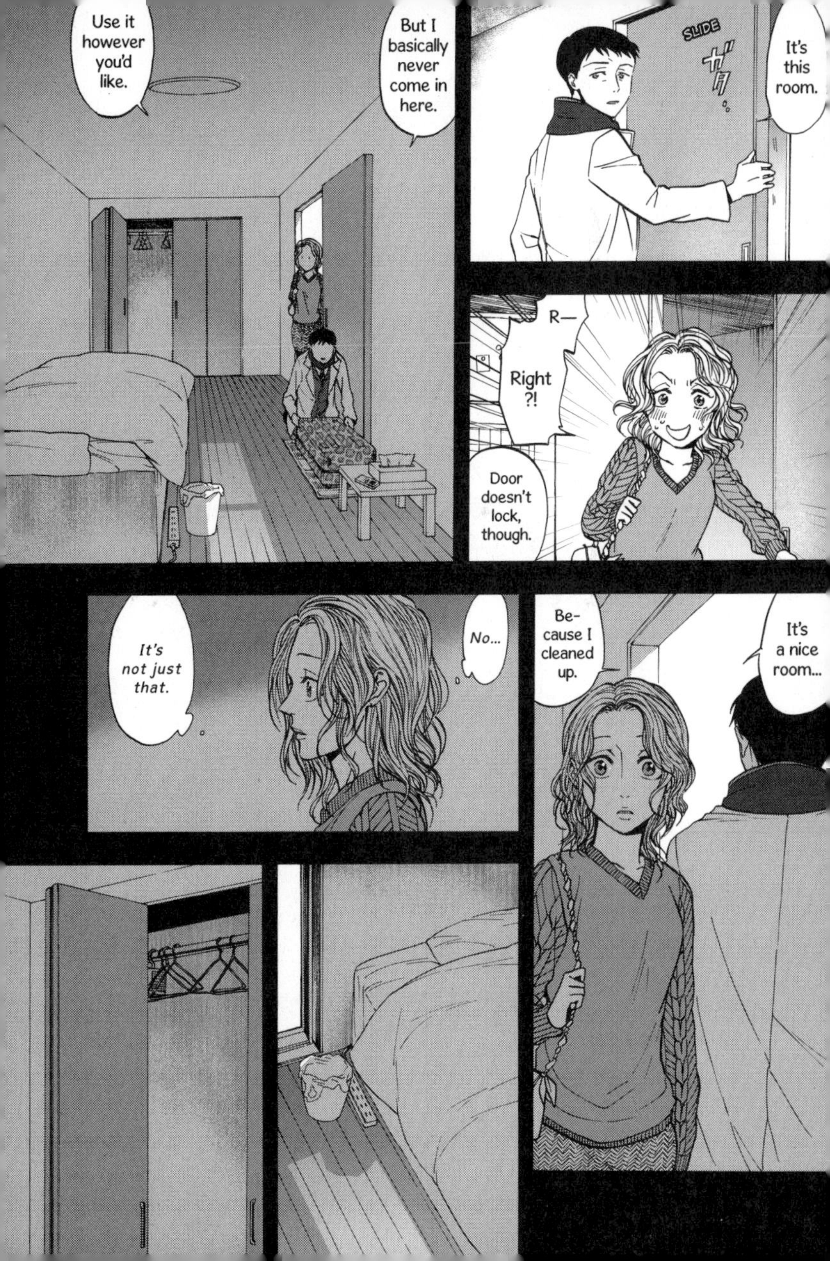
SLIDE
ガタ
It's this room.
R—
Right ?!
Door doesn't lock, though.
But I basically never come in here.
Use it however you'd like.
It's a nice room...
Be-cause I cleaned up.
No...
It's not just that.

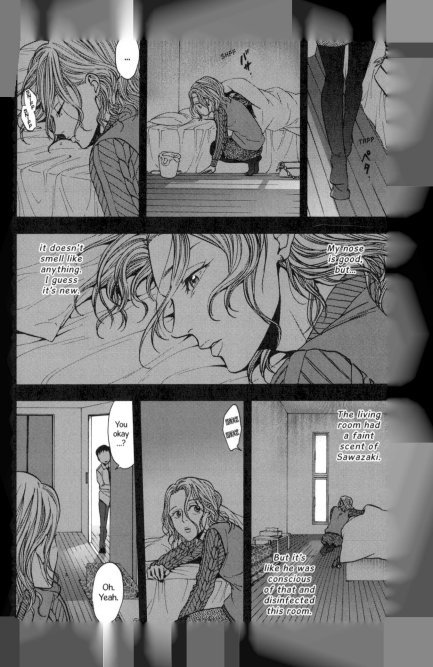

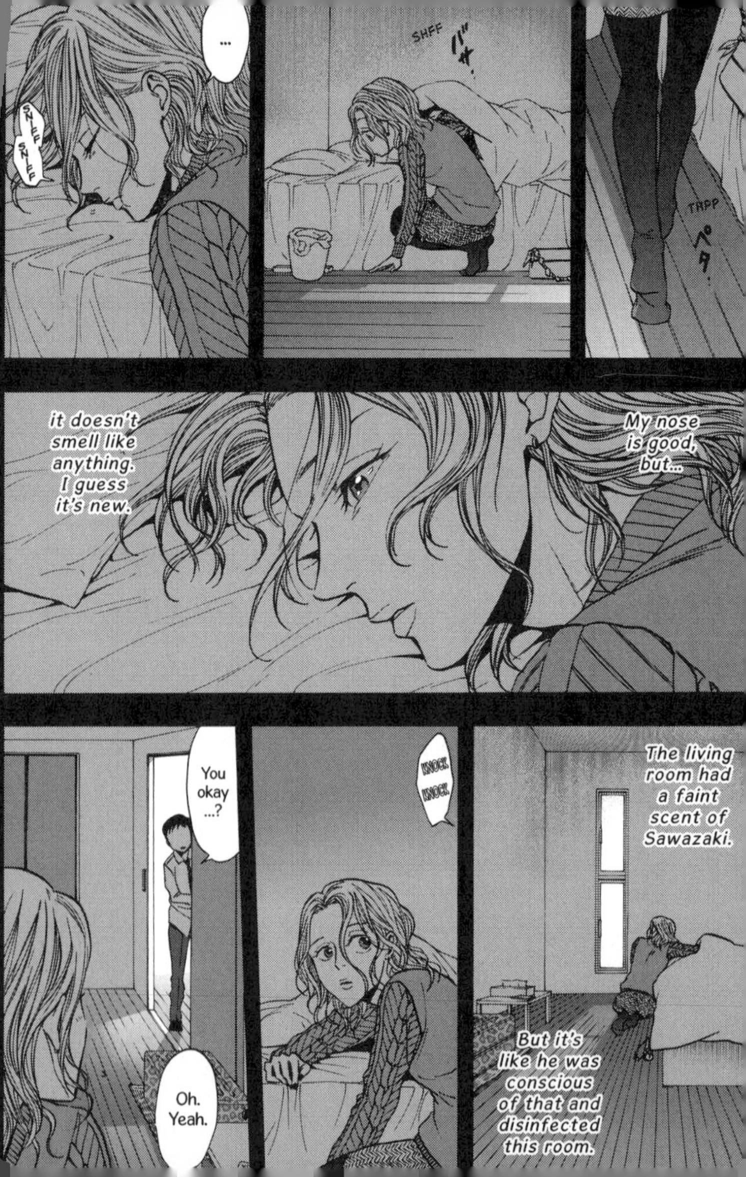
TAPP
ペタ
SHFF
バサ
...
SNIFF SNIFF
My nose is good, but...
it doesn't smell like anything. I guess it's new.
The living room had a faint scent of Sawazaki.
But it's like he was conscious of that and disinfected this room.
KNOCK KNOCK
You okay ...?
Oh. Yeah.

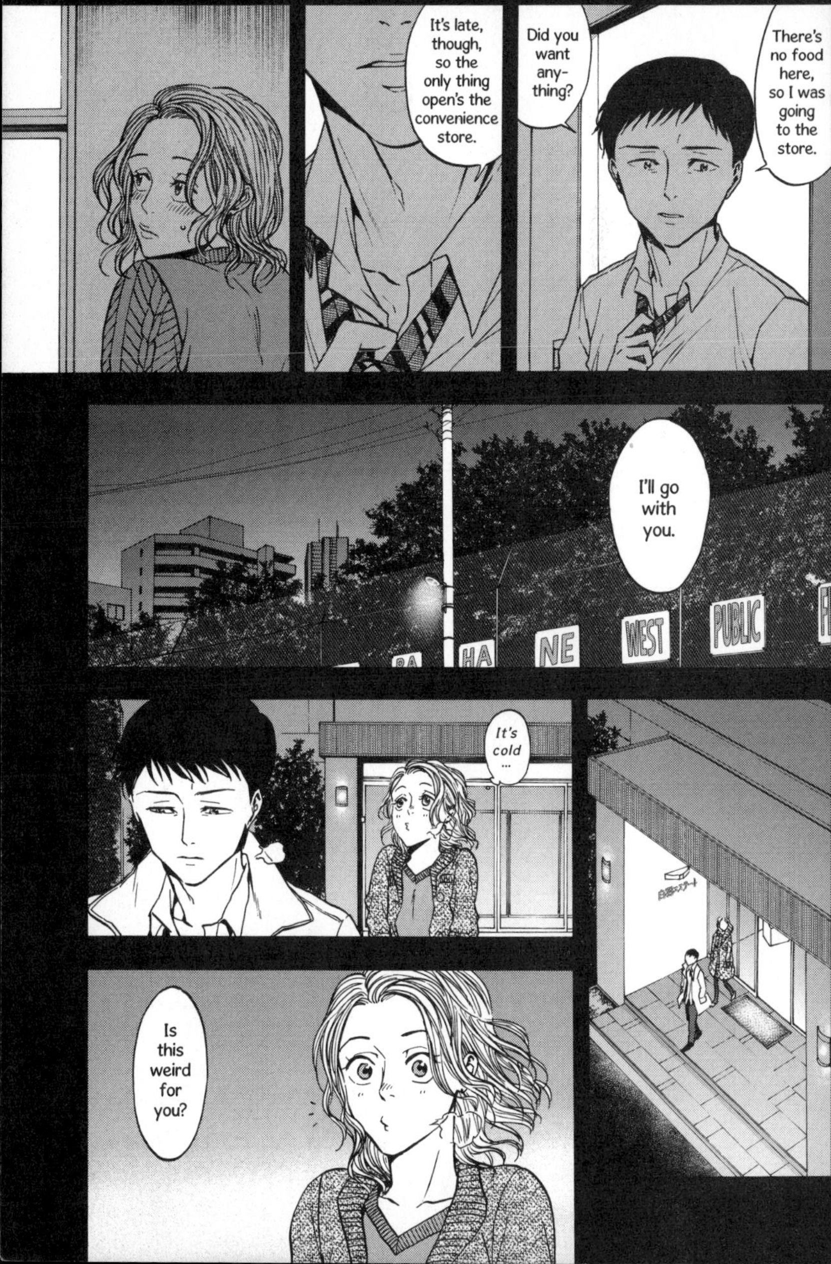
There's no food here, so I was going to the store.
Did you want anything?
It's late, though, so the only thing open's the convenience store.
I'll go with you.
HA NE WEST PUBLIC
It's cold...
Is this weird for you?

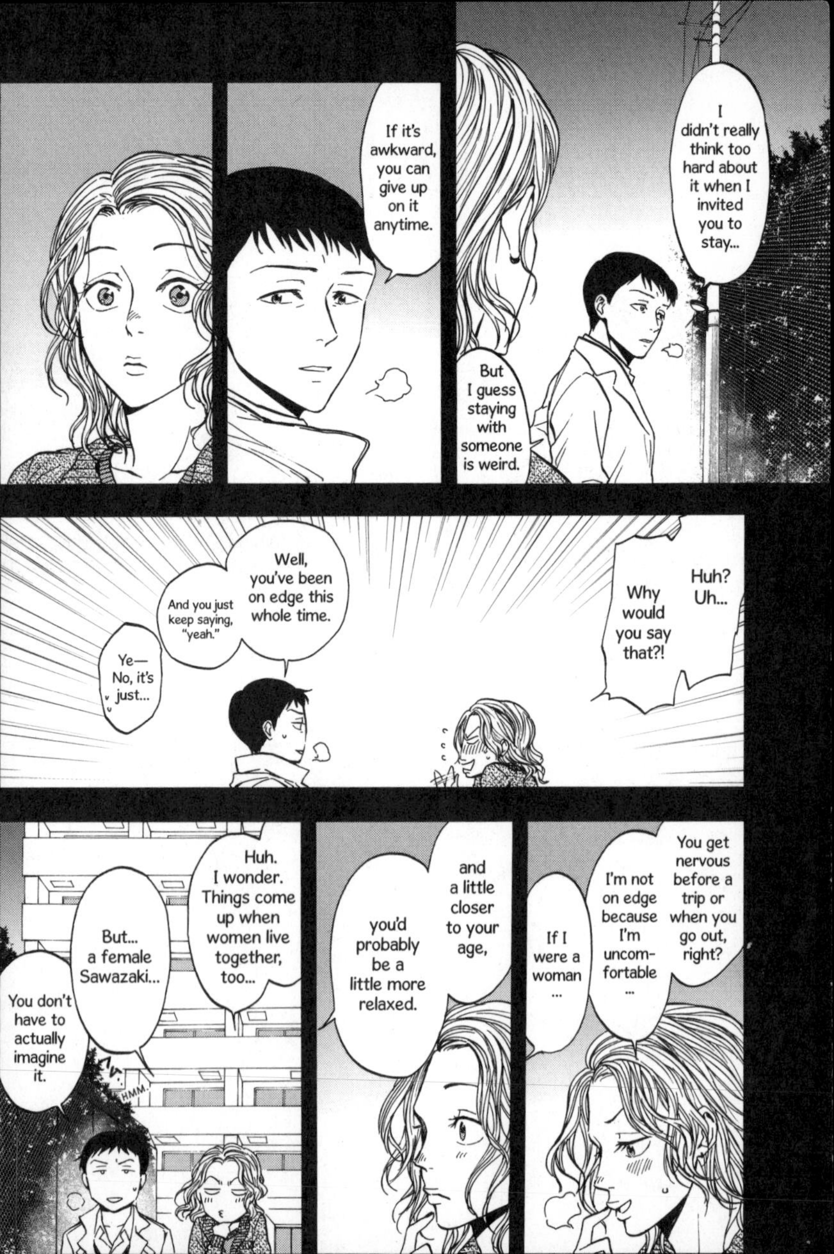
I didn't really think too hard about it when I invited you to stay...
But I guess staying with someone is weird.
If it's awkward, you can give up on it anytime.
Huh? Uh...
Why would you say that?!
Well, you've been on edge this whole time.
And you just keep saying, "yeah."
Ye— No, it's just...
You get nervous before a trip or when you go out, right?
I'm not on edge because I'm uncom- fortable ...
If I were a woman ...
and a little closer to your age,
you'd probably be a little more relaxed.
Huh. I wonder. Things come up when women live together, too...
But... a female Sawazaki...
HMM
You don't have to actually imagine it.

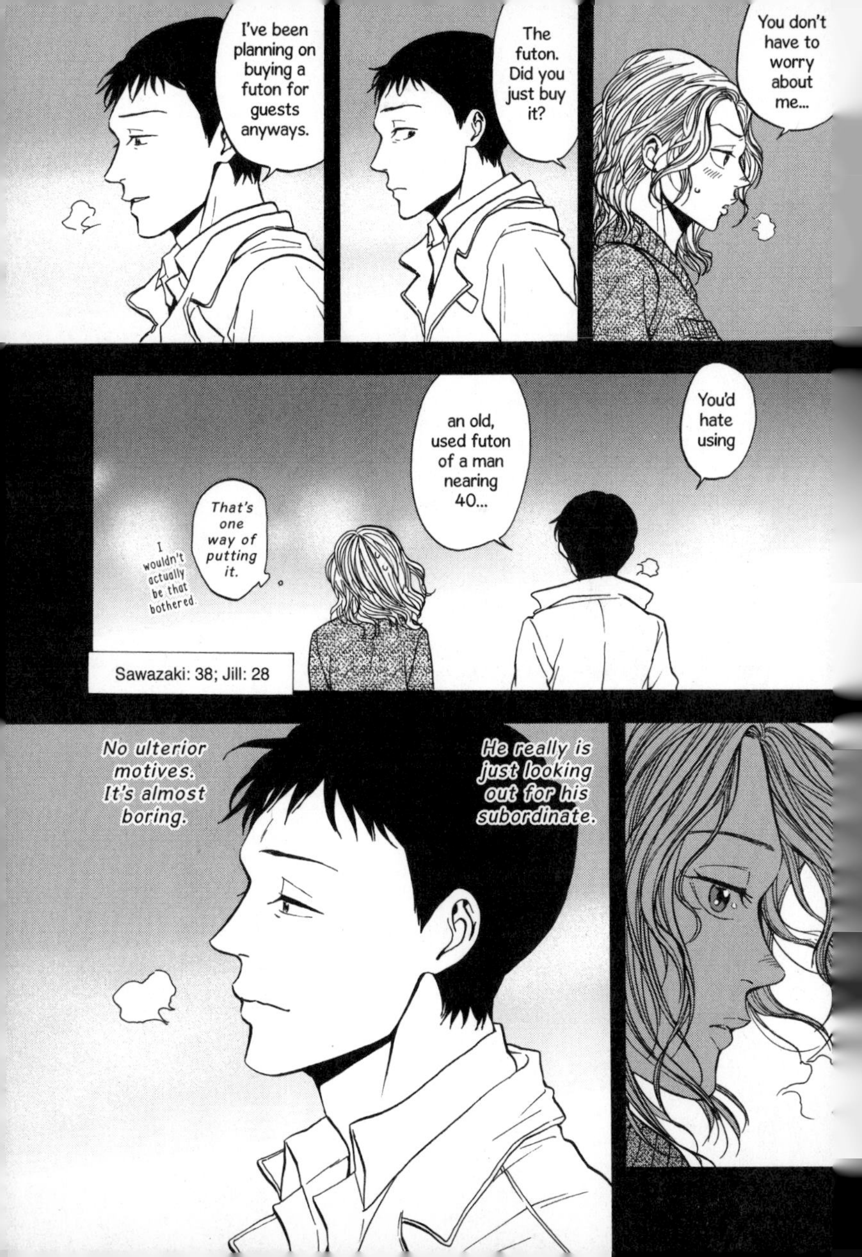
You don't have to worry about me...
The futon. Did you just buy it?
I've been planning on buying a futon for guests anyways.
You'd hate using
an old, used futon of a man nearing 40...
That's one way of putting it.
I wouldn't actually be that bothered.
Sawazaki: 38; Jill: 28
He really is just looking out for his subordinate.
No ulterior motives. It's almost boring.

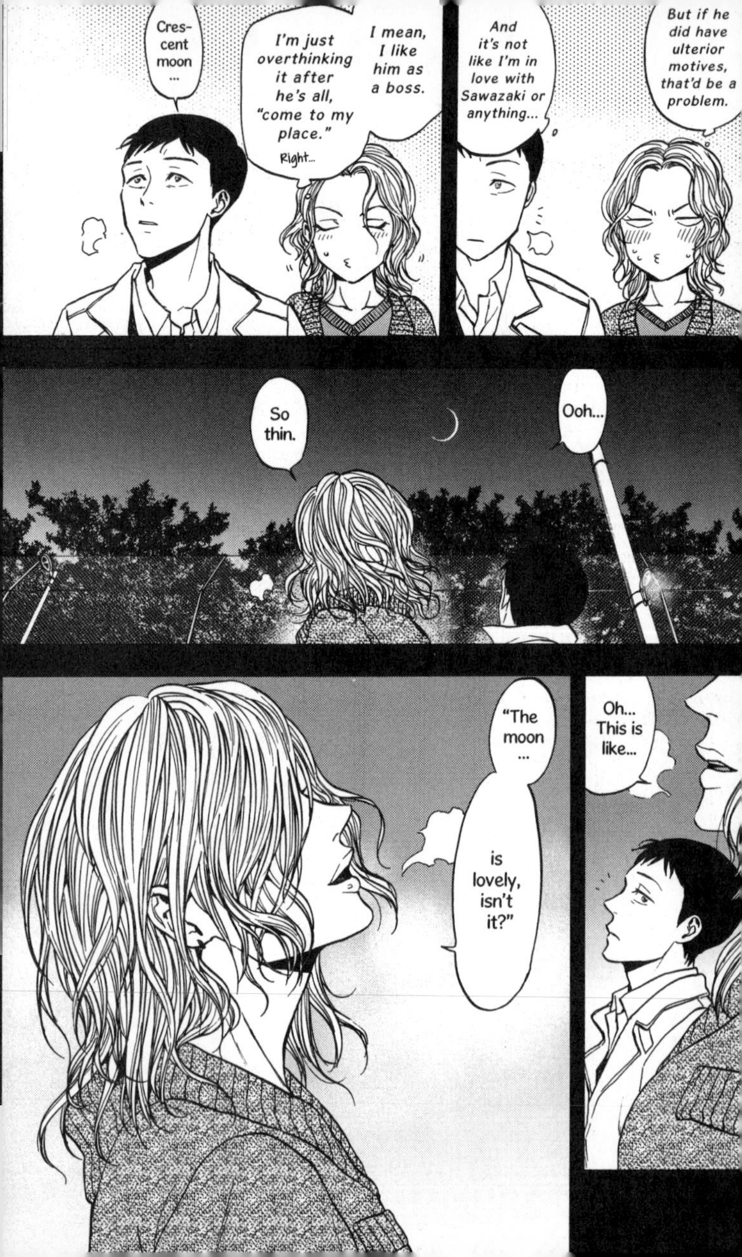
But if he did have ulterior motives, that'd be a problem.
And it's not like I'm in love with Sawazaki or anything...
I mean, I like him as a boss.
I'm just overthinking it after he's all, "come to my place."
Right...
Crescent moon...
Ooh...
So thin.
Oh... This is like...
"The moon...
is lovely, isn't it?"

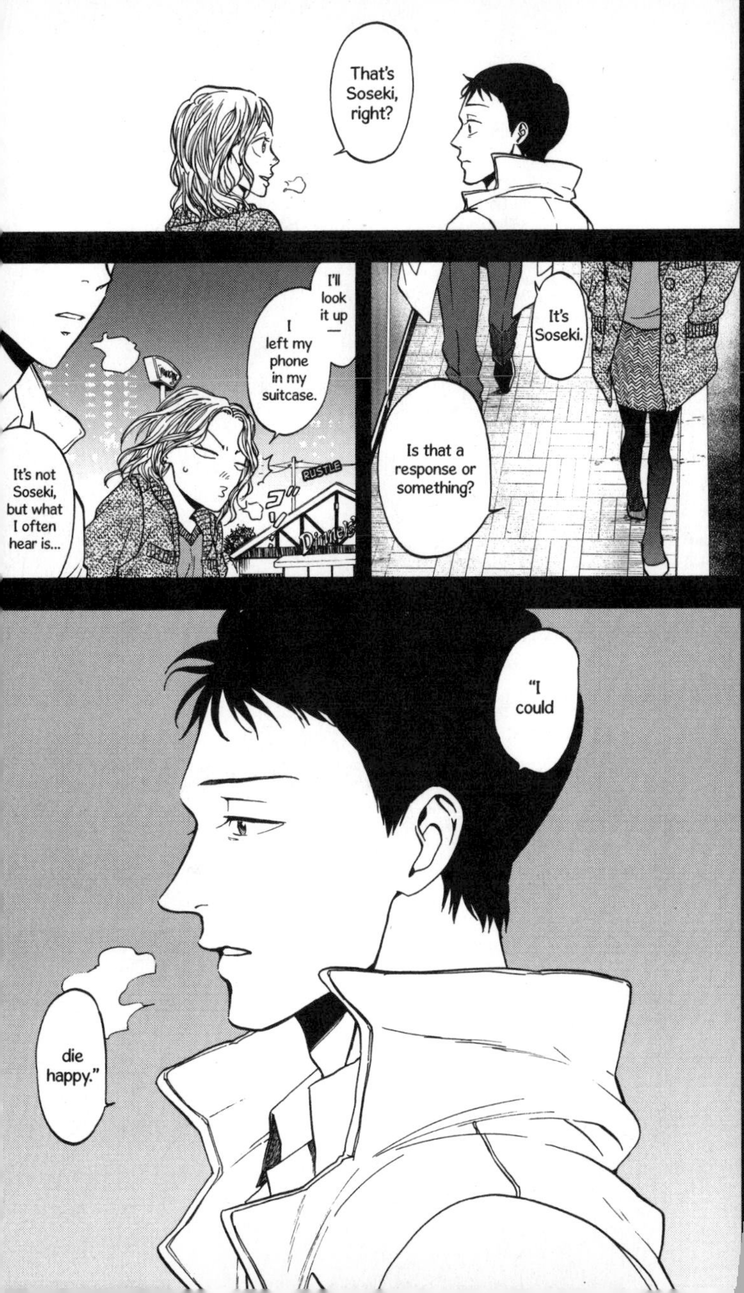
That's Soseki, right?
It's Soseki.
Is that a response or something?
I'll look it up—
I left my phone in my suitcase.
RUSTLE
It's not Soseki, but what I often hear is...
"I could
die happy."

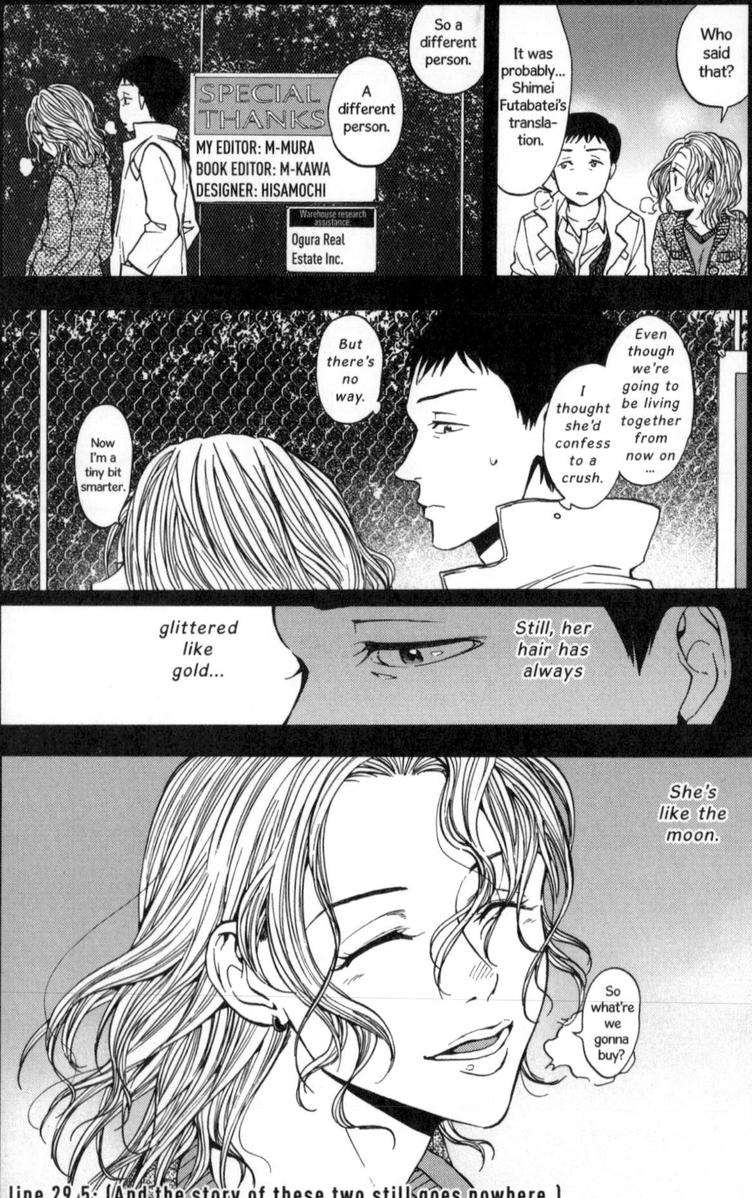
Who said that?
It was probably... Shimei Futabatei's translation.
So a different person.
A different person.
SPECIAL THANKS
MY EDITOR: M-MURA
BOOK EDITOR: M-KAWA
DESIGNER: HISAMOCHI
Warehouse research assistance:
Ogura Real Estate Inc.
Even though we're going to be living together from now on ...
I thought she'd confess to a crush.
But there's no way.
Now I'm a tiny bit smarter.
Still, her hair has always
glittered like gold...
She's like the moon.
So what're we gonna buy?
line 29.5: (And the story of these two still goes nowhere.)

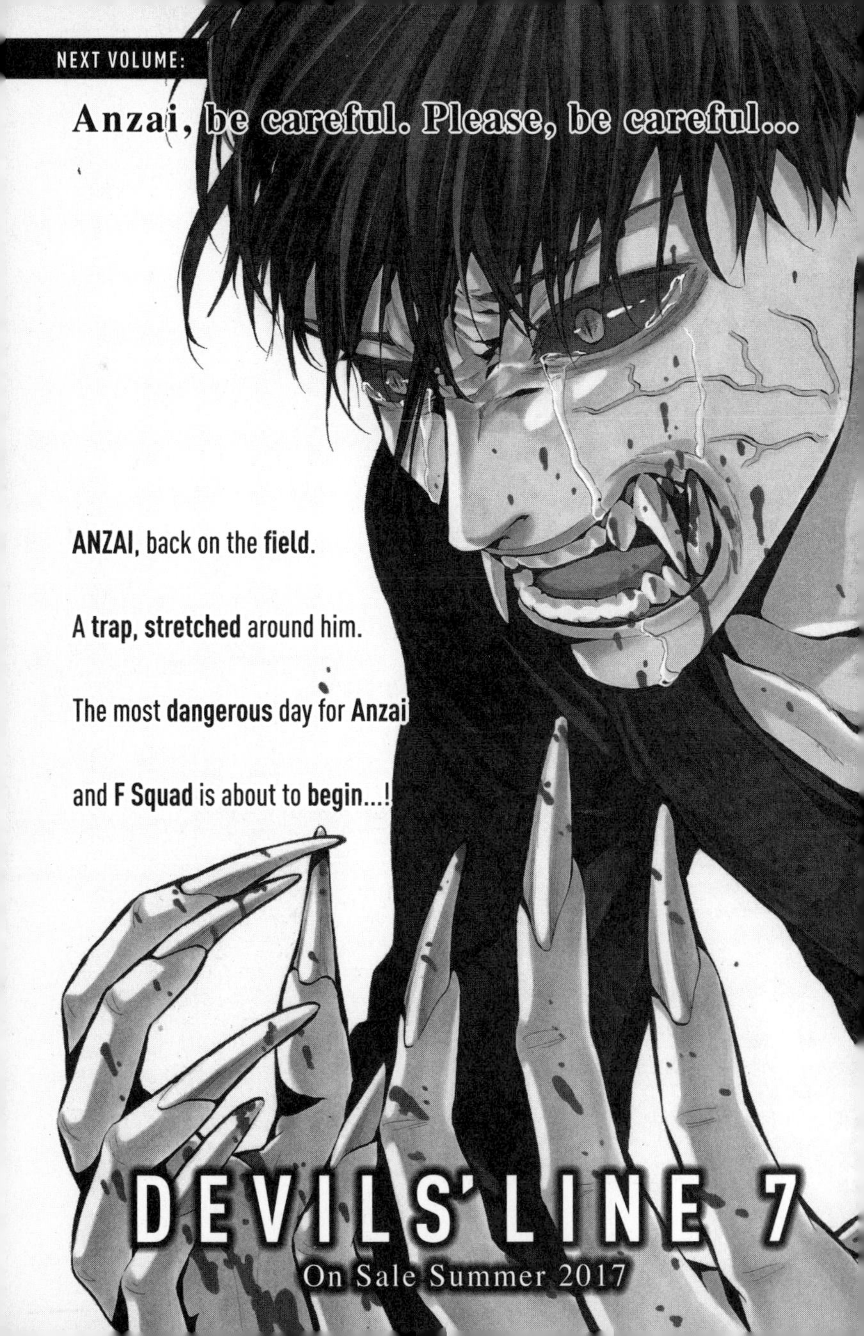
NEXT VOLUME:
Anzai, be careful. Please, be careful...
ANZAI, back on the field.
A trap, stretched around him.
The most dangerous day for Anzai
and F Squad is about to begin...!
DEVILS' LINE 7
On Sale Summer 2017

DEVILS' LINE 6

A Vertical Comics Edition

Translation: Jocelyne Allen
Production: Risa Cho
          Lorina Mapa

© 2017 Ryo Hanada. All rights reserved.
First published in Japan in 2015 by Kodansha, Ltd., Tokyo
Publication rights for this English edition arranged through Kodansha, Ltd., Tokyo
English language version produced by Vertical, Inc., New York

Translation provided by Vertical Comics, 2017
Published by Vertical, Inc., New York

Originally published in Japanese as *Debiruzurain 6* by Kodansha, Ltd., 2015
Debiruzurain first serialized in *Morning two*, Kodansha, Ltd., 2013-

This is a work of fiction.

ISBN: 978-1-942993-91-9

Manufactured in the United States of America

First Edition

Vertical, Inc.
451 Park Avenue South
7th Floor
New York, NY 10016
www.vertical-comics.com

Vertical books are distributed through Penguin-Random House Publisher Services.